THE MINOR PROPHETS

THE MESSAGE OF SOME

OF

THE MINOR
PROPHETS

OF THE

OLD TESTAMENT

By
J. Todd Ferrier

THE ORDER OF THE CROSS

ISBN 900235 02 1

Published by
THE ORDER OF THE CROSS
10 DE VERE GARDENS, LONDON W8 5AE
1976

Printed by
H. H. GREAVES LTD.
106/110 LORDSHIP LANE, LONDON SE22 8HG

FOREWORD

There are many lovers and students of the Old Testament who in their search for Truth have sensed, but could not find, a deeper meaning in the Messages of the Major and Minor Prophets. These seekers will understand the awe with which Members and Friends of the Order of the Cross heard the Founder of the Order, the Rev. J. Todd Ferrier, unveil the Cosmic significance of the Messages of these Prophets. As the living gems of Truth were separated from their false settings, their inherent Divine Light flashed forth not only illumining the understanding of those who listened, but also nourishing the heart and satisfying the Soul-hunger. They realized they were hearing a Message of Divine import revealing GOD's Purpose in the rescue, redemption and regeneration of this planetary system with her freight of Souls, which would find fulfilment in this Age.

These Addresses and also the essential text and logia of the Prophecies were given by the Author either at the Headquarters of the Order in London or at the Summer Schools for Members at High Leigh, Hoddesdon, mainly between the years 1927–1935; and most were revised and published by him. In 1931 he issued his book on *The Message of Ezekiel, A Cosmic Drama*, and in 1934, *Isaiah, A Cosmic and Messianic Drama*. The text and Unveilings of many of the Minor Prophets were published by him in *The Herald of the Cross*, Vols. viii and ix; and after his passing in 1943 the Addresses on these Prophets which he had not revised, were edited according to his instructions and published in later volumes of *The Herald of the Cross*. Editorial insertions are denoted by square brackets.

The Trustees of the Order have felt for some time that it would be helpful to seekers for Truth to have all the Author's writings on the Minor Prophets under one cover. And as a most valuable introduction, the opening chapter of the Author's volume on *Ezekiel* has been included, as it not only gives deep insight into the nature of true prophecy but also the meaning of the names and the Messages of the Prophets of the Old Testament.

Though not named as a Minor Prophet, the prophecies of Balaam were shown by the Writer as being of Divine import and have been included in this volume. Together with the other great prophecies of the Old Testament, when the essence of them is set forth, they not only throw light upon the tragic and tumultuous conditions of today, but also reveal continuously the unfailing Divine Ministries towards the healing of the peoples.

In the Teachings of the Order, but not included in this volume, much is unveiled relating to the ministry of the Prophet Elijah. Interested readers may find illumination concerning this Prophet in the Author's book *Life's Mysteries Unveiled* and in *The Herald of the Cross*, Vol. xxv and also in many of his other writings.

It may seem to some readers that only fragments of the text of the Biblical Prophecies are given. The following quotation from the Preface of the Author's book on *Ezekiel* may help to give the reason for this: "The logia of the Prophet as herein presented, were recovered by the Writer. In so far as it was found possible, the terms made use of in the Book as found in the Old Testament, have been retained. In the original Message, many great Truths were revealed to the Elders of Israel which, through the redactors and translators not understanding the Masonic use of the signs and symbols, are quite veiled in the various MSS. and translations.

. . . the Writer would have the reader understand that he makes no personal claim whatever: what is claimed by him concerns the Message alone—that it is from the

Divine World whence the **Prophet's Message** can alone find the true interpretation."

It is our sincere desire that this volume may not only bring enlightenment to all who read it, but also new hope and encouragement for the future, and the assurance that we are indeed living in the Days of True Redemption and Regeneration for all Souls.

KATHLEEN E. SPENCER

on behalf of the Trustees
of the Order of the Cross

1976

CONTENTS

INTRODUCTION

The Office of a Prophet

INTRODUCTION

The Office of a Prophet

A TRUE Prophet is the Servant of the Most High. He is not a resultant of human education, for no scholastic centre could endow him with more than human knowledge. If scholastic colleges and ecclesiastic seminaries could have bestowed such a gift upon their students, assuredly this world would have been the home of vast communities of true Prophets.

Thus-wise a Prophet is not made. He is God's direct creation. He is God-begotten, fashioned and illumined. A Prophet is one who has taken Divine Masonic degrees in the Heavens. In his Being he has ascended from one state of spiritual consciousness to another, growing in spiritual attribute through his contact with Angels and Gods until he has attained the status of *an Illumined one*. In this exalted inward state he can receive Divine Illumination and communicate it: he can henceforth fill the office of Divine Prophet.

Such an office implies universal sympathy. Though the Prophet will derive his personal equation through family and race, yet he will transcend these; for to be dominated by the thought of family, tribe and race would place the prophet under great limitation. And that could not be if his sphere of illumination were associated with the realm of Universal Being, and his message to the Eternal and the Soul. For the message given him to proclaim would be of universal import which would necessitate the transcension by him of the limited bounds created by personal, national and racial relationships. And herein will his message exceed in significance and scope and differ from that of many who might be regarded as prophets, but whose message is related to the prophet's own people or race.

These latter are minor Prophets indeed. The true great Prophets have a message of universal value, and speak of Soulic, Celestial, and Divine Events. Therefore, it should not be difficult to differentiate between the messages of the

2

true Prophets because of their universal significance, and those who are merely political and national enthusiasts, denouncing at times their own people, and upon other nations pouring forth judgments. It will be readily conceded by students of the prophetic books of the Old Testament, that there are two orders of prophetic utterances found in those books, the one relating to what could only be accounted local and national, and the other to themes and events of transcendent nature, themes relating to the Mysteries of Planetary, Celestial and Divine history, and of great Soulic value.

It is in the light of such revelations when these are fully unveiled, that the message of the real Prophet of GOD is distinguished from the most mixed addenda of the writings of the local and national teachers (though bearing the name of prophets), introduced by the various scribes, editors and redactors, and mixed up with the true Divine Message to the latter's obscuration. For it was in this way that the ancient Scribes and Pharisees made void the Law and the Testimony from GOD given unto and through HIS illumined ones.

MESSAGES TRUE AND FALSE

True prophetic messages are written in cryptic terms. They are something more than interpretations given to local and national religious ideas. The message of a true Prophet is something profoundly greater and loftier than any statements that are imbued with the spirit of national political bias and racial religious prejudices. Of these latter the books of the Old Testament are full. They are to be found side by side with the real Message and are the work of the priestly scribes. And this must be borne in mind if the reader of the Old Testament prophecies would discern between the true and the false, the illumined message of the illumined Soul and that message in a false setting, changed and placed there to support traditional beliefs of a local, national or racial character.

3

Jewry claimed the Prophets and Seers, and these were made to speak for Jewry. The JEHOVAH Who reveals HIMSELF unto the Prophets and Seers as the Most Holy and transcendent ONE, *who filleth all things*, is so changed into an anthropomorphic GOD that HE becomes one with like passions and humours as possessed the people. To the real Prophet HIS is an unchanging Love; but to Jewry HE is ever changing towards them with every change in the religious or national life. HIS mercy flies like a radiant cloud across the Heavens, followed soon by clouds of judgment. Though the most sacred Name by which HE was known in Israel became known to Jewry because it belonged to the terms used in the Mysteries which came into their possession, yet the most glorious ONE Whose Name was above all earthly names and was signified by the Tetragrammaton, was reduced to the conception of an eastern potentate who reflected in himself the changing emotions, desires, ambitions, loves and hates of the nation's own fallen states.

The deep shadow of such a tragedy as this degradation of the Divine Nature, Love and Wisdom, lies athwart the threshold of all the prophetic Books of the Old Testament.

THE PROPHET ILLUMINED OF GOD

The true Prophet was an illumined Soul, and his message was an illumination. Being illumined of GOD the message he had to give could not misrepresent the Divine Nature, Love and Wisdom. In such a message there would be nothing derogatory to the Divine Love and Wisdom. Whatever the nature of the message, it would always be of transcendent character and worthy of HIM concerning Whom it spake. To know the Divine Presence even in the degree in which a true Prophet must know that glorious ONE, would ensure that the Prophet could not represent HIM as if HE were like a man, governed by the changing degrees of desire and passion characteristic of fallen humanity.

4

In the real message of the true Prophet, the LORD, the GOD of Sabaoth, was as unlike the representation of HIM in the denunciatory parts of the prophetic Books, as the transcendent glory of a perfect day is unlike the deep darkness of the night where not even a star shines to relieve its gloom. Unto the true son of Israel who had risen into the realm of high illumination and become GOD's Prophet, the LORD GOD of Sabaoth was also the LORD of the Inner Sanctuary and the Shekinah overshadowing the Soul's Shrine. HE was the Voice whose vibration spoke of Love and Wisdom, compassion and pity. Yet, through the misrepresentations of HIM by the teachers and priests, the people of Jewry dreaded HIM. HE was thought of as ONE whose demands, laws and statutes were inwrought with judgments and punishments, and Who wrested obedience from HIS children by the elementary means of promises of rewards for obedience, and sufferings for disobedience.

THE CRYPTIC LANGUAGE OF THE PROPHET

The transcendent Visions and Messages found in the Old Testament are the true prophetic Teachings. They are often cryptographic; and frequently hieroglyphs are used to set them forth. For the innermost Mysteries conveyed in the messages had to be guarded from those who would have wrested them and put the knowledge to wrong uses, with the danger of bringing disaster upon themselves and others, and even upon the Planet, as had been in other ages when great minds made wrong use of the knowledge of Planetary secrets, and caused great catastrophes to befall the elements, seas and outer planes. That is the reason why in the prophetic Books the innermost Mysteries were presented in the language of glyph, so that only the illumined could come into the true knowledge of them.

This Divine provision accentuates in all the Books of the Old Testament the difference between the message of the real Prophet of GOD Who was the medium of the revelation of the Mysteries, and the local and national so-called prophet whose interests were chiefly Jewish, and very often only tribal and personal. In the Old Testament the contrast between the voice of the true Prophet and that of the priestly Scribe is most obvious from Isaiah to Malachi, and even long before the books which bear their names became part of the Jewish Canon. The two voices have different messages, and these are mostly at variance. That of the true Prophet calls to the Inner Life, and deals with the Mysteries of the Heavens and the Earth, GOD and the Soul, the Sun and the Planet; that of the priestly Scribe calls to obedience to outer temple-ceremonial and ritual, and emphasizes the Divine necessity and value of these. The true Prophet is not oblivious of the beautiful outer aspects of religious expression, but he sees the danger of these when unaccompanied by Divine illumination and consecration. He knows that where the innermost significances of the Mysteries are apprehended and applied, the outer worship will express the inner beauty and glory of Life. But the mere tribal, national and racial priest and scribe, see not the inner relationships to the outward ritual and ceremonial. To them the former may be experienced by the few; whilst the latter must be observed by all. Yet the office of the true Prophet and that of the true Priest is of the sublime Mystery of GOD, and should ever have been in harmony; and the outer ceremonial and ritual should always have been the articulation of the inner motion of the Divine Spirit and the shadowing forth of the Mysteries.

* * * *

Prophecy is usually associated with the prediction of coming events in the immediate or distant future. The prophetic is here brought down from its realm of exalted spiritual vision to that of the occult or even the astral realm. Many who are far from the state of spiritual consciousness necessary for the true Prophet, and who could not possibly fill his office, have nevertheless been able to foretell coming events upon the outer planes. Many of the things foretold whose action is upon the outer planes may be known beforehand because they are the results of activities upon the astral and occult planes. Very few clairvoyants see beyond these planes; and it is there that outward events are shadowed forth. On the higher occult plane many render beautiful ministries; and there are times when those who minister there are permitted to communicate what may have been seen or heard. Most of the spiritualistic experiences and communications through mediums are from that plane.

Such experience and communications are, however, very different in nature and character from those which are the outcome of true prophecy and the office of the true Prophet. The Prophet of GOD does not function within the astral and occult realms. His office is of such a nature that he is borne aloft in his consciousness far beyond the realms of the ordinary medium. He shares the motion of the realms of the true spiritual and angelic life and ministry. He hears the Voices of the Inner World, and communes with Angels and even Archangels. His Message is from the Divine: the Voice of the Eternal ONE makes all his planes vibrate and respond to the Divine motion. The Four Breaths move through him; the Four Living Creatures or Divine Atmospheres within him are the recipients of the Breath. His Rings, or Wheels, or Planes (they are the same), go whithersoever the Spirit goeth; and they are full of Eyes or the light of heavenly perception. The cherubic motion of which he speaks he will understand, his knowledge of it will be through cherubic motion in himself.

UNDERSTANDING THE SIGNS AND SYMBOLS

When the Message of the true Prophet is understood, the interpretation of the hieroglyphs will throw light

upon the world's darkness. It will unveil the Divine
Drama of the Soul, reveal the meaning of the Earth's
tragedies and the Soul's travail, and interpret the Divine
Purpose. And to understand the Message even after the
hieroglyphs are interpreted and the cryptic signs uncovered, the seeker must approach in reverence and from
the standpoint of the spiritual realms. No mere textual
criticism, however valuable it may be accounted from the
traditional or scholastic standpoint, can possibly give an
insight into the Divine significance of the Message.
Indeed, textual criticism has not only missed the mark in
failing to effect what was hoped for from it, but the critics
have closed the doors to many of the entrants who would
fain come into a knowledge of the Divine and Celestial
Mysteries set forth in the prophetic Books. The spirit of
hyper-criticism has often prevented the scholar from
entering into the kingdom whence the Vision and the
Message of the Prophet have come; and it has left un-
opened the gates to the Temple of the Mysteries, and thus
failed in its ministry to those who have desired to enter
into the Divine Pantheon of prophetic Revelation. Ultra-
criticism has not provided the Realities for all who have
earnestly sought the truth; but it has shaken the foundations of religious belief in many. It has not thrown light
upon the way into the Kingdom of GOD; alas! it has only
too often obscured the inner vision of those who have
brought the criticism of the mind to bear upon things
essentially of the Soul and the Divine Kingdom.

*　　*　　*　　*

There is only one way of approach to the true understanding of the messages of the divinely inspired and
illumined Prophets. It is the path of Soul enlightenment.
But all enlightenment is from within. Knowledge gained
from without informs the mind, but it does not enlighten
the Being. Many have held the Mysteries in the cryptographic body of their presentation without finding the

inner meaning of them. For witness to this we have the Christian Church of to-day that holds its Seven Sacraments as the Mysterious Rites by which the Soul of man finds GOD; yet the Church has no real illumination concerning the Divine Soul significance of each Sacrament. Of each Sacrament it makes a masonic rite of great import to the individual; and it does this even whilst it condemns all masonic rites expressive of the Mysteries, if these are rendered outside of its own communion. By the path of illumination the Mysteries become Revelation to the true seeker. The terms in which the Mysteries are expressed are the various masonic Signs, Symbols and Passwords contained within the degrees in their ascending scale. Each Mystery is a cryptograph; each term a cryptogram.

THE TEACHINGS OF THE PROPHETS

Such was the character of the true prophetic Teachings. Of such character may those Teachings be seen to be now by all who come into the realm of light. These Teachings contain Divine Secrets. The Secrets had to be guarded. They had to be protected from those who sought knowledge for personal ends, who would wrest nature's secrets from her for personal ambitious purposes, and make use of them to dominate and conquer. For it was through such a misuse of the secret potencies of the Planet that many great disasters befell the Earth's outer planes. And such minds would also wrest from the Soul of man its Divine Secret; for which reason the Mysteries concerning the constitution of the Soul have been veiled from all but those who attain to the Divine Consciousness.

The Teachings of the true Prophets were related to the Divine Kingdom and contained illuminations on

The Secrets of Creation:

The constitution and fashion of the Earth:

The nature and place in the Heavens of the Solar Body:

The creation, fashioning and evolution of the Sons of GOD.

9

The creation and generation of the Children of this world:

The fall of this Planet and, in some degree, as a result, the whole system:

The primary cause of "the Fall," and the disastrous results to the whole Planetary Household, to the Sons of GOD, and to all those who caused it to take place:

The ministry of the Divine World with a view to effecting the Planet's restoration:

The nature of those ministries which had to undergo change from time to time because of the new unforeseen difficult conditions which arose:

The tragic things which befell the outer planes of the Planet and all the races upon them:

The rending of the Planet's Kingdoms, written of under the guise of the Kingdom of Judah and the Kingdom of Israel:

The Divine Purpose expressed in the coming of the Messengers, and very specially in the Messianic Advent revealed in and through the Master known as Jesus Christ:

The nature of the Redemption to be accomplished on behalf of the Sons of GOD who bore the cryptograms of Israel and Zion:

The effect of that Redemption upon the Kingdoms and planes of the Planet, and upon all her children:

The path of the Oblation, its nature, burden and duration:

The resultant of the Oblation revealed in the Regeneration of the Sons of GOD and their restoration to their long lost Divine Inheritance:

The rehabilitation of the Ancient Christhood, and a corporate Messianic Manifestation through restored Israel:

The ultimate triumph of the Divine Love and Wisdom
over all the fallen astral and occult forces and conditions, and the re-establishing of the Christ-
regnancy in the restoration of the ancient Theocracy.

Such is the burden of the Teachings of the true Prophets.
These Teachings constitute the Great Mysteries of the
ages. They are gems of Revelation which have been overlaid by their settings, hidden beneath priestly ceremonial
and national traditions, and the local, tribal and racial
application of them to Jewry. Even the apparently
personal names assigned to the Books are cryptic, and
indicate the subject-matter of the Revelation. The understanding of the terms is the "open sesame" to the hidden
truth. These terms have no more relation to the Prophet-
servant of the LORD, than had the sacred terms Jesus
Christ the Lord to the personal Master, though the terms
were given to Him as personal names, notwithstanding
that the real meaning of them is found in His Mission.
And thus with the true Prophets. The Servant took the
term signifying the Office. To analyse the Names of the
Prophets in relation to the Message which they were
appointed to give, is interesting and illumining. Thus:
(See page 12).

All this will indicate the wealth of sacred story that
came into the hands of Jewry through the Schools of the
Prophets. Alas! the Scribes and Priests did not understand the inner meaning of the various messages. They
misinterpreted them, with the result that often their
misrepresentations were accepted as the real message, and
chronicled as such. Thus the real vision was veiled by
them, and the true Treasure buried amidst the elements
of their own national and racial history.

Yet the Messages of all the Prophets, Major and Minor,
make up one grand Symphony of Divine Revelation of
Motion, Purpose, Travail and accomplishment on the
part of the Divine World on behalf of Israel and Judah.

THE PROPHETIC BOOKS

THE MESSAGE	NAME	MEANING OF NAME
The Drama of the Oblation	Isaiah or Ye-shá-yah	The Burden of the Spirit of JEHOVAH
The Divine Lament over Israel, Judah and Ierusalem	Jeremiah or Je-remai-yah	The appointed of JEHOVAH
An Unveiling of Planetary History	Ezekiel	In whom is Divine Strength
A History of Israel in Allegory	Daniel	The Divine Judge or Separator
The Flight of the Beloved	Jonah	The Dove or the Beloved One
The Way of Salvation	Hosea	The Saviour
A Divine Reveille	Joel	JEHOVAH is the LORD
The Travail of the Planet-Soul	Amos	The Burden-bearer
The Way into the Holiest	Micah or Michiyah	JEHOVAH is our Strength
Assurance of the overthrow of the Great City (Nineveh)	Nahum	A Son of Consolation
Counsel concerning guarding the Message of GOD	Zephaniah	JEHOVAH is our Guardian
The Process of Regeneration	Habakkuk	Divine Embracement
The Overthrow of Edom and Esau	Obadiah	Worship GOD only
The Coming of Triumph	Haggai	The Feast of YAHWEH
The Sanctuary Restored	Zechariah	The Divine Omniscience
The Refiner's Fire	Malachi	The Messenger of YAHWEH

12

THE STORY OF
BALAAM

THE FOUR ORACLES OF BALAAM

I

THE SEPARATENESS OF ISRAEL

From the heights hath Balak brought me down,
Even from the Mountains of God's Orient.
The King of Moab would have me curse Ya-akob-El,
And pour out wroth against God's Israel.

But how could I curse Ya-akob-El?
Or pour out wroth upon God's Israel?

For God hath blessed Ya-akob-El,
And showered tender mercies upon Israel.

Upon the summit of the Earth I behold Ya-akob-El,
And from the Mountains I look upon Gods' Israel.

Israel is a people that dwell alone
And account not themselves of the Earth's Nations.

Who can reckon the children of Ya-akob-El?
Or name the four divisions of Israel?

Truth cannot die upon my lips;
By it the Just shall live.
So would I that my Life may be.

II

THE KING IN THE MIDST OF ISRAEL

Arise ye, Balak, and hearken unto me!
God is not like men; He does not lie;
He is not as the sons of men that He should repent.
Hath He purposed? Shall he not fulfil it?
Hath He spoken? Shall not His Word prevail?
Behold His commandment unto me is of Blessing.
He hath Blessed: who can reverse it?

He holdeth not iniquity against Ya-akob-El,
Nor remembereth against Israel the perversity that smote them.

The Lord Who is with Ya-akob-El is his God;
And the Voice of Jehovah is regnant in Israel.
God bringeth them up from the darkness of Egypt,
And giveth power to again ascend the Hills.
No enchantment shall prevail against Ya-akob-El;
Nor the divinations of Egypt overthrow Israel;
For the power of the Most High shall be upon Ya-akob-El,
And there shall be revealed what great things
The Lord hath wrought out for Israel.

III

THE VOCATION OF ISRAEL

Thus speaketh the Stranger who is a Son of the Lamp—
The Man whose eyes are once more open—
Who in audience doth hear the Voice of God,
Who beholdeth the Glory of the Almighty,
And boweth low before the Splendour of His Presence—

How goodly are thy tents, O Ya-akob-El!
And glorious your Tabernacles, O Israel!
Amid the valleys are they spread forth
Like watered gardens by the river-side
Upon whose banks there grow those Trees
Of Life whose planting is of God.

Israel shall be as water-carriers whose pitchers
Shall pour forth living waters unto many.
Their King is high above all earthly kings;
His Flame shall cause His Kingdom to prevail.
God hath brought them forth from Egypt
And given them the strength of exalted powers
By which they shall subdue all enemies
And pierce them to the marrow by Truth's arrows.

IV

The Coming of the Star
AND
The Arising of Israel

Thus once more doth the Stranger speak,
Even one who is a Son of the Lamp of God,
The man whose eyes are opened though once closed:—
Who hath had audience of the Word of God,
And seen in open Vision the resplendent One,
And knoweth Him Who ever is the Most High—

I see Him coming, but it is not yet;
I behold Him becoming, though He is not yet nigh—
There shall arise a Star for Ya-akob-El,
And the Sceptre come again to Israel.
Then shall be smitten all the land of Moab
And her sons of tumult be overthrown;
Then shall be re-possessed the Edom-land;
When Israel have all regained the land of their Inheritance,
And Ya-akob-El's dominion be once more restored.

NOTES ON TEXT

The Story of Balaam is fascinating. Balaam with his Ass is more than an eastern fable. The names and the strange terms used are mystical. Some day in the near future it may be permitted to unveil the allegory. The true story has been corrupted and changed, and what was left of it has been sadly misinterpreted. It is an allegorical Story of Planetary History. Balaam is a stranger; he does not belong to this Planet. Balak King of Moab is the embodiment and impersonation of confusion and that which makes void. Balaam represents the state of Israel—Prophet, Seer and Priest; Balak is the resultant of the betrayal. He may be likened unto the Betrayer who set out to curse Israel and make void the manifestation and ministry of the Christhood.

From the heights of God's Orient had Balak brought down the whole House of Israel. Yet Ya-akob-El remained at the head of the Planet, and Israel continued a separate People from those on the Earth.

There is great majesty here in the Prophet's challenge to the spirit that makes void. God is the Eternal Truth. He does not create that He may destroy, nor promise and then withhold. His purpose is not changed though conditions upon such a world as the Earth may change and become militant against the fulfilment of His Will. Nor is there cause for repentance in God such as is frequently indicated in the Old Testament. He never has to repent that He has created Souls, Worlds and Systems. His Laws are perfect and their outworking makes for perfection in all realms of manifestation. If any untoward conditions arise through deflection of thought, desire, motive and ambition such as overtook this System through the manifestation and practice of the spirit embodied in Balak, the Eternal World grieves. But it is not overwhelmed, for it knows that in any System where there is the perfect freedom Divine Love gives, mistakes and misdirections may arise. But when they do, the Eternal World gives such accommodated ministry as will correct them. No fallen Earth-spirit, nor even Celestial Star, can acquire the evil power of divination that makes void perpetually, and blights by its wrong use of Divine Gift, the Works of God.

The expression "Son of the Lamp" is an exquisitely beautiful form of recognition of the Light of God that lighteth all who rise up out of the world. A Son of the Lamp is one who seeks his Light from interior illumination from the Heavens. He becomes Prophet and Seer. Balaam is likewise Baalim—a worshipper amid the Gods. He had known great things, but had lost the Light. Then he recovered the power to see, hear and realize. He beheld again the Glory of the Almighty and bowed amidst its Auric Splendour. The Divine Voice once more could speak within him.

He knew Ya-akob-El. He was familiar with the history of Israel. He understood the regnancy of the Divine Vicegerent, and how and where the members of his Hierarchies tented—that is, where the various Angels of the Divine, Celestial and Angelic ministrations of the Planet, dwelt and served. He knew the purpose for which Israel was upon the Planes of this Planet, saw them as once they had been upon the Celestial Spheres when they had been ministered unto upon the Solar Bethlehem, and thence descended to minister upon the Earth's Heavens. And he knew who was the chosen Mediator unto Israel. Hence his vision and prophecy concerning the Christhood.

Here is revealed the exalted state that had been reached by Balaam. He had had audience of the Word of God; this implies very intimate and direct contact with the Eternal Mystery. He had in consciousness stood in the Presence of Adonai and received counsel and empowerment from Him. The great shadow that had fallen upon him had passed sufficiently for him to be capable of such restoration as would enable him to look out upon the Divine and Celestial Drama enacted by the Eternal World through Sol, Ya-akob-El, and Israel. Amid the Earth's dark night of spiritual bereavement, he is shown the coming of the Messenger of the Lord whose Message would be luminous as a Star, whose shining would restore the Kingdom of Ya-akob-El, and raise the Divine Regal Sceptre in the midst of Israel—by which is cryptically implied, the full restoration of the glorious days of The Theocracy.

I

BALAK AND BALAAM

Part i

YOU all know something of the story of Balak and Balaam as the record is found in the book of Numbers.* We will first, by way of prelude, look at it as set forth there, and then see the inner significance of it in relation to the planetary constitution and history, and then in relation to the Oracles said to have been spoken by Balaam.

Prelude

Perhaps the chief thing of interest which you will remember, is associated with what is known as Balaam's ass, which is said to have spoken. Balak is represented as king of Moab, who beheld a people coming up out of Egypt stronger and more numerous than his own, [a people] whom he comes to fear lest his own land should be overrun by them and his people swamped. That he had belief in the power of blessing or cursing is evident from the story, [which indicates] that he also believed in the dark forces and that there were prophets of such who were prepared to bring the blight of those forces upon individuals and peoples, especially so for earthly gain. It is reported that he sent to Balaam. That he had heard of such a prophet and that he probably knew Balaam, must have been in the thought of one of the writers who composed the story, which, by the way, is threefold. It is said that he offered to Balaam great treasures, and even a high place of honour in his kingdom if he would bring those dark forces to act upon the people, known as Israel,

---

* *Vide* Numbers, Chaps. XXII-XXIV.

who had come up out of Egypt. Balaam had some conviction that the GOD of Israel would not permit such a curse to be uttered against HIS people, and sent back word to Balak that it could not be done. But the king of Moab sent again to him, urging him to come. He sent, with his emissaries, presents to tempt the prophet, and it is said that Balaam yielded.

Now, there are two sets of stories which are quite distinct. The first omits entirely that of the ass on the journey, but the other gives the story of the ass. In the first, GOD permits Balaam to go to Balak. In the second, Balaam sets out without asking permission and is rebuked on the way by means of the ass. There is even a third influence in the narrative which becomes manifest at the close of the fourth Oracle where three other minor Oracles are uttered wherein other nations are cursed.

Those of you to whom the story is familiar will remember that in the second part of it, where Balaam is said to have set out upon his ass, he had a trying experience, for the ass on the journey refused to go further and seemed affrighted, and it is said that the Angel of the LORD stood in the way of Balaam's going and that the ass beheld the Angel. And then it is narrated that the Angel of the LORD told Balaam that the ass had saved his life, for, if he had persisted on his journey without permission, he would have been slain by the sword of the Angel of the LORD. Such is to refresh your memories.

Another most important point is that, prior to the utterance of the first and second and third Oracles, seven Altars are built, upon each of which an ox and a ram are offered in sacrifice—all highly significant when the mystical nature of the story is apprehended. For that for which the seven Altars stands cannot be attained without the erection of such Altars on the way; nor can the sublime realizations which are indicated be entered into, until those sacrifices signified by the ox and the ram are offered upon each of the Altars.

Having thus refreshed your memories with this outline, I would approach it with you now from the Inner Worlds.

THE SIGNIFICANCE OF THE TERMS USED

It is a mystical story concerned with the planetary constitution and fall, and the coming and travail and restoration of Israel. All the terms used are mystical. They have spiritual significations, whether they relate to the realms of HIS transcendent Presence, or to the realms of the darkness which overtook this World. Balak and **Balaam are** personifications, just as the term, the Devil, is the personification of the spirit of negation that destroys; Satan personifies the mind that betrays, and the Dragon, the will that oppresses; the Beast personifies the sensualizing influences at play in the World; and even the Beast that spake like a Lamb but had the power to become one with the Dragon, personifies the false spirit that cloaks itself under religious nomenclature. When will the children of the FATHER-MOTHER cease to seek for the real meaning of things in merely outer significations? When will they come to understand that the language of the Heavens has to be spoken in signs and symbols; that the Mysteries of GOD and the Soul, of the Planet and the Sun, have to be signified for those who can perceive, through the cryptic terms which are used as signs and passwords into the realms where alone such Mysteries can be known to be understood? When will come the hour, even the day which will herald the hour, when all those who believe, or profess to believe, in those old-world stories as real stories, will have their eyes opened and become Sons of the Lamp of GOD, so that their vision be once more unveiled and their ears unstopped, that they may look upon HIS Glory as it is made manifest, and hear the reverberations of HIS Word even unto great understanding of all that it signifies for all the children of the World and of the System?

Balak represents the spirit through whose motion the planetary life was betrayed to pass out of the life that was radiant with the light of the joy of beautiful childhood, into the darkness that smote all the children with the sorrow of great loss. Balaam represents the effect of that betraying spirit upon many of those who were of Israel, one-time prophets and seers within the kingdom of their GOD, the LORD of BEING. Thus the story is planetary.

As I indicated to you, there are three portions of the narrative, and these have been worked up by different editors, one of whom took the manuscripts and put the three portions into the story in the book of Numbers in the Old Testament. It is there presented as the biography of a man who was a Son of the Lamp, and who was asked to exercise his GOD-given gift in other than blessing, and was promised as a reward great gain, even a place of honour. In [connection with] this temptation there is something [indicative] of the allegorical meaning of the ass which Balaam is said to have ridden all his life; for the ass represents the vehicle of manifestation on these planes, and it can be so used on other planes. The ass is a vehicle through which a Soul makes manifest. It is thus said of the Master in the New Testament, as you find it there quoted from one of the prophets, "Behold thy king cometh unto thee riding upon an ass and the foal, or colt, of an ass,"—signifying the vehicle through which the manifestation should be made. Nay, it is even said He was borne down into Egypt upon an ass by His mother, accompanied by His father—another allegorical story, as those of you know who are familiar with the Teachings, having its full significance in the Travail of the Oblation.

The Mystery of the ass speaking, is a Mystery that is allegorically set forth in other religions. You have [a similar instance] in the [ancient] Greek religion. Was it not in the experience—as presented in the Greek story— of Achilles, whose horses, drawing his chariot, foretold his passing? There are many details into which I may not enter in explanation, which, bye and bye, will be set forth; for I would hasten to deal with the two outstanding features of the story, that in relation to the Planet, and that in relation to Israel.

THE STORY IN RELATION TO THE PLANET

The writer of the story was verily a Hebrew of the Hebrews—that is, one who knew of the planetary disaster. He was one (I am referring to the original narrative) who knew what Israel had been in the Heavens, and what Israel had become within the planetary constitution in ministry, and what Israel must needs become again ere the planetary life could be restored. That one could have been no betrayer of the glorious Word of the LORD of BEING. He could not have accounted earthly gain of any value in comparison with the truth which he knew, and which he must restore to Israel. He was a prophet, or Son of the Lamp; a Son in whom the Lamp of GOD burned so that the Light of the Eternal was his Light. He beheld in vision the Resplendence of the Glorious ONE, and in that Light was able to interpret all that had over-taken this World in its sad and disastrous experience. The prophet of the LORD looked out and saw what this World once was in its former estate, before the shadows fell upon its threshold, and the glory of its day was changed into the darkness of night. He knew not only Israel, for he was one of Israel, but he knew Jacob-El, or Ya-akob-El, who was none other than the chief Planetary Angel, whose ministry had to do with the generation of children unto the FATHER-MOTHER upon the planes of Judah, this World.

Balak was the evil spirit that materialized this World into such a state that it could not obey and so fulfil the Divine Purpose through responding in perfect motion to the Divine attraction. That evil spirit, which is personified in Balak, represented those who came to this system determined to change it and make of it a solidified

22

world, in the materialistic sense in which you understand
solids today. There is set forth in the story the desire of
those who came to bring a blight upon the world of Ya-
akob-El, the Planetary Angel. Ya-akob-El is very specially
named in the Old Scripture because of the special
ministry he had to render to this World. And with the
desire to blight all the energies and ministries of Ya-akob-
El there was the desire so to smite Israel that the
planetary life could not be restored again to its ancient
glory, but remain a smitten and lost world. Though it
was not accounted lost by that spirit of Balak that brought
about the Fall, yet it was lost—lost to Him Who is ever the
Great Love and Wisdom, and Whose ways are beautiful,
ever spiritual, ever glorious in their Celestial motion,
ever transcendent in their Divine action. So it is a story of
the cursing of this World unto its Fall, though the
endeavour to repeat, emphasize, intensify [that cursing],
has often been made.

You know this World was once beautiful. There are
many elements in it beautiful now, many of its manifestations exquisite in form and colour, and wonderful in
their ministry. But it was once a far more beautiful
World than it is to-day. There were no desert sands, not
only mystically but literally, for they themselves speak
of the tragedy that befell this land of Judah. There were
no wildernesses denizened by evil-minded creatures hurtful
to the children and to one another, for all life upon this
World expressed, from the lowliest to the highest degrees,
the Love and the Wisdom of the FATHER-MOTHER. The
former glory of Jerusalem, the Heavenly World, the
World flooded with Heavenly Light, the World that
was a World of Joy for the children and full of heavenly
peace, that former glory passed away when the World
became stricken with evil, the evil of the negativing
spirit named the Devil. This is no person, but is the
negativing spirit in any man or woman anywhere in this
World, or any World, if it can persist anywhere. The

Devil is that spirit that denies the exquisite glory of the FATHER-MOTHER expounded in a Human Soul, in Human childhood, in planetary childhood, planetary Soul life. In those days Satanas did not exist. The Maya that seemed to be was but the mists that envelop the Soul through which it must needs break, peer, penetrate, to come to the great vision beyond, and still greater vision in the beyond, and still beyond. But there was no betrayal. There was no falsifying. There was no inversion. There was no mirage of the truth. The World was beautiful.

It is difficult for some people to receive this divine truth. There are those who cannot bear to hear that this World was ever better than it is to-day, and that to-day is not a glorious exposition of ages of evolutary motion. Why, the civilizations of ten thousand years ago were greater than the civilizations of today! But what was understood then by civilization is not what is understood to-day, for civilization today is commercial and racial and national success, not the culture of the mind in the truest sense, and of the spirit, and the elevation of the life, and the teaching of the children how to interpret all that they see; to interpret rightly, and relate all that is beautiful to the Divine and the Eternal FATHER-MOTHER of all. We are suffering to-day the effect of the betrayal even of those earlier civilizations and their materialization, for the Zeit-geist in this World has always been a materializing spirit of the very nature of Balak. But the World was beautiful, and its redemption is the bringing of it back to what it once was in glorious estate.

So the story, on the first hand, is a parting of the veils that those who can understand may glimpse how Balak came to this World in the betraying spirits who smote Ya-akob-El, whose iniquity is not held against him (in the old meaning of the word, iniquity is mistake), whose iniquity is not held against him by the Divine. The Divine does not hold anything against HIS children. Why, who could be saved—that is, who could be restored,

healed, who could evermore be rejoiced—if the Divine
Love and Wisdom held anything against His children?
Such is a perversion of the Divine Love and Wisdom, an
inversion of the action of that Love and revelation of that
Wisdom, a betrayal of the attitude of the FATHER-
MOTHER unto all His children. Nor could HE remember
the perverseness that smote Israel—that is, the Children
of Israel. In many, many ages they scarcely knew where
they were because of the awful conditions amidst which
they had to function and serve. The Great Love knows.
HE remembers HIS children. HE remembers all the perverse conditions in which they have had to toil, travail
and sorrow, carry their burden, be oppressed by the
conditions. HE remembers not only the heights which
once they climbed, the glories amidst which they once
dwelt, but HE remembers also the low estates into which
they had to go, into which they were taken down, and
where they had to abide through ages in order to be as the
salt preserving this World from utter loss, that it might be,
in due course, borne back again to the bosom of GOD; that
is, on the bosom of Love to a redeemed and healed state.
For perfect Love in a Human Soul expressed in ministry
and taking to itself the burden of a World's travail, is
verily the Love of GOD taking to its bosom a World's
sorrow and burden.

Now I will address myself to the Oracles, to the glorious, prophetic unveiling. It is a Revelation, the beauty
of which some day you will see when you are able to read
those Oracles* with the explanations which have to be
given in detail; but for this hour I will unveil enough to
show you what the Oracles signify. That they are masonic
is obvious to one who understands.

THE SEPARATENESS OF ISRAEL

The first Oracle speaks of the aloneness of Israel in
this World, and their separateness from all the other

---

*Vide pp. 14-17.

nations of the Earth. This might seem to indicate pride and vanity on the part of a people, as if the people said within themselves, "We are holier, we are nobler, we are greater than all the other nations". Such a thought never entered the heart of Israel in the unfallen days, and any such shadow of it afterwards was but the affliction which overtook many, the result of the travail of the people in this distraught World. The first Oracle speaks of the separateness or apartness of Israel. The writer knew. He understood that the Children of Israel were not of the nations of the Earth. They did not belong to the Earth. In their inner life they were not like the children of the Earth, because they were older, they had had experience far beyond that of the children of this World. Therefore they were able to be teachers of the children of the Earth, and for that purpose they were sent. For great ages they remained apart from the nations of the Earth before the diaspora, or the scattering of them, when they had to melt away, as it were, into the heart of all the nations. This was not the Jewish diaspora, but the dispersion of the House of the Christhood. Before that time they were as a separate people, a nation that did not account itself a nation in the earthly sense, a people who had come for ministry, a household, every member of which was a priest of GOD, that is, one in mediation, in mediatorial service. The Children of Israel were always apart from the children of Judah. They knew Ya-akob-El, the Planetary Angel. They knew the other Angels. They knew the yet higher Angels, that is, those beyond the planetary constitution. They were familiar with the Solar life. They drank in of the breaths from the Solar Body. They were children of the Light. They were children of the Sun. When they came they were familiar with the glories of heavenly, Angelic, Celestial ministries, and many of them had touched the threshold of the Divine.

You can understand the meaning of their separateness therefore. This was not a standing apart, but functioning as a community of Souls for a special ministry. It is remarkable that through the great ages since the diaspora took place, none of them have ever been at home in this World; they never find the same pleasure and joy in this World. They did not in its perfect days. How much less could they in these days! Their highest joy is in service; they love to serve. Their supremest moments are those in which they are called upon to make sublime sacrifice for their LORD. They have been the Saints through the ages, not only in the Christian ages, but through all the ages of their history in this World. The prophet sees them still as a separate people. Though they had to intermingle with the nations, they never became of them. They were always in some strange way apart, seeking in their innermost life that aloneness which could come to them only in the places of the silence, seeking indeed *the* Silence, which is the place of HIS Dwelling in the innermost Sanctuary of Being.

Here is a testimony to the origin of Israel, the ancient heritage of Israel, a testimony from unexpected quarters that Israel as a community of Souls formed the Elect People, the people elected to come here; elected, but in a Divine sense, and elected to come for ministry for the Divine. So the prophet saw them still as a separate people alone in the World in their travail. To think of them [at first] as separate links of an inner and glorious golden chain that at one time bound the Earth through their exposition of the Divine Love and Wisdom, [and then] to think of them as separated, contains an element of sadness, yet it had to be because of the conditions. True, they met, some of them, on the way; they met each other and formed themselves into schools, into spiritual communities for Angelic ministry, and very specially for hours of talk upon those latent memories of theirs which are associated with the Ancient Mysteries.

It was thus the later or intermediary periods of the masonic schools arose, for Israel were at the founding of them long before they passed into mere centres of occult instruction where Souls, irrespective of the beauty of life and the seeking for the transcendent vision, became neophytes and initiates merely for outer knowledges, outer brotherhoods. This is no reflection upon those societies that are to-day the vestiges—that is, the remnants—of the ancient heritage of Israel, but just to show you how they have come down through the ages; how they have passed, bearing within themselves something of the high masonic vision and ritual and signs and wonders of ancient Israel.

THE KING IN THE MIDST OF ISRAEL

The masonic sign of the second Oracle is "The shout of a King,"—the King, the royal crown. Here the prophet sees Israel as once they were, as once more they are to become. He sees the days of the glorious Theocracy when GOD was King in the midst of Israel as Israel reigned and ministered in the midst of Judah. The "shout of a King" signifies that the volume of life, in responding to the Divine regnancy, interprets GOD's dwelling within each Son of Israel and in the midst of the great Christhood community of Israel. On the part of the Seer it is no mere recovery along historical lines of the days of the Theocracy as understood in the book of Judges. No, that was not a day of the true Theocracy. For the real Theocracy has not been in manifestation since Israel went down into bondage great ages ago, because of the result of the diaspora. Yet whilst GOD reigns within a true Israelite— yes, even in the depths of Sheol or the land of the Shadows, and the Hadean world, the land of the shades; yes, even though he might have to go in his ministry into the Tartarean world, or the hells of life, for the healing of Souls—[whilst GOD reigns within a true Israelite,] there is that in the very foundation of his spiritual constitution which holds the Being to the central [pole] which is the Regnant Presence within the Soul's Sanctuary.

28

The Theocracy is GOD's Regnancy, as once it was in every Israelite and through the communal life expressed in all Israel's service. It is the shout of a King. It is not an earthly noise. When GOD reigns you do not require to shout it to the Heavens. No; though men and women may have to hear of those things. But where GOD moves the motion is as the great deep, silent but tremendous. Where GOD reigns all the powers of the Being are in response to HIM. HE comes silently. HE indwells silently. HE makes HIMSELF manifest silently; but all the powers, as it were, unite in proclaiming HIM. And that is what is meant by the shout of a King. Why, when GOD reigns in you, you will not seek to hide it, nor will you seek to call attention to it as such. No, that would be vanity. When GOD reigns in you, wherever you go HIS Breath will pour through you; wherever you go HIS resplendence will illumine your auric flow, so that its outflow will affect the atmosphere, will affect the very breaths, the inner breaths, of those whom you meet in the way. When GOD reigns in you, you just love to be even silent with HIM, for HIM, because of HIS tremendous Theocratic motion within you; but the motion goes out in its effects to touch all the life that comes within the compass of your environment, and the touch of your ministry. When GOD reigned in Israel, Israel reigned in their tents, that is, in the covered house, in the tabernacle Sanctuary where there was ever the perfect Overshadowing of the glory of HIS Presence.

Who could blight the life in whom GOD reigns? No one. No one, if that one walks in the consciousness of the Indwelling of that glorious Presence. Even Balak, the evil, devilish, Satanic spirit, would utterly fail to smite, to bring a curse—that is, a blighting effect—upon the life. Oh no! Where GOD reigns everything is delightful. You need not fear anything if GOD reigns within you; not the future, nor to-day. You need not fear the power that seems oppressive around you. If GOD be regnant within

29

you, your life is Theocratic. HE is its principle, its centre, and HE will become its circumference. HE is [the sum of its] attributes. HE is its potency. HE becomes in sublime fulness, at last, its perfect life. You need not fear if GOD be regnant within you. An Israelite indeed must be Theocratic—must be. This does not mean that there would be no earthly kings. If good men and women, ever thinking for the children of the FATHER-MOTHER, [seek to] minister, to mediate for them, to help them, well, that is the truest form of earthly government. That earthly kings have so largely passed away is because there has passed from them the true vision of their ministry unto the people.

THE VOCATION OF ISRAEL

The Vocation of Israel is indicated in the third Oracle. It is clearly indicated that they are all Aquarians. This is not in the merely modern interpretation of Aquarius in his influence upon lives, but that which Aquarius signifies in the Celestial and Divine administration. Aquarius speaks of the water-carrier, the water-bearer, and the out-pouring of that water. The vocation of Israel was this; that they were water-bearers, water-carriers. They came to this World with their pitchers full of living waters of the knowledge of the Divine Love and Wisdom. They came to this World full of the knowledge of the Angelic Heavens and Celestial ministries. Thus they out-poured their knowledge for the Divine, as waters that brought yet greater life to the children in the unfallen days; and through great ages of the fallen days they have been also the water-bearers, that is, the water-carriers. They are the children to whom the inner truths of the Kingdom appeal; they are arrested by them; they can understand them; they are drawn by them. Their vocation is ever to receive of the Water of Life and, having received it, and been enriched by it, to pour it forth again from their pitcher, which they should have full to overflow. The vocation of Israel all through the ages, from the unfallen days even to these days, is that of the water-carrier. It does not mean that they are all Aquarians in the astrological sense, but they are all Aquarians in the Celestial, Divine Celestial sense, bearers of the living waters, those waters that revitalize whilst they refresh all the Being.

This is just by the way of indication to you, for Israel is to be restored to this office once more, as is indicated in the fourth Oracle.

THE COMING OF THE STAR
AND THE ARISING OF ISRAEL

The masonic signs are those of a Star and a Sceptre. The Star shall arise again for Ya-akob-El, the Planetary Angel. The Redeemer shall come for him, for his system; for Judah, the land of Judah. And the Sceptre shall be restored to Israel; for the Sceptre is the regnancy, the sign of the regnancy, the sign of authority, of the children who have Divine authority. This is not in the human sense. For one who has Divine authority never exercises it in the sense of a human superiority and power. One who has Divine authority is one who can speak from out the Presence, from the very heart of the Presence, of HIM Who is the Word of GOD, Who is the living Truth, Who is the Regnant ONE, Who is the Immanent Presence within us, Who is none other than the LORD of all BEING and FATHER-MOTHER of all. Divine authority comes to a Soul, not through being conveyed to it from without, but through the Soul's realization within itself of HIM Who is the LORD of the Sanctuary and High Priest of HIS Temple, Mediator and Shekinah in one, the Living Bread, the Living Wine, GOD's Mass for HIS Children, HIS Mass in HIS Children realized. It is the coming of the Messenger, the Star; the Messenger, the Illumined One.

But the Messenger is not to be thought of as any man or woman. No! The LORD is the Messenger, though HE

31

has His servants, in the Celestial Heavens, in the Angelic Heavens, and even functioning upon the Human Kingdom. He has His Servants, but He is ever the Messenger, for He is the Message. The Servant is but the conveyor of the Message. It is the Message, *the Message*, you understand; no man or woman, though the Messenger or Servant must be one with his Message; he would not understand it if he were not; he would not understand Him of Whom it speaks if he were not one with it. For only through being one with the Message has he become able to be Servant of the Message for the FATHER-MOTHER unto His children.

The Star for Ya-akob-El, the Planetary Angel, for the Angels of the LORD who were involved in the great declivity, the awful Descent, and whose mistake has overwhelmed themselves and all the children of Judah unto the rending of Judah's kingdoms and the filling of her once glorious planes with spiritual darkness, the Star and the Message have come back. The Star has arisen for Ya-akob-El, and he rejoices to see this day.

And the Sceptre is coming back to Israel. For every Israelite who returns, that is, every Soul who rises up into the consciousness of real childhood to the FATHER-MOTHER, to live the life of Jesushood and Christhood, through that life, in that life, the Sceptre is coming back. That is, the power to reign upon the Earth for the FATHER-MOTHER, to reign with Christ, Christ reigning in you and through you. The Sceptre of GOD is the sign within you of His Regnancy, that you can reign for HIM, reign with HIM, thus making manifest the glory of His Presence come back again.

Ah, the Seer said, "I see His Coming, but not yet. I behold His Arising, yet the becoming is not just now." But it shall be when Israel, *when* Israel is restored; when the land, when the Edom land, the land of forgetfulness, becomes again their possession, and they forget no more the greatness of the loving-kindness of the LORD with them, recover again the goodness of GOD unto them, and attain once more their ancient inheritance, that All-transcendent Christhood, to be for HIM as Jesus Christ in this World unto its healing, unto its illumination, unto its redemption.

May these fragments out of a great history, broken as they have had to be, as it were, into very small pieces, nevertheless be such as to be worthy of your gathering and partaking of unto the arising of your own Being to manifest for HIM Who is your LORD.

O Lord God of Sabaoth, the Lord of Ya-akob-El, the Lord God of Israel, may each of Thy children here who seek unto the knowing of Thee, find the veils which have hidden Thee parting, even until Thy glory streams unto them, upon them, and into them, to fill all the Sanctuary of their Being! We would that all Thine Israel once more come to know Thee and be again for Thee amongst Thy Judah children who are of Ya-akob-El. Thus would we ever adore and worship and praise Thee, in life and service and motion of blessing for Thee.

I

BALAK AND BALAAM

PART II

THIS morning I return to the subject of last Sunday
to speak of the two aspects then only indicated. Those
of you who were present will remember that the subject
was *Balak and Balaam*, the one said to be the king of Moab,
and the other a prophet given to divination. I would
remind you of some of the salient features spoken of last
week by me; primarily, that the whole story, except for
some vestiges gathered and worked up into it, is non-
historical on the outer planes in a merely human sense,
but is very specially historical in a mystical soulic and
planetary sense; and that it is a compound allegory of
the betrayal of this World and its children, with, added
on to that, the betrayal of the House of Israel.

You will remember that Balak represented the evil
mind that brought about the desolation within the land of
Judah, this Planet; and how, having accomplished so
much through the materialization of the planes of the
Planet, that evil mind sought ever to pursue Israel, the
representatives of the Divine World—that is, they were as
ministrants from GOD unto the children of this World— to
pursue them with its curses, its blighting influences, which,
even with such knowledge as you may have of Israel,
will become most obvious as you read these Old
Scriptures.

That such a disaster overtook this World is only too
obvious to everyone, though they may not relate the
conditions to such causes as I have indicated. That such
disaster is to be healed is gloriously true, and the healing
is in process of being accomplished in this very hour.

34

Though ages have intervened and the time may have
seemed long for the accomplishment of so glorious a work,
yet it takes a long time for a Soul to grow into the
consciousness of the Divine, and, as you will have experienced in this life, it sometimes takes much travail to
return, and overcome states, and get back into the
Sanctuary in your consciousness, where you may hear
His Voice and look again upon the glory of His Vision.
And if such be so, how much greater must the effort and
the time be for the accomplishment of the Divine Purpose
necessary for the recovery of Ya-akob-El, the Planetary
Angel, with all the glorious—one-time glorious—household of Judah; the healing of all the hurt that befell, not
only its planes, but all its children, and even the healing
of the hurt, not only of Judah, but of Israel.

So, though the ages have seemed great in number,
they are after all but as the passing years in your own
experience. The Great Love has waited, waited until the
time when the accomplishment of so desirable an end
would be possible. Thus the Manifestation in the days
of the Master was the forerunner wherein was the revelation again of that estate Israel once stood in and
made manifest; it was the forerunner of that Travail
which was to accomplish the return of all Israel, and all
the house of Judah from Shittim to Gilgal, and beyond
Gilgal up to Pisgah, and beyond Pisgah, as we shall see.

Such is a succinct presentation of the Mystery with
which we dealt last week, so that you will understand
better the things I would now address myself to and speak
of to you.

Apart from the Four Oracles which I read to you last
week and spoke on, concerning *The Separateness of Israel,*
The Regnancy in the heart of Israel, The Vocation of Israel,
and *The Coming of the Star and Sceptre,* there are those two
outstanding elements in the story:—the Ass of Balaam,
on which he rode to meet Balak, and the Seven Altars
with dual sacrifices on each, repeated three times in the

experience of Balaam before he proclaimed, or in his ministry of proclamation of, the Four Oracles. Though the allegory of the ass comes first, as it is immediately related to the possibilities of a Soul ascending, we will take it after we look at those fragments of human and divine sacrifices set forth in the story.

THE SEVEN ALTARS

Balak offered upon his Altar sacrifices of oxen and sheep, it is said. After he had done so, Balaam asked Balak to build Seven Altars and offer upon each Altar an ox and a ram. This was done on the heights of Baal. Baal is thought of as a heathen God. Doubtless the term was applied in that way. But Baal had relation to a Solar story, also. Thus you have it in many combinations. Even the modern term of Baalbek is none other than the City of the Sun, changed by the Greeks to Heliopolis, or City of the Sun. The name Baal was brought down just as was the name of the ELOHIM, and that most sacred unutterable Name that came to be spoken of as YAHWEH, and we speak of as JEHOVAH. For the heights of Baal represented for the time being the human aspect of the endeavour of a Soul to approach unto the Presence.

There are three distinct ascensions presented. The first is to the heights of Baal; the second to the heights, the summit, of Pisgah; and the third is to Peor, Baal-Peor, or the mountain of GOD with the cleft in it. It is an indication, in the true story, of how a Soul must return. Balaam is said to have left Balak at his own Altar, even to have left him behind when he built the Seven Altars upon the heights of Baal and sought the Presence.

THE ASCENSION TO THE HEIGHTS OF BAAL

Now you will note this, that Balak offered sacrifices of oxen and sheep. Balak represents the betraying principle. One of the great betrayals that overtook the children of this World was the descent from their true childhood estate to the FATHER-MOTHER, to become as ravenous creatures eating flesh. For the habit of flesh-eating is a part of, as well as collateral to, the offering of the sacrifices of creatures to appease the Divine. For the eating of flesh was to appease the false desires within the body, even as the mind offered the creatures, believing that that ONE Who gave to the Human Soul the Mystery of its consciousness and potency, Who gave to it its love-principle and its love-streams to flow through its system, could demand such sacrifices to be offered to HIM to help HIM to be beautiful towards them.

Do not you see the nature of the betrayal that overtook all the children, [part] of which [is the practice of] flesh-eating by men and women who are worshippers of Baal in the fallen sense even unto this day? That which Balak did before he asked Balaam to consult GOD was a perversion of sacred Mystery. For, remember, that those who betrayed this World at one time knew the Mysteries, yes, knew the Mysteries. You remember a passage in the Old Scripture that says, "O Lucifer, one-time Star of the morning, how thou hast fallen! For though thou wast exalted even unto the Heavens, thou hast been brought down to hell"—that is, in state, not in place; the state makes the place. So those who betrayed this World knew many, many of the Celestial Mysteries, and even some of the Divine Mysteries, though there had to be hidden from them the Mystery of the Tree of Life lest they should partake of it and in evil state persist forever. That is how it is presented in the Allegory stating the Fall, in the book of Genesis. For, originally, the ox and the sheep, especially set forth as the ox and the ram, were terms used in the Mysteries to hide secrets, secret significances concerning the life-forces—the life-forces of the Being and the life-forces of the body, and the life-forces as made manifest in the ascensions of the Heavens, that is, the different degrees of the Heavenly estates. So Balak's offering reveals the degradation of his own estate.

Of course, as I said to you, Balak represents a principle, the evil mind, and is not to be thought of simply as a man. So is it with Balaam, who is considered a false prophet, a lover of divination and the gain that comes from divination. But no one can be a real prophet and be false. I read but a day or two ago in a commentary on this very subject how possible it was for a man to be a true prophet of God and yet to be an evil man. But that is not possible. The motion by which a Soul becomes evil also closes its gates, draws its veils again so that its spiritual vision becomes closed to it. A prophet is an illumined one. If the prophet seeks to do evil [the gates of the Soul are closed]. I am not speaking of human, earthly mistakes which may arise, not through choice at all, but as the result of the conditions amidst which the prophet ministers—those things which he has to do in order to enable him to give his prophetic message to the World. To be evil would be to *choose* the evil. A prophet is a God-inspired and God-illumined man or woman Soul. This is not to be understood in the personal way, but he or she is an illumined Soul. And to be false would be at once to cause the operation within the inner Sanctuary of the Being of those Laws of God which are in our very constitution, by which the veils would be drawn.

Balaam represents, as I indicated to you, the effect of the betrayal of the whole House of Israel, and very specially of many of them. But he has to be thought of in relation to the Son of the Flame, the Son of the Lamp, the Lamp with the living Flame, without which there is no illumination. And that illumination is set forth in the four wonderful Oracles which I read to you last week.

Now that which Balaam is said to have requested to be done—the Seven Altars to be built, and upon each Altar an ox and a ram offered in sacrifice—was a mystical and masonic statement. For the ox represents the body. The ram represents the Divine Principle in us. He is the symbol of Ramah who is said to have been a Messenger.

Each Altar has the ox and the ram, and there are Seven
Altars, seven on the heights of Baal. Why, they represent
the Altars upon each plane of our consciousness, each
plane of our experience, each plane of our life on the
seven circles or spheres of our experience! And you cannot
get anywhere without such sacrifice, such consecration in
sacrifice of the body, which is the ox, and the sacrifice
and consecration of the Divine Principle in you, the ram.
There is no way of ascension unto the heights of the
Heavens but by the way of sacrifice. And Sacrifice means
Altar, and Altar means Mediation, and Mediation means
Consecration. Even in the more human aspects—that is,
in the lower degrees, or the first of the three great ascensions—there must be the sacrifice of the vehicle, as
well as of the inner principle of our life, unto all that is
true and pure and noble and beautiful and good, all that is
Divine. We cannot rise without such sacrifice. We cannot
approach the Divine without such sacrifice. We cannot
have our lives ratified by the Fire that gives Divine
Energy without such sacrifice. You will note that the two
[sacrifices] are offered upon each Altar, and they represent the seven degrees within the life in all the ascensions,
but the seven degrees are from the outermost to the
Innermost. There must be complete sacrifice.

It is said that after such sacrifices the LORD as the
ELOHIM, met Balaam; and that Balaam had a vision of
Israel. It was partial, but it was the prelude to greater
things to come. He saw again the ancient estate of Israel,
the separateness of Israel from this system, the communal
Christhood, as once it was, of Israel in this world. He saw
how they could never be accounted as one of the nations
of the Earth. Thus far: for it is said that Balak said to him,
"Why! you have sung glorious things of Israel, and in
such statement blest them. Come! that is not the way to
aid me in my work of materialization." For Balak
represents the materializing spirit.

THE ASCENSION TO THE SUMMIT OF PISGAH

In the allegory it is said Balak took Balaam to another height, Pisgah. We have to forget the apparently human aspect of the dramatic story, and to understand that it hides the Mysteries of the Soul's motion. Having accomplished so much on the summits of Baal, or [that estate of consciousness] where it feels its first great inter-relationship with the Solar body, the Solar ministry, the Divine radiating Presence, the Soul goes through yet another ascension—it ascends Mount Pisgah. Pisgah is the Mount from which it is said Moses viewed the Promised Land. It is the Mount on which the Glorious, that is, the Divine Messenger can give to the Soul the vision of its ancient and future inheritance, the Land of great possession. He does not take it into that possession, but *shows* it the possession, into the inheritance of which it must go bye and bye.

But here again you have the repetition of the Seven Altars and the fourteen sacrifices; that is, the sacrifice, the dual sacrifice, upon each Altar is repeated. And you will note how in each instance it *is* dual. There must be the *Vehicle* and the *Principle*. We have vehicles wherever we are. Some think they will have no vehicles when they pass from here to the other world; that they will be amongst the great aetheric mists that you behold sometimes with the eye. Wherever you go there must be a vehicle, there is a vehicle. The Divine Principle is at the centre of all things; but when HE, as the Principle and the Centre of all things, makes manifest, HE has HIMSELF a Vehicle. Thus, what is the Sun but the Vehicle of tremendous Divine Embodiment for manifestation?

So wherever you go in the ascension of your life, the vehicle has to be consecrated. It is that which is represented by the ox, as the principle is by the ram; the Divine Centre, and that which is related to the circumference; for it is through the vehicle that the circumference

40

of life becomes manifest. There is no way upward, even to Pisgah, but by the way of sacrifice, by the way of the Altars of GOD, not one but seven. As you rise out of the astral-occult conditions of this World on to the purified Planetary Angelic Heavens, you have to make sacrifice upon your Altars. As you ascend further in your estate, in your consciousness, in your power to make manifest the Divine within you, you have again your Seven Altars, and on the way you must needs place upon them your dual sacrifice. There is no way inward and upward but by the consecration of whatsoever vehicle you have, and always as the exposition of the motion of your Divine Principle, Ramah within you.

You see, it is a masonic story, and the very terms themselves were meant to hide the Mystery. Not to hide from those who could discern, but from those who would betray. And it is because those who translated the Scriptures, who have translated those Scriptures, knew nothing of the masonic Mysteries at the heart of those Scriptures, that we have them in the state in which they are presented in the Old and New Testaments. True, they have been terribly corrupted in the way, even those of the Mysteries that were truly set forth in cryptic terms; for there have been such accretions, during the ages, associated with Jewish story, and these have all been added on to the real gems of truth found in those Old Books to the hiding of many things that would have been apparent in meaning to those who could discern.

THE ASCENSION TO THE MOUNT CLEFT IN TWAIN

At Pisgah the Son of the Lamp beheld the Presence, spake with that Presence, and had the vision of the Divine regnancy as once it was in Israel, and as it was again to become. Hence the second Oracle. Yet that was not all. For Israel was in high estate at one time, and so it was given to the Son of the Lamp to see yet further and to behold how the ancient estate was to come back to Israel.

And so he went yet higher into the third ascension. He went to the Mount of GOD that had the cleft in it. There is only one mountain spoken of specially in the Old Scriptures which is said to have been cleft in twain. Around Sinai the radiations of the Presence played. In dioramic fashion there moved upon the summit of Horeb the passing of the glory of the Presence. But it is recorded that when HE comes, Who is the LORD of BEING, HIS feet shall stand upon Olivet, and that in that day the mountain shall be cleft in twain, and that there shall be from the wilderness unto the land of promise a highway along which all the House of Israel shall move, even until the ancient inheritance is re-possessed.

So the prophet is taken to the mountain of GOD with the cleft in it. Even in the term "cleft" there is masonic significance; there is the opening for vision, there is also the power of veiling. And there he sees Israel, full once more of Divine Vocation, carrying unto the children of this World, as in the ancient times, the Waters of Life with which to heal all their woundings, to refresh them, to re-exhilarate them, and even to bring them into the conscious experience, the degree in which they were able consciously to realize the beauty of the power of the Love of the FATHER-MOTHER. Nay more! As he looks through that cleft away from the wilderness that is behind, he sees the Sun, the Star rising, the glory of Christhood once more ascending the heavenly arcs to ultimately fill the whole dome of the Heavens of the Soul, and therefore of all Israel, with HIS glory; and, as a result, the return of consciousness to the individual Israelite, and through that possession to the communal Israelitish embodiment, of the glorious Sceptre of the LORD, when HE shall have dominion in their midst, and through them restore again to a Ya-akob-El dominion over the whole planetary life. For, as I said to you, Jacob, spoken of so much in the Old Scriptures, refers to the planetary constitution, and Ya-akob-El was the Planetary Angel at the head of his planetary hierarchy, administrator for the Great Love in the evolutionary exposition of that Love and Wisdom in the planetary life.

Thus again, if you would see the Star and regain the Sceptre, you must make, even in the Innermost, in the higher ascensions, your Seven Altars and offer your sacrifices. Whatever vehicles you may have, they must be consecrated absolutely for the service of your LORD. The Divine Principle in you must needs have its motion within all the ascensions unto HIM, taking with it all your powers, even [that symbolized by] the ox within the Celestial realms, all the powers of your Being in high consecration unto HIM.

These are but glints and gleamings of the Mystery, yet they are such as to emphasize this great Truth—and it needs emphasis in these days continually: *you cannot get anywhere without sacrifice, consecration, noble endeavour, sacred and holy purpose. You cannot reach the Innermost and the highest without absolute consecration of your Being. It cannot be done.* The Soul who essays to reach the Innermost without such consecration would, like those who fell, go down, yes, go down even to the prison-houses written of in Scripure, but little understood, indeed, if at all, by those who read concerning those Mysteries.

We cannot reach the Divine except by the Divine Way. It is the way of purity, the way of noble purpose, the way of sweet and blessed endeavour. It is the way of lowliness and true humility, which, permit me to say, is not a grovelling in the dust of earthliness in any sense, or the loss of dignity. No! No! The Humblest ONE in the Universe is that ONE Who is the very Heart of all our heart's motions, the Secret of our life, the Centre of its Mystery, the Fulness of its experience, the energizing Potency by which we live and move and have our Being; the most Dignified ONE. All HIS works speak of dignity. There is nothing lacking in beauty in HIS works. There is nothing in HIS expositions that would humiliate your thought and bring down in your vision the divinity within you. God is the most perfect Artist. All perfect art is an exposition of HIMSELF. HE is the Lowliest yet the most Majestic. So we can ascend only in the measure in which we become like HIM in our ways upon all the kingdoms; in the true Human Kingdom, purifying our life and following no longer the ways of Balak, the evil mind; exalting our life by the raising of the Altars upon every plane; in the Human experience, in its Angelic experience, in its Celestial experience; and then the Soul can glimpse, glimpse that which it will yet more fully enter into, even the Mystery of the Divine.

BALAAM'S ASS

Now I would speak to you of Balaam's ass, which is a part of the allegory. There are stories that would seem to be reflections of the truth, lying at the heart of that one found in ancient Egypt, stories associated with the ancient Egyptian religion and with Greek myths, with Babylonian lore, and even with tradition and superstition in South Africa. For in the Bible, Balaam's ass is not the only creature that is said to speak. Even in a wonderful parable we read of a tree speaking; and then in the early history we have the story, as it is told, of the serpent speaking and betraying Adam and Eve. In Egypt there was the sacred cow that spake, and I referred last week to Achilles, of whom it is said in the Iliad that the horses that drew his chariot turned and predicted his end. And there is also a mystical story in South Africa of the ass speaking. Why, it is a mystical presentation in the allegory of the Soul in its motion, in its setting out, in its trend, not only the downward, but also the onward and upward trend.

The ass is a vehicle of transit. It is the body's mind. The colt of the ass is the body. The mind, or the vehicle in the body through which the mind can operate is the ass in our constitution, just as the powers of the body are symbolized in the masonic term of the cow or the ox. The ass was said to have been ridden by Balaam all his life. For the ass rebuked its owner, and said that all the days of his life he had served him faithfully until now. Our vehicles are for transit and for manifestation. By means of them we proceed; by means of them we reveal; through them we serve. Our vehicles carry us; they bear us through all our earthly days and through all our history. For we have other vehicles than those observable to the human eye.

Balaam, setting out, rides his ass. It is his vehicle. The beauty of the masonic presentation is revealed as you unfold it. As he made his journey to offer sacrifice, he desired that the ass should proceed more quickly, and it is said that the ass could not, but that the ass spake to him. Can our bodies speak to us? Is speech confined to the intonation through language, or are there other forms of speech? GOD utters HIS Voice, it is said; the Earth melts. There is the speech, the inward speech, that cannot be intoned, that cannot be expressed outwardly. There is the greatest speech of the Being that can find no language to articulate it. Has your ass never spoken to you of how you have been driving it; your mind, the higher mind—as the horse of Achilles represented—your higher mind desiring to accomplish something that the lower mind and your body even resented, felt the burden of too greatly? Have you never sought to drive your ass whither it did not wish to go in the ways of your life, in your desires, in your actions? Have you never smitten your ass, hurt your vehicle, made it less competent to bear you where you desired to go? Have you never caused it to be held up on the way? For the ass, as an ass, can see only on to the planes of reflection where the trees are reflected; because to see an Angel would mean that the veil of the Soul was drawn, and an ass has not in this life, and whilst it is an ass, reached the Human Kingdom. (But, as I have indicated, the noble horses, and the mules, which belong to an offshoot, and the asses too, were at one time functioning as very little children in Human consciousness upon the Human Kingdom before the last great descent of the whole Planetary constitution. That Mystery lies at the heart of many of the tales told in ancient Persian, and later Babylonian, and ancient and later Indian and Greek myth). The ass speaks, "What have I done that thou shouldst smite me so and drive me whither I cannot go? Cannot you see an Angel stands in the way?" There are circumferences in the operations of the Laws of GOD that you cannot go beyond. Life is so constituted that if you attempt to do so you are held up, your ass is held up, on the way. You do not see the cause of the holding up. You do not see the Angel in the path. You would drive your ass when you do not know the danger which the Angel would inform you of, and does afterwards inform you of when your eyes are opened. Why, the story of Balaam's ass is a living story, without any contradictions of natural law within it; for it is the mystical presentation of how a Soul setting out in life will ride its ass wherever it desires to go!

And then the ass comes to a passage (it is put as a cleft) in the rock, through which it cannot proceed because an Angel stands in its way. When you seek to do a great wrong to anyone, if you ever feel like that, an Angel will stand in your way. You may accomplish it, but it will be to your hurt. If you seek to violate the Divine Law within you, the Angel will stand in the way speaking to your vehicles and then speaking to you. Your ass will speak to you, though you may smite it.

How lacking in consideration men are unto their asses—their bodies and their minds! How lacking in thought when indeed there are even those who teach that the body is nothing to be regarded with concern or especially to be regarded of high estate. Why, it is a glorious representation upon the outermost planes of the Fashion of GOD in the Inner Realms; that is, the Fashion of HIS Potencies, the Fashion HIS Potencies take! It is a

glorious representation of the forms within the Inner
Kingdom, which are in all the Kingdoms right from the
Divine out on to the Human Kingdom. The body is
something to be regarded; not in a self-regarding way,
but to be valued as a vehicle, a vehicle of transit, a vehicle
of manifestation, and a vehicle of service. So that to care
for our bodies in the truest way is to care for that power
that can convey us from place to place, and help us in the
motion of the ram within us in the manifestation of the
Divine Love, and aid us in our exposition of God in our
daily ministries wheresoever we are, wheresoever our
ministries may be. Care for your ass that has borne you
all your life—your body and the vehicle for the mind to
operate through. And when you are held up in the hour
of your extreme pressure on your ass, think, "There must
be an Angel in the way, though I see not his flaming sword,
nor hear his voice. But I would hear his voice and behold
his flaming sword; I would understand the truth." Then
the Angel of the LORD will speak to you.

Nay more! You cannot get to your Seven Altars, to
build them, whereon to offer your sacrifices, without your
ass; whether it be the ass which is the accommodation to
these planes, or the ass, the vehicle that will be an
accommodation to you in other planes, you must ride your
ass.

The prophet cannot escape it. He must ride his ass.
Would he ride the heights of Baal, the Mount whereon the
Solar vision first comes upon the Soul? Then he must ride
his ass. Should he meet Balak in the way and fall in with
Balak's wishes, woe betide him and his ass! But if he ig-
nores the desire of the evil mind, then blessing unto him,
for he will build his Altars and offer his sacrifices, taking
the first ascension, a great degree with seven degrees within itself. And then he will take his next ascension, a
greater degree with seven degrees within itself; for each
Altar represents a degree. And he then will proceed to
take his third ascension wherein he comes into the

47

consciousness of Celestial things. The first ascension is Angelic; the second is the Higher Angelic or the Lower Celestial; the third is the Higher Celestial wherein he enters into the consciousness of a Solar order. He can stand on the Mount with its cleft. It is the Mount of Divine Vision, the Mount of Divine recovery. He can see the past of Israel and of Judah. He can see that which the LORD would bring to Judah through re-glorifying HIS people Israel.

May these most precious truths broken in most fragmentary form—necessarily so in this hour—so arrest you, so draw you, that you will come along riding joyfully upon your ass unto the high places of GOD, to re-institute your Soul's sacrifices; building your Altars unto HIM, for HIM; offering your life for Earth's service, for Angelic service, for Celestial service upon the Earth, for Divine service, even to be HIS perfect exposition, from Ramah in the very principles of your life, even unto all the potencies and powers of your body, making your ass part of yourself as your mind rides forth a divine victor, conquering and to conquer.

O our Father-Mother, the wealth of Thy Love is beyond telling; Thy ways upon the great deep beyond fathoming! The glory of Thine Approach, and Thine Encompassing and Overshadowing, and Thy Most holy Outworking, are greater than tongue can tell, yet such as Thy children may realize.

Ever Blessed be Thy most glorious Name!

I

THE MESSAGE OF THE BOOK OF
JOEL

Upon my holy Mount Zion, blow ye the Trumpet of the Lord!
Sound the Reveille unto all the Children of Zion, that they may
awaken, arise, and come forth to greet their Lord:
For the Day of His coming is at hand; and He Himself is nigh.
Like the morning breaking upon the mountains, and its glory
descending unto the plains, after a night of dense darkness cast by
gloomy clouds, until the darkness flees away and the night is no
more, so shall be the coming of the Lord.
His People shall be great and strong. Their like shall not have
been seen for ages within the land of Judah; nor for many coming
generations shall there be their equal.
His Cloud of Glory shall go before them; His Pillar of Fire
encompass them.
The land before them shall become an Eden through their pro-
ceeding; and the desolate wilderness behind them they shall know no
more.
In His Chariot of Fire shall the Lord go before them, and they
shall follow Him; arrayed shall they be as His Army of Horsemen
to run His race and accomplish His Will in the land.
As the Hosts of the Lord shall they be led by His Chariot of
Fire unto the Mountains of God; and their motion shall be as the
procedure of the Sacred Flame.
Before the bowed Heavens the whole world shall be moved;
with the fervent heat of the Sacred Flame shall the Earth melt,
and all things become changed.
The Sun and Moon shall no more be veiled; nor shall the
Stars in the Firmament withhold their shining.

* * * *

Blow ye the Trumpet of the Lord in Zion!
Sound ye the Reveille unto the citizens of the Holy City!
Call them together into a sacred Assembly. Say unto them:
Thus saith the Lord your God, O Israel!
Fear not, O People of mine Inheritance; but be glad and shout
for very gladness.

Be not afraid, O ye afflicted creatures of the field, for the day of your deliverance draweth nigh.

The Earth's wilderness shall be changed, and green pastures shall spring forth.

The Trees shall bear their fruit, even the Fig-tree and the Vine shall yield of their richness. For the Earth shall be renewed.

Be glad, therefore, O ye Children of Zion, and rejoice in and before your Lord!

For He shall gather you together as His Hosts, and make His Name glorious in your midst.

None amongst you shall be ashamed; for all nations shall come to know that the Lord God of Israel is in the midst of you.

And it shall come to pass when My Spirit is breathed through all your substance, that, as My Sons and Daughters, ye shall prophesy of those things beheld by the Ancients of Israel in the land of their nativity when as yet they were young men.

And those who serve before you shall behold the wonders made manifest through the motion of My Spirit; for there shall be given signs in the Heavens for the dwellers upon the Earth, even the Blood of the Everlasting Covenant, the Chariot of Fire and the Cloud of the Glory of the Lord.

*   *   *   *

All who turn unto Him shall know the deliverance He doth give unto Ierusalem through the holy Assembly of His children upon Mount Zion.

And all the nations shall know that the Lord God of the Heavenly Hosts dwelleth in Zion in the midst of His People Israel.

For, thus saith the Lord God of Sabaoth—

Behold! I will gather together all peoples within the valley of Jehoshaphat.

And I will perform My great work of judgment in their midst, and cause to take place the overthrow of all those who be enemy unto Mount Zion;

For by the Blood of the Everlasting Covenant will I cleanse the Earth, until the whole land of Judah be redeemed, and Ierusalem be once more as the Holy City.

THE MINOR PROPHETS

NOTES ON TEXT

A FRAGMENT OF RECOVERED LOGIA FROM JOEL'S MESSAGE

The Book of Joel is a mere fragment of an ancient prophecy concerning the House of Israel. It is a Message from YAHWEH. It is couched in many Masonic terms which were familiar to the House of Israel. Only the high Initiates, the Sons of GOD, knew their hidden meanings. Mount Zion and the Holy City, referred to the Christhood, and belonged to the Solar Kingdom. The Cloud of Glory hid the Mystery of the Presence of LORD ADONAI. The Pillar of Fire spoke to the Sons of GOD of the Spiral of Being. YAHWEH's Chariot of Fire was a Password to the Innermost Circles of Initiates, and signified the Eternal Mystery as manifested in Energy. The Vine and the Fig-tree were masonic symbols of the Divine Love and Wisdom.

The Messianic Manifestation, with the Redemption and Regeneration are clearly heralded, and also the conflict and victory within the Valley of Jehoshaphat—the Armageddon within the Planet's Heavens during the Oblation.

I

A PROPHETIC REVEILLE

THE MESSAGE OF THE BOOK OF JOEL

THE book of Joel in its compass is quite short, comprising some three chapters. In the prophetic records it is old, believed to have been proclaimed as a prophecy some eight hundred years B.C., and therefore has preceded all the other prophets given after the Psalter, that is, from Isaiah to Malachi. It is a strange book. It is so mixed, even though so brief; so contradictory, though so revelatory. It undoubtedly has suffered, as the other books have suffered, through the introduction of the racial, national and geographical influences which were so evident in the history of Jewry.

The book [sounds] a triumphant note. It takes me far back in my vision; that is, to all that it calls to and anticipates. In its brevity it nevertheless contains tremendous teachings which I will endeavour to unveil to you, in so far as the hour will permit.

We have a presentation of Mount Zion; of the LORD's Trumpeter and HIS Reveille; of the Appearance of the LORD unto Israel; of the Transformation of the whole House of Israel; of the further Transformation of the Earth as the result of the Transformation of Israel; of the restoration to Israel of lost Offices, such as true Seership, Prophetism, and Mediatorial Ministry; and then of the coming of the Great Day when in the valley of Jehoshaphat, the LORD GOD of Israel would accomplish such great things through HIS people, for HIS people, and then through them unto the healing of all the nations and the redemption of the Earth.

At some of these aspects of the teachings contained in the prophecy we will look; and we will take them in the order in which they appear in the book. They are not obvious in the reading of the book, except in two instances, but when the gems are re-gathered out of their false settings and stand in the light which HE throws upon HIS Word, the beauty of them is marvellous, and their glory transcendent.

MOUNT ZION

It is upon the holy Mount Zion that the LORD calls. The holy Mount Zion represents the Christhood. It represents the regnant estate of Christhood. It is the exalted consciousness in the Heavens represented by Christhood. It is the exalted state into which a Soul enters when it attains to Christhood. It is that great altitude wherein the Soul, having ascended the Mountain, realizes the great Silence, and wherein it has partaken of what that Silence means— the perfect awe of HIS approach, of HIS Overshadowing, that intense realization of the coming of the King of Glory unto the Being, to fill the Being as a Sanctuary for HIM-SELF with HIS Glory, which means to cause the motion of HIS Indwelling Presence to become so intense that the magnetic radiance produced fills the whole Being with the glory of the Presence.

Mount Zion is oft-times associated with Israel because they were the Children of Mount Zion. You will remember how a part of Jerusalem became associated with Mount Zion; that it was the upper city within the greater city, seemingly a lesser city within the greater city, a higher city standing above Jerusalem itself; and how it was there that the temple, the earthly temple, is said to have been reared. If time had permitted, it would have been most interesting and truly educative and illumining to trace how the ancient Sons of GOD, in order to preserve the titles, gave names to places and brought them thus into divine association. It was thus that Ierusalem arose, and Zion within it, and even the earthly house of worship, before the corrupting influences of material and creature sacrifices [polluted it]. It was thus that Ierusalem had gates [which were] given names associated with the

Mysteries, and [thus also] Mount Zion. Mount Zion was even said to have contained within its precincts Mount Moriah, upon which the great temple is said to have been built. These [names] all belong to the Mysteries; and in the days when vision grew dim, [the Sons of GOD gave names to places] in order to preserve in name the sacred associations of the terms, and thus hold in geographical situations and earthly exposition the remembrances of what was once the heritage of Israel. It was thus that the sacred Mysteries came to be associated with that land of Palestine, just as they have been with other lands we could name.

THE LORD'S TRUMPETER AND HIS REVEILLE

The holy city of Zion, the Mount Zion upon which the city of GOD is reared, is none other than the Christhood; and the call of the LORD unto HIS Children from Mount Zion is the call of the Christhood. It is as the Voice of the Eternal Christ calling unto all those who understood Christhood in the ancient days. The Voice is from the summit of Mount Zion, the city of the LORD. Therefore it is the Voice of the Christ, the voice of no man; though every man and every woman who becomes a Child of the FATHER-MOTHER and enters into high estate hears the Voice from Mount Zion, and will ascend that Mount even unto realization of the Christhood.

This is the first meaning of the prophetic presentation. It is full of tremendous meaning. It is not the voice of a man calling amidst the wilderness of Judah, though the Message originally was spoken through an Elder of Israel; but it was conveyed to that one through the Messenger. It was the Messenger of the LORD speaking unto one who could hear unto the receiving of the Message and the transmission of it unto Israel—*"Blow ye the trumpet of the Lord in Zion."*

What is the Trumpet of the LORD but the Divine Vehicle through which HE can cause HIS voice to be heard,

C

the reverberation of it to be felt, the Message revealed in the intonation of that Voice. The Trumpet of the LORD is the Divine Voice sounding the Divine Call to all Israel. I have used the word this morning which is associated with earthly things, because I know of no better. In the prophecy it is, "Sound a *warning* unto Israel"; but it was not a warning in the sense of a warning of coming judgment, although so presented in the book. It was in very deed a Divine Reveille, a call to all the people to arise, to awaken spiritually and arise and come forth from their dwelling-places, and ascend once more the holy Mount Zion; to come up into the realm of the Christ vision, of the Christ realization, of the Christ ministry. Remember when this prophecy is said to have been uttered—nearly a Naronic cycle and a half prior to the days of the Manifestation.

Joel hears the prophecy. He prepares for what is coming. The great revelations which were given unto Israel covered some two hundred years; the revelations given after Joel in Isaiah and Ezekiel, and, in minor degree, in Amos and Hosea, containing great things hidden in the language in which they are presented in the Old Scriptures. Then follows Micah—Michaiah—and the transcendent vision of Zechariah, closing with the astonishing prediction, through Malachi, that Israel's inner sense, their book of life, would be opened.

THE APPEARANCE OF THE LORD UNTO ISRAEL

The message of Joel was prophetic. It was a vision looking forward to the days when the Trumpet of the LORD would proclaim, with a voice unmistakable, HIS own coming unto HIS People. How HE was to come is set forth in beautiful metaphorical language; that HIS Word was to be proclaimed; that HE was coming; that Israel was to awaken and arise and ascend the Mount so that they could meet HIM. Then there is the presentation of HIS approach, said to be as a host of chariots upon the top of the mountain. The LORD came in appearance, it is said, as a Chariot of Fire, and with horses of fire, and before HIM went a flame—a devouring flame, it is recorded, a consuming flame. Oh, it is an energizing flame, and, when necessary, it is redemptive and regenerative. It is the transmutory flame of the Divine Presence that acts upon all the elements, not only upon the Earth, but in all the Worlds, when the elements have to be even changed for other degrees of service. It is a symbol of the Divine potency in action upon the elements. Herein is a great Mystery, as you will note.

But the LORD came to Israel as a Chariot of Fire. What is a Chariot of Fire but the Divine Embodiment of the spiral motion of the sacred Flame? That spiral contains the Mystery of GOD Who, in exposition in Stellar or Planetary or Soul formation, is the LORD. HE comes upon the top of Mount Zion. HIS Chariot moves from the mountain top down the slopes. HIS appearance is glorious to behold as the Soul can endure the approach of the Presence—the Energy of the Divine motion within itself. The LORD comes as a Chariot of Fire to Israel—remember it is to *Israel*; the all-energizing ONE Whose sacred Flame is to re-light every lamp within the Temple of the Soul's Being until that Temple represents HIM perfectly in every aspect of it, in every degree of it, in every court of it, in every sacred vessel of it.

The LORD is coming. It was a prophecy unto Israel to be of good cheer; to be encouraged in the way; amidst their travail to know that they were not forgotten. But from time to time they had to be awakened, recalled, re-energized, drawn up, as it were, up the slopes of GOD's hills. And as many as were able to climb yet further to endure the more rarefied atmosphere, were lifted up on to the slopes of the great mountains, as the prophets and seers had to be.

The LORD comes as a Chariot of Fire. Do you dread HIS coming to you? That was a prediction. To-day is the realization, as we shall see. That was so long ago, as we count time, but as yesterday in heavenly motion; a long time when reckoned as to ages of travail, and yet the day will come when it will seem but as yesterday, when it passes. The ages of travail when anticipated, as in the Gethsemane prior to the Oblation being undertaken, seem a long period, yet being past, it seems but as yesterday, a fleeting time in comparison with the great ages during which the LORD has been operating within this World and moving unto its redemption; indeed, in relation to HIS people, dwelling here and travailing as HIS seers and priests and interpreters and teachers, and, in many ages, redeemers.

It was a prophecy that the LORD would so come. HE has come from time to time to the few who could receive HIM as the Chariot of Fire descending upon holy Mount Zion, descending from the summit of Zion to meet the Children as they were ascending, and calling them through HIS Trumpeter, the Angel of HIS Presence, the One Who holds that glorious power of proclaiming HIS Word. This is no human word, no; but HIS Truth as it is alive like the sacred Substance and Flame of Being. It was a prophecy anticipating the coming of Israel. It is to be fulfilled to-day, as we shall see.

But are you able to endure the Chariot of Fire? Do you fear the approach of the Divine? Do you feel as if you would run away when the transcendent vision breaks within you, and you are conscious of the play of the magnetic streams upon you, and you feel as if you could not endure them? Are ye prepared to receive the LORD as the Chariot of Fire? It is unto this end that our School has been held. It is unto this end we have had fellowship together. It is unto this end that there have been such Unveilings from HIM, such as HE purposed according as ye have been able to receive. It is no vain thing to anticipate HIM. It is no vain thing to ask HIM to come. It is no small thing to pray that HE may be realized within the

Being in His motion. It is a most tremendous reality to the Soul when He approaches it as the Chariot of Fire descending from the summit of holy Mount Zion; that is, coming down from the very slopes of the Christhood estate to find the Soul where it is, and draw it upwards, touch it with His own consuming, energizing Flame, changing the very substances of the Being that they may be able to rise and become of service for Him in more exalted estates of consciousness and therefore of realization, and so of service unto others of His children. It is said that when the LORD comes, HE comes as a refiner's fire, a purifier of all things. But when HE comes to Israel, HE comes as more than that. HE comes as the great Energizer, the Elevator, the ONE Who dynamically raises the Soul up the slopes of Zion until it can rest upon its summit and look upon His Chariot of glorious Mystery. For it is in the exalted state of the Christhood that a Soul looks upon HIM as the Chariot of Fire, for there HE is ELI-YAH.

THE TRANSFORMATION OF THE WHOLE HOUSE OF ISRAEL

Now, in the prophetic story it is represented that all the Children of Zion, the Children of Israel, are awakening, arising, responding, and are gathered together—that is, in the prophetic vision—and that when the LORD came down the Mount they proceeded to meet HIM, and they followed HIM, and they became, it is said, like an army or host of horses, clothed in fire, and that the noise was as the noise of battle. Language fails even the Prophet in describing the Divine Mystery of transmutory processes and the exaltation of Being and the realization of Soul which come through following the LORD. The whole Household of Israel became as an army of horses and horsemen, and they were as the horsemen who could run beside the LORD. They were glorious in appearance. They had part in the same Flame which proceeded from the LORD.

59

What is signified by the whole House of Israel becoming
a host of horses drawing chariots of fire whose flame
proceeds from the centre outward? Why, the horse is the
symbol of the mind—the mind in its exalted state. A
horse of fire is the symbol of the mind exalted in its
understanding and intuition, in all its reflective potency,
and in its creative potency to the estate wherein it can
cognize and follow the LORD and endure to look upon HIS
vision and be as one who, like a horseman, runs with the
LORD. This is no slow process, but has the potency of
quick motion—inward, Spiritual, Divine motion; no
dragging of wheels; no stopping on the way because there
is a stone to be got over; no fear lest the chariot should be
upset and the rider thrown, lest the horses themselves
should be thrown down. No! It is to have Souls so energized that there is no longer any fear in them that the
Divine will forsake them or that HIS potency will fail
them; no longer any fear lest they should miss finding the
slopes of Mount Zion and the power to ascend even unto
the summit as the Host of the Lord.

You see it is not the inner Being of Israel that has been
in the darkness of the night, though Israel's mind has
been veiled. Israel's Being has yearned through the ages,
and has written those wonderful stories in the ancient,
real ancient Scriptures, and breathed forth the passion of
the Soul in the glorious Psalms, those uncorrupted ones,
the real Psalms of Israel, the real songs of Zion. The mind
of Israel was brought into captivity; it was brought into
the land of the shadows; it was overtaken by the night of
the world. *The mind lost its energy to rise.* It could purpose, it
could strive, it could think, it could endeavour to create,
it could seek to execute, but it was upon the plains
and even in the valleys, and not upon the slopes of
Mount Zion. But the coming of the LORD in HIS Chariot
unto HIS Children is to restore them to such a degree that
they themselves shall become as Chariots of Fire, drawn
by the horses, minds; that is, led by minds purified,

exalted in their vision, in their purpose, consecrated absolutely for the service of their LORD.

It was a prophecy. Surely it is being fulfilled? It was anticipated. Surely the day has come when the LORD in His Chariot of Fire has verily come to Israel, and HE has moved from the Heavens to the Earth? The Reveille for Israel has been sounded in this Message from the LORD GOD of Israel. Many Messages have come to help Israel on the way. Even the Manifestation was but a help on the way to present to Israel—if that Manifestation in its description had not been corrupted—to help Israel to realize afresh the meaning of Mount Zion, the real meaning of Christhood, and to retain that realization whilst the valley of Jehoshaphat was being cleared of the enemy through the judgment of GOD. His Trumpet, the LORD's Trumpet, is being blown from Mount Zion by His holy Messenger, the Angel of His Presence. This is not only as that Angel is said to accompany all Israel, but that Angel as understood in the Innermost realms in relation to the LORD of BEING, that Angel Who is Gabriel, Gabriel proclaiming again the coming of the LORD.

Here is something for you, to fill you with hope and with joy; if it fills you with heart-searching and mind-wonder, yet surely also with hope. It is the day—though I do not think any of you doubt it now—it is the day of His Coming, and there shall be no more backward motion for Israel; for Israel, hearing His Voice, arises and follows, which surely shall be done. Surely each one of the Children of Israel, hearing His Voice, will with alacrity respond, and, with sublime reverence of Being and spontaneity of spirit, come unto the LORD and say—

"Here am I, Lord, I come even with my attributes that have been smitten amidst the darkness. I come as I am. Thy sacred Flame will purify them, will energize them, will enrich them, will transmute their powers and exalt them for greater service for Thee. Thou shalt thus restore Thy Zion in me and make Thy Zion

*manifest through me. Thus, Lord, O my Lord, would I follow
Thy Chariot of Fire and take on the glory of Thy Presence, even
to become as Fire for Thee, that the Chariot of Thy Presence
within my Being may be drawn by powers fully illumined from
Thee and entirely directed by Thee."*

It was a prophecy, but is glorious to know that, although
it seems so far off, it was the harbinger of great events. It
anticipated Isaiah and Ezekiel and others who came—
that is, the Message anticipated them; and it anticipated
the Manifestation, and it anticipated this day unto which
it looked forward. The very word Joel means "the Choice
of GOD, JEHOVAH; JE-HO-VAH is my GOD." So it is the
choice of Israel again to think of their LORD GOD as the
real JEHOVAH, and not that semi-human, semi-planetary
potency imagined and sacrificed unto in the heart of
Jewry.

THE TRANSFORMATION OF THE EARTH

Now, as the result of the approach of the Chariot of
Fire unto Israel, with Israel's arising to meet the LORD
and their becoming even as the Chariot of Fire and as
Horsemen with their chariots running with the LORD, it is
said that in their proceeding, through their transformation, the Earth became transformed. As they proceeded,
Eden rose before them, and the wilderness was left behind
them; that is, the past states and conditions were no more,
and the new life became a part of the manifestation upon
the Earth-planes. The wilderness was changed, its confusion gave place to harmony, and the life that rose out
of the very heart of the wilderness and the desert became Edenic, a life of purity, of goodness, of beauty, of
love, of the motion of praise, of exquisite embodiment, of
glorious fellowship, of sublime service, of exalted realization wherein the Soul again walked with GOD. The night
of the wilderness was no more for Israel.

That is to be the resultant of the whole Household of

Israel's rising to recognize and to follow the LORD of BEING as the Energizing, Purifying, Regenerating, Transforming and Glorifying Presence in HIS Chariot of Fire, in you individually, in you collectively, for glorious manifestation. In the measure in which the Hosts of the LORD realize the LORD Who is their Overshadowing ONE and also their Leader, the ONE Who goes before; in the measure in which they realize the motion of the sacred Flame within them, so shall this World become Edenic, the wilderness of confusion give place to a life more in harmony with divine harmonics, the desert places, the arid sands, be changed in every life into a garden where the roses bloom and all the flowers grow once more, and even the Rose of Sharon has its place, that glorious life of Spiritual Christhood which, surely, is to come back to the elder children of this World, and gradually unto all the children of this World. The prophecy that was uttered ages ago, is to-day in the day of its fulfilment.

Oh, think of it—that it can be written concerning you in that glorious Message of the Heavens given under the title of Isaiah: *"For them in their coming shall the wilderness rejoice and even the desert blossom as the rose!"* Think of it—that it can be spoken concerning you and all who will obey the Voice, respond to the Voice of the Most Holy ONE! Unto such, Carmel shall restore its excellency; that is, the mind will be a reflector of HIS Excellency Who is the LORD of BEING. HE is the most Excellent in all the Earth. HE is the Most Holy and Most Excellent ONE to be adored. And Carmel, the Mount of the Mind, shall give to HIM adoration and praise and worship and perfect service. The glory of Carmel shall come back again through the glory of Sharon. Nay, not only Spiritual Christhood, but even the glory of Lebanon shall be restored; that is, you will glimpse again the heights of the Divine World; you will drink of the radiant streams of that World, you will dwell in the consciousness of the vision proceeding from that World.

Oh, it is a wonderful prophecy and should fill the heart, the Being, of every one of you with great hope and joy. You should be, to use the prophetic language, like those creatures who skip upon the pastures and slopes of the hills, and even those who are able to ascend the great heights, for very joy that the Divine Love has so come back to you in manifestation to re-energize you. You should rejoice at the energy that has been poured into the chariot of your Being. You should rejoice that the motion of the sacred Flame once more moves through your spiral, with all its glorious creative service within you, in order to fit you to be perfect vehicles for His glorious manifestation.

With the coming of Israel, preceded by their LORD, with Whom they are said to run as horsemen in a race to accomplish His Holy Will, the Earth is to become Edenic, and its wilderness to pass away. It may seem a dream, a vague dream in these days when you look out upon the World. That is not so if you could see it all from the within. Things are not what they seem, even where Planetary conditions are distressing and great Solar activities are taking place. There is a meaning behind them all. The LORD is the Chariot of Fire, moving through the Solar Body tremendously in His ministry unto Israel, and, of course, unto this World; and His Flame shoots out from HIM unto the purification of life upon these planes. But the primary call is unto Israel. The primary work is to make it possible for Israel to arise; to fully respond to His call; to be true—true citizens of His holy City of Zion; and to respond at once to the Trumpet Call of His Holy Messenger, even the Angel of His Presence. It is coming. I see it coming. It is coming to you. It is coming in you, coming through you. You are going back to make manifest, as you have not done for great ages, the reality of His Presence with you and within you.

The Restoration to Israel of True Seership, Prophetism and Mediatorial Ministry

Now, as a glorious result of the Children of Israel's following the LORD in His Chariot of Fire and then being sharers of His living Flame, they become once more restored to their high Offices of the ancient times. In Joel you will remember a passage, quoted in the story of Pentecost in the Acts of the Apostles—"Your old men shall dream dreams, and your young men see visions", etc. There is much more in it than merely old men dreaming dreams and young men seeing visions. You will note how I read the transcription to you: all Israel shall come back to have the power of Seership; [they will be of] those who see into the Spiritual realms. This is not simply to see reflected images upon the magnetic plane of the Planet; that is a clairvoyance which belongs to the personal equation. True, the Soul may have visions of the planetary conditions as well, through an inner clairvoyance; that is to be also for those who are to interpret. They will have that Seership which enables the Soul not only to see into the heart of the planetary conditions, which is given to the Messenger, but to see into the Angelic World; to have real Seership restored again, to be able to look into that World, not in night-dreams only but in day-realities as well as night-dreams, which are also night-realities of ministries; to have restored the power to see divinely again; and to have restored the prophetic office, the power to interpret that which is seen and realized; to have the power restored of high Mediation, to be able to mediate of the Mystery of the FATHER-MOTHER, thus to be the Prophets and the Seers and the Priests once more of the LORD of BEING. This is promised.

The Prophets were Seers, the real Prophets were Seers first and interpreters after. You cannot interpret that which you do not know. You may be Seers without having clairvoyant vision. You can be Seers seeking the truth, perceiving the truth, perceiving the truth taking form, perceiving its simple relationships, its manifold relationships, its most intricate relationships to the Soul, to the race, to the Divine World. To have those powers restored is a gift from the FATHER-MOTHER. It was predicted that Israel would have it. It is coming back. There is coming back to all the Children of Israel, heavenly perception, the real opening of the vision, the drawing of the veils of the inner Temple even, so that the Children will perceive heavenly secrets and be able as GOD's Prophets to interpret those heavenly secrets to all who desire to know them, who desire to follow, even if it may seem to be afar off to them or to you, still to follow the Divine Reveille, the Call.

And the result of this restoration is to be that the Sun shall no more be darkened, nor the Moon refrain from giving her light, nor the Stars hide their glory, but the Mystery of the LORD as the Sun of Being shall be fully unveiled to the Soul, so that you shall know in the light of HIS Countenance; and the Moon [as the mind shall again be] the reflector of HIS glory unto the Soul. [Celestially, as] the companion [of the Earth] amidst the night of the travail, though giving only reflected light through great ages, nevertheless [the Moon has been] serving a beautiful ministry before the LORD and on behalf of HIS children. [For] the Moon on its other side, where its pole is held Celestially from the Divine World, which no man can look on but which the Gods understand and which is seen from the Inner World, is magnetically full of the splendour of the Presence—representing your own mind whose magnetic pole has to be balanced in HIM, having the side that reflects outwardly to the Earth, and the side that reflects inwardly to the Heavens. The light of the Moon shall be restored; the mind will be able to receive the glory of the LORD thrown upon it, and to illumine those courts of the Sanctuary which are lit up from the Moon as it is made radiant from the LORD of BEING.

The Sun in His glory, the Divine Presence within, shall no more be darkened, [for] the Light of the everlasting Day shall be within; nor shall the Moon refuse to give her light, to receive it and to distribute it; nor shall the Stars be hidden any more, for the gloom of night will have passed away and the glory of the Christs shall fill the Celestial Firmament of the FATHER-MOTHER, even that Firmament by which Israel is overshadowed. For the sacred Flame of every Israelite, in the measure in which it ascends, is reflected within the magnetic plane of that Firmament, so that the Angels, looking upon the Firmament, know where the Stars are, or the Sons of GOD— another great Mystery of our FATHER-MOTHER built up into us and into His Heavens, an exposition of His glorious revealing and ministry unto His children.

THE SIGNS OF THE COMING OF THE GREAT DAY

As the result of the restoration of Israel through following the Chariot of the LORD Presence and becoming one with His sacred Flame, horsemen running the race of life to fulfil His holy Purpose upon the Earth, Children who are re-transfigured after being re-transformed, and whose glory goes out before them as part of the holy energy of His Chariot of Fire within them, revealing thus the potency of the sacred Flame, transmuting the conditions around them, and changing the wilderness into the Eden of the Presence once more, and, as the result of their following of His Chariot, the restoration to them of their ancient inheritance, their ancient powers of Priesthood, Seership and prophetic utterance, with all the adaptation of these in the more lowly degrees of teaching in ministry for HIM, the Firmament will thus be filled with the Signs of His Coming, so that those upon the Earth will see the Signs of His Coming. Those Signs are to be the Blood of the Everlasting Covenant, the Chariot of Fire and the Cloud of His Radiance. These are to be made manifest, first, through the sacred Lifestream of the Children. The

Blood of the Everlasting Covenant is none other than HIS own glorious, sacred Ætheric Lifestream full of Divine magnetic potency flowing into and through them and out through every life, out from the heart of each one; that Blood that cleanses from sin; that sacred potency that makes pure where impurity has prevailed; that power that transmutes even the elements within conditions which make the conditions such as they are. That most holy and sacred Blood of the Everlasting Covenant is the Lifestream, GOD's Covenant within us, GOD's Writing within us which is the fashion of HIMSELF. That is HIS Covenant within us. HE has made us in HIS Likeness. The Lifestream which flows into us and through our spiral, apart from the Flame, is that Lifestream called the Blood of the Lamb, the Blood of the Everlasting Covenant. And the Earth shall witness the effect of this flow. It will be the Sign that the LORD is coming.

The World does not know the LORD, does not know what HE is like, does not understand HIM as a Chariot of Fire, though the World might think of HIM in planetary potency and stellar manifestation. But [how] HE comes to a Human Soul, and how HE makes HIMSELF manifest through a Human Soul and ministers to the elements through the auric outflow of a Human Soul, the World does not understand; but it is to understand something of the potency in us and making itself manifest through us.

The Blood of the Everlasting Covenant is to set its seal upon every Israelite. It is the Sign of the Presence within us, that which is the Eternal Love in its sublimest and most transcendent and all-conquering power. Ah! it is Divine Omnipotency embodied through HIS Immanence in a Soul, brought into manifestation through that Soul as the Soul realizes HIM. How is the World ever to know HE is coming back except through the healing stream, the Blood of the Everlasting Covenant, purifying everything? How is it ever to understand that HE is a Flaming Fire Who will consume all stubble, all dross, all that is alloy, yet not hurt HIS Children? HE can put them into the fiery furnace, as it were, created by HIS Chariot of Fire, without their being hurt; but they would all come out purified, everything Spiritual and Angelic and Celestial and Divine made more glorious. Yes, they are even to see, it is said, the Cloud of HIS Glory; that is, they are to become conscious that those men and women who [seem to be] turning the world upside down [are indeed turning it] inside out, changing it; not disturbing its true polarity, but changing it back to a right polarity, affecting the elements, bringing with their presence an atmosphere which is other than that begotten amidst the daily service of Life amidst the workshops of the world, amidst the travail of the Soul's sorrow; an atmosphere which speaks of peace and of delight; an atmosphere that makes the children feel they can shout for the joy of life, that they can be glad before the LORD, that they can even dance before HIM and come to a time when they can dance before HIS Ark. This means that the Being in the very innermost, in the sacred motion of its Being, can accomplish the perfect praise of HIM before HIS secret, the Ark of the Covenant, whose sacred Lifestream is unto the healing of all flesh, all substance; the revealing of HIMSELF as the Glorious ONE; the Overshadowing by HIMSELF of HIS children, that they may dwell in the Cloud of HIS Radiance, and be radiant, yes, *be radiant*.

This does not mean that you will have no travail. The Children of GOD will have travail in this World until it is healed and redeemed, but there is a great difference between travailing because you are carrying the burden of others' sorrow, and travailing because of your own states. There is a great difference. There is not much joy when the Soul is travailing to get out of the night and to free itself from the shackles which have held it in bondage, to liberate itself from fallen desire and to clarify its vision of the impure things that have been given it on the way. It is a time of sorrow, oft-times, of weeping and of crying unto the LORD to know whether HE has forsaken HIS Children. You have been coming through that; you have come through that way. Now you are to understand the travail of bearing the World's burden, in which travail you can have supreme joy, delight even. With the burden of a World on your consciousness you may yet skip upon the slopes and from hillock to hillock, and ascend the hills and even climb the great mountains.

The World is to know you through your love. *"Love ye one another; even as I have loved you, so love ye one another."* The World is to recognize you through the energy of that Love, its Flame, its potent outpouring, invisible, but felt most truly by every Soul who contacts you. Let your love cause its light to so shine that you will be as the city on a hill, the Hill of Zion, no longer to be hid; your light no longer to be hid, but to shine there, to show the wayfarer up the slopes on the way of attainment of the redeemed life, and then the regenerate life.

The World is to know you through your radiance. Even as the energy of your love is to be revealed as a sacred Flame, so its motion is to clothe you with radiance. Oh, let your eyes speak of your love. Let your countenance carry its radiance. So love ye that the glory of Love will pour itself in great streamers through you. The auric splendour will be one with the Glory of your LORD, and the World in its conditions will become healed, so that many will turn to call upon the Name of the LORD; that is, to seek unto the understanding in some degree of the secret that fills you, that reveals itself through you and of your love that brings this strange atmosphere that gives energy to those whom you meet on the way, and that pours itself forth from you as those who dwell in the Presence of their LORD and enjoy the radiant life, as children of joy.

Thus, sing aloud for very joy, all ye who were captives in the land of Judah and sharers of the travail of Ierusalem, for the LORD has come to HIS holy Mount Zion. HIS

Messenger blows HIS Trumpet. The LORD HIMSELF through HIS Messenger, pouring HIS Word forth, sounds the Reveille unto Israel. Shall there be one who is Israelite indeed who fails to hear HIS Voice, and with all the Being respond?

*   *   *   *

Great and glorious are Thy ways, O my Father-Mother! How wondrously Thou hast ministered unto Thy children, even through the long night of their travail! How exquisitely beautiful has been Thy stooping unto their every need, so that in this day their faces are Zionward turned; and their ears are opened to hear Thy call; and their eyes to behold Thee; and their heart's motion to welcome Thee; and the whole Sanctuary of their Being to greet Thee lowlily, profoundly, in high reverence and awe of Thee!
Ever Blessed be Thy glorious Name!

I

THE MESSAGE OF PROPHET

AMOS

THE PROPHET'S WARNING

Woe unto all who are at ease in the land of the oppressor, who seek not unto Mount Zion[1] but are content with the valleys of Samaria:[2] who call themselves the chief of nations unto whom the message of the Lord came through the House of Israel!

They pass by the way of Calneh[3] because they behold not, and go down unto Hameth[4] the great, even unto Gath[5] of the Philistines that they may enlarge their borders and extend the greatness of their kingdoms.

Woe unto all who dream that the evil day is afar off though they cause the habitations of violence[6] to arise in their midst.

They make beds of evil to lie down upon, and cause life to abound with superfluities; they eat the lambs of the fold and the calves of the stall, and make of the creatures offerings unto Moloch, even whilst they chant the praises of the Lord and raise altars unto His Holy Name.

But they grieve not for the affliction of Joseph,[7] and continue to fill His cup with the gall of the works of their hands; they anoint not Him with the precious ointment, pure, sweet and ennobling from the Orient of the Divine Love; for their ways are those of bondage, whither they would draw back again those who have found deliverance.

NOTES ON TEXT

[1] Mount Zion is the Celestial Christhood.

[2] Samaria represents the life of the world.

[3] Calneh, the Soul encompassed from the Divine.

[4] Hameth the Great was the defence sought and built up by man—physical fortifications.

[5] Gath of the Philistines was the way by which the Philistines or oppressors of the life made the children of Israel to pass, viz., through "the wine-press."

[6] Abattoirs, Shambles, Physiological Laboratories, Breweries, Distilleries, Drink Palaces, etc.

[7] The Adonai as the Supreme Cross-bearer.

I

LIFE SMITTEN FROM THE LORD

I saw the Lord standing beside the Altar within the Sanctuary[1], and He spake unto me, saying—

Son of Man[2], smite the lintels[3] of the doors of the houses wherein the people dwell until they shake; by the sword of the Lord[4] bring them down until not one remaineth.

Though they may have gone down into hell,[5] yet will I find them to bring them back again unto the Heavens from whence they went away.

If they have hid themselves on Carmel[6], I will seek them out to bring them once more unto the heights of the Mountains of the Lord.[7]

If they have descended into the bottom of the abyss[8] where the great serpent biteth, and are no more able to return because of their wounding, even there shall my Love seek them until the accomplishing of their deliverance and the overthrow of their enemy.

The Lord of Hosts is He Who toucheth the land of the people with the sword of His power, Who raiseth up the land which the flood from Egypt overwhelmed.[9]

He it is Who buildeth His Ascensions and Spheres in the Heavens,[10] Who founded the children of the Earth, Who called upon the Waters of the Great Deep to pour out their fulness upon the Earth: the Lord is His Name.

NOTES ON TEXT

[1]"The Altar within the Sanctuary—the innermost of the system of the Soul."

[2]"Son of Man"—A term used to denote the Celestial Christhood.

[3]"The lintels of the doors," etc.—The entire life of the body when its senses dominate the Soul. It is the House whose doors must have upon them the sign of the Deliverance from Egypt, i.e. the purified life.

[4]"The Sword of the Lord"—the Divine Word whose truth is like a two-edged sword.

[5]"Down into Hell"—The Valley of Gehenna where the fires of the senses burn.

[6]"Carmel"—The worship of Baal, or the materialization of the Divine Mysteries.

[7]"Mountains of the Lord"—The Divine states into which the Soul is called.

[8]"The Abyss"—The Astral world whose lowest spheres are ruled by the arch-enemy of the Soul, viz., Matter, or that state which leads the Soul into a state of Negation.

[9]"The Flood from Egypt"—the Soul overwhelmed by the Sense-life.

[10]"Ascensions and Spheres"—The various Kingdoms and Spheres within each Kingdom in the Heavens: Human, Angelic, Celestial and Divine.

I

THE MESSAGE OF

OBADIAH

A FRAGMENT OF RECOVERED LOGIA
OF ISRAEL

The Vision that came to Obadiah concerning the land of Edom and those who dwelt in it.

The Word of the Lord went forth into Edom to do battle against all who afflicted His people.

When it became known to the Edomites what the Lord had purposed to accomplish by means of His Ambassador, there was great commotion amongst them.

They stirred up strife everywhere; and all the Edomic people united to oppose themselves to the one sent by the Lord.

* * * *

Thus saith the Lord, the God of Sabaoth:—

In the pride of thine heart hast thou exalted thyself to be a dweller with those who have known Me, children who dwelt in the clefts of the Eternal Rock and whose habitation was in the Most High;

And in thy pride thou hast boasted that none could hinder thee nor cast thee out from the midst of My children whom thou hast smitten;

Yet shalt thou be brought down and thy powers overthrown.

For though thou hast had flight like the eagle's, to soar into the heights and there make thy dwelling, and though thou hast had ambition to reach the Stars and reign in them, yet shalt thou be brought low;

For My Servant shall conquer thee utterly.

* * * *

The things belonging to Esau shall be searched through and through; and all those powers hidden in his Mystery shall be shown up and revealed.

All thy confederates shall be brought across the borders, and also those who sought after peace within thy land but were deceived by thee;

For though they did eat of thy bread, yet didst thou most grievously wound them, and none could understand it.

* * * *

In the Day of My coming, saith the Lord, through My Servant who is Ambassador unto thee from Me, the wisdom of Edom shall be as if it were not, and it shall be shown that there is no understanding in Esau.

Even those who were the mighty ones in the day of Teman shall be dismayed when they witness the dethronement of all the dwellers upon mount Esau.

The humiliation with which Esau did cover his brother Ya-acob-El shall come upon himself when the Servant of the Lord doth unveil the mystery of the history of the House of Ya-acob-El.

When those who were enemies brought his powers into captivity, and aliens entered into his Gates and cast lots for the possession of Ierusalem, Esau stood on their side as one of them.

He looked on whilst the foreigner smote Ya-acob-El; and he rejoiced over the destruction of Judah and all her children, and magnified himself in the day of their distress.

He even entered into the City by the Gate belonging to My people Israel, and laid hands upon their substance in the day of their affliction when through the smiting of Ya-acob-El calamity overtook them.

He stood in the borders of the City to cut off the retreat of those who sought to escape, and put into bondage those who were unable to deliver themselves.

* * * *

Now the Day of the Lord draweth near.

It is the day wherein all things shall be judged.

The Lord Himself shall separate and redeem His people.

The works of those who have smitten Ya-acob-El and Israel shall recoil upon themselves, until it shall be as if they had not been; for all nations shall be delivered from the power of Edom and the Edomites.

For even as Edom did once drink of the streams flowing from My Holy Mountain, so shall all nations drink of their waters.

And upon Mount Zion all who have escaped from Edom shall find deliverance, and they shall be once more holy unto the Lord;

Then the House of Ya-acob-El shall regain all the possessions of which they were dispossessed;

And once more the Sacred Fire shall burn within it, and the House of I-o-seph be lit by the Sacred Flame whose heat shall consume the stubble left in the land of Edom, until Esau also becomes purified and redeemed.

Then the powers of the South (Teman) shall possess those of the mount of Esau; those of the intermediary planes shall possess Philistia; together they shall hold the land of Ephraim and that of Samaria; and Benjamin shall regain the inheritance of Mount Gilead.

The hosts of the Children of Israel who were of the captivity shall come again into the land of Canaan, even unto Zarephath; and those of the captivity who belonged to Ierusalem shall re-possess the land that is in Sepharad of the South.

Thus shall it come to pass that the Messengers shall again sit upon Mount Zion, and the whole of the Kingdom of Ya-acob-El be full of the Regnancy of the Lord.[1]

NOTES ON TEXT

[1]The Message of Obadiah comes as a Ray of Light from the Eternal World projected into the midst of intense darkness. It may seem to be only a single Ray, yet it is of Sirion power, and brings with it great illumination. To the reader it may seem as if all its chief references were to outward histories, for it names in a special way the Houses of Jacob, Judah, and Israel, and also the House and Kingdom of Esau and land of Edom. It is a mystical story of Planetary, Celestial, and Divine import, and is as a lightning flash of the radiance of the Heavens. Great things are revealed in it concerning the House of Ya-akob-El and the Ancients of Israel.

Though it is the briefest prophetic Record amongst the Books of the Old Testament, yet it has had given to it a place in that Sacred Record apparently far beyond its outer value; and this place of importance has been vouchsafed to it by those who are accounted the greatest scholars and authorities in Textual Criticism, both evangelical and heterodox.

But amongst these scholars there is no real unity of thought and inter-pretation concerning the meaning of the Book, nor even the date of its prophecy. Some have thought it was given as early as the ninth century B.C., whilst others have assigned it to the fifth century before the Mani-festation. The like incertitude obtains with them respecting its personal or impersonal nature, whether to consider the name Obadiah as that of a man who was a Prophet, or as relating to the theme.

However, to this purely mystical story of Planetary and Celestial things, they have given an outward historical interpretation. The things that belong to the Unseen are made to relate to the Jewish people and the nations surrounding them, their inter-racial conflicts, the alternating victories and defeats, and the judgment of the Eternal World upon one nation, and its favour unto another. And in this last the Jews are blessed by the Heavens at the expense of many others. They are to have great possessions in land restored to them, and even the kingdoms belonging to other nations handed over—as if the Divine Love and Wisdom could ever do an unjust thing to any of the Children, even to those who had gone furthest away from the way of righteousness and truth.

In such interpretations there is a clear revealing that the Light that illumineth the Understanding cometh not from without. Whilst we appreciate the work of a true scholasticism and recognize the value of Textual Criticism in much needed road-breaking and road-mending, yet it is most obvious how greatly the intuition and vision have been veiled in those who, pursuing that path, have become wedded to it. *Never was it more evident, than in the results of such pursuit, that the letter killeth, but the Spirit giveth Life.* From some of the most profound and transcendent passages in the Old Testament the ETERNAL ONE is driven out by the literalism of the translator, and the failure to recognize the mystical and innermost significance of things.

The Book of Obadiah, though so brief, so earthly in its statement as translated, and apparently Jewish in its outlook and appeal, is a wonderful gem of Revelation of Divine Purpose.

The Burden of the Book concerns:

1. Edom, or the Land of Forgetfulness;
2. Esau, the Celestial who was brother of Ya-akob, and who sold his inheritance;
3. The Coming of the Messenger of GOD whose work was to overthrow the Edomites or hurtful conditions, and restore the land to its unfallen state;
4. The Redemption of Esau, and his restoration;
5. A great Recessional of All Israel, followed by a transcendent Processional into the ancient estate of Christhood;
6. And crowned with the full restoration and re-instatement of the whole House of Ya-akob-El.

I

THE MESSAGE OF OBADIAH

THE burden of the Message may be divided into five
sections, viz.:

The Land of Edom;

The Mystery of Esau;

The Messenger sent for the overthrow of Edom and the
redemption of Esau;

A Grand Recessional of Israel;

A Transcendent Processional of all the Tribes, together
with a restitution of the Houses of Ya-akob-El.

THE LAND OF EDOM

The term Edom has been translated in different ways·
Sometimes it is used for *red*, or for *blood;* and it may also be
related to the Soul's consciousness.

The latter was the meaning given to it in the Mysteries.
But the two former meanings have also mystical signific-
ance; for the *red ray* is vital to Life. It is even vital to the
Life-stream of the Body, though the reference is to that
Life-stream which gives energy to all the Being. It there-
fore represents the Elohe of the Ruby Tincture.

It is this energizing action that enables the Soul to rise
in consciousness, know and remember. But when it goes
down into Edom in the fallen significance of the term, it
forgets. For the Land of Edom is that of lost memories.
It is the country of spiritual forgetfulness. In the Mysteries
it came to mean the state of consciousness wherein the
Soul lost all memories of the past, and where it even forgot
its LORD.

The reader will find in the [Messianic] Book of Isaiah
a remarkable passage in the revelation given through the
Prophet wherein Edom is associated with the Oblation.

It opens with these words:—

"Who is this that cometh up from Edom?
His garments are red-dyed like the raiment of those who have
been treading the Wine-vat.
It is he who went down from Bozrah arrayed in glorious
apparel, to travail for the people.
In the strength of Him Who is mighty to save, even the Lord
of Righteousness, went he down.
Wherefore cometh it to pass that his garments are dyed red like
those of one who has been treading in the Wine-press?
When the Lord appointed His Servant to go down into Edom,
it was that he might travail on behalf of the Children of men."

The one coming up out of Edom with garments red-dyed is as a sojourner coming back from the Land of Forgetfulness. And the passage is realistically descriptive of the Return from the Travail of the Oblation. For the accomplishment of such a work the glorious garments and apparel of Bozrah had to be laid aside whilst he went down into the Land of Edom.

*　*　*　*

But Edom is applicable to all Souls upon this Planet, including the Sons of GOD and the Planet's Angel. In the Land of Edom the powers of Life were smitten from the lesser Children to the greater, and even to the heights of planetary administrative realms. There is a profound depth of meaning in the words of the Message of Isaiah addressed to Ya-akob-El and Israel:—

"O Ya-akob! Why sayest thou
'My way is hidden from the sight of God'?
O Israel! Why speakest thou thus
'In His Judgment hath the Lord passed over me'?
Unto whom do ye liken Him?
Compare ye Him in His ways towards you, with those who bear
not His Likeness?

Have ye not known Him of old time when His Voice spake unto you concerning the Word of His Message?"

The dominating influence of the Edomic State smote with spiritual death the whole of the Household of Ya-akob-El, from the youngest of the Children who had spiritual memories, to the eldest members who had such memories in great measure, and who still had vivid dreams by night and day of the one-time Golden Age. And, not only was the effect felt by the whole of the spiritual Household of the Planet, named Ierusalem, but to a great extent Israel likewise became smitten. The Chosen People of GOD—the Sons of GOD sent to this world for ministry, and who were so richly endowed that they came laden with the Treasures of the Heavens—lost the consciousness of who they were, whence they had come, why they were here, the ministries they had been sent to render, and that which was meant to be accomplished. Edom smote them from the crown of the head to the soles of their feet, from the realm where in consciousness they had dwelt beneath the overshadowing Cloud to the realm of the Understanding where Divine Illumination is the heritage of the Being.

When the Mind forgets its Divine Inheritance and the Source of all its Life-powers and attributes, Edom smites it. And the influence of Edom upon the Mind is to turn its vision wholly outward and downward, away from GOD and the realms of Light. And the more the vision becomes veiled, the more is it stricken. The perceptions become dulled and the intuition veiled. When the doors into the Sanctuary of Being are closed, men and women forget GOD. Then the powers of Edom dominate them. With their vision turned earthward, and the influence of the material life becoming regnant; pride of mind and heart and even spirit, may overtake them and conquer all that is best in them. It is in this way that conflict within and without comes to have a place in life. It is thus that war arises and is pursued; for all war upon any kingdom, is the result of the influence of Edom. Though men and women think they hold GOD in remembrance during war, and pray to HIM for success and conquest, yet the state of conflict reveals how sadly they have forgotten the Eternal Love and Wisdom. War is diabolical; the ETERNAL ONE is the LORD of all Good.

*   *   *   *

In the Prophet's Message it is stated that Edom became lifted up in a wrong way. It indicates the Mind exalting itself. It implies pride of heart. In the course of its journey, the Soul had passed through many high experiences. It had dwelt in the heavenly places and drunk of the streams of GOD. The Mind had known true exaltation of state through illumination and understanding. It had shared the Soul's glory. Then something happened to it. The Source of its origin, and all its powers and inheritance, were forgotten. Its ambition to ascend into the Heavens by doing the Will of GOD gave place to self-regarding ambition. Pride possessed it. Its selfless Divine Urge was changed into self-regard, till its desire was to reign amongst the Stars and be as a God, and even as GOD.

Such was the state of the Mind that brought the whole world down to disaster. And in that state the Mind would have all the Stars forget their heritage, their glorious Divine-derived Potencies, their magnificent endowments from the ETERNAL, and their share in the Eternal Mystery of the FATHER-MOTHER revealed in their magnetic powers and electric forces.

It is such a Mind that would to-day, interpret for us the Universe as a merely materialistic System, the home of matter, great embodiments in Stars and Systems burning themselves out.

For such a Mind is in Edom. It is in the Land of lost Consciousness. The Presence of GOD is not there; HIS Glory is eclipsed. Edom-state smites the Being and fills it with dread and unbelief. It robs the Soul of Divine Realities, and leaves in their place the darkness of fear or uncertainty.

It was in this way that the Heavens of the Earth were smitten, the perfect reign of Ya-akob-El was intercepted, and the manifestation of the ancient Christhood of Israel made impossible. The regnancy of GOD's plenipotentiary as the Planet's Angel, was opposed by the founder of Edom who, historically, was spoken of as Esau, brother to Ya-akob-El. The embodiment of Human Angelic Life in the Ierusalem which was Edenic, was overthrown. The Glorious Revelation of the ADONAI in and through the Sons of GOD as the radiant City of Zion, was crushed out by the opposing forces generated and called forth into action by the fallen Mind and all its empowered emissaries.

To all earnest students of these Teachings it should become obvious how the Earth became a fallen world, and Humanity a family of distraught Races. And they should also come to recognize something of their own inner and outer history in the most obvious travail of the whole Planet; for they also must have had a share in that travail, either as members of the ancient House of Israel or as Children of this world who had attained in the past to some degree of spiritual enlightenment and power.

THE MYSTERY OF ESAU

Esau plays an important part in the drama of which Obadiah speaks. Every reader of the Old Testament will be familiar with the story of Esau and Jacob. In the Bible story Esau is the hero of an unhappy episode, and Jacob is represented as a supplanter of his brother. Esau is said to have sold his inheritance for a mess of pottage, whilst Jacob, who has the consciousness of having bereft his brother and has become afraid of him, is also presented as the chosen of the Heavens. It is even written concerning the ETERNAL ONE that HE said in respect of the two

brothers, "Jacob have I loved, but Esau have I hated."
And if it were true, then it would only deepen and intensify the tragedy of the story. But its very falsity is a
most tragic betrayal of the Divine Love and Wisdom.

In the ancient Mysteries the story had an individual
and planetary significance. Its application to Life was
most beautiful in meaning; and its revelation in relation to
the Planet, was most illuminating. In the Message of
Obadiah the unveiling of Esau has relation to the planetary constitution.

In the individual Life, Esau represents the man who in
mind and heart is merely earthly man, whilst Jacob is the
spiritual man who has gone down and is seeking his way
back. Esau founds the kingdom of Edom. He is the man
who has forgotten GOD. Jacob is man full of uncertainty
and fear, but struggling back to the Land of Spiritual
things. He is man having recovered the power to pray, yet
so earthly that he would even barter with GOD. The
grounds of his loyalty are gifts and blessings—a way with
many Souls even in this day.

Over Esau it is said GOD grieved, whilst in Jacob HE
delighted. The Heavens rejoiced when they beheld the
spiritual nomad, Jacob, like the prodigal, returning from
the far country to seek real spiritual succour and inheritance.

Thus it is not to the Esau-man, but to the Jacob-Soul
the vision of the ministry of Angels is given in the night-
watches, though he cannot see or hear them in the daily
pilgrimage. In heavenly dream he sees the Ladder of GOD
let down to him, and has the privilege of even sensing the
ETERNAL PRESENCE above the Ladder. To him is given
the further revelation of the Angelic Hosts and their
ministry, though as yet he cannot openly commune with
them. But he knows himself accompanied. And then,
having grown in spiritual strength and deepened in Divine
Purpose, he is laid hold of by the Spiral Breath of the
ETERNAL, and made to realize the Divine Immanence.

D

He is translated to Peniel where he looks upon a transcendent vision; then he is transfigured at Penuel, where
he beholds the glory of ADONAI in the rising Sol, and
becomes garmented in HIS Radiance.

Thus there is made obvious the Human element in the
story, and its intensely interesting relationship to those
Souls who once knew the LORD, but who were smitten in
their mind and heart and carried down into the Edom
Land where they forgot the vision of the Beloved's
Countenance. For all these, like Jacob, have now to
return to find again the vision, the company of Angels,
and even the realization of the Divine Immanence.

* * * *

Now consider the Cosmic side of the Story as it related
to this Planet as a System. That which was true in relation
to the individual, became specially so when applied to the
Planet. The whole Household of Ya-akob-El was affected.
The Household embraced the City of Ierusalem and its
Environs, as well as the triple Hierarchies who administered for the Divine World. Ierusalem and its Environs
took in the whole Planet as a Spiritual House, including
its Atmospheria, its Heavens, and its Vortexya. The
Hierarchies were composed of Minor and Senior Sons of
the Gods; and these directed the Elements, guided them
in their motion, worked within the various kingdoms of
the Planet, supported the Planet-Soul Judah in the
evolution and development of all her Children given her
by the LORD OF BEING, and provided the conditions
necessary for ministries of a purely Soulic nature from
the encompassing Angelic World. At the head of the
entire System of the Earth reigned Ya-akob-El, as Divine
Vicegerent. He was of the Gods who are appointed by the
Divine World to be the heads of Planetary Households.
He was therefore the Angel of the Planet and the Archangel of the Household.

With this illumination it will be readily recognized

what a serious thing happened in the betrayal when the whole System was brought down; and what a tragedy was enacted when the Betrayer went out from the Divine Presence, and set in motion the influences that brought about the downfall of this one-time most glorious Emerald Isle amid the Great Deep. For that one who became brother to Ya-akob-El, and who has been known as Esau, sought only the pottage of a materialized System, and the venison of Life slain. Jealousy filled his Heart and swayed his Mind, till he became its slave. In his slavery he founded the Kingdom of Edom, and smote the Realm of Ya-akob-El. He pursued the members of the lower Hierarchy, till he so influenced them that they fell into the materializing snare, and he prevailed upon Lucifer to change the Planet's motion and cause the outer Planes to become in great part fixed.

The result was the descent of the entire Household into new and difficult conditions, amidst which the Children of Judah suffered tragically; for they gradually underwent spiritual impoverishment, until the Mind of the Race took on the nature of that of the Betrayer. Even the Mind of the lovely Planet became as Esau. For the aliens took possession of its field of spiritual activity, and the foreign powers smote it. These marshalled themselves against the House of Israel, robbed all the members of their Divine Inheritance—the Christhood—and so impoverished them that they became as those bereft of all that had been most dear. And Esau is said to have aided all the foreigners and rejoiced in the overthrow of the Houses of Israel and Ya-akob-El.

THE MESSENGER SENT

Obadiah proclaimed the Word of the LORD. ADONAI was to send HIS Messenger for the overthrow of Edom and the ultimate redemption of Esau. He was to change the conditions until Edom ceased to be the Land of Forgetfulness for the Children, and once more became rich with the treasures of GOD. The Law of the ETERNAL was to be restored; Righteousness and Equity were to give balance to all Souls. Esau was to be redeemed and fully restored, and the Land which he had made desert watered from the Divine Fountain and healed.

When the Message went forth that ADONAI was sending a Messenger to Edom, all the Edomites were greatly disturbed, and they combined to oppress the Messenger. In this we may recognize an Overture built up of the main theme of the Oblation. The Manifestation is the fulfilment of the promise of the Messenger, and the Oblation the process by which Edom is changed and Esau redeemed. What marvellous gleamings the Prophets had of these sublime events and the supreme importance of them! Though their glimpses may seem but momentary, and especially so in the Message of Obadiah, yet we may witness the portrayal of the Ambassador entering Edom, his going down into the Edomic states until in the midst of his ministry his garments became red-dyed as he trod the world's wine-press. The Ambassador went down into Edom, for the Word of the LORD sent him.

It was the Word of the LORD that disturbed Edom and rebuked Esau. The revelation of Truth disturbed error and rebuked falsity. It always has done so; and it has the same effect to-day. It is the Word of the LORD that conquers. The power is of no man though Prophet or even Messenger. It is alone of GOD. It belongs to the Divine Passion. Whatsoever ministry a Servant may render, the power to do so is of the Divine LORD. It is HE Who effects that which is realized. The Servant embodies, reveals, and interprets the Message, but the Divine Passion in him belongs to his LORD. Therefore be it ever understood that when the Ambassador was sent to Edom and Esau, it was the Divine Love Who spake and acted through him. And the whole Land of Edom was shaken in the Divine approach, and Esau made to bow in lowly reverence.

Such events did take place in the planetary circles when

the LORD's Ambassador arrived for manifested and redemptive ministry. Edom and Esau did not like it; but their opposition was overcome and the conquest of the Land made.

Such an experience of the intermediary realms, is likewise true of the individual life. It has been the experience of the House of Israel. If you who read this Message can do so with Divine discernment, the Word will come to you from the Inner World, and you will recognize how truly it describes your own experience. Many who to-day gladly welcome the Teachings given in the Message the Writer is here to proclaim, were at first deeply disturbed by its revelation, its claim, and its appeal. In its claim it is impersonal and from the Divine World; in its revelation it speaks only of HIM Who is the ETERNAL FATHER-MOTHER, Source of all Being and Nourisher of all Worlds and Souls; and in its appeal it speaks directly to the Being of every one, and, in a very special sense, to those who once knew something of the Presence of the LORD of Love and Wisdom in their own Sanctuary. Yet the Edom and Esau states in many were disturbed, and not a few of those who should have welcomed the Message, rose up to oppose it. Perhaps some who now gladly read these words may recall how they questioned the Message in the Truth of its Revelation and the Authority it claimed and must ever claim for itself.

The Edomites always do battle against the Message of the LORD of Love. The Truth disturbs them. It calls to the Life of purity, justice, righteousness, equity, compassion, pity, gentleness, humility and peace. Those who love contention do not love it. Those who agree with and follow the unjust ways of the world resent its appeal to them. Those who forget to reveal justice, righteousness and equity in their ways, close their audient chamber to its call. Those who are full of self-love and vanity will be shaken by it into a selfless love and life, or they will repudiate its claim and reject its call. For in this Message from the LORD GOD of Sabaoth, there is no half-way house on the Road of the Soul's Journey to the Celestial City, where the lovers of Edom and Esau may make a prolonged stay, rejoicing in the ways of Edom and the regnancy of Esau, whilst looking askance at the Path to the Celestial City, the while proclaiming the fact that they had to set out to reach its Citadel.

The Word of the LORD is sure in its effect upon those who receive it. All that is wrong is put right. Everything, feeling, desire and purpose, becomes clean and beautiful. The Word makes its recipients like the LORD HIMSELF Whose Love and Wisdom are perfect. If it gives pain, it is unto the healing of the cause of wrong states. If it makes great demands, it is for the regeneration and exaltation of those to whom it proceeds from the LORD. If it becomes overwhelmingly revelatory, it is in the process of overthrowing all the Edomic states of darkness and forgetfulness, and restoring to the consciousness the long-lost memory of the Divine Countenance and the Soul's Inheritance. If the Word searches you through all your Being, making your foundations shake and all your powers tremble, it is unto your full restoration to Sonship to HIM, wherein Christ shall again reign within you, from the poles of your Being, to the rivers of etheric breaths that flow around you and form the circumference of the field of Divine Magnetic Action. For all that has been accomplished in the Heavens of the Planet by means of the Oblation, must needs now have its counterpart in your Regeneration. In the Planet's constitution, Edom with all its inhabitants has been conquered, and Esau has been changed and reconciled to his brother Ya-akob-El. (Herein is much Mystery, of which more may be written, bye and bye.) And the corresponding results are looked for in all Israel. The Sons of GOD are now being called Home in this Message; not to be taken out of the Earth, for the latter sorely needs them, but to become again the glorious Children of Divine Inheritance wherein the

Divine Presence is realized, and be once more the Vehicles of the ETERNAL CHRIST.

A GRAND RECESSIONAL OF ISRAEL

As a result of this Divine re-conquest of all the Sons of GOD, there is to be a Grand Recessional. Such a procedure is to take place within every one, that there will be a recessional from all that Edom and Esau stood for. This the Prophet foresaw. He proclaimed the Return of the Sons of GOD from the Land of Egypt and its bondage, the country of Edom with its forgetfulness of GOD; and their entrance into Canaan, the Land of the Radiant Presence. And such a prophecy is being fulfilled to-day in your own Return. You are coming out from the Land of Shadows into the Divine Country whose paths are full of Divine Light, and whose Hills and Mountains are again unveiled so that the Glory of the LORD may be beheld by you. If you continue to follow the Light of HIS Message given through HIS Servant, it will lead you into the most ancient Inheritance of Israel which was once your possession.

If every reader of this Message will now join in the Grand Recessional, then the Heavens shall be rejoiced, and there will be a living hope for this world. Divine Regnancy shall be again expressed in and revealed through the Vicegerency of Ya-akob-El. Ierusalem once more shall become a true Spiritual Home for all the Children of Judah. The Planet-Soul shall also be raised once more to feast with the Gods in the Paradise of the ETERNAL, and her Sphere of Ministry be reclaimed from all foreign yoke, and acclaimed again to be The HOLY CITY. Israel of the Captivity shall return from Babylon to repossess the Land of JEHOVAH which HE gave unto Abraham. Benjamin shall again ascend Mount Gilead; for the Intuition shall be recovered for the Soul and lit up with the splendour of the Eternal Light, and all its treasures re-discovered and poured forth in Service for the LORD. Ephraim also shall be found again and brought into accord with Israel and

93

Judah; for Ephraim is the Mind endowed for administration and ruling. It was, unfortunately for Ephraim, pride of Mind that brought down that marvellous community of Celestials, and perpetuated the disasters that befell the Household of Ya-akob-El and crushed the yearning spirit of Israel. The great Intellects, the administrative Minds and those endowed with constructive and scientific Genius, are of the great ancient House of Ephraim. For assuredly the day is coming when the House of Ephraim shall be redeemed, and the great ones in it shall again possess the Mount Ephraim—the state of exalted illumination of the Understanding from the LORD. And in that day shall all Israel ascend to Mount Zion and there dwell, and thence minister; for they shall once more be the re-formed House of the Christhood through whom ADONAI speaks and reveals HIS Glory upon the Earth, and they shall be evermore with their LORD, knowing in blessed fulness HIS Overshadowing Cloud and HIS Indwelling Presence.

A TRANSCENDENT PROCESSIONAL

As the natural outcome of the Grand Recessional of the whole House of Israel from Edom, followed by all the Children of Judah and the Household of Ya-akob-El as represented in redeemed Ierusalem, there will be made manifest upon the Earth a Transcendent Processional. This Divine Event will be no mere earthly display of ceremonial of an ecclesiastical character which those love who parade their religious goods for sale. It will be of an order of such spiritual moment, that it will speak of GOD in its embodiment, and in its Processional reveal and interpret HIM; for it will be atmosphered from the Inner Sanctuary, and send forth as the result of its motion, the Angelic Breaths. Israel as a Kingdom of Priests of the Most High ONE shall be able to lead the multitudes into the Sanctuary of GOD, and to the various Altars representing degrees of initiation. And even those who are found able to present themselves to the Presence in the Inner Sanctuary, the Elders of

Israel will be equipped of GOD to guide; for they shall once more become the true Shepherds of Israel, and the Mediators of GOD's Covenant unto all HIS Children. As ADONAI through HIS Servant goes before Israel, so shall the Sons of GOD go before the People.

In that day shall the Messengers stand upon Mount Zion, the Citadel of the Christhood. This is the promised resultant of the work of the Ambassador; for he shall have made the ETERNAL manifest unto Israel, and accomplished the Redemption of Judah and Ierusalem through the conquest of Edom and the reconciliation of Esau. Through the mysterious Work of the Oblation, the LORD hath accomplished great things for HIS People. Not only has the Messenger who was appointed Ambassador from the Divine World, come back again in the Message of the Christhood and the restoration of the Sacred Teachings given by the Master Ioannes, but those who are to be the Manifestors and Interpreters of that Message are now appearing to make the Way of the LORD clear, so that the full effects of the Sublime Manifestation and Oblation may be realizable upon the Earth.

But concerning these latter, even as with the LORD's Ambassador Messenger, this word of counsel: do not think personally. The Messengers who are to be the Interpreters of this Message will make no personal claim. They will exalt the LORD who reveals HIMSELF in the Message, and not themselves. They will acknowledge HIM in all their ways, and as the Source of the illumination that has come to them. Of them will many be able to say most truly —"*How lovely are the Messengers who bring back the vision of the Soul and her Lord!*"

How many of those who read this Message will respond? How fully will those who may respond arise and make consecrate their lives for the great redeeming and interpretive Work? The Call of my LORD is unto all who are able to hear and understand. Who will take up the Burden of the Divine Passion for Souls, and serve HIM WHO has given so immeasurably? How many readers will again become true Children of the Cross, and share in the Great Work of this World's Healing? How many will leave all things that are of Edom and Esau, and follow on into the Spheres where the Divine Love and Wisdom call for absolute sacrifice? Who will be from the Divine Centre of Life within them, to the outermost field of their activities, the Vehicles of the FATHER-MOTHER in and through whom HE may, through the Beloved ADONAI, become incarnate upon the Earth and make manifest HIS Glory?

* * * *

Ever Blessed be HIS Glorious Name, Who, having sought unto the finding of you in Edom, though the work red-dyed HIS garments in the Servant, calls you back to the Land of your Divine Nativity, and into the rich Inheritance HE once gifted unto you!

To those who know HIM, HE is irresistible; for HE is Chief amongst all the Gods, and the altogether Lovely ONE.

* * * *

O Transcendent Lord! How wonderful Thou art in the Way of Thy Love! How glorious in Thine approach unto Thy Children!

With what Wonders as tokens of Thy Presence Thou dost enrich them as Thou unlockest the Gates of the Eternal World for them that they may look within Thy Holy City, even the City of their ancient Inheritance, and behold Thy Glory within its Sanctuary, as once they knew it.

Thy Children would adore Thee in Divine Embodiment. They would worship Thee in all their Service. They would Praise Thee in the full rhythmic Motion of their Being.

O Father-Mother, the ever Radiant One! Our Life would be lived unto the revealing of the Fashion of Thee in us; our activities would be expressive of Thy Will and interpretive of Thy Love; and the entire Motion of our Being, from centre to circumference of Life, would intonate Thy Allelujahs and Hallelujahs. We would share with all the House of Ya-akob-El the Blessing Thou bestowest upon us.

Unto this end may our Lives become Living Sacrifices upon Thine Oblatory, to be offered evermore in the service of Thee.

Amen and Amen.

I

THE MESSAGE OF
JONAH

THE ISLES OF TARSHISH

Lord, God of Abraham, Isaac, and Ya-akob! What great things Thou hast wrought for Thine Israel!

When the enemy smote them, even unto death, Thou didst find them in the graves wherein they had been buried, and Thou didst raise them again to Life.

In the midst of the great Sea where they found only trouble and sorrow, Thou didst walk upon the waters of tumult and cause these to cease their raging.

When enemies deceived Thy Sons and bore them into a strange land where they were made bondservants, from Thy High Heavens Thou didst look with compassion upon their travail and impoverishment, and didst send Thy servant Moses to effect their deliverance from the thraldom of Egypt.

When the oppressors pursued them in their flight from the land of their captivity, Thou didst cause the Whirlwind of Thy Majesty to overthrow all their chariots and horsemen.

The great Sea into which they drove Thine Israel in their hatred of them as Thy Sons, Thou didst cause to become their tomb when Thou madest the tempestuous waters to engulf and destroy all the armies of the false Pharaoh, which had been sent to overtake and hurt Thy People.

O Lord, God of Sabaoth! Great and glorious art Thou in Thy ways even when Thou veilest the Mystery of Thy Motion as Thou movest through the waters of the Great Deep to accomplish Thy Holy Purpose.

When the Isles of Tarshish became the dwelling-places of those who opposed themselves to Thy Will that they might make impossible the accomplishment of Thy Purpose towards this Earth, Thou didst command that Thy Servant whom Thou hadst named a Beloved, shouldest make journey unto those Isles in an Argosy of Thine Own appointing.

In Thy Love and Wisdom Thou didst purpose to change all the conditions within the great Sea, dethrone the evil powers which had established their principalities within the Tarshish Isles, and by purifying them to make of them fit habitations for the Children of Judah, and seats of regnancy for Thy people Israel.

The overthrow of the apostacy that seized those Isles Thou hast accomplished through Thy Servant Jonah whom Thou didst send as Ambassador for Thee, that he might voyage upon the great Sea, even from Isle to Isle moving in the fulness of Thy strength, casting down those who had falsely represented Thee, restoring the Law of Thy Love and Wisdom within each Isle, making of them centres of Angelic Ministry from Thee for those who seek Thy Blessing, the Redemption of all their powers, and the Healing of their wounded attributes.

Thou art indeed most glorious in Thy regnancy throughout the Universal Heavens of Thy Dwelling. Before Thee the Hosts of Thy Creation bow in their majestic strength in which Thou hast founded and endowed them, full of the Holy Awe of Thee, that they may testify of Thy Love and Wisdom, and in the Fashion of Thy Glory, Adore and Serve Thee.

O Lord, God of Abraham, Isaac, and Ya-akob! Would that every Soul upon this System joined the greater Hosts in Worship and Praise of Thee! For Thou hast done mighty and marvellous things on its behalf.

Unto it Thou didst reveal Thyself in glorious embodiment through thy Servant Abraham. For Thou didst array him in High-Priestly robes when as Melchizedek Thou didst meet him in the way of his journey, and Bless him in his Patriarchal ministry.

Thou didst enrich him with the wealth of Thine Own realm, and the full regnancy of all the Kingdoms of the Sun.

Thou madest him a Divine Vicegerent for Thee,—and his Household, a Home for the Sons of Thy Love. Through these, his ancestry was to cover the land of his regnancy, and through them were all the Earth's Sons to be blest.

Through Isaac Thou didst reveal Thy Glory as Thou hadst promised; for the Abrahamic Blessing Thou madest manifest in Solar Radiance till all the Earth was filled with the laughter of pure joy.

Through Isaac Thou didst thus make to be revealed the glory of Thy Love and Wisdom as these were found embodied in Abraham; for when Thou revealedst Thyself unto him in Mamre, Thou didst cause him to be filled with the laughter of all the Gods, for Thou madest unto him the promise of High-Priesthood under the regnancy of Melchizedek, and the out-pouring of Thy Glory by means of Israel in intensified Solar Radiation.

From the loins of Isaac Thou didst cause to come forth into manifestation, the regnancy of Thy servant Ya-akob-El, assisted by all the Tribes of Israel; for, in opening the Gates of the Solar World for ministry unto Judah, Thou didst establish the triple estate, and give to her for government of Thine Elders, that they might sit upon the thrones of regnancy and reign with Ya-akob-El their head, in the accomplishment of Thy Holy Purpose.

O Lord, God of Abraham, Isaac, and Ya-akob-El! What wondrous things Thou hast wrought out on behalf of this Earth and her Hierarchies! How marvellous Thy Love! How glorious Thy Wisdom! How exquisitely beautiful Thy Patience!

When the whole Earth went down into Egypt and found only a House of Bondage, Thou didst not forsake those whom Thou hadst appointed administrators, nor withhold aught of Thy Love; but didst reveal it anew in full measure of outflow.

Thy Beloved Thou didst send unto them as Liberator and Redeemer; and though the whole Heavens were bowed down through His setting out for such redeeming ministry, and the Solar Glory had to be veiled, yet Thou gavest out of the Greatness of Thy Being that Thou mightest find all Thy Children and bear them back Home.

O Lord, God of Abraham, Isaac, and Ya-akob! Great art Thou in the Glory of Thy giving of Love and Wisdom! May all Thy Children hasten to Praise, Worship, and Adore Thee!

I

THE MESSAGE OF JONAH

THE NARRATIVE

The Word of the Lord appeared unto Jonah, the Beloved, the inheritor of the Eternal Spirit, and spake unto him concerning the voyage to be made by him unto the great City of Nineveh.

For wickedness had prevailed within its borders, and had smitten all the inhabitants thereof until they knew not right from wrong, nor any longer possessed the power to write the true story of Life upon its Walls.

But the Compassion of the Lord was great unto them, and He purposed to redeem the City and save all Souls within it.

Therefore He requested His Servant Jonah to be His Ambassador unto Nineveh, and effect the redemption of all the Souls who dwelt within its borders.

* * * *

To accomplish so great a work it became necessary for the Servant who was to be Ambassador and Redeemer, to leave the Heavens where he dwelt. Therefore, when the time appointed for the voyage drew near, he went out from the Presence within Whose radiance he had dwelt for great ages, that alone and separate from the Presence he might accomplish the great mission.

For the first part of his journey he took an Argosy that was adventuring to the Isles of Tarshish where Souls worshipped many strange Gods.

Those who accompanied him could not understand the nature of his office and mission, and he could not tell them all that he was appointed to do.

Whilst they wondered at and questioned concerning him, he went lower down into the Argosy, and went to sleep.

Whilst he slept the sea became tumultuous, for the storm winds arose because of the nature of his mission, and amid the tempest many precious possessions in the Argosy had to be abandoned. The Breaths that the Heavens caused to move for the purpose of the mission, fought with the Titanic elements which smote the Argosy.

Many there were who dreaded the storm-conflict between the elements, and cried out for deliverance; and they prayed unto their Gods that they might understand the meaning of the tempest.

*   *   *   *

When it became known to those who were bearing their burden to Tarshish that the voyager with them had come out from the Presence of the God of Gods, they became more afraid. For they had asked him concerning the God he worshipped and served; and when he told them of Him, Who He was, and of His Majesty, they became sore afraid and felt as if the condemnation and judgment of such an exalted Being had fallen upon them for the part they had played in having him in their Argosy.

In dire distress they turned to him for counsel, since the storm continued and they could not reach the land whither they went. It was then that he informed them that the tempestuous conditions were the outcome of his journey and the mission on which he had been sent; and also that he must now leave them and make his journey through the great Deep without them. Such was the lot that had fallen to him.

So Jonah went forth upon the bosom of the great Deep to contend with the elemental spirits that were in conflict, that they might be quelled and overcome.

For three days did he wage battle against the evil powers that had smitten Nineveh and gained dominion over all Souls within its kingdom. But his journey took him even deeper into the tumultuous waters as he passed from state to state, and visited the forty Isles that came within the scope of his mission. For the Heavens had proclaimed to him that after the forty times of his visit to those Isles, the great system known as Nineveh would be destroyed, though the Souls within its gates would be saved.

For three days which were as nights to him, was Jonah lost to all who had known him, whilst he dwelt amid the waters of the great Sea.

BEFORE THE SETTING OUT

O Lord of my Being, in Thy calling of me Thou searchest my thoughts and desires.

Thou knowest me from the Within of my Sanctuary to the circumference of my attributes.

My going away and my returning Thou understandest even whilst they are yet afar off.

Even as Thou now dost ensphere me, so shalt Thou encompass me in my path as I go down, and be acquainted with all my ways.

From Thee there shall be nothing hid of all my voyaging, for Thou alone knowest all that Thou hast purposed to accomplish through me.

In the midst of Thine ensphering of me in the Cloud of Thy Glory, Thou has laid upon me this burden of service.

The realization of such an honour overwhelms me; to attain to the height of its fulfilment is beyond my powers.

Yet, since Thou hast so laid Thy Hand upon me, it must needs be that I go to fulfil Thy Will; for in Thee is my strength.

Whithersoever Thy Holy Spirit leadeth me must I go. Yet how may I flee from Thy Presence?

Thou fillest all the Heavens of my Being with the Glory of Thy Presence; Thou art ever with me. How then shall it be when I must needs pass through the great deep of the sea, even unto its uttermost Isle?

Surely even then Thou shall be with me till the morning breaketh and the night of my travail hath passed away!

For, in Thy Right Hand Thou ever holdest me; and amid the darkness I shall still be with Thee.

Amid the Tumultuous Sea

By reason of mine affliction amid this sea of trouble, do I cry unto thee, O Lord, God of my Being.

Oh, vouchsafe Thy help to me! For I have found only sorrow and pain in the depths of hell.

It is to me the place of woe, and it doth seem as if I were cast away from Thee, and that I should see Thee no more.

Unto Thy Holy Temple within me Thou didst come; but now it is as if Thou hadst forsaken me.

In their tumultuousness and anger, the waves of the sea dashed upon the bulwarks of my Soul. They bore me to the lowest depths

*and wrapped weeds around my head; they drove me to the outer
bounds of the Earth and smote me as with iron bars.*

*Amid the tumult of their motion my whole Being grew sick
even unto spiritual death, and I would have succumbed to my
tribulation but for Thee.*

*For, even when Thy mission was no more before me, and my
Soul had no longer its remembrance of Thee, nor the Glory of Thy
Presence dwelt in before my journey began, yet Thou didst cause
Thy loving-kindness to reach unto me, and upon Thy Right Arm
Thou didst bear me back from the land of darkness and death.*

*Thou didst speak unto me amid the mysterious conditions that
engulfed me, and deliver me from the fearful pit whither my
journey for Thee took me.*

*Upon each Isle Thou didst put strength in me to do Thy Will
and accomplish Thy Work, that the wickedness of Nineveh might
be blotted out, and all false powers wither as a gourd of the night.*

*Thou hast in these things confirmed my vow unto Thee, and
ratified and glorified the sacrifice which Thou didst request of me.*

*O Lord, God of all the Gods, and of my Being, truly Thou art
marvellous in Thy ways as Thou ridest upon the sea, and makest
the wind and the waves to obey Thee.*

NOTES ON TEXT

The Message of Jonah is in the form of an allegory. Though some terms
and names used are associated with geographical positions, yet these are
cryptic. They are used only because of their esoteric meanings, and to veil
the Mystery lying at the heart of the allegory. For the story and Message
of Jonah form an *Idyll of the Oblation*. It is wholly mystical, and, in the truest
sense, altogether impersonal, though the Servant, Jonah (The Beloved),
becomes the vehicle. Nineveh, The Isles of Tarshish, the Argosy, the Sea,
the Ship's Wares and the Sailors, are all cryptic. And so is the great Fish—
the Piscarian Mystery that swallowed the Servant.

I

THE ISLES OF TARSHISH

IN this unveiling, a sublime Mystery is revealed. To most students of the Old Testament, the story of the prophet Jonah is fascinating, yet impossible. It has been the cause of conflict in various schools of Biblical exegesis, and on the field of Theology great battles have been arranged for and fought. Its purpose in the Scripture Canon has never seemed clear, nor the place given to it amid the prophetic writings, other than confusing. Those who have followed the path of a blind literalism, have accepted it as Revelation without knowing what it revealed beyond the supposed disobedience of the prophet. Some have deemed the Book an allegorical setting of the captivity of the Jews in Babylon, with Jonah as a type of his people who failed in their true mission; and that the Book was written by a learned Scribe some time after the return from Babylon. But there have been many who have rejected the Book as spurious; and the cynics have enjoyed hilarity over the whale that swallowed the prophet.

Yet the story is full of Revelation. It is a Divine Allegory. It is a cryptograph of the Oblation. Divine Mysteries are communicated in cryptic language and are expressed through symbol and allegory. And the Book of Jonah is of like order. It chronicles a Divine Event which had been projected. It reveals the Eternal Purpose, and interprets the Divine Love and Wisdom.

THE DIVINE ALLEGORY

The Book of Jonah is said to have been referred to in a very special way by the Master. It is stated in the New Testament that He applied some of the events narrated in the story, to similar events that would take place in His own Mission. The writer of this article knows that He did so speak of the allegory, but it was not after the manner in which it is found in the Gospel Records. The reader may remember the statement found in the Gospel attributed to the disciple Matthew. The Pharisees ask of the Master some sign that His Mission is what He claims for it; and His reply is thus given:—

"An evil and adulterous generation seeketh after a sign; and there shall no sign be given to it, but the sign of the prophet Jonas:

For as Jonas was three days and three nights in the whale's belly; so shall the Son of Man be three days and three nights in the heart of the earth."

* * * *

The Truth has been veiled and corrupted by those who wrote of the incident in the Gospels of Matthew and Luke. The occasion of the utterance was a most intimate meeting between the Master and His Friends. The reference to the story of Jonah was made during a profound unveiling of the Mystery of the Oblation. The gathering was most select and secluded. It was amid one of those rare hours that He loved to spend with His beloved ones where He could open out His Being to them, that the allegory was interpreted. The unveiling could be made only to those of His Friends who were able to endure to hear of the Divine Travail. It was in such an hour that the allegory was unmasked, and the revelation given of its Divine intent.

To my Friends who may be able to receive the interpretation of the allegory which follows, it will be a further revelation, if such were needed, of the reality of the Oblation, the Work purposed by the Divine World, the path of its accomplishment, the Deeps that had to be explored and the nature of the descent necessary for such exploration, the Travail that would accompany it, and the Glory of the Eternal Love whose Passion was all-conquering and whose giving was immeasurable.

The Servant Jonah

The name holds Divine Values. In relation to the Mission, it is full of Divine significance. It breathes the

Breath of the Eternal. Usually it is rendered *The Dove*. But the Dove is used as a symbol of the Spirit. Therefore, the name had relation to the Eternal Mystery. It was a Sign whose meaning was hidden. It was a cryptogram of the Holy Spirit. But it also had another hidden meaning, and was related to the ADONAI. It stood for *The Beloved*. It had a similar meaning to that of Ioannes.

ADONAI is always *The Beloved*. HE is such in the Divine World; but HE is likewise always The Beloved amongst the Gods. In every Celestial System there is present in active service, a replica of the Divine World; and ADONAI as The Beloved is at the heart of each System. All revelation is from HIM; all administration is for HIM.

The Story of Jonah is, therefore, intimately related to HIM; for it was the Mission of The Beloved, in a Work of redemption which HE only could accomplish. But in such a Work, HE operates through a Servant. A Son of GOD is chosen and set apart; he is in due course consecrated for the ministry. And he is endowed for the Mission. Amongst his endowments is the Sacred Name. He is given the Royal Insignature, the Seal of his Office. He becomes Jonah, or Ioannes, The Beloved, as the Vicegerent and Ambassador for ADONAI. It is not a personal name. It is not even the name of the individual. It is the insignia of the one appointed, denoting his spiritual estate and the degree of his realization of the Eternal. And it is also connected with the Mission on which he is sent. All Souls are beloved of the FATHER-MOTHER. But when one rises in state into the Divine Kingdom he becomes *a Beloved One;* and to the System wherein he has been appointed to minister as the head, he will become known as The Beloved.

Thus it was with Jonah. He was the endowed Servant bearing the Signature of ADONAI as the Seal of his Mission. As the Servant of his LORD, he was Iona—I-ON-A, the Divine Messenger from the Sun who was to carry the

Cross of the Redemption as the exposition of the Passion of his LORD.

In the "fulness of time" he came, the Dove alighting upon him. With the Sacred Name written in his fashion, he went forth to accomplish his Mission.

THE MISSION TO NINEVEH

The Mission was redemptive. It was to go to a great City, take away from it a specific burden, redeem its inhabitants, reconstruct the Life within it by a righteous administration that would be revelatory. All Souls within the City who had fallen under evil domination, were to be restored and set free, and know Divine healing.

Gross darkness reigned in the City of Nineveh. It symbolically meant the darkness in which the children of this world dwelt, and the influence of that darkness upon the Christhood. The children of men, spoken of as the inhabitants of Nineveh, did not know right from wrong. They had no spiritual Light; they had become children of the darkness. No spiritual radiance shone, therefore they had no true understanding of heavenly things. Life was misinterpreted; its purpose was veiled; and its streams were misdirected.

The City represented the great system of spiritual darkness that lay upon the Earth and enshrouded all peoples. From that darkness the Earth is just beginning to emerge. Unto this planetary system, the dawn has not yet broken. It is, however, being heralded. It is now near the Planet's gates. It can now be heralded because of all that has been accomplished in the magnetic circulus of the Planet. For within that circulus there shines a radiance that has not been known for ages. Within the Astral Sea a mighty Work has been accomplished, and those spiritually dead have been liberated. For that was the sea that was said to give up the dead that were in it. Those who have heard the voice from out the Eternal World, have come forth from the grave of spiritual death. For such Souls it is the resurrection morning. For them the Dawn has broken. These are ascending out from the graves of material bondage to begin their climb up the Hills of GOD, and attain again to those altitudes of Vision, Life and Consciousness within whose radius shines the Glory of the Eternal.

Nineveh has been redeemed, and all the Souls within its compass have found liberation. Now they may learn how to write their names, which means, that they can now have opportunity to live as children of GOD, and receive constant Angelic helpful ministry to enable them to regain the purity and joy of true spiritual childhood. For the great City is no longer governed by those who became oppressors of Souls, the terrible taskmasters crushing all spiritual growth and making Soul unfoldment impossible, even when the children of this Earth passed into the Planet's Heavens. For the Kingdom of the oppressors was up there within the great Astral Sea. From thence they affected all Life upon the Earth; and when Souls passed on to the spheres of the Heavens of the Planet, they found the same conditions, oppression, domination, and crushing burdens, amid atmospheres that made Angelic ministries unto them impossible. Their passing from the lower to the higher, from the outer to the inner, was not a passing from darkness and sorrow to light and joy. They knew no spiritual change in the conditions of their environment. They remained in the darkness, shut up within the Astral Sea, or house of spiritual death.

*   *   *   *

The realm of the planetary Heavens has been redeemed, and in the process of its redemption those powers that set up false principalities and sat in high places (the storied circles of the Earth), have been cast out. Their Kingdoms have been overthrown. Their power has been broken. For those who were responsible for the growth of the system of Nineveh with all its disastrous outworking, have been cast down. Their reign within the Heavens of the

Planet is ended. No more shall they have power over the Souls who pass into the intermediary world, or Heavens of the Planet, to make of it a realm of pandemonium wherein the demon-spirits may find dominion and scope for their crushing regnancy; for their principalities have been thrown down, and they themselves have been cast out.

Upon these outer planes many of those awful spirits are making manifest. They seek power that they may dominate the mind and emotion of men, and rule over them even in their spiritual Life. The meaning of much that is being made manifest in our midst to-day, is to be found in this interpretation of this Planet's history, past and present. Light from on High reveals the meaning of the terrible evils in our midst—the sins of individual, national and racial pride; the spirit of domination, unrighteousness and greed; the love of self in individuals, communities and nations.

But the manifestation of those oppressors and their crushing regnancies, is unto the abolition of them; for they are hastening to the day of their overthrow when they too shall be cast into the abyss, or place where they shall no more find any foundation on which to rear their false principalities. As the Eternal Love has been triumphant in the Planet's Heavens, so shall it be upon the Earth. The day hastens in its coming when, *as the refiner's fire*, HE shall make HIS appearance in a new spiritual régime wherein righteousness shall be regnant. In that day, historical Christianity will be exchanged for the presence of a living Christ in everyone who seeks Truth, Divine Honour, Equity and Love. The failure of the mirage that arose in the name of Christ, will be replaced by the triumphant manifestion of the Divine Reality that was meant to grow out of the Teachings given in the days of the Manifestation by the Master. Then the world's real healing will be assured. The flesh-pots of Egypt will be forsaken. The oppression of the various creatures will cease, for over them will be extended the wings of true pity. Compassion, or the tender mercy of Love, will be regnant and made manifest towards all Souls. None will lack. None will know oppression or injustice. Selfless Love will shine within the firmament of the Earth's Life, and all service will bear the mark of the regnant Presence of the LORD of Being.

THE PLACE OF JONAH'S MINISTRY

The field of the ministry was within the great Astral Sea. The Servant had to make a long journey to reach this Planet and the realm wherein his Mission had to be fulfilled. The Astral Sea was a most strange place for him to approach and voyage upon. It was so conditioned at that time that it was the negation of all he had been accustomed to.

You who read this story may often think that your own life is full of travail amid Earth's elemental conditions and world states. You may think that the waters of life for you are most frequently tremendously tumultuous, and that they often dash against the bulwarks of your inner life. Yet, it would not be possible for you to fully realize what the Astral Sea was when the Mission was undertaken, nor how greatly changed it has become as the result of the Oblation. Now you can rise to glimpse the Glory and even realize the splendour of the Vision; then few could rise above the outer planes. Amidst the Astral Sea the multitudes were lost in the awful spiritual darkness; and few there were who did not toil in their rowing and none were able to reach the Land even though they desired it.

But to-day, all who desire to reach that Land of Light may do so. For the power to smite of that sea, is broken, and its waters are all changed. In that one-time land of strife, peace now reigns. That House of sorrow has been changed into one of joy. For the Divine Love has found the way whereby His Children could be liberated, and their return to Eden assured. His exquisite patience has been rewarded in the great Work accomplished.

* * * *

The voyage of the Servant was made in an Argosy of Divine appointing. The Argosy was a vehicle suited for the purpose of his setting out. He had to be prepared to ship from the Kingdom unto which he had been raised and where he served. He had long dwelt in the Presence and ministered before Him. He was in High Priesthood. His Office was after the Order of Melchizedek. He mediated from the Altar within the Sanctuary of the realm unto which he had been appointed. To leave that glorious Home for an unknown country, was no light undertaking. To leave it upon such a mission required absolute trust in the Divine Love and Wisdom. And great preparations had to be made, the secret of which was hidden in cryptic terms in the allegory. He had to descend to where the magnetic conditions were not only less than in his own Kingdom, but where those conditions were all out of harmony.

For his work he had to have various Argosies. He had to have a number of Argosies. These represented the various states into which he had to enter. In the first Argosy he made his journey in part from the Divine World into one of the Celestial realms. There were those appointed to accompany him as far as they could. The Argosy of Divine Appointment was the ship or vehicle provided for his Divine descent. Then he had to assume another vehicle magnetically conditioned and polarized to suit the realms to be entered. Some also accompanied him on the Celestial descent, but could not go further. Then other vehicles had to be found and other means for his ministry. The first Argosy represented his own Divine Estate; others that followed, the Stations of the Cross reached; and then the various Argosies—forty in all— necessary for his work amid the Astral Sea, revealed to the Heavens the states he had entered.

When he reached the great Astral Sea, his own vibrations disturbed its waters. The purpose of his Mission was opposed by the elemental states and those who ruled by means of them. To enable him to make effectual the Work he had come to do, the Divine Wares in his Argosy had to be cast out. The language is cryptic and hides the mystery of his humiliation, and the imposition by the Divine Love of necessary limitations. It was the process of the descent. He had to lay aside his garments worn in the Presence, and appear as one who had gone out from that Holy Atmosphere. His riches, powers and attributes, had all to be laid on the Altar of Oblation and veiled, whilst he accomplished his forty days of Lent, and wrought out the Planet's Redemption from the evil powers that filled and dominated its Heavens. The Beloved ONE travailed in and through the Servant who was known in the Heavens as a Beloved One, in order to effect the healing of the great Astral Sea.

In the journey he went from Isle to Isle. For the Isles of Tarshish were the various states within the Astral Sea that had to be entered into, changed and conquered. They were once the resting-places of the Soul on its journey through the planetary Heavens. They had all become fallen through the mal-administration of the evil powers. His visit to each of those Isles synchronized with one of the forty incarnations necessary for the accomplishment of the Work. Those were the Isles that waited for his coming as Redeemer; and they are the Isles that are to welcome the Divine Régime of a world redeemed.

* * * *

To the reader the Allegory will surely now be revelatory. The Divine Purpose should be revealed. The height and depth of the Eternal Love must stand unveiled. Those who follow closely the restored Message of the Christhood, will surely behold in this unveiling, the wealth of the Divine Love and Wisdom. The devout will be full of reverence before the Message of the Servant who speaks for the Beloved ONE of all. To all sincere seekers and illumined Souls, the tragic significance of the Oblation will be most obvious; but likewise will the beauty of the Christhood stand revealed when sublimest sacrifice is made in sweet obedience to the command of the Eternal Will. Those whose perceptions are illumined must indeed witness in this unveiling the motion of ADONAI through the Servant unto the salving of this distraught member of a system that was, at one time, most glorious amongst the Gods and the Sons of the Gods in the Celestial Spheres. Unto each one I would have come the flight of the Spirit, raising each to transcendent heights of vision and realization, and experiencing the rehabilitation of all the lost Christ-potencies, so as to make Christ manifest again upon the Earth, and bear it back to the land of Light and Hope, Love and Peace.

THE GREAT FISH MYSTERY

The objective of the Oblation was the Planet's Heavens. The Divine Purpose was the purification of these. The path of the Travail was amid the Astral Sea whose waters had been terribly hurt. The work to be accomplished had to be effected by visiting all the Isles of Tarshish. Upon each Isle a new régime had to be introduced and a new Life established. Each state had to be so greatly changed that the Divine Will could be expressed in the new administration, and that righteousness and equity would be regnant.

But during the grand processional from Isle to Isle, from the time the Divine Argosy entered upon the Astral Sea, he who was the vehicle of THE BELOVED ONE, even of ADONAI, became lost to all who accompanied him on the earlier parts of the journey. Just as he had to go out from the Presence of the Glorious One in order to accomplish the Will of the FATHER-MOTHER, so had he to leave all his brethren. His Mission in the great Astral Sea caused him to be as one lost to them and the Heavens. He was swallowed up by the Great Fish or Mystery of the Oblation. The Fish is the symbol of the Great Deep. He came from out of the heart of the Great Deep. He came soon after the dawn of the Piscarian Age. He landed upon the Earth's shores in the Argosy given him for the Manifestation. He brought with him the riches of the Heavens to distribute unto his brethren. For a time these accompanied him, during which period he unveiled to them the Divine Mission on which he was sent. Then the hour came when he must needs leave them, even as he left those who had journeyed with him from stage to stage of the Divine Processional. When he passed from them amid the Syrian hills, they saw no more of him until the Work appointed unto him to fulfil had been wrought in the place whither he went. He became lost in the Sea of Divine Mystery. The Great Fish of the Oblation swallowed him and hid him through the Piscarian Age. In the bowels of it he went down into *the deeps* of the Earth, the while suspended from the Divine World like a mysterious dependent triangle, himself the apex, the sides the magnetic holders, the Centre the Divine Container of the Eternal Electric Force for the redemptive work to be accomplished.

For three days, which were as nights for him, he was in the womb of the Great Mystery, hidden from all but the Divine World, and the special Angelic Presences who had been appointed to wait upon him and supply his needs. As he moved from Isle to Isle or state to state, he was borne from the heights to the depths. The conditions of the Earth smote him as with iron bars, and wound around his life the evil growths of an evil sea. To the high places where the infamy of the betrayers had found most powerful and disastrous expression, he had to be carried by the Spirit, and empowered to overthrow their false systems and destroy their regnancy. For these self-seeking administrators had changed the one-time glorious Isles of Tarshish into centres of evil dominancy. For the Planet's

Isles were once most blessed Houses of Spiritual nourish-
ment and enlightenment for the Children of the Earth,
and were planetary expositions of such Isles as obtain
within the Solar Body and all Celestial Systems, and even
within the Divine World.

AFTER THREE DAYS

Jonah's journey occupied forty days. These days are
related to those mentioned in the Temptations in the
Wilderness. They signify the Forty Lives of the Oblation,
and have no relation to time, as such. For the duration
of the Oblation covered three Naronic Cycles. These lasted
from the close of the Manifestation to quite recent years.
He came in the "fulness of time"—a term relating in a
most intimate way to the Celestial arrangements, and the
position of certain members of the Celestial Gods. He
came within the Piscarian Celestial ruling, and his Oblatory Processional continued to almost the close of it.

In all this the reader may behold how true the Divine
Story is, even in detail, and how profound the meaning
of the cryptograph! The Veil is lifted, and now the
earnest-seeking Sons of GOD may know the truth concerning the Divine Passion. The Divine Truth is full-rounded.
It is of the Light whose radiance it is. It illumines all that
it touches.

When unveiling and interpreting this story to the inner
groups of Initiates, the Master said—

*"For even as it is in this allegorical foreshadowing of the
Oblation, so shall it be with me in the process of the redemptive
Work. There shall be three cycles of Naronic duration whilst the
Isles of Tarshish are visited, the evil principalities overthrown, and
the great Sea changed, that those Isles may again become true
Spiritual Homes for the Children of Judah, and noble states
wherein the regnancy of all Israel may be once more restored.
Therefore, in the day of the Return, those Isles shall await the
coming of the Christhood regnancy through all Israel. For the*

whole House of Israel must be saved. Unto this end came I into this world; unto this end go I forth to accomplish the Work, given me to do from the Father-Mother."

The Three Days have been accomplished and the Oblation has been fully made. The Vision is restored. The Christ has arisen. The Great Fish has yielded up its secret. The Beloved has conquered. The Message is brought back and the true interpretation is given unto it. It is the day of the re-proclamation. The first was concerned with all that had to be accomplished; the second reveals and testifies of all that has been wrought out by the Divine Passion. But in this re-proclamation the Divine Reveille is sounded. That which was borne and accomplished for the House of Israel is now to bear its full fruitage. Arise ye! O House of Israel, and reign again in Christ-radiance amid the great Sea and upon the Isles! Show your Blessing and Praise, your Worship and Adoration, in your Life's Oblation and Service for your LORD.

Surely every one who reads these words will understand.

The Three Days are fulfilled. The Work has been accomplished. The Piscarian Mystery now stands revealed; the Oblation is made manifest. It is of no man. Surely all lovers of the Teachings have learnt to relate all Divine Revelation and all Sacrificial Ministry unto the FATHER-MOTHER. It is through HIS Love we are preserved; it is through HIS Wisdom and Power these Mysteries are unveiled. In relation to these things, think of HIM! In the motion of your Being, Praise HIM! In all the motion of Life, express and reveal your oneness with HIS Will. Let all of Life's Service in thought, speech and act be the Worship of HIM. Let Life's purpose be the embodiment of HIM, for that is true Adoration.

Beloved Friends! In and through this further Revelation of HIS Love for you, behold also the exquisite beauty of HIS Wisdom in accommodating HIS Message unto you, and gradually leading you into the realm of HIS Radiance that grows ever brighter and stronger as HE bears you up into the Glory of His Resplendence, that ye may understand His Will and fully respond to His Call.

*   *   *   *

O Father-Mother! Ever most blessed art Thou!

Who could tell the measure of Thy Love?

Who could find tongue golden enough to rightly intonate Thee and unveil Thee?

Yet our limited endeavours Thou acceptest and crownest with Thy Goodness.

Beyond all telling Thou art ever Lovely as revealed in Thy Beloved One.

I

THE ORIGINAL MESSAGE OF THE BOOK OF
MICAH

A GREAT PROPHECY

The Word of the Lord as He came unto His servant Michaiah:
Hearken unto Me, all Israel!
Hear Me, all who are dwellers on the Earth!
Let the Word of the Lord God of Sabaoth
Who proceedeth from His Holy Temple
Be His sure Witness amongst you.
Behold ye, how the Lord doth descend to you;
From the Holy Place of His dwelling
Doth He stoop to touch the Earth.
Hear ye now what He doth proclaim:

"Arise, O Israel!
Address yourselves unto the Mountains of God;
Let all His Hills hear your voice!

"O ye Mountains of God,
And ye sure foundations of the Earth,
Hear ye and behold the motion of the Lord,
As unto Israel He doth approach
And with His people plead!

"O Israel, My people, wherein have I failed you?
Let the Word speak and testify.
Ye have grown weary in the way
Because ye have not understood what I have done.

"From the land of Egypt I brought you;
From the House of Bondage I redeemed you;
Unto you I sent My Servant, even Moses,
And with him Aaron and Miriam.
Remember the purpose of their visitation,
And all My Acts to restore you and bring you
From the land of Shittim even unto Gilgal.

MICAH

"Forget not Balak, ruler of Moab,
Whose sons of confusion have been overthrown;
Nor that one who became the Son of the Flame
Whose message was from the Word of God
And spake of restoration unto Ya-akobel
Through the arising of God's Star
To shine within the midst of Israel
And make God's Sceptre have dominion."

*   *   *   *

Doth Israel ask wherewith to come before the Lord
    And bow at His High Altar?

Come ye with the Being's Offering energised and make
    your Sacrifice.
For though your gifts be like the yearlings of the flock,
Yet will the Lord be gracious in accepting them,
And bless you till ye have regained the powers
To exalt His Ram and make Sacrifice supreme
Of all your attributes, and cause the Oil-streams
Of your Being to flow unto Him,
Even the full fruition of all your Powers.

Thus doth the Lord again show to his Israel
The Way unto the Eternal Good,
That they may be dwellers in his Righteousness,
And Mediators of His Tender-Mercy,
In lowliness as they walk with Him.

Therefore, hear this, My Word, all ye Angels of Ya-
    akobel,
And all ye Princes of the House of Israel!

The Lord by His Spirit shall remove the effects of the
    transgression of the House of Ya-akobel,
And blot out all the sins of Israel.

*He shall again restore the Watch-towers of Samaria
And sentinel them with the Sons of Light.
No more shall Night encompass you with darkness,
Nor the Prophets' vision be veiled before the Lord;
And ye shall be once more able to divine the Truth;
For your Sun shall no more go down.*

* * * *

*In the latter days shall it come to pass that the House of the
Lord shall be established upon the Mountains of God;
Unto it shall all the House of Israel come.*

*Many amongst the nations shall likewise be drawn to the
Mountains of God and come into the House of the Lord when
Ya-akobel is restored and his throne re-established.*

*For then shall they be taught the Way of the Lord, and how to
walk in His paths.*

*For the Law of the Lord shall again go forth from Zion, and
His Word obtain within Ierusalem.*

*And in that day shall the whole House of Israel sit under the
Vine and the Fig-tree;
There shall be none to make them afraid; for in their midst
shall dwell the Lord of Hosts,
And in Mount Zion He shall reign over them for evermore.*
(Recovered Logia from Michaiah)

I

THE BOOK OF MICAH

IN its present form the Message of Micah and its original teaching could be but little understood. Even the greatest Hebrew scholars, who make it their special work to examine such literature, acknowledge that it can only be a fragment, many fragments, which have been gathered together by some scribe into the present form of the book. Indeed, there is no certainty that most of the book belonged to the original document. I name these things because of what I will have to say to you.

In its present form the book claims to be a voice unto Israel and Judah and Jerusalem, and unto the city of Zion. It is full of judgement. It is predicated in it that the land of Samaria shall be smitten with evil, and even Judah —the idea of which is gathered up into the term Jerusalem —shall have a share in the judgement. The Glorious Divine ONE is represented—as HE is so often represented under the racial Jewish thought and in many of the wonderful Old Scriptures—as a tribal GOD Who is almost continuously angry with HIS people, yet is moved to compassion towards them. HE changes day by day like the elemental kingdoms of the Earth, from judgement to promise of healing, from threats of captivity to promises of deliverance and redemption, and from the taking away of all that is valuable to Israel to the restoration again of all that Israel had inherited. The glory of Micah's Message is lost in the book as you find it. Try to read it as an exercise from beginning to end.

But the original book of Micah, or Michaiah who was a Messenger, was delivered in the period covered by Isaiah; and its burden, though different from that of Isaiah, concerns itself with planetary history, the Sons of GOD, the Children of Israel, the Holy City of Zion, the fall of Samaria, the fall of Judah and her Holy City Jerusalem.

It is full of the glorious promise that from Bethlehem, the city of David, would arise the Deliverer; that Israel should again come back to the Holy City of Zion and be once more the chosen of GOD in manifestation.

There are indicated in the prophecy two Returns, the first a lesser Return, and the second a great Return; the issue of the latter being the outpouring from the Heavens of Universal Being upon all the Earth. The very terms that are used in the book are mystical, even as the name is, for Micah is an abbreviation of Michaiah, which is the Message representing "the Fulness of GOD"; that is, the Outpouring upon Israel, the Divine Pleroma come unto Israel. The bondage of the Children of Israel, the story of their wanderings, their travail, are all mystically portrayed. The reason for their travail is revealed in the fall of Samaria and the captivity of Judah and the destruction of Ierusalem. For Samaria is the land of the Watch-towers, the spiritual uplands of this Planet at one time, where the Watchmen were, wherein the real Bethlehem was contained; and the land of Judah is the Planet-Soul's sphere of ministry, and Ierusalem her spiritual household. The Message is a message concerning the planetary descent, the fall of its land with its estate, the descent or declension of its children and their descent into the bondage of material and occult powers; the bringing down of the land of Samaria—not that parcel of land in Palestine, but the land of the Watch-towers—and the destroying of the Middle Kingdom by the occult powers which had dominated the World for some ages and brought her into such bondage. For the bondage of this World has been through occultism in its worst form, the inversion of spiritual and divine things by inverted mental vision, and the misappropriation of spiritual and divine forces for personal, individual, communal and racial ends. Why, the children of men live in a realm of darkness concerning the history of the World which they people, and even the Children of Israel have forgotten their past and all that they have gone through in the ages of travail through misuse of spiritual and divine powers!

Such is the burden of Michaiah, or Micah. The full story, which touches the condition of the House of Israel, and gives the reasons for the fall of Samaria, is embodied in the real prophecy, [as is also the reference to] the land of Judah and the once wonderful spiritual household called the Holy City of Ierusalem. It is a Message unto Israel preceding that of Isaiah. Isaiah follows it. Micah interprets the conditions of Judah. Isaiah reveals the burden of the Divine Passion as it is to be made manifest in the redemption of Israel and the healing of the land of Judah. Micah anticipates the Messiah, the coming of the Redeemer. But this is not merely as a Servant in the human sense, but as the coming of the Regnancy of the Divine LORD. HE is to come through Bethlehem, and through the house of David, and become once more unto Israel Daysman and Redeemer. Such a revelation unto those who could receive it of the household of Israel, explains what follows. The fragment I read to you from the book itself, but now re-read to you in another form, reveals the awakening of Israel, the First Awakening. It was anticipatory of the coming of the Manifestation; and the Second [Awakening is] of these days in which we ourselves are making manifest.

Now I will address myself to the great question, and the answer with its resultant.

THE GREAT QUESTION

"O Israel! My people Israel! Have I failed you, that you should murmur at the conditions, that you should mourn as if you were never comforted, as if there was nothing that could comfort you? O my people Israel! Have you forgotten the ages? Are your memories so veiled that you cannot recall how I sent Moses unto you, Moses the Messenger who brought to you the consciousness again of high priesthood, the true Aaronic ministry; and even Miriam,

who is said to have sung the song of praise and rejoicing on the recovery of the Soul of Israel?"

Moses is the Light of GOD shining again upon Israel; Aaron is the motion of the Presence before the high Altar of the Being; and Miriam, which is the Hebrew form of Maria, is the Soul awake to recognize that priesthood and the radiance of that Presence.

"Have you forgotten?" Thus the appeal. And it is presented as if Israel, as the household, was led to enquire, *"Wherewithal shall I come before the Lord? How shall I return into the consciousness of Him, and, in returning, how shall I present myself before His High Altar?"* And here you will remember what I read from the book—*"Will the Lord be pleased? Shall I come with burnt-offerings, with calves of a year old? Will the Lord be pleased with thousands of rams and oil?"* These latter could only be poetical expressions, if meant to convey the truth. *"Shall I give to Him my firstborn for my transgression, and the fruit of my body for the sin of my Soul?"*

Oh, how these wondrous Scriptures have been perverted! It was beautiful to add, even as a scribe must have done, *"What doth the Lord require of thee? Not these outward sacrifices",*—though all outward life is touched with the sacrificial spirit when that spirit is true in its motion— *"What doth He require of thee? To do justice and love mercy and walk humbly in the sight of God."* Although in some ways these terms are beautiful, they hide the Mystery at the heart of them.

THE PATH OF SACRIFICE

"Wherewithal shall I come back into the consciousness of my Lord and present myself before His High Altar? I would come before Him with burnt-offering, with the sacrifice of my Being touched with the fire of His Divine Power."

There is no other way of coming before the LORD. It must be a burnt-offering, an offering ratified from the Heavens. Therefore it must be an offering that can be ratified from the Heavens. For offerings that are not real, true, that are not of GOD in the Being, cannot be ratified from the Heavens, and when an offering is ratified from the Heavens it is said to be a burnt-offering, that is, energized from the Divine Presence by the Divine Fire. We cannot pretend to do things before the Divine. HE knows our downsitting, and our uprising, the innermost thoughts of our Being and our motion from the lowest plane to the highest, from the outermost kingdom to the innermost in our conscious functioning and volition.

I would come before HIM with the burnt-offering of my Being. I would come before HIM with calves of a year old? No, no! Even the Hebrew, as you will find it in the margin of your Bibles, interprets that expression "calves" as "sons". Shall I come with my powers, though they be young, even as the yearling, apparently young in the recovery of them, in the exposition of them, in the use of them? Yet I would come giving all my powers in the sacrifice unto the most Holy ONE. It is the only way. For GOD would have us give ourselves, our gifts, our attributes, though they may seem to be but as yearlings, young, lacking in experience. Experience enriches, it is true. But with the enrichment the responsibility of full giving is implied. It is commanded by the very experience of our Being.

Here we have a revelation of the Soul's return unto the FATHER-MOTHER, the coming again unto the high Altar. The consciousness, with the attributes, have been impoverished in the way, and the recovery of their potencies makes them appear to be young and inexperienced. I would come with my burnt-offering, even with such gifts. For HE can enrich them again. HE can make them beautiful. HE can clothe them with divine potency. There is no growth in any other way. No, even for Israel who had grown into the consciousness, in other ages, of that glorious ONE, there is no other way in the return than by offering the attributes, even though they have been smitten in the way, impoverished in the travail, to present

them unto HIM. HE delights in HIS children even bringing
a maimed attribute to HIM with the confidence that HE
can heal it, touch it and make it whole again; that HE can
restore its power, restore it with the majesty of spiritual
fulness of strength for manifestation and service.

I would bring to HIM the horns of the ram. You know
it is put as "thousands of rams". No, for a thousand, one
thousand, ten thousand, all eventuate, in progressional
numbers, in one. I would bring to HIM the Ram of my
Being. [This signifies] the majesty of HIS secret, with
the dual horns or powers of that divinity which is
within you. And I would make sacrifice of such so that
I become absolutely HIS own. I would be once more
as Ramah, a dweller within Ramah, the Kingdom of HIS
Holy Presence. For there is no entrance into that Kingdom
—that is, into the Kingdom of High Realization—but
by the presentation of the Ramah in you, the Divine
in you. Give to GOD that which is HIS own, that is, your
Being. There is no return otherwise. You may seek the
powers of the world. You may rejoice in them. You may
think they are elevating you and bearing you forward.
But there is no ascension of Being by means of them; none.
The true ascension of Being is by offering GOD's, the
Ram's, horns, the dual power of the divinity which is
resident with you, making the Divine Principle of your
life a sublime sacrifice in its dual motion, centrifugal in its
outflow, centripetal in its inflow; centrifugal in its creative
power, everywhere you touch, everything you touch,
everywhere you minister; in its centripetal or indrawing
[power], nourishing, upholding, enriching; making the
presentation of the dual divine power within you. Shall
HE be well pleased with less? HE asks for all. The divinity
in you pleads to be so presented unto HIM. For thus alone
can the divine realization which is all round you and over
you come into full realization within your own Being. The
good pleasure of the FATHER-MOTHER is to realize HIS
Will. HIS Will is realized through the presentation of the

divinity within us to the Eternal Divine. GOD is not well pleased as a man or woman is in getting what they want. For HE is no man, no person, but HE is BEING, Eternal and Universal BEING. When HE has presented to HIM that which has become individuated from HIMSELF, it is presented that HE may fill it with HIS Pleroma, that the Micah of the Message may fill the Being. Then, if I may use such a term concerning HIM, HE is rejoiced. For nothing can satisfy the Divine Heart but the perfect return of the child in whose Being that Heart in its Divine motion makes exposition of HIM in its systolic and diastolic motion.

Surely that seems a sacrifice complete, the burnt-offering of our life, the offering of our life to be ratified by the energy of the Divine within unto the outer vehicle, the giving of all our attributes once more, though they may seem but young because of all that they have lost in the way; the giving of the divinity within us even unto all fulness, with its dual power, creative and fashioning, active and passive, the ascending and the descending arc of our Being.

Yet there is something more: "*Will the Lord be pleased with ten thousand rivers of oil?*" Though you have it put poetically you begin to think that it had to do with a great deal of earthly oil poured out upon the Altar. That is not the meaning at all. The dual powers of the Ram come into exposition when the oil of the Being is presented, for it is none other than the secret stream of our Being, which, in the outer vehicle, flows through the spinal column and up and down the Two Witnesses, little known, even physiologically little known; the Witnesses which support the central cord of the spinal column, but in our inner Being are represented by the Two Olive Trees in the wonderful vision of Zechariah*, whose oil is poured into the sacred bowl that crowns the seven-branched candle-stick. For without oil there is no high illumination, there is no perfect enrichment. The sacrifice of the oil of our

*See pp. 183-184.

Being is the sacrifice of our very bone and marrow. Those terms are used, but mystically they mean the marrow, the very secret stream of our Being that flows through what is called the vehicle; mystically it is all a part of the super-structure of our inner life, having its corresponding expression even in the outer vehicle. But the oil is the oil of the sacred essence of our Being.

Anoint your sacrifice with the oil of your Being. Give up everything. Give up everything to HIM. LORD! I am thine, even to my bones and my marrow that fills them; that is, to the life-mystery which vitalizes all the vehicles through which my Being is brought into fashion and manifests itself. Will the LORD be pleased with such? [Will HE be] rejoiced? The Heavens are rejoiced when a Soul offers, sacrificially, the very marrow or oil of its bones, mystically meaning the very life-stream of its Being, for the fruit of the life is expressed in and through that life-stream.

"Shall I give my firstborn for my transgression, the fruit of my body for the sin of my Soul?" Here you have an adaptation by some scribe who was anxious to help Souls in their return from dark ways to purer ways of living. *"Shall I give my firstborn?"* Who is the firstborn in you? Is it merely a human equation, or is it a divine statement? *"Shall I give my firstborn for my transgression?"* No, no, but I do so in the sacrifice. Shall I be transgressing my own Being in doing it? No, I shall be but fulfilling the divine law in myself in offering that firstborn of high divine consciousness where-in I recognize HIM Who is my LORD, which cognition enables me to behold HIM at the High Altar, and moves me to offer my sacrifice, even unto its being ratified by the Fire of HIS Spirit, even unto the giving of all my powers, however wounded they may have been in the way, yes, even to the giving up of my will, the Divine Will in me in its dual manifestion, to make the sacrifice divine in its nature and in its completeness. And with such [I would give] the oil of my Being, the lifestream of my Being. And with such [I would also give] that which has been the

resultant of its motion through the Ram of my Being, the consciousness which makes me consciously His child; more—that which gives to me that heritage of Israel, that which made the Children of Israel as members of the great household of the Christs of GOD.

To give the firstborn, is not simply to give that which is born first in us, but that which is the highest and fullest of all the births in us, that which comes first in its fulness. You see the term has brought the meaning of the name, Michaiah—"the Fulness." The Message was unto the fulness of the giving of the Being, giving the Pleroma of GOD that is in you unto HIM; the Christ consciousness, the Jesus Christ consciousness in our terms, the consciousness of the SON of GOD in you, the consciousness of your relationship to the City of Zion, as a dweller in the Holy estate of Zion. Shall I give this? Yes! What do you live for? Why, to realize HIM. And why do we realize HIM? Surely to fulfil HIS Law operating within us. And we realize HIM to give that which we realize unto HIM. No man liveth unto himself [alone]. If he does, then he does not succeed. He cannot. He may become a world man, a world conqueror, but he is not a divine man whilst he is in such states. And therefore no man liveth unto himself. That which he attains he gives. We acquire to serve. We acquire to give in our service. We attain that we may lay our attainment on the Altar of sacrifice. It is the only way. Shall I give my firstborn, that which is highest in me? Yes! The fruit of my body? Oh no! That is only the outer plane aspect of it. The fruit of my Being unto HIM? Yes! Yes, LORD, all my Being, to be THINE from the very apex of life down through the standard of the Being, through all the planes, manifesting through all the vehicles, even to the body, until the body is caught up of the innermost and is one in the sublime act of consecration; that the outer life is lived as the inner life is lived, as a life given in service for THEE, O LORD of my Being, LORD of your Being, LORD GOD of Israel.

Such is the path of sacrifice. You see how exquisitely beautiful it is, the burnt-offering, the attributes, the divinity in you, the oil of your Being, the realized Christhood in all the potency of the Jesus Christ life; the fruit of your Being, even the sublime joy which comes as a resultant of the realization of the Jesus Christ consciousness dwelling in HIM; the fruit of your Being, to give sacrificially in service to HIM.

THE RESTORATION OF THE ARK OF TESTIMONY

Israel, my people Israel, have ye forgotten the way ye have been led? Are ye overwhelmed because Samaria has fallen and Judah gone into bondage, and Ierusalem been levelled to the dust? Yet, saith the LORD, I will bring thee back again. Samaria shall be restored. Samaria is restored, *is* restored. The house of the Watch-towers is restored through the Oblation. And the land of Judah is undergoing the process of liberation, redemption from bondage. And even Ierusalem is having new foundations laid, [that she may] be rebuilt. And the Holy City of Zion is in process of arising again to be the manifestation of the glory of the LORD, through the return of yourselves and all the House of Israel.

O Israel! My people, Israel! Are ye grown weary because of the travail, and have ye forgotten the days of Joseph and of Moses and of Aaron and of Miriam? Have you forgotten how these days have been brought back again through the vision and the motion of that high priesthood before the High Altar and the restoration of the vision of the Soul? Behold! saith the LORD, MY Covenant is now restored, and the Ark of MY Testament revealed. For the Covenant is the relationship of the Soul to the Divine Mystery, and the Ark that testifies of HIM-SELF is HIS Holy Tabernacle within you. *How lovely are Thy tabernacles, O Lord of the Heavenly Hosts. They are full of the beauty shed by the glory of Thy Presence. There the sparrow hath found shelter, and the swallow a home for herself, a nest where she may lay her young.* In the true vision of the Ark of Testimony within yourself, even the lowly things, the humble things, the homely things, find a dwelling, a share. The sparrow is a homely bird, and it is but the symbol there of the homely things, the homing feelings which express themselves through into the Earthplanes. Even such are to find a place, a share, in the lovely dwellings of the LORD of Love; and the swallow with its flight through the upper airs; thrown down only when those upper airs are dense and heavy, the swallow, the flight of the emotion, hath found a nest where she may lay her young—the children begotten of the emotions, the beautiful generative desires, feelings, children reflecting the Love that moves through the emotion, revealing how the very Tabernacle of GOD is one from the within to the without, and how the without reflects the sweetness, the gentleness, the homeliness, the divine sublimity of the innermost.

THE GRAND RESULTANT

Now the resultant may be seen by you. Michaiah is the Message that makes life full. It is from the Divine threshold. It is that revelation of the Divine unto a Soul that makes it complete. Unto Israel it is the story of the history of their own travail, of their own ministry, of their past estate and of the estate which befell them during their ministry upon these planes. It is a call unto Israel to return to make once more that sacrifice which, in its fulness, exalts the Being to the very threshold of the Divine World and brings it face to face with HIM Who mediates before the High Altar in the Sanctuary of Being. It calls for that fulness of sacrifice that holds nothing back, but makes of life one sublime whole, an offering full from the innermost to the outermost, worthy of the divinity with which HE hath crowned the life, worthy of Sonship to HIM.

Here is the grand result in manifestation expressed in these simple words, applied to encourage men and women:—*To do justly, to love mercy, and to walk humbly with God.* That is an exquisitely beautiful, poetical, yet spiritually lowly form of interpretation for the daily life of every child of the FATHER-MOTHER; but for an Israelite there is far, far more lying behind it. Men and women oft-times measure their justice in the World, and their mercy too. And what is meant by walking humbly with GOD? That is a gospel for the World that would do it good if every man and every woman acted justly and manifested mercy, and walked humbly through life. But for an Israelite there is far more than that implied. And the Message was unto Israel. The unveiling of the sacrifice was unto Israel, for only an Israelite could have understood such a divine motion within the Being, such an intimate relationship, such potency, such fulness of Divine Indwelling, and endure to be called to the giving unto the absolute surrender of the will and all the powers controlled from its divine magnetic centre. Oh, the result is that the life is a dweller in the realm of Righteousness; that is, the life is equipoised, it is balanced. Those three [phrases] represent the balanced Life, the magnetic Life, and the Pleroma, the full Life.

To Do Justly

To be a Son of Righteousness is to be a Son of divine balance; to be balanced in mind, in heart, in will, in Being. That is why the will had to be sacrificed in order to attain the balance. There can be no perfect balance until the will is sacrificed unto the Divine. For the will is seated in the Arche or magnetic Centre of our Being. It is one with the Ram; it is of the Ram; the dual horns of the Ram are the dual powers of that will exercised. A righteous man is a balanced man—balanced in thought, balanced in desire, balanced in judgement, balanced in all his planes, balanced in all his vehicles; he has the power of control over his planes, over his vehicles. It is not of self, but of the Divine in him; it is of the divinity at the centre of his Being. To offer one's self in such sacrificial glorious offering before the High Altar of GOD is to attain unto the estate of Righteousness, perfect balance. It is GOD's standard and GOD's equity. To walk justly is to walk as a balanced life. Oh, it is a high standard, but it is the standard to be sought for. It is a divine standard, but it is a standard that is possible, otherwise we should not be asked to attain to it. GOD never asks of HIS children that which they cannot attain. And if HE asks Israel to get back to a life which is a sacrifice to Him, and manifest before the world as a balanced life, balanced in mind, in heart, in will, in the whole of the potencies of the Being, then HE is calling HIS children back to that life which alone is a perfect exposition of HIMSELF.

You will understand many of those sayings in the Old Scripture where Israel is appealed to—"*O Israel! My people Israel! Have ye forgotten the past?*" The outer history? No! No! That is the way that the Jewish scribes wrote into the history and interpreted it for racial and religious and national purposes. Israel was a race of the Sons of GOD, and therefore not confined in vision to any earthly, racial outlook. The Children of Israel were members of a divine community, and therefore were actuated always by the divine motion within them, so that that motion became manifest through them. Thus the appeal to them as Children of Zion, to return unto Zion; that is, to the holy estate of the Jesus Christ manifestation of the LORD of BEING. Yes, to make such sacrifice is to attain to be a dweller in the house of GOD's Righteousness, [to lead] the balanced life, the equitable life, the life of exquisite oneness with HIMSELF, and, as a resultant, to be a mediator of HIS Mercy.

TO LOVE MERCY

To be a mediator of His Mercy. You will recognize that though love can always express itself in beautiful merciful kindness (would that there was more of it in the World, for the children of the FATHER-MOTHER as a human race have that Love-principle within them, and there is far more kindness at the heart of them than becomes out-wardly manifest, because of the corrupting traditions and habits of great ages and the blindness where the light is supposed to shine in traditional beliefs as these are expressed before the high Altars of earthly worship), yet to be a Son who can mediate the Divine Mercy is to be one who understands through the very balance of life what God is, how HE loves, how HE ministers, what HIS Mercy is. What is it? It is never strained. No, because it is Love itself, Love itself in the exquisite beauty of its power in its outflow. Where Love obtains and prevails and triumphs, Mercy has not to be *spoken* of: it is there *manifest*. To be a mediator of HIS Mercy is to be a priest, a real priest, within the Sanctuary of HIS glorious high priestly ministries; to mediate of the Glowing Stone, even sharing the Seraphic ministry from HIS High Altar. To mediate of HIS Mercy is not a light thing. To be merciful is not to be weak. I say, *to be merciful is not to be weak*. It is to be strong in Love. It is to be majestic in Love. And the Soul who makes the sacrifice of all the Being comes to know the Mercy of God as none other can know it; that is, the Love in its flow through the standard, reveals itself in the exquisite balance in the very fashion of the Being, in the motion of the Being, in the outflow of the Being. There is Mercy that is the sweet healing of the breath of Love in the very aura of a Human Soul who loves divinely. Ah, but the aura is as the very Mercy of God in exposition. It is full of healing, but it does not hurt. It does not heal here and hurt there. Oh no! There is nothing of that in a balanced life. The balanced life hurts nowhere. It is of God, ever beautiful, like HIM. For such a life, you see, walks with HIM.

To Walk Humbly With God

What is it *to walk with God?* Simply to be as the people think, religious, walking in the consciousness that HE is good, and that His Name is Love?—all very beautiful, but it needs definition; it needs apexing in the triangle of life into a radiant centre. To walk with God is to walk in the consciousness of His Indwelling Presence, to be enshrined in His Glorious Radiance. It is to walk in communion with Him; that is, learning continually what He purposes for the life and through the life. To walk with Him is to walk so that the whole auric outflow is the revelation of Himself. Oh, when the Sons of God again walk the Earth, God will be walking with them, because He will be realized by them through their sublime sacrifice. He will be the Dweller within their Sanctuary. He will again be unto them, Moses; that is, the radiant revealing of Himself. He will be unto them, Aaron; that is, the glorious High Priest of their Being, whose divine Rod of Power changes everything, giving to them the triumph of Divine Omnipotency. He will be to them, Miriam, the sweet song of the Soul. Of Him the Soul will sing, always, ever of Him, interpreting Him, His conquests within it, His conquests for it, His conquests through it.

Oh, to walk with God! You could not but be lowly if you walked with God. There is no pride in God. He is Divine Dignity; He is Divine Majesty; but He is Exquisite Lowliness. There is no real quality you could name, no quality worthy of the name, which is not from Himself, because it is of Himself. And we acquire it because He has given it to us as a part of the fashion of our life to expound and reveal Himself. So you cannot walk with God without being lowly. No! He will give you majesty, that is, divine dignity. But that is not human pride. No! There is no such thing in the Heavens.

Look now at the fulness of the Message of Michaiah; the bringing back out of the turmoil, through the ages of travail, of Israel who came to minister unto Judah and enrich the Holy City of Ierusalem by revealing all that

Zion meant, through the establishing of Zion as a glorious communal Christhood, fellowship and ministry of exposition, revealing, interpretation; and [the showing] how HE would have all HIS children come back again to be the dwellers in the house of Righteousness, to mete out the real meaning of HIS Mercy as the mediators from the house of HIS Love, and to walk with HIM; to be majestic children, yet always lowly, majestic in life, yet always humble of heart and lowly of mind, majestic in divine potency, yet so selfless as never to be obviously conscious of being different from others; majestic and lowly, to be the expositions of the universal majesty of HIMSELF, Who, though so high as the Magnificent (how inadequate words are!) Potentate of all the Universe, nevertheless stoops to find exposition of HIS sacred Mystery through HIS lovely children, yet though lovely, lowly children.

That is HIS Message to you in this hour, a re-vision of the days of Michaiah, or the revealing of all that the FATHER-MOTHER had in store for HIS children, and the call it gave them to prepare for the Return; that which was to be the Return following the Manifestation, which was intercepted through the Occult World by those who did not like the restoration of the Christhood and have never desired it, have always worked against it, though many of the vehicles that World has used have been unconscious of their own opposing ministries as they have been handled to smite the new-born Christhood; and then the latter arising when the Oblation was accomplished; Samaria, the land of Samaria, the land of the Watchtower, restored, so that the Angelic World could approach again the outer realms of this Planet and pour down the spiritual oxygen to revitalize all its Kingdoms and re-inspire and illumine all the children who were able to respond.

The Return is now, that which was foreseen. And the call is unto you, now that ye are able, now that HE has enabled you to make the sacrifice and to be once more His children, dwellers in the house of His Righteousness, mediators of the streams of His Mercy, and thus, like Enoch, to walk with God.

O Lord of all Being, of Thy children's Being, of Thy Servant's Being, may the day hasten when Thy glorious outpouring shall be so fully received by Thy children that the sacrifice in its degrees will be made, and the house of Thy Righteousness and the mediation of Thy streams of Mercy once more become manifest as Thy children walk with Thee.

We would ever bless Thy Most Sacred Name.

I

THE MESSAGE OF
HABAKKUK

A FRAGMENT OF RECOVERED LOGIA
OF ISRAEL

THE VISION OF HABAKKUK

O Lord, Thine address to me have I heard;
the Awe of Thee overwhelms me.[1]

How marvellous are Thy ways!
Thou has made them manifest
throughout the Ages, for Thou hast
preserved and kept alive Thy Children.
   From Teman[2] *Thou didst come as their God,*
as the Holy One from mount Paran.[3]
   Thy Glory filled the Heavens,
and the Earth was full of the Praise of Thee.
   Thy brightness was as the glory of noon-day;
the streams of Light proceeded from Thy Side;
but Thy Right-hand hid the secret of Thy Power:[4]
   Before Thee the pestilence fled;
at Thy footsteps the fires ceased to consume.
   Thou didst stand to measure the Earth
and didst behold the nations driven asunder;
the Mountains of the Everlasting were not,
the Hills were all bowed down to the Earth.[5]

I saw the dwellers of Cushan in affliction;[6]
they were compassed by Midian; their curtains did tremble.[7]
   The Rivers were risen as when the floods come;
the people thought the Lord Himself was wrathful towards
them.
   But Thou didst ride upon the Sea in Thy chariot,
Thou didst bridge its Waves and drive them as Horses.[8]
   And thus didst Thou bring Thy Salvation nigh for Thy
Children.

*   *   *   *

Thou didst uncover Thy bow unto the Tribes of Israel,[9]
and send them Thy Word as Thou hadst promised.

Thy Word divided the Rivers of the Earth;
Thy voice was heard once more within its Deep;[10]
Thine Utterance made the Mountains tremblingly unveil,[11]
and Thy Right-hand opened the flood-gates of Being.[12]

The Sun and the Moon kept within their Habitations; they
moved in obedience to Thy magnetic Radiations, for Thy Radiance
played upon them like glistening spears.[13]

Through the land of Midian Thou didst march as Conqueror;
upon its threshing-floors didst Thou make Thy conquests;

For the Salvation of Thy People wentest Thou forth; through
Thine Anointed didst Thou smite the seat of wickedness, and
uncover the nakedness of Midian's foundations;[14] *even unto the*
head didst Thou reveal the evil things, and through Thy Whirl-
wind didst Thou scatter their dwelling-places.[15]

* * * *

When I heard Thee, my Solar Body trembled;[16]
my inward parts did quiver at the sound of Thy Voice.

The Foundations of my Being were shaken,
and my lips could utter no speech;

Yet prayed I that in the day of trouble I might know Thy
Rest.[17]

For then, though the Fig-Tree does not blossom,
nor fruit be within the vineyard;

Though the strength of the Olive-tree may fail,
and the fields of service yield me no meat;

Though the flock be absent from the fold,
and there be no herd in all the stalls;

Yet will I rejoice in Thee, O Lord,
and have joy in Thy Salvation; for Thou art my Strength.
Through Thee shall my feet again stand within the stalls of Thy
Temple, and walk upon the high places of Thy Dwelling.

NOTES ON TEXT

[1]Though a Soul need not be afraid of THE ETERNAL ONE, for always HE is the Compassionate ONE, yet the sublimity of the Vision of His Glory becomes overwhelming. To look into the midst of a Celestial System takes from the Soul the power of utterance; how much more so to behold HIM in

some concrete manifestion Who is the Heart of All Things! The Spirit of Divine Awe is of the ELOHIM.

[2]This represents THE ETERNAL approaching in the power of the Divine Passion. Teman signifies the southern motion of the Eternals, or Divine Dimension. It speaks of the redemptive motion of the Divine Passion.

[3]The Eternal Mystery. The word signifies the hidden things or places. GOD came out from the depth of HIS Mystery and made manifest.

[4]The streams of Light radiated from HIS side relate to Divine electric force; but the Secret of Divine Power was hidden. By this it is to be understood that no one can discover the Divine Secret; but it becomes known in Realization upon the Divine Kingdom.

[5]The Mountains of the Everlasting were the Divine Altitudes of Consciousness which were once manifest upon the Earth. They were not, because they had become lost to those who once were of the Christhood. Even the Hills or foot-hills of spiritual experience, were brought down by the Earthgeist or materializing spirit.

[6]The dwellers of Cushan relate to those who are kept in the darkness. Where no spiritual Light shines, there is cushi—the blackness of night.

[7]Amid the darkness the Midianites smote them. They caused them grievous afflictions, and broke down their defences. For the Midianites are lovers of strife. Their spirit is quarrelsome and dominating. They make war upon every Kingdom where they can find an entrance, and within every plane where they can find foothold. It was they who caused the Earth's hills to become bowed down, and the Mountains of the Everlasting to disappear.

[8]The Chariots and Horsemen were the Powers of the Heavens, riding over and amidst the tumultuous conditions, and quelling, for the time being, the raging of the storm.

[9]The revelation unto the Christhood of the presence of ELOHIM in their sevenfold ministry. To uncover the Bow of the LORD was to reveal the Glory of ELOHIM as each ELOHE operated unto the changing of the tumultuous conditions. For these fulfil the Will of the Word, EL ADONAI.

[10]The Voice of The Eternal was heard by Judah, the Planet-Soul, in the midst of its Spiral Mystery as the ELOHIM ministered.

[11]The Everlasting Mountains gradually reappeared within the Spiral of Being.

[12]All the Soul's avenues were liberated and opened with power to receive and give.

[13]A glorious revelation of Celestial action in ministry, and how the Divine World commands Sun and Moon.

[14]The effect of Truth where its flash-light is thrown upon the false systems which obtain in national life, commercial habits and ways, and religion whose spirit is midianite and whose teachings are contributory to the maelstrom of racial and national strife. For the materialistic Church is the Head of the false system.

[15]The play of tremendous Solar activity, by which the conditions are to be broken up and changed. The seats of wickedness in individuals, communities, nations and races shall be revealed, uprooted and swept away.

[16]The effect upon all the nerve-centres and vehicles of the revelation of the Eternal ONE. Such a vision shakes the Being to its foundations.

[17]Perfect equipoise in GOD, wherein is found the Great Peace. In such a state the Soul regains perfect trust in the Divine Presence, and full assurance of victory.

I

THE MESSAGE OF HABAKKUK

THE DIVINE EMBRACE

I WOULD speak to you this morning on an old-world Vision that has very special relation to our own times, and to the needs which are pending. The Logia in which that Vision was set forth I read to you last week, from a re-transcription of the Vision of Habakkuk. It is a Prophet's Vision of GOD in HIS Giving. It is supposed to have come to a Prophet who took the name of Habakkuk, during the period in which Jeremiah is said to have been prophesying. Therefore, although it is placed amongst the Minor Prophets, and classed with them, it is, from a literary standpoint, a very old document, but so greatly changed that only the Light of Heaven could possibly reveal the hidden meanings couched in the real Logia.

The name Habakkuk means "Divine Embrace", and the Vision was concerned with the Embrace of GOD. It has an individual aspect, and a Cosmic aspect in relation to this World and this System, so that those two aspects will run through the whole of the unveiling of the hidden meaning of the wonderful Vision.

We all understand on the human planes and within the motion of the human kingdom, as it is called, the meaning of embrace. How beautiful it is to a beloved one to receive the embrace of one greatly beloved. We can understand such an experience. It seems human, very natural, such as our heart longs for, and the natural fulfilment and expression of the deep motion of the love within our Being and within another beloved one. It is less easy, probably, for the human mind to transcend the human estate, to rise out of any consciousness of the human kingdom, to enter into the larger realm of the whole planetary constitution, and even to transcend it and enter the realm of the Solar Body, and try to apprehend what it could mean to the Soul to be embraced as an individual in planetary estate, or in Solar estate, by the Eternal Mystery we name the FATHER-MOTHER.

To help you to follow me, I will take you along this path—

The Vision:

How GOD comes to the Soul and to the World:

HIS Revelation unto Israel:

HIS uncovering of the Soul and the Earth through HIS Approach:

HIS Majestic Ride through the land of Midian and HIS Conquest, with the splendid resultant to the whole House of Israel and the House of Judah, this World, and consequently to the Solar Community.

THE VISION

Here I should indicate that there are certain key words in the prophecy, the understanding of which—for they are mystical words—enables you to see something of the Mystery of GOD'S Approach. One of these words is Cushan, which means the Night, or the Darkness of Night. [Then there is the word] Midian, thought of as a land and people whom ancient Israel is said to have contacted and fought, for Midian means the Land of Strife; therefore the Midianites are those who loved strife, or who used it for their own ends. Then there is the word Teman, "GOD came from Teman and the Glory of the Most High shone from Paran."* Teman, in a general interpretation, means South; really the Southern aspect of the Four Eternals, or the Southern avenue through which the Divine Ministry proceeds; therefore it represents the Divine Passion. And Paran means the Radiant Place. When HIS Glory shone from Paran, it was the revelation of HIS veiled Mystery unto the Children of Israel.

---

*Vide Habakkuk, ch. 3 v. 3.

Now the Vision said to have come to a Prophet is the same as that which comes to every Soul. Those of you who have had the privilege of looking through a great telescope to observe something of the expanse of the Celestial Realms, will easily recall how full of wonder the mind felt, how full of awe the heart. And if at a given time you had been privileged to see some of the greater Celestial wonders in that way (in so far as they could be seen and known, for they are not really known, only the outer garment of the Revelation of the Eternal Mystery is known through the telescope, or through any mental vision or reasoning), and if the occasion were a great one, you would remember how even your tongue was dumb, there was no speech or language in you to express the wonders of such a Universe as the Home of our FATHER-MOTHER, and the exposition of HIS Most Holy Mystery. If you had been privileged—provided it had been possible —to look upon, say, Sirius brought quite near to you, the Vision would have become so overwhelming that the Being could have felt it was unutterable. Even to take a voyage in any measure of realization into the heart of the Solar Body—which you know now from the Message is no mere physical body but a glorious Spiritual, Celestial, Divine Home, with Angelic, Celestial and Divine King-doms, with ten thousand times ten thousand, aye millions, ten thousand millions of Glorious Beings dwelling in the midst of it and ministering through its magnificent ele-ments and by means of its potencies unto this World and other members of the System—if you were privileged to take such a voyage into the heart of the Solar Body, you would be filled with amazement (the word is utterly inadequate), overwhelmed with the Glory; yes, and if, as you voyaged within, there gradually unfolded to you the Vision of ADONAI as HE is represented, even in the Solar Body, you would have felt overwhelmed, as the Prophet is said to have felt when the Cosmic Vision broke within him, and he saw the Presence of the Eternal ONE.

Is it possible to have such a Vision, even in realization? Oh yes, yes, it is possible! It is as truly possible to see such an inward vision as it is for our eyes to look Heavenward, and when our own Sun sets, by whose electric force during the day our atmosphere is lit up with glory, when he sets and the glory gradually passes so that there is no absorbent light to prevent us from seeing something of the Starry Hosts, it is as true that we can look on HIM as that we can in that most miniature way [gaze] upon the Universe. For although the Universe is so vast, it is but a miniature to the vision. Those Worlds are so vast in themselves, though they look like specks amidst the azure, the vaulted arch of the Heavens.

It is possible to have a Cosmic Vision of GOD. Many think that they have that Vision when they have but a representation of ADONAI in a planetary constitution even like this one in the unfallen days, but that is only a comparative Cosmic Vision. You will understand that to see HIM in a constitution like even our World in its perfect day, is most glorious, but not to be compared with beholding HIM, the same ONE, in HIS Fashion at the heart of the Solar Body. Yet even greater and grander is HIS Fashion in a Divine Kingdom, as in a Realm like Sirius. And yet still greater and grander is HIS Fashion when another form of Cosmic presentation of HIMSELF is made to the Being, as if the whole Universe were gathered up into one concrete exposition of HIS Sacred Mystery as it is in the Divine Vision of ADONAI, when HE is seen as KING, the Regnant ONE of all the Reigning Kings of the Worlds, and LORD of All, the Administrator, the ONE Who gives and receives, Whose Law commands and it is fulfilled.

HOW GOD COMES TO THE SOUL
AND TO THE WORLD

Now it is not unnatural to feel overwhelmed with Divine Awe in the conscious approach to the Eternal ONE. We cannot be too reverent. Do not confound, however,

reverence with grovelling in the dust of religious superstition. I do not mean that that is reverence. No, no. When
HE approaches, our Being bows before HIM; the whole Being,
not simply the body through genuflexion, but the Being
bows before HIM. You will understand how, when that
Prayer of Prayers* is spoken as we spoke it this morning,
and as we do at our morning services, it comes to pass that
I myself feel as if I must represent the dual motion, the
centrifugal and the centripetal, in the hands and arms
making the Sign of the Cross before HIM Who is THE
SIGN OF THE CROSS, as we pray to HIM that Prayer so
Soulic, so intimate, so lowly, so transcendent, so expressive of our Childhood in our absolute dependence
upon HIM.

Here I would say to you, do not be afraid of any degree
of the Cosmic Vision that may come to you, though do
not seek for it as such. It might be that in your very striving the Veil of your Temple would part for a little time
and you had a Vision you were unequal to receiving, in
which case you would not only be dumb, but moved to
the depths of your Being in such a way that it might take
you days and weeks, or even longer, to recover. But whilst
you should not strive, no one should strive, merely to
attain that Vision, yet each one should seek to live the
Life that leads ultimately to the Vision, and be full of the
Divine Patience and await HIS Coming; live anticipating
HIS Coming, but await HIS Coming.

*Oh, the Vision of God is a Reality! I cannot impress this upon
you too much; to make Him the Living Agency in every hour of
your life, in every feeling of your Being, in the power of your
motion, in the power of your vision, in the power of your expansion
and descension and ascension.* HE comes to you as you are
able to receive HIM, but do not be afraid of HIM. Oh, no,
never be afraid of GOD, never! If men and women could
trust each other as beautifully, selflessly, as they may trust
GOD, there would be nothing wrong with the World any

*The LORD's Prayer as given in THE LOGIA or SAYINGS OF THE MASTER.

more, for it would soon right itself. But they do not trust each other, nor do they trust GOD. Merely to proclaim their trust in HIM in song, or in prayer, does not mean that men and women trust GOD. If they did, they would live the Life HE asks them to live, and trust in HIM that it would lead them whither HE reveals in the Message of HIS Love and Wisdom. Men and women trust GOD in so far as they think it is outwardly profitable, commercially, socially, nationally and racially. It is the lack of that trust expressed in the individual, community, people, nation and race, which is behind so much of the tribulation that fills the World to-day. For to trust GOD is to believe in HIS Righteousness and HIS Equity; it is to believe that what HE asks of us is the true way, *and to live it.*

The Vision that came to Habakkuk (and the word means "to be embraced"), came to the Prophet, embraced him, caught him up into the Whirlwind of the Divine Presence, the Spiral of the Divine Presence. He was filled with the Spirit of Divine Awe. The Mystery of it, the Majesty of it, yet the Lowliness of it, that the Eternal should descend, condescend to ensphere him, gather him up, uplift him, overshadow and crown him with the consciousness of the Presence! Nothing will steady you so much in life as the consciousness of GOD with you. If you live equipoised in HIM you will not wobble in your planes, for there will be true magnetic balance. If you live in the consciousness of HIS ensphering, you will be able to electrically transmit HIS Energy as HE fills you from the Fountain of HIS Being in the degree in which you have become one with HIM. You will not go here and there seeking for something to establish your faith, as it is called —your mind, your heart. Oh, the thought of it! That those who once knew HIM in HIS Sacred Mystery [should participate in] anything that is beneath the dignity of a Son of GOD and such a Message as HE, the FATHER-MOTHER, gives to HIS Children, in the estate of Sons of GOD!

His Revelation unto Israel

How did the Vision come to the Prophet? In the motion of God, the Presence from Teman. He came to him in the form of the Divine Passion. That is not always to be thought of as relating to the Oblation, which was a special Act and Ministry unto this World for the healing of it.

You will remember, those of you who were present, my speaking to you in recent months of the Four Eternals, the North, South, East and West; and when God comes as the Presence to reveal His Love in its majestic ministry, He comes from Teman, and His Glory shines out from the heart of His Secret, illumining the Soul that receives something of His Passion. For you cannot know God except in His Passion as Divine Love; you cannot realize God except through Love. Love is the Divine Passion in us. The beautiful term "passion", you know has been degraded, materialized, until you can scarcely recognize it. True Passion, Divine Passion, is the whole Being moved from the Inner Worlds in ministry unto the fulfilment of His Will Who is the Father-Mother, because the Being lives to do His Will, allows nothing to stand in the way of accomplishing that Will—within itself, I mean.

God comes to you from Teman. Can you endure His Passion? Can you endure to receive Him in the Passion of His Love? If you can, then you will be Children of Love henceforth. If you can receive Him, you will be interpenetrated by His Own Mystery until He, Himself, lives in you, manifests through you, and you become the chalice of His Love, and the revelation of that Love as it is poured forth in blessed ministry. It is only in that way we realize God. We cannot know Him in any other way. We know Him in the Three Eternals through the Passion of His Love. When He comes from Paran, out of the heart of the Mystery, His Glory shines. It is North-Eastern— and here terms fail, for to use such a term only makes you think of the earthly definition.

GOD comes to you in the Passion of HIS Love. It makes your Solar Plexus ache when it is intense, but if you respond in sweet willinghood unto the call which the motion of HIS Presence gives to you, you will be able to live in harmony, to be in harmony with HIM. Instead of pain, you will have exaltation; lowliness with exaltation; humbleness, though crowned with HIS Majesty; gentleness, though filled with HIS Own Might, HIS Omnipotence (the word we use is the synonym for Almighty). HE fills you with HIS Potency. It fills you in the degree in which Omnipotency can be revealed in you and unto you and through you, so that you are one with HIM in HIS Omnipotence. Think what it is to be so embraced of GOD! Think what it means to be so embraced of GOD till every part of your Being quivers through HIS Encompassing and Overshadowing Presence; trembles, it is said; oh, quivers, responds, feels the effect of HIS Electrical Forces, and HIS Great Heart Magnetism, in which HE draws you ever nearer in consciousness to the realization of HIS Holy Mystery.

Here you may glimpse what it means for a Community to be embraced of GOD, and for a Planet, a World like ours, to be embraced of GOD. HE comes in the Avatar with HIS Encompassing Hosts. HE comes, not simply through external means. The external means are only the phenomena resulting from HIS motion within and through the Angelic Hosts and all HIS Children who are on the Earth-planes. For HE comes to embrace the Earth; first through embracing the individual, and then through embracing HIS people as a whole, HIS people Israel. How?

HE revealeth HIMSELF through HIS Bow. It is said HE uncovereth HIS Bow. It is not a bow and arrow, no; it is the Sacred Bow, the Arch of the Heavens, the Glory of the ELOHIM. HE revealeth unto Israel. Why? To recall them again to their ancient heritage, to bring them back again by means of such ministry unto the realization of their ancient Christhood estate. To call without is not effective to the Soul, though such a call may embrace the body; it may embrace the mind. But the Being has to be called within its own Kingdom, and so HE calls there to every one of you, and to Israel as a whole HE uncovereth HIS Bow.

Has HE not revealed HIS Mystery to you in these latter days? Has HE not given to you as ONE from Teman, in Divine Passion of Love for you? Has HE not descended from Paran—out of what is translated Paran—out of the Great Mystery whose depths are impenetrable by the mind, by the mental vision, even by the perception, until the Being has realized HIS Glory within the Sanctuary? HE has come to you. Unto what end? That HE may embrace more effectively the World. The Avatar has come back, the planetary life is embraced; it is encompassed by the Angelic Hosts, great multitudes are visible, their ministries can be felt, recognized, realized. The Avatar is with us. GOD, through the Solar Body, has come nearer to this World—not spatially, for space is not everything, you understand; but through the intensification of the ministry of the Divine Kingdom, the ministry of the Solar Body, HE has come nearer to the World. Greater outpouring proceeds day by day, hour by hour; greater still is to come. But first of all must come the recognition of HIS Children who have been embraced by HIM individually, who have come into the consciousness of HIS Ensphering and Overshadowing, who are to recognize HIS Bow in the Clouds of the Heavens; that is, the Sign that HE is with them.

The Glorious ELOHIM minister. Each Soul is specially ministered unto by its own ELOHE, but in combination all the Children are overshadowed by, interfused from, and must become the vehicle for, the ELOHIM.

GOD is embracing the World. The world is shaking to its foundations, its Solar Plexus is disturbed. It has to be so. It trembles in every fibre of its outer and inner bodies. It is the result of the Embrace of GOD, the Avatar.

His Uncovering of the Soul and the Earth
through His approach

Now in that coming, the FATHER-MOTHER doth uncover the Earth. Uncover? What is the meaning of that?
HE reveals; HE reveals the state of the Earth. HE found
that the Mountains of GOD were not, and the hills were
all brought down, that there were no altitudes of consciousness, no real spiritual consciousness of HIMSELF
operating in the World. HE measured the Earth; HE came
to embrace it. It is mystical language, but it is most real.
We have to use terms that are utterly inadequate, but we
do the best possible to impress HIS Holy, Holy Mystery in
such terms as we can command in any tongue, excepting
the tongue of the Divine Heavens of realization which has
to be learnt by each individual Soul. HE is uncovering the
Earth. What is HE doing? HE is revealing to you, if you
will accept it; HE is revealing to you that in the reper-
cussion of the conflict of Armageddon which was accomplished in the Intermediary Realms by means of the
Oblation, and is now taking place on the outer planes
of the Earth, evil is being uncovered everywhere, not
only unto the exposure of it, but that, through the uncovering of it, it may be recognized in the communal,
national and racial life, and healed by the application of
Righteousness and Equity.

When GOD comes to uncover, HE reveals HIS Truth.
HIS Truth, like a flashlight, sheds its Glory upon the world
of untruth. That is, where things are untrue, they are
revealed. We are witnessing the great activity to-day—
it is more than an adumbration, it is an actual reper-
cussion and repetition, but on the outer planes and without such power for permanent hurt—of that [evil] which
obtained in the Intermediary Realms prior to the work
of the Oblation. It proceeded throughout the ages of the
Oblation, but was gradually overthrown until at last the
powers and the principalities that sought high places, that
reigned over the Elemental Kingdoms, were cast down,

and they are on the Earth now. [These are] lovers of power over men, over individuals, over communities, over nations, over races; not merely individual lovers of power, racial lovers of power; [setting] one race against another, one community against another, and man against man. But the leaders, those at the heart of it, were cast out of the Planetary Heavens into that pit which shall be bottomless, the abyss wherein there is no foundation; that is, there shall be found no more any place where there is ought of darkness, superstitution, unrighteousness, iniquity, hatred, malice.

His Majestic Ride through the Land of Midian

The Lord Himself rides amidst the Midianites, the lovers of strife, the makers of strife everywhere. If you have ever felt strife coming to you, and the Lord is approaching you, He has shaken up your Solar Plexus until you would have been glad for the time being to have had other than such an experience of His Ensphering of you and Over-shadowing, but He shakes up His people as He shakes the Earth.

We cannot do anything that is wrong, and escape the shadow that it casts and the hurt that it brings; and the one who does the wrong ultimately suffers more than the one against whom, or upon whom, the wrong was done. Oh, the Law of the Lord is immutable, perfect! You cannot change it. His Righteousness is Eternal and His Equity in every Kingdom, from the Innermost Realm down into the humbler degrees upon the Earth-planes.

So He shakes the World to its foundations, and rides in His Chariots upon the waves. Here is a word of comfort for you. In His Chariot of Divine Power He rides upon the waves of the tumultuous conditions of life; He controls them for His Children. The tumults must continue whilst the people require to be shaken up, and the Streams of the Heavens cannot be other than disturbing to the streams of the Earth; but He is the All-Conquering

ONE, and HE rides upon the white horse of perfect Divine
Intelligence, real Omniscience, perfect Purity. HE rides
in the power of HIS inherent Love, the All-potent factor
that quietens, ultimately, all strife. The Nations will never
cure strife by being in an attitude of anticipating it, being
ready for it. You never cure strife in another whom you
know, by having it working underground in yourself so
that you are ready for a revelation of strife in that other.
You can heal the strife in another only through the Peace
that is in you, the power of the Peace, the power of Love,
the power of Truth shining out, causing the flashlight of
HIS Presence to shine through you, and strife itself will
either be forced back, or changed. Its spirit cannot stand
in the Light of HIS Radiance.

But how great is the responsibility for us who are here
manifesting in these days, with the consciousness that we
have not only been embraced ourselves, but that the
FATHER-MOTHER is embracing this World unto its healing, its redemption, its exaltation! HE hath revealed HIS
Bow in the Heavens to you. Dwell in the consciousness of
it. HE hath called you from the heart of HIS Glory. Live
in the memory of it, but let it be a memory that hears the
repercussions of HIS Voice within you. HE has come in
the Majesty of HIS Passion to fill you, to lay hold of you.
Oh, think of it! The honour of it, *the honour of it!*—the
sacred privilege, to be laid hold of by GOD that in the
Divine Passion HE may reveal HIMSELF through you!

Lord, when Thou callest, surely we must respond!
O my Father-Mother, Thou art irresistible in Thy Love and
Glory. I would follow whither Thou leadest, even unto the con-
sciousness of Teman and the radiance of Paran. I would follow
Thee, even into the Land of Cushan where the darkness still is;
bearing with me, through Thy Presence, Thy Radiance. I would
follow Thee amidst the tumultuous seas. I would ride with Thee
in Thy Chariots of Love and Wisdom upon the waves of human
trouble, individually, communally, nationally and internationally.

I would ride with Thee, sharing in Thy Ministry unto the Earth as Thy Child, Thy Servant, honoured to be such from Thee, for I would have the Earth most fully embraced by Thee, even as Thou hast embraced me and lifted me up, though but a little Child, into the realm where there is the knowing of Thee.

Such, Beloved Ones, is my prayer. I would have it yours, and if it be so, though we are apparently a small Community, yet the Message travels thousands of miles even in this hour in other Realms, and the resultant will be glorious. Great multitudes are here, sharing with us. Great multitudes minister Elsewhere to share with us that ministry that is to accomplish the perfect Avataric Embrace of the whole Earth unto its healing, and the restoration of all its children to the Edenic state, and the joy of a perfect Childhood to HIM. Why should not the children have joy? Why should they always have either false joy, or sorrow, until there seems no healing? Help them through your own Divine Joy to learn that the FATHER-MOTHER would have them filled with joy in their Childhood to HIM.

Unto Thee, Most Glorious One, be all the resultant in our own individual life, and all communal life, and all the Planetary motion unto the fulfilment through realization of Thy Perfect Law and Will.

Ever Blessed be Thy Name within us, and through us, in the service that is without.

I

THE MESSAGE OF
HAGGAI

THE PROPHECY OF HAGGAI

The Word of the Lord as He came unto the Prophet Haggai concerning the restoration of the Temple of the Lord, and the work to be accomplished by Zerubbabel the son of Shealtiel the governor of Judah, and also of the service to be rendered by Joshua of Josedech the high Priest.

The Lord of Sabaoth spake to me concerning the people who affirmed that the time had not come for the restoration of the Temple of the Lord.

But the Lord said unto me, speak thus to Israel:—

"It is now time for the Holy People to re-build the Temple of the Lord.

Ye dwell in beautiful Houses, yet ye have no Sanctuary wherein to Worship and offer your sacrifices unto the Lord.

Hitherto ye have sown much and reaped but little; ye have food but it never satisfies you; ye have water to drink but your thirst is never assuaged; all that ye have gathered has left you poor.

But why is it that these things have befallen you?

Because your heart is not in the things that ye do.

Ye do much looking, but it comes to naught; ye carry much to your houses, but it is taken away.

The Heavens above you have been stayed in their giving of the Dews of Hermon, so the Earth is stayed in her bearing of fruits.

The drought upon the land has been great, and the corn and oil have suffered; nor is there a renewal of the Vine and its fruit.

Even the Mountains of the Lord have not been able to shower down upon you the blessings He is wont to give you."

*   *   *   *

Then was Zerubbabel moved to undertake the rebuilding of the House of the Lord.

And Joshua joined himself to Zerubbabel;

And all the people hearkened unto obedience to the Law of the Lord, and they set to work to re-build the Temple.

They went up to Mount Lebanon and brought down wood blest by the Lord for service in the building of the House.

* * * *

The Word of the Lord unto Zerubbabel:

"O Zerubbabel! Be strong in Me and fear not. My Spirit is upon thee. Thou dost bear the Signet and Seal of the Most High, for thou art chosen to build His House. The Lord of Sabaoth is with thee.

Build ye My House and fear not though in the proceeding the very Heavens of the Earth are shaken, and the great Sea, and the land of Judah.

For then the Desire of all Souls shall come, and the Earth be moved to her foundations; for the Glory of the Temple of the Lord shall be even as great in these latter days as it was in the times of the Ancients.

The Cedars of Lebanon are mine with which ye shall build the House; and likewise are the Silver and Gold in vessels with which ye shall enrich it.

And the Glory of My Presence shall fill the Sanctuary, and it shall go forth unto all the Earth.

I, your Lord, am with you."

I

THE DESIRE OF ALL SOULS

THIS is an unveiling of the original prophecy of the Prophet who, in the Old Testament, bears the name of Haggai. The Message is placed with that of the other minor Prophets, and is not considered of first-rate importance. In the record of the Old Testament, four themes are presented, and these are crowned by a fifth which lends great value to the Message.

In the first theme there is a distinct chiding of the people by YAHWEH, for their unbelief, and their lack of enthusiasm concerning the rebuilding of the Temple.

The second theme is concerned with comparison between the original Temple and that which they had been asked to build, because many affirmed that the glory of the first great House could not be equalled by anything that Israel could raise.

This is followed by a great promise of blessing unto Israel, providing they heartily undertake the work and properly build the Temple.

Then the interest is transferred to Zerubbabel who throws the full weight of his influence into the project, and, as a result, is called by and endowed of YAHWEH, and the enriching of him with Messianic Light, Potency and Authority to accomplish the Divine Purpose.

These themes are crowned by the prophecy that, in the midst of the Work, the Earth should be shaken to its foundations, also the Great Sea and the Land of Judah, and that ultimately there should be a great response from these.

Such is a brief outline of the prophecy as that is stated in the Book of Haggai. But I now ask you to follow me as the true inwardness of the Prophet's Message is unveiled under these aspects:—

A. The First House that was Built but Destroyed;
B. The House that is to be Rebuilt;
C. The Instruments of the Restoration;

D. The Riches with which it is to be Endowed;
E. A Glorious Messianic Resultant.

A

THE FIRST HOUSE THAT WAS BUILT BUT DESTROYED

The Message of Haggai was Cosmic. It was a part of the whole prophetic Revelation unto Israel. Therefore, the reference to the first Temple had no connection with an earthly Sanctuary. The meaning belongs to the Solar World. Commentators dwell upon the earthly side of the story of the Temple of Solomon; but whatever gorgeous House was reared by the one who is written of as King Solomon, the true meaning of the event is not to be found on the Earth. It belongs to the Heavens. The Solomon of GOD, was a Divine embodiment upon the Solar Kingdom, and his Temple was Soulic and Solar. The Temple that was destroyed upon the Earth was none other than the Cosmic Christhood of the Sons of GOD, which was built upon the Earth-planes in the sense only that it was a Solar manifestation of Christ through the Twelve Tribes of ancient Israel, who were originally the Sons of GOD in the Solar Celestial Spheres, and who were deputed to come here on a mission of manifestation and interpretation unto the elder races of this Planet.

* * * *

An earthly Temple may be of great value as a centre of worship and service. To consecrate its uses to the Holy ONE, surely is a most sacred act. And it may become the centre from which great spiritual radiations will be poured forth. For a true Sanctuary upon the Earth should be a house of Divine Love, Life, and Light; and these should be radiated to all who come near its Courts.

Sanctuaries, whether on the Earth or in the Heavens, are for worship and service. *For perfect Worship is also perfect service.* We possess the Adoré in the exact measure in which we serve in purity of heart, lowliness of mind, and

165

humbleness of spirit. And according to our degree of such a realization shall be our power to make manifest the Divine Love and Wisdom.

It was thus with the first Temple. It was a most glorious House let down from the Heavens. The radiance of Christ shone through it. The Divine Love and Wisdom found exposition through its manifestation. It was the Home of the Worship of YAHWEH. The Glory of ADONAI filled all its Courts. The Holy PRESENCE moved through its aisles, HIS Voice was heard throughout its triforium and clerestory. HIS Cloud overshadowed the Oblatory, and the motion of Cherubim and Seraphim was everywhere manifest. The transcendent Cross was there above and beyond the Oblatory, the radiations of which were resplendent like the Sun in his power; and the seven-fold Glory of ELOHIM was revealed in all the Sacred Tinctures.

Such was the first House of GOD upon the Earth. It was the Temple of Solomon, the manifestation in embodiment of the Holy Mystery of YAHWEH, energized from the Eternals and clothed with Solar radiance.

* * * *

Thus must it be obvious to the earnest mystical student of this Message that the true story of the building of the Temple was spiritual and Cosmic; and it should be readily observed that it had very special relationship to the Christhood. Also, that it was this most sacred House that was destroyed during the conquest of this world by the enemies who came to this Planet, or House of Judah, to make it the scene of their activities wherein, by means of materializing processes, they changed the nature of the Elements and brought about the fixity of many of them, gave wrong direction to the magnetic streams with disastrous results, and gained the dominion of all the outer spheres of the Earth.

* * * *

For Jewry it was doubtless a calamitous thing to have their earthly Sanctuary which they had built upon the Hill that had been named Zion in the north-east corner of the City of Jerusalem, destroyed by those who had been turned into enemies. But even such an event was a small local affair, and not to be compared with the destruction of the Solar Temple of the Christhood, brought about by those who did not appreciate the manifestation of the Divine Love and Wisdom in the constitution and exposition of the Earth. For it was the defeat of the purpose for which the Sons of GOD came to this Planet as Divine Teachers, Interpreters and Manifestors. As a glorious Body of Solar Christs, they were sent here to educate in the Divine Love and Wisdom the elder children of Judah. The sacred Temple which they composed had been reared by Angelic and Archangelic ministries within the Solar World; and the coming to Earth of such a Temple, was the revelation of the Glory of the FATHER-MOTHER. The auric splendour of the manifestation was even as a reflection of the resplendence of Sol. It was indeed the Temple of Solomon.

* * * *

Such a manifestation was necessary. Souls can understand the Wisdom of GOD only as it is interpreted by those who know the Wisdom. And the interpretation has to be in the degree in which the Soul can apprehend, and in relation to the Divine Revelation on the Earth and in the Universe. All the perfect things upon the Earth are still reminiscent of the glorious Wisdom of GOD. They speak of HIM.

It is too sadly true, even unto this day, that the people see much but understand little; that they hear many things concerning GOD, but have no right vision of HIM; and that they neither perceive nor apprehend the things of the Spirit. They gather much knowledge on the way, yet possess not that inward vision out of which Divine Realization grows and becomes inheritance. *Divine Scholasticism is lacking. The world is impoverished through lack of true interpreters of Life and Celestial manifestation.* In looking out upon the world, few there are who seek to understand the Mystery lying behind all manifestations of the FATHER-MOTHER in hill and dale, tree and flower, blossom and fruit, the zephyr breaths, and when the wind majestically sweeps through every avenue. Such things are thought of only as relating to the Earth and, rarely, if ever, as Heavenly phenomena. Yet they are as truly Heavenly as many Soulic experiences. No man can make them, though he may mar them. When permitted to rightly fulfil the Law of their Kingdom, they are products of the operation of the Eternal Laws of the Divine Love and Wisdom.

*　　*　　*　　*

This Earth was once a Heavenly House. It was clothed with Divine-World glory in the degree in which it could make that glory manifest. There came to it as a gift from God, the Cosmic Solar Christhood. It was a most wonderful Temple of Divine Manifestation resting upon the Earth's Bethlehem. It was the Holy City of Zion, the radiant Body of the LORD in Solar exposition, radiating upon the Earth the glory of the LORD. The embodiment was a remarkable revelation of Divine Love and Wisdom. If you could, even for a few moments, glimpse the radiance that streamed from it as auric radiation, you would understand that it is no vain story you are asked to consider, but *the blessed Revelation of God.* It was the House of GOD in Israel, whose constituent elements were altogether spiritual, and whose fashion was an embodiment of the ETERNAL ONE. In the formation of its quadruple square, it was Celestial. Its illumination and inspiration were from the Divine World.

But with the changing of the Kingdoms of the Earth and the shattering of the Planetary constitution as a Temple of the Divine, the Temple of the Christhood was brought down, and its stones (the individual members of the Christhood) were levelled to the dust. The Sons of GOD were dethroned from their Divinely regal position and state, and driven out of the Land of their Nativity to become wanderers amid the wilderness conditions of the Earth. They hungered for the Bread they once ate of; they thirsted for the Living Streams that once sustained and refreshed them; they longed for the glorious communal Christhood, the Living Temple with its sacred worship, fellowship and service. *They were Celestial Mendicants*, poor and needy souls.

The overthrow of the ancient Temple of Solomon was a sad story. It was the utter destruction of the first glorious House of the Christhood within the spheres of the Earth. In a vital way, it was the defeat of the manifestation of the Divine Man, individually and cosmically; for it was the frustration of the Divine Purpose and the negativing of the ministry of Solomon, who was a regnant one for GOD, high Potentate within the Solar Body, and Divine Administrator.

B

THE HOUSE THAT IS TO BE REBUILT

After such a vista of the nature of the Temple of the Christhood and what befell it, you will not be surprised to learn that such a people wandered in a strange land for ages, oppressed by the elemental conditions, sorrowfully contending with the play of forces that were ever in conflict with their own desires and aspirations, smitten by the very breaths that prevailed which were set in motion by the astral powers, and plunged into the darkness caused by the powers that ruled within the Planet's Heavens and upon its fixed planes.

These Sons of GOD were the people dwelling amid the darkness who came to see a great Light in the Prophetic Unveilings. For they were the only Souls upon the Earth who could understand Heavenly things. When they truly saw, they knew; when they heard the Divine Call, they understood. And often when they saw and heard, they would fain have risen out of the awful conditions that had enmeshed them. But the elemental powers were too great for them. They had therefore to remain and endure oppression in the land of their captivity, the while acquiring Divine content and patience.

Many were the efforts made by the Heavens to restore the Temple of YAHWEH as the Living Christhood. Messengers came. They brought the Revelations which are still to be discerned underlying the great Religions— Patriarchal, Brahminical, Zoroastrian, Osirion and Rama-han, Hermean and Jovian. Prophets and Seers arose as interpreters of these. Their ministries encouraged and strengthened the Sons of GOD often; but all efforts to fully restore the Cosmic Christhood upon the Earth failed, for the elemental conditions opposed themselves to such a high manifestation. The Heavens of the Planet were dominated by powers whose purpose it was in their activities, to defeat the effort to regain a Christhood embodiment. They essayed always to frustrate the work of the Divine World. The Gods and the Sons of the Gods who had been appointed to give special direct ministry, had to work through the most difficult conditions. There were times when, if the Sons of GOD who had formed the Christhood could have risen high enough in state, it might have been possible to fully rescue and restore them. But the task proved too great; for they had been terribly afflicted by the conditions generated by the enemy.

Yet the Divine World found the way in the fulness of time to defeat the enemy, and make possible the rebuilding of the Temple of GOD. That was a glorious accomplishment effected by means of the Oblation. After that great event, the restoration became possible.

The Temple to be rebuilt is none other than the Christ-hood. All that that most glorious Home of Divine radiance and mediation was when let down from the Heavens, is to again become embodied in and through the Sons of GOD. *That which the Manifestation signified, is to find perfect fruition in the restored House of Israel.*

C

THE INSTRUMENTS OF THE RESTORATION

In more recent days you have had unveiled to you with an ever-increasing fulness, the Divine Mystery of the Oblation. You will remember that that sublime though tragic Divine Work in Sacrifice, was the outcome of the prevailing inimical conditions; for these latter had become so great, and were of such a nature, that, to break their power and change the conditions, the Divine World, in order to enable Israel to arise, specially intervened by projecting and carrying through the Work of the Oblation. By this means they were to be able to come up out of the darkness and begin the rebuilding of the Temple of the Christhood.

Now is "the fulness of time." The Divine Event has come to pass. Haggai's prophecy is being fulfilled. The Heavens were shaken by the Oblation. The great Astral Sea was changed and purified. That Sea was made to give up the dead who were in it—those who were spiritually without Life. The Souls who had died in their vision and realization amid the impure astral conditions and elements, have been liberated and delivered by the Oblation. The upper and lower circles of the Atmospheria, were purged of their evil states, and the freedom of the Sons of GOD assured. And now they must be the instruments of the yet greater arising.

Through the Light of Heaven brought to you by means of this Message, you may be able to rightly interpret history during the Christian Era, and witness something of the effects of the Oblation in process, upon peoples and nations, and especially upon the religious conflicts and the planes of the Planet. For, in its grand processional, the Divine, Majestic, painful Travail of ADONAI through the

Solar ministry, and in and through HIS Servant Whom HE chose as Vehicle, moved the Heavens of the Earth, and even the lower reaches of the Planet, and shook them all to their depths. By means of it was fought the Astral and occult Armageddon, and the powers of the air were cast down. The conflicts witnessed to-day between races and nations, people and elements, are part of *the aftermath;* and in a sense they are the fruitage of the Oblation. The Armageddon that took place in the intermediary realms, is now reflected upon the outer Kingdoms. The powers that were cast out of the Heavens and thrown down to the Earth and which now seek to dominate the nations and peoples, are being gradually overthrown, and will ere long be cast out of the Earth. The Divine Heavens are triumphing, and the processional back to Edenic conditions has begun.

These things are being accomplished. The vision of the Temple of YAHWEH has been restored, and now the sacred House is to be rebuilt. The Festival is proclaimed again. The Message of Haggai is recovered and interpreted. *Proclaim the Reveille!* For the realization of the Message of Haggai is with us. It is the grand Festival of the Christhood.

* * * *

It must be recognized that Sanctuaries of stone cannot save the people. Many most beautiful Houses have been built and dedicated to the service of the Most High ONE. These have been as sacred to those who built them, as history says the first Temple in Jerusalem was to Jewry. Many of those Sanctuaries have been put to beautiful service. The Saints have passed through them and made them consecrate. Indeed, many of the great Builders upon whom the Afflatus rested, and whose illumined genius was used to rear them, were of the ancient Christhood. Yet, notwithstanding this, the raising of those Houses has not saved Humanity, not even spiritually illumined the Nations. Indeed, the Church itself, though possessing those wonderful works of Celestial formation and Angelic symbolism, has failed to perceive the inward meanings, and has worshipped the very stones of the earthly House whilst missing the Divine Significance of the things made manifest on the outer kingdom. If Salvation could have come by this means, then surely Europe would have become a Garden of Eden ages ago. But such blessing has not come to it. The Home of the Great Catholic Church is no nearer the Light than when Savonarola sought its redemption. Germany is no nearer the true understanding of the Faith professed for ages, than Luther was when he denounced Rome. France has worshipped Joan of Arc as a great liberator but is as much in bondage now but without the consciousness of it. Her Houses of Rheims and Notre-Dame to-day cannot be said to be full of the Glory of the LORD.

Nor can much better things be said of these Isles. Most lovely Sanctuaries are scattered over the land. Glorious Cathedrals as Homes of Light were raised by the Saints; yet darkness prevails. The people are still needing saving, redeeming and regenerating. The failure of Calvin and Knox is as obvious as that of Luther and Savonarola. The great Sanctuaries reared in their memory have not brought Redemption one day nearer. And though the real Redemption of the nations is nigh, and the Regeneration of Israel at hand, such events are quite outside the religious activities of the nations. They are the fruitage of the Oblation made manifest as the Sons of GOD arise to build anew the Temple of the Christhood, which is in verity the Temple of Divine Life.

It was of this Temple, Haggai spoke. His Message was prophetic. That prophecy is now being fulfilled. The House to be reared was the Temple of Life in each Soul; then the communal expression of that in a Cosmic Christhood. This latter is to become the Body of the LORD in manifestation. The real Body of the LORD is not found in earthly elements though sacramentally consecrated, though there is a sense in which all the Elements may be related back to their primal state as that Body in the realm of outer manifestation. The real Body is realized in Divine Substance and the Blood of the Eternal Mystery or Life-Stream. When a Soul reaches high Christhood it becomes part of the Body of the LORD for manifestation. Its whole Being is built up of the Divine Substance, and its Life-stream is that of the Eternal magnetic and electric Force. *Herein the Soul becomes an exposition of Yahweh.*

Everyone who realizes Christ is an instrument for the building of the Temple of the LORD. Everyone who lives in the consciousness of the Divine ensphering and over-shadowing, is contributing to the appearing of the LORD in the Cosmic Christhood. This is the Divine Revelation in this Message. It is for all who can respond. Ye who have sat in the darkness may now come into the Light shed by the Dawn of HIS Day. Open your eyes and behold! Unstop your ears and hear the Voice that speaks within your audience chamber! Open the floodgates of your Being, and the Presence will fill your Chalice-reservoir to overflow.

* * * *

The Festival Day has come. It is Haggai's day. The celebration of the inception of the rebuilding of the House of YAHWEH is now to begin: it is "the fulness of time." Will you share in the Work? Do you say the time has not come and we must wait better times and conditions? Do you desire to be accounted of those who in speech and conduct retard all those who long to be Christ-workers? Will you be so laggard that it may be said of you that you actually aided those influences that are always inimical to the Christhood? Surely your prayer will be:—

Lord, here am I to do Thy will in whatsoever Thou askest me.

* * * *

Remember, all ye who hear this Message, that ye are always Sons of God. Therefore ye must be of the Christhood, the Temple built up of Living Stones.

174

The coming of this Festival Day is also the becoming of The Beloved of the FATHER-MOTHER. It is the opening of the Soul's Vision; the enriching and energizing of the streams of the Being; the appearing of the Presence within the Sanctuary and the shedding of the Radiance of the FATHER-MOTHER through all its Courts; the Celestial assumption and the crowning of the Soul "with power from on High" to become as a Beloved One for HIM.

The world and all its children are to be saved. Assuredly it shall be so, for the Heavens now declare it. This one-time beautiful member of the system could not be left to perish. But if the Will of the Heavens is to be accomplished in the restoration of the Planet (the Land of Judah) and all her children, to the conditions of purity, spiritual light, and radiant happy childhood such as obtained in the Edenic Days, then the Temple of YAHWEH must be rebuilt, the glorious Solar Christhood made manifest, and Ierusalem from Above again descend to dwell upon the Earth. FOR ONLY THUS CAN HE COME WHO IS THE DESIRE OF ALL ISRAEL, AND WHO IS TO BECOME THE FULFILMENT OF THE DESIRE OF ALL SOULS.

In urging you to arise and come back into the Christhood estate, individually and communally, I hope you will not misapprehend my meaning, and imagine that such a return to Christhood means for you a declaration to those around you that you are different from them and superior to them. For, when Christ comes He is not announced. He is manifested. When a Soul is in Christhood, there is no personal claim, nor is there even an individual consciousness of the estate. The Christs of GOD do not call attention to themselves. They are ever in a state of blessing unto all Souls; yet when the Radiance of GOD streams through as auric glory, they are quite unconscious of it. They dwell in the realm of Divine Realization. The Message embodied into concrete manifestation will reveal Christ. And the Christhood so revealed, will ultimately draw many to recognize that GOD is indeed once more incarnate upon the Earth.

D

THE RICHES WITH WHICH IT IS TO BE ENDOWED

In the Prophet's vision the Cedars of Lebanon were to occupy an important place in the new superstructure. For the House was to be built of Cedar-wood from Lebanon. Here the Prophet in symbol unveils a Divine Mystery. The Substance and Life-stream of the ETERNAL of which Christhood is upbuilt, as such never descend below the Solar Atmospheria. The slopes of Lebanon are the Celestial Spheres adjacent to the Divine Kingdom, the lofty White Mountains of the Divine Estate, and Home of the Eternals.

The Cedars of Lebanon were, therefore, the Solar Christs. They grew up on the slopes of the Divine King-dom as expressed in the Solar World, attained to an estate of consciousness and realization wherein they could dwell in the Majestic Presence as that Holy Mystery was accommodated to the Solar Celestial Kingdom, and drink of the Eternal Streams which flowed from the summit of the Great Mount. They ministered before the LORD as HIS Priests serving at the Table of the Shew-bread—the Sacramental Bread of Angelic Love and Wisdom for all who were ascending in the Arc of Life within the sphere of their ministry. That Bread was the Divine Sub-stance accommodated to the Mind and Heart states of the Soul. And likewise with the contents of the Chalice wherein was preserved the Wine of GOD. But those who were in yet higher estate became the recipients of the Bread or Divine Substance within the Ark of Reservation— *the Bread that was the Food of the Gods.* And they partook of *Wine named the Blood of the Lamb* whose Mystery of Deity the Ark concealed even whilst the Son of GOD mediated of it unto all who had so attained to inherit such a degree of the *Deific Force.*

Such high endowments are to be restored to all who once possessed them for the blessed ministry of the Christ-hood. Therefore, all ye who still sleep, hear the Voice of the ETERNAL calling you through HIS Servant! Awake! awake! all ye who yet slumber! Arise, and let GOD's Christ in you come forth to make manifest! Ascend once more into the realm of your Ancient Inheritance. Put on the radiant robes of Christhood. Know HIS Regeneration as well as HIS Redemption. Get up again to the high mountain of true Celestial Vision and realization. If you have been grovelling in the dusty realms of mere mentality, personality, and all earthliness, then quit these now. Arise in the power of the flight of the Spirit, and get you up on to the Mount of GOD. It is the Voice of your King calling. HE desires to see you in all the beauty of your ancient Estate and Priesthood.

*   *   *   *

O Wondrous One! The glory of Thy Love is immeasurable, Thou givest so abundantly to Thy Children. Everything connected with Thine Israel, Thy manifestations unto them, Thy exposition of Love and Wisdom through them, and Thy transcendent revela-tions unto them, speaks of Thyself, of Thy Loving-kindness, of Thy great Tenderness, and Thy exceedingly great Patience.

Thou art most Glorious, O Father-Mother! How honoured we are to be Thy Children! How rich we are to be sharers of Thy Holy Mystery!

E

A GLORIOUS MESSIANIC RESULTANT

Did you grow upon Lebanon as one of GOD's Cedars? Were you of the Ancient House of the Christhood? Many who hear this Message and find in themselves a strange response to it as something related to them, are asking the above questions. The Being cries out to know for certainty.

177

Yet you say that you have no remembrances of such experiences.

All the members of the Christhood suffered such affliction and privation that they forgot even the vision of His Countenance Who was and is their LORD. If you love this Message, that in itself is testimony to your heritage. The veil that is upon you is the result of ages of travail amid the darkness. Being veiled, you have lost the memory of The Beloved ONE, and those whom the FATHER-MOTHER sent. Even the most intimate relationships have become dimmed in your vision and now appear like a vague dream of long-past ages.

But in many there is a great awakening proceeding, as if those memories were being stirred through the over-shadowing of the Divine World. For all the stones which comprised the Temple of Solomon are to be raised from the dust, re-energized and adorned to take their place in the new manifestation. As Living Stones they are to form the Living Temple of YAHWEH, and know again the Chief among ten thousand and altogether lovely ONE, even the Solomon of the Divine World.

O Solomon of God! Thou art more than solar radiation and glory, and even more than one from the Realms of the Gods! Thou art indeed none other than Adonai, The Beloved One, ever the Chief amongst all the Gods, and the lovely sum of them all!

It was promised that the House to be rebuilt for YAHWEH should be equal in form, beauty and glory to the first House. That promise implies tremendous things. And all who can hear and read this Message are called to contribute to the coming of such Messianic Glory. If you respond your endeavour will not be fruitless. You will not escape criticism. The cynics and those who are out to crush every good that comes to birth, will say of you, *Look how those who profess to follow such an exalted Message fail.* The critics of the Work of rebuilding are many, but the true labourers are few. Most who sit in judgment have a false view of the values belonging to Jesushood and Christhood.

The outlook of historical Christianity is far removed from that which belonged to the Message of the Master. The message of historical Christianity turns the true vision of the Master upside down. In the light of all that He stood for and taught, it is difficult to recognize Him in the superstructure that has His name written all over its externals. When the new House of the LORD is again reared upon this Earth, there will be no mistaking it for the House and System which pose as founded in and built upon Christ. At present that Temple of high purpose and glorious fashion, is only in process of erection. But the foundations can be seen. And the walls rise ever higher. Even the beams and rafters may be witnessed of as they take their place. The House grows, though the necessary outer scaffolding hides its form and beauty. Bye and bye these will be also seen.

Therefore, have patience. Be faithful to that which has been restored to you. Let Wisdom reveal itself. Make Love to be triumphant. Radiate the glory of Truth in wise conduct. Let your aura reveal the Beloved ONE. The Glory of GOD is one, whether it be in a multiple Star or one that is alone; whether in a great or a small embodiment. Therefore, be encouraged. Let nothing daunt or dismay you. Seek the realization of your LORD, then it shall be well. Then verily you will share in the Great Work, and, in doing so, bring salvation to unexpected quarters.

* * * *

The manifestation of such a Christhood will be irresistible, and its power will reach to the Heart of Judah—the Planet-Soul. The Earth will retake her primal estate, and all her powers be young again. Art will be illumined till it reveal HIM; Music will express the perfect Praise of HIM; and Science will no longer be a dead language, but the living interpreter of HIS Wisdom. Religion itself will be clothed in Heavenly garments and not in lifeless creeds and dead shibboleths. Then also may we hope to see the earthly Sanctuaries reared in the name of Christ become like those of the Heavens and take genuine part in the glorious work of the building of the House of the Christ-hood. Then indeed shall the Work of Zerubbabel be made manifest, His special Solar ministry be crowned with Divine Glory. For it will be a cosmic achievement. And the full relationship between Him and Israel will be restored. Then also may it be possible for Him to unveil again the Mystery of the Golden Candlestick with its seven-fold Lamps of ELOHIM.

May all who hear of these most sacred things, so respond to the call that they may share in the glorious resultant.

O my Father-Mother! There is no end to what Thou revealest of Thyself unto us, nor to the mysterious language which Thou dost inscribe upon the walls of the Sanctuary of our Being.

We would evermore adore Thee. We would live for Thee. We would be Living Stones in Thy Temple of Being. We would be once more Thy consecrated Children, and serve as Thy Priests in Thy Sacred House.

Thy Name is ever glorious and blessed unto us.

Amen and Amen.

THE MESSAGE OF
ZECHARIAH

A PROPHETIC VISION

In the midst of this world's night, when no star shone in its firmament to guide the wayfarer, nor voice spake from out of the Great Silence, the Angel of the Lord stood by me that I might not be alone, and that I might again witness the opening of the Heavens and receive from the Lord revealings concerning His Holy Purpose.

In Visions did He speak to me. He showed me one who sat upon a red horse in the midst of a grove of Myrtle trees. Accompanying him there were other riders and horses of varying colour, and one white.

When I enquired the meaning of the Vision, the Lord through His Angel enlightened me that these were the powers of the Eternal Love and Wisdom making manifest His Presence unto any who might be found awake amid the darkness. They moved to and fro in the Earth, representing the dual motion of the Elohim. Yet the whole Earth remained still as if it were asleep.

Then the Angel who was with me spake unto the Eternal One, saying—

"O Lord God of Sabaoth, how marvellous Thou art in Thy loving kindness. Thy Mercy in all its tenderness, Thou has made manifest unto Judah that all her woundings might be healed, and the Holy City of Ierusalem within her borders might be restored."

Then the Angel cried aloud—

Thus saith the Lord of Sabaoth:

"In My return to the Holy City of Zion, My House shall be rebuilt:

"All the affliction of My people shall be healed, and I shall comfort them:

"Those who smote them because of their jealousy shall be overthrown in the way, and their evil work defeated;

"And from the Holy Place of My Temple when it is restored there shall go forth a stream of blessing unto Ierusalem that will heal her states, upraise her children, rebuild her walls, and restore all her gates."

After these things, I saw in vision four Horns. These signified the powers that had overthrown Ierusalem, Judah and Israel, laid waste the Holy City and desecrated the Sanctuary.

And the Angel said unto me,

"Fear not, the Lord Himself shall work great things on behalf of Israel. He shall yet break the powers of the oppressors, cast them down from the seats of their regnancy, and deliver and redeem all the House of Israel and the Children of Judah. And Israel shall be clothed in His radiance, and Ierusalem be once more a City of Light and Beauty. And the Lord shall be as a wall of Fire round about them, their defence and their glory."

I

THE GOLDEN CANDLESTICK

The Angel of the Lord once more drew near to me; and He parted the Veils of the inner Sanctuary and led me to the High Altar of the Most Holy One.

Upon the Altar I beheld the most Sacred Mystery of the Eternal God.

In Fashion He was like a Golden Candlestick.

The Form of the Candlestick was like a glorious Spiral.

Seven Branches proceeded from its Standard, and rose one above the other like ascending Arcs of Light.

Each Arc had its Light different from the other, and together they made the colours of the Rainbow around the Spiral.

The Standard of the Spiral was crowned with a Sacred Bowl wherein burned a White Light, which to look upon was ineffable.

From this Bowl all the other Arcs derived their power to shine, for there were conduits from the Sacred Bowl to each of the Lamps.

On either side of the Spiral stood an Olive Tree, and these poured of their Oil into the Golden Bowl by means of two Golden Pipes.

Then the Angel of the Lord revealed to me the meaning of the Two Olive Trees and the Spiral with its seven Branches and seven Lamps, and the Sacred Golden Bowl on the top of the Spiral.

And I bowed my whole Being before the Sacred Mystery of God revealed in the Sacred Spiral and the Two Olive Trees.

I

CROWNS OF SILVER AND GOLD

The Word of the Lord came unto me in the midst of the darkness that lay upon the Earth and commanded that I should find those of the Captivity who belonged to the Houses of Heldai, Tobijah, Jedaiah and Hen, and convey them to the Houses of Joshua and Josedech the High Priest.

He also commanded that all the Silver and Gold held by those Houses should be given unto me, that of these precious elements I might fashion crowns for Joshua and Josedech; for a crown of Silver was to encircle their brow, and a crown of Gold rest upon their head.

And He further said unto me—

"Thus shall you speak unto them,

"Behold, one cometh who shall be the Servant of the Branch! He shall grow up before Me and take his place in Israel, making manifest My Branch, and rebuilding My Temple.

"And you shall share the Glory that shall follow his coming, and participate in the regnancy of My Branch as He reigns over the whole Household of Israel. For His Throne shall be raised within Zion and His dominion extend to and embrace the land of Judah; and His reign will be glorious."

And the Lord commanded me to make crowns from the Silver and Gold and place them upon the heads of the Houses of Heldai, Tobijah, Jedaiah and Hen.

These crowns were to be as memorials of the coming of the Branch of the Lord and the Glory of His Reign; and the Light of the Crown of Silver was to show forth the Radiance of His Presence, and the golden rays proceeding from the Crown of Gold were to fill the Temple with the resplendence of His overshadowing, and testify of Him as the ever-present Eternal Light.

Thus saith the Lord unto the House of Zion—

"Behold, I come to dwell in the midst of thee!

"Rejoice greatly, O daughters of Zion; let your hearts be glad and full of the Songs of ancient times;

"Sing of all that hath been done for all My children!

"Then shall the children of Judah behold and know that I am in your midst, and come unto Me that I may heal them and make holy their land.

"And the House of Judah shall regain its inheritance, and Ierusalem her peace and glory."

Oh! That the Earth could enter the Silence and hear His Word, and know Him once more.

I

THE MOUNT OF RECOVERY

Behold the day of the Lord cometh when His chosen shall stand upon Mount Olivet[1] which lieth Eastward[2] from Jerusalem.

And it shall come to pass in that day that the light of the Soul shall not be clear in some ways of life and dark in others, but the light shall be as one continual day before the Lord: at eventide the light shall be full.[3]

In that day there shall flow Eastwards from Jerusalem the Living Waters[4], half of them towards the former land and half towards the latter land:[5] and in the outflowing of them shall healing be found for all peoples.

NOTES ON TEXT

[1]"Mount Olivet"—The Mountain of Recovery of the past by the Soul.
[2]"Eastwards"—Towards the Divine.
[3]The Divine Spirit filling the Soul with light.
[4]"Living Waters"—The Divine Love and Divine Wisdom flowing into and from the Soul.
[5]The former and latter lands being the Divine Estate and the Human Estate the true worship of the Divine and true service unto the Human Race.

I

THE MAN WHO WAS A BRANCH

Thus saith the Lord of Hosts unto His children—
Behold the man who becometh a Branch[1] that he may grow up
before the Lord and build the Temple wherein the Lord may dwell!

He shall build the Temple[2] of the Lord in which the glory
of the Lord shall be made manifest, and which shall contain the
throne of the Divine Love whereon sitteth the Lord as one who
ruleth: and the man shall become a priest unto the Lord and be
filled with His Peace.

And in that day shall the people also come from afar whither
they have wandered, to build up the waste places[3] and to inquire
within the Sanctuary; for they shall know that the Lord hath
been amongst them.

NOTES ON TEXT

[1]The Christhood Estate.
[2]The Soul Redeemed and Illumined.
[3]To restore the Social Organism to the Redeemed Life in all its ways.

I

THE MESSAGE OF ZECHARIAH

LIKE Micah, of whose Message I spoke to you last week, Zechariah is accounted one of the minor prophets. He is supposed to have prophesied during a period about one and a half centuries later than Isaiah, and immediately after the return of the Jews from their captivity in Babylon. It is, indeed, believed that he was associated with that strange captivity and the liberation from it under the edict of Cyrus.

The book of Zechariah has been the subject of great controversy. Its subject matter is so mixed, and the latter half of the book is even disputed entirely as belonging to the prophecy of the prophet who is named. Yet, notwithstanding its most mixed character which makes it almost impossible to read without pain, it contains some of the most astonishing teachings concerning ancient Israel and the restoration of the Sons of God. Apart altogether from the Jewish historical elements which came to be inwoven into the real book, the fragments remaining are most precious, and although they are like jewels in false settings, and at times so overlaid that most of their light is obscured, yet they do from time to time give forth something of the radiance they once possessed as Teachings for the Sons of God in the days of their travail amidst tremendous occult and astral forces, bearing within them not only the Light of the Eternal Presence reflected to bring light to the understanding, but also the message of a great hope.

The book contains nine visions, one of the chief of which I read to you concerning the golden bowl, standard, and the pipes, and the olive trees.* And mixed up with that astonishing vision of Divine Secrets there is introduced Zerubbabel, who was supposed to be one of the Jews born in Babylon who returned about the time of

---

*The recovered logia of some of these visions, may be found on pp. 183-6. These should be compared with the book of Zechariah, chs. I to VI.

Ezra, and who had committed to his care the rebuilding of the temple—at least so far as the prophecy indicates—at which things we will look presently. If these Old Scriptures of major and minor prophets do one thing more than another, it is to reveal the awful darkness which obtained and prevailed throughout the ages from the day wherein the vision for Israel seemed to close, so that there was no open vision any more for ages; and how, when the revealers of the Divine Will came, that which they revealed was made use of in a personal and national and racial way. Thus the most precious gems are mixed up with tragic Jewish history, as if the book were one garment woven with many different threads; whereas the real book of Zechariah speaks of the Secrets of GOD and not much about Jewish history, and then only in the little indicated where it has relation to Israel in the midst of the once Holy City of Ierusalem, or Spiritual Household of the land of Judah, and how that Household was to be built after the sacred Temple had been restored.

The book is essentially Messianic. This is not affirmed because some mystic teachers in the Church in other ages have thought so; though even they have made the mystical interpretation entirely personal in relation to the Master when He came in the days of the Manifestation, thus missing the Divine Purpose, the Divine Vision, and the glory of that Vision, through making it personal. For a Manifestation, though given through a Servant, is never personal. The personal oft-times has to veil, sometimes it actually veils because of the conditions, that which has to be made manifest. But the Manifestation is impersonal; it is of the Eternal. It is therefore Spiritual, it is Soulic, it is Angelic, it is, when it is a high Manifestation, Celestial, for it has relation to the Gods, and it is Divine because it is always of the FATHER-MOTHER. As the Master so often said, He spake of the FATHER-MOTHER. It was *His* Will He came to reveal, and *His* Work to accomplish.

Under its Messianic character the book takes specially two aspects in its unveiling; the first is the individual, and the second is the communal. In relation to them both there is the very name itself wherein that which is revealed is implied—Zechariah. Many men have been so named, doubtless, for the Jews loved to choose names with spiritual meanings, which heritage they derived from the Sons of God, the ancient House of Israel. Now the word Zechariah is Ze-char-i-ah, that is, it is associated with the revelation of JEHOVAH in HIS Omnisciency. You will note this, those of you who have read in the second volume of THE DIVINE RENAISSANCE concerning Zachariel who is related to the realm of Divine Omnisciency, as the great Archangel of the Third Sphere from the Divine centre outward. Thus the book of Zechariah is Ze-char-i-ah, or the revelation of one who remembers YAHWEH; that is, whose knowledge is in YAHWEH or the Divine Presence, the Divine Mystery. Thus, as will be unveiled to you, it comes to pass that the prophet is said to have unveiled a great Divine Secret. That Secret is related to Zerubbabel. He is spoken of as the Branch. Isaiah also spoke of the Branch—"*There shall come forth from the rod of Jesse a stem, and from that stem a branch,*" *the* Branch—and the glory of the Presence, called the Spirit of the LORD, would sit, rest, in reality would overshadow the Shekinah of that one. In Zechariah the Branch is spoken of in relation to Joshua the High Priest. This is so presented sometimes, and there is such confusion, that you scarcely know whether the scribe who edited the book as it is, meant Joshua the High Priest or the Branch as Joshua the High Priest, or whether Zerubbabel is the Branch.

Zerubbabel is not simply the one born in Babylon, as the name would seem to imply, who came forth to be Servant of the Most High ONE; the term has a far deeper meaning. It is the Divine Master-builder born amidst the conditions of the Babylonian states which obtained and prevailed through the world at that time. It is a prophecy of the awakening once more, and the coming forth into manifestation of the glorious Christhood. Preceding that awakening and manifestation as set forth in the story of the book, there comes the remarkable indication of the conflict of the children of the FATHER-MOTHER, the warfare with the powers, the four Elemental Kingdoms, named under different symbols; those Kingdoms smitten by four horns which arise, and then the overthrow of those powers which went to and fro on the Earth; that is, the dominating occult powers which sought to destroy even the spiritual estate of the Four great Atmospheres of the Planetary constitution, and consequently those Atmospheres in relation to the Human Soul, by their misuse of the powers of the Elemental Kingdom. In the Unveiling there is the conflict of the Kingdoms to such an extent that the prophet is said to see four horses, like the Four Horses of the Apocalypse, proceeding within those Four Atmospheres and entering into conflict until the time came when the Branch accomplished the victory overall within the four great Atmospheres, or the contending forces within them. For the horse as a glyph symbolizes the higher mind. The understanding in a state of deflection in polarity and in conflict is symbolized by a dark horse, a pale horse, a red horse, in conflict with all that is white and pure and beautiful. But amidst the conflict, unto those Sons of GOD who could receive such a re-unveiling of the Secret of GOD within the superstructure of the Being, there is unveiled once more the Temple of GOD, even in its fashion in the individual life.

We will look at the individual aspect first.

THE INDIVIDUAL ASPECT

In every man and woman there is that which is represented by the Branch; there is the Mystery of GOD. Unto every man and woman there comes in due time an unveiling—which is gradual, but it has so to be—having its ultimate in perfect vision; in the wonderful opening up of the whole Being in vision, which ultimately becomes realization. In the vision we have given to us the masonic Mystery of the superstructure of the Soul, and the masonic ritual of the ministry unto it. How far men and women are from *understanding* that Secret, and rightly interpreting the ritual that is there revealed, is made manifest in even what we have to speak of as scriptural interpretations, religious expositions of the Soul of man as a unit, man as a microcosm, man as a miniature of the sublime majestic Mystery of the ETERNAL BEING.

The Temple of GOD not made with hands is none other than the Temple of the Human Soul. It has one sublime Standard: it is the Standard of the Cross. To that Standard all the parts of the Being are intimately related. That Standard holds them—not in bondage, no; there is no fixity in spiritual elements and divine qualities. They are all volatile; that is, they have the power of operating at any moment. And the Standard holds elements which, though formulated most distinctively so are nevertheless volatile in their power of response and in their motion. In the vision of the Golden Candlestick it is said to be seven-branched; but in the true rendering* it has no fewer than forty-nine pipes, each lamp having seven conduits, the whole crowned with the sacred bowl. The vision is not only represented in the Seven-branched Candlestick, which really represents the Elohistic ministries in the Divine World and to the Soul; but each lamp has given to it a seven-fold ministry from the Standard by which the conduits are held, through which the sacred oil flows to replenish the lamp, each lamp, until the whole life is one. It appears as a glowing stone, but not in a human sense. It is a glowing radiant Stone of Divine Ætheria; the glorious Stone of the Divine Mystery whereon the seven sacred Signs are written, the seven names of the ELOHIM;

---

*See p. 183 and cf. Zechariah, ch. IV.

which, in accommodated ministry, are also the names of
the seven great Archangels; which again in their accommodated ministry take the names of members of the
Heavenly Hierarchy.

The coming of Christ, the Messianic idea, you see,
even in the individual life, is not simply the coming of a
story concerning Christ; not even the coming of a Messenger to reveal and make manifest and interpret Christ. It is
the coming of that true Messianic influence through its
Standard which builds up the Temple of its Being as a
Temple of Christ, a Temple for Christ, a Temple representing the Christ Mystery, a Temple whose every stone is
precious, whose every court represents a court of service
for the LORD, whose Altars are all Altars consecrated to
the service of the Most High ONE, and whose high Altar is
the scene of the mediatorial ministry of the great High
Priest of Being within the Sanctuary of the Soul, where
the Soul comes into the consciousness of HIS Presence
canopying it as Shekinah.

Into the middle of the vision* there is introduced the
question, "Who hath despised the day of small things?"
then follows the work of Zerubbabel. I would re-interpret
the passage for you. *Who hath despised you in the day of small
beginnings, the day of small manifestations? For ye shall be
made to rejoice in that day when Zerubbabel within you, the great
Divine Builder, builds up the temple of your Being until it is
crowned with the consciousness of that Sonship which gives you
the right, that is, the power to realize, the right to enter into His
Immediate Presence and share in His high priestly mediatorial
ministry.*

The Secret of the Soul's superstructure is GOD's
Secret in every man and woman, and you cannot discover
it physiologically, nor anatomically, nor psychologically
—as that word is used, or rather misused, to-day. You
cannot get to the secret of a Soul by means of psychology

---

*Cf. Zechariah, ch. IV.

as it is understood and interpreted to-day. For true psychology is the Logos of the Soul; it is the Psyche, the Logos, the Divine Mystery within the Being, and only there can you know the Secret of GOD. It is GOD's Secret in yourself. Who knows it? Men and women may be despised unless they be great in the earthly sense, in the world-power sense, in the world-enrichment sense, great in the sense of domination, great before men and world-Gods, that is, the spirit that would make of this world other than the theatre of the exquisite dramatic exposition of the life of real childhood, full of the joy of it, unto GOD, before HIM and for HIM.

These Old Scriptures reveal how the glory of manhood was brought down and degraded, even until they are full of judgement. Why, notwithstanding the nine visions, which were glorious in their true presentation, notwithstanding them, the book is full, like Micah, of judgements, of misrepresentation of the Divine Goodness, of a glamour of promise of forgiveness and restoration, without a clear revealing of the tenderness and the compassion, the universal Love of the FATHER-MOTHER, because it was made national and racial. *All true prophecy is the spirit of interpretation of Divine Events. It is therefore of the Universal Being and belongs to all time and all Souls.*

Now witness the exquisitely beautiful and masonic ritual of the upbuilding of the Temple of a Human Soul as presented in that simple yet most sublime story of the prophet's vision. Note that it was whilst he was with the Angel of the LORD that he saw it; whilst he was with the Angel of the LORD, the Angel of the Presence. Why, to be with HIM is to be in *the* Presence. Great Divine Visions do not come to you anywhere and anyhow; oh no! You may have reflected visions upon the magnetic plane of the mind, but great Soul visions come only within the realm to which they belong, as your Heavens open.

The prophet is represented in the Book of Zechariah as not having any interest in that which was presented to

him; but also in the story there is represented the earnest
enquiry of the Angel of the Presence concerning the understanding of the meaning of the vision—"Knowest thou not
these things"—that is, do not you know them? Why, you
must know them. If you do not, if you have never known
them, you cannot now. No. For understanding is not
flashed within the Being in a moment. The understanding
has to grow through illumination. Life is one great process of growth in understanding, by means of which there
are repeated acts or initiations through great degrees
which are the evolutary acts by which the Soul ascends
into higher arcs of consciousness and realization. No Soul
could understand the Mystery, the Secret of GOD within
itself, within another, within the constitution of a World
like this, unless it had grown to that estate wherein it
could be as Zechariah, one who can enter the realm to
receive the vision of Divine Omniscience. Only through
such Omnisciency in the Soul could the Soul understand
the secret as it is unveiled in that most wonderful Vision.

Behold the ritual wherein there is unveiled the Divine
process by which the whole life is upbuilt. The olive trees
are none other than the Divine Love and Wisdom, to
the right and to the left, supporting the Standard of Life.
They do not pour their oil outside. There is nothing wasted.
They pour their oil into the sacred bowl, and from that
bowl through the manifold conduits; first through the
seven branches, the main conduits, but each conduit has
seven sub-branches. Here you have the seven great nerve
centres of the life; the seven points of magnetic contact
between the inner Being and the Divine World; the seven
centres that enable you to contact the realm of the Archangels, the seven great Archangels; the seven that enable
you ultimately to receive from, and endure the influx of,
the Elohistic motion, magnetic motion, upon each of your
centres, so that you become one in your motion with all
the motion of the ELOHIM.

And from those seven centres there proceed seven sub-conduits, each one representing a quality. For the sum of life is fifty; in the evolution of numbers it is the five of the Divine Man, the masonic number. In actual data it is the fifty or Jubilee wherein the Soul can sing its Jubilate. It is the realization by the Soul of the seven qualities which operate from and unto each centre, and being unified in the Standard they have sublime unity of motion, of ministry. It is thus, it is through such realization, that the seven planes become perfectly balanced; having the power to deflect, apparently, but only for ministry; always *magnetically* in balance, having the power to descend and the power to ascend, the power to go forth and the power to return, never losing their contact with the Centre, never being deflected in their polarity from that Centre. It is through the operation of the seven main conduits bearing the oil into the sacred bowl, and its flow through all the Being, that the planes are kept in equipoise, that they are always in true polarity, and that the vehicles themselves become nourished, *the vehicles become nourished.*

You think about the nourishing of your body, but perhaps it is the only vehicle you ever think about; whereas *each* vehicle has to be nourished. Your mind must be nourished. Your heart must be nourished. Pure vision nourishes the mind; it makes inroads to the understanding, carrying glorious light to chase out from the understanding any darkness that may be there. The heart is nourished, even the heart of the body is nourished, through Love; Love itself being the magnetic action by which the whole Being is held, even as our body is held, held by the action of our heart. The body is not held as upon a standard, no; but is able to fulfil its ministry through the beautiful dual action of our heart. Even the outer heart is nourished through Love; and if that be so how much more the inner heart of which it is the outer exposition! We have the outer temple. It is not the outer temple that is the Temple of the Holy Guest, no. It is man's Being that is the Temple of the Holy Guest, the Indwelling Secret of GOD individuated into the consciousness of a Human Soul. So the body ultimately becomes the temple of that Being who comes to know the Secret of GOD; and the outer vehicle becomes an exposition of the effect of knowing that Secret, and becoming one with the magnetic motion of the streams that are connected by means of the conduits with the Standard and the planes, so that all the vehicles become nourished. The equation of a Human Soul is infinitely more than even philosophy has ever dreamt of, and it contains the Secret of GOD, GOD's Mystery.

"What a responsibility!" you say. Yes, what a treasure. But *what* a treasure! What a trust! What an endowment! What a Life to be gifted with from the Eternal, capable of realizing HIS own Secret, to know HIM in fashion, in feeling, in vision, through realization as one dwelling in the Temple of HIS Immediate Presence. For when the Soul realizes that which the vision presents, it is conscious of dwelling with HIM, of being in HIS Presence before HIS High Altar; it has the consciousness not only in vision, inner vision, but in realization of the marvellous Cherubic motion; it has the consciousness of receiving from the marvellous Seraphic motion increased power because of an increase born of the Glowing Stone, the sacred Mystery; yes, that Glowing Stone, that sacred Mystery, not only the White Stone of Templary, that Stone which is the everlasting Bread for all Souls, that Stone whose glow is Light, the Radiance of GOD, that Stone whose motion is begotten of the hidden Fire of GOD within it; but also conscious of having the Jewel, that Jewel called the Seal of Solomon, that Jewel which gives to the Soul the six sacred realizations by which it becomes empowered and able to enter into the most secret realm, crowned a Son of GOD. This is the true Messianic idea, that you become as Christ.

The Communal Aspect

Then in relation to it there is the communal presentation. There is the prophecy of the coming of the Branch. There is an indication that the great spiritual Household is to be reared, and Ierusalem itself to be redeemed and healed. There is a portrayal of the nature of the Branch. And here I would just indicate to you that many commentators have thought that some of the Messianic portions of the prophecy where it portrayed the suffering of the Redeemer, had relation to Zerubbabel. He seems to come from nowhere. He seems to pass to nowhere. He is like the Divine Mystery itself, coming and going. Yet in relation to him there are these prophecies. He becomes prophet; interpreter of the Divine Purpose. He becomes Seer; he beholds the glory of the Presence. He becomes High Priest; he is the great mediator in the building of the Temple. He becomes shepherd; he is the shepherd of his people whom the LORD doth give into his keeping. He becomes the suffering one as a rejected shepherd. There is even the indication not only of his rejection, but of his betrayal and his crucifixion. Yet as the crucified one, to whom the world will some day look, it is said, as the one men pierced, he becomes redeemer and revealer; and as a result of the redemption and the revelation of the Secrets of GOD, all Israel is restored, the Temple is perfectly reared within the Holy City of Zion, Jerusalem is once more redeemed, its sacred vessels brought back. It is so far redeemed, that is, raised, in its estate, that the LORD HIMSELF doth encompass it with fire.

Here we have a picture of the Days of the Manifestation, the things expected as the result of the Manifestation, the prophetic office as the interpreter of the Divine Love and Wisdom in the Message in those far-away days, the Seer Who looked into the innermost Heavens and beheld not only the Beloved ONE, but also that glorious divine Hierarchy set forth in "THE LOGIA"*, and found in the fourth

*See THE LOGIA or SAYINGS OF THE MASTER.

chapter of the Apocalypse; beheld the Mystery, and the meaning of the Mystery, of the LORD Regnant amidst the great Sea with the Four Divine Eternities, the great Kingdoms, the Elemental Kingdoms of the Divine World, called the Living Creatures, who ever worshipped at the Throne of the Eternal; with the twenty-four Elders, or the glorious divine attributes in their positive and negative motion of ministry, GOD's Hierarchy, which is also HIS Mystery expressed through all the Hierarchies of the Stellar Universe and the Angelic World, even unto the Soul. For that which is of the communal and the divinely racial—that is, the race of the Sons of GOD, not only those who came to this World to be the teachers, and, in later days, the burden-bearers, and in some measure the redeemers, and such are to be the redeemers in these coming days again; but all the glorious race of the Sons of GOD, or all Souls who attained to the consciousness of Divine Sonship—even such communal Mystery is reflected into the individual, so that in the building of the individual Temple, of which I have spoken to you, you have a representation of the Divine and Celestial and Angelic Hierarchies.

It is because of such that you are able to get into direct contact with the Angelic Hierarchies, and ultimately to understand them and to be sharers of their glorious ministry, and on and on through the realms, even unto the attainment of direct contact, that is, in consciousness, with the Divine Hierarchies, so that you know yourself henceforth and for evermore touched in the seven centres of your Being from those glorious Ones, and held, as it were, by them whilst you are continued here for ministry as Souls realizing the Secret of GOD in the innermost, yet let down to such planes and Kingdoms as these are for purposes of prophetic ministry—interpretation; seership— seeing and interpreting the Divine Love and Wisdom; priesthood—mediating through your life ministry, as well as through your interpretation, of the sacred Mystery of His Love and Wisdom.

Oh, the Messianic idea is not the idea of a man. It is of GOD, the Universal. It is of the FATHER-MOTHER Who reveals His embodiment in every man and woman who can attain to the Messianic estate, the estate of a Christhood, a Jesus Christ estate, an estate revealing Jesus in all the foundation thoughts and feelings and desires and ambitions and outflow of the life; radiating Christ, one whose very countenance is lit up with the glory of the Indwelling, radiant Presence, where there is no gloom even in the midst of sorrow, no gloom, for light is there; even in the hour of travail, no doubt as to His Presence, though the travail may bring sorrow and pain and even anguish and divine grief.

The Message of Zechariah is the Message of the rebuilding of the Kingdom of Messiah. It is the restoration of the Christhood. Now look at what it will mean communally if, individually in the realization of our Being, we are associated through our nerve centres with the glorious Hierarchical ministries from the Divine World down from the Angelic into the Human estate; if we realize those ministries in all our nerve centres in the innermost (of course, such power is reflected into the outermost vehicle also, but I am speaking of the fashion of the Being); if we realize this relationship so that we have actually within ourselves Angelic Hierarchy, Celestial Hierarchy and Divine Hierarchy. Why! HE sits upon the circles, it is said, of the Earth; yes, upon its planes. HE sits upon all the planes. HE rules upon all the planes. HE rules through His representatives, so that each plane has its corresponding ministrant. This may seem difficult to apprehend at first, though verily it should be—for most of you at any rate, and should become for all of you—clear as the radiance of the noonday when the Sun is full of splendour because of the conditions permitting it to reveal His glory. It is thus the Messianic Kingdom within a man

199

is not single nor even dual, nor is it only a triplicity, nor quadruple; it is sevenfold. A Christhood even in manifestation is sevenfold.

If you do not fully apprehend the significance of these statements, you will bye and bye in your own motion of Being as you grow in your coming back, as you ascend in your entering into the returning consciousness of what once you were and of the inheritance that was your possession, that is, of divine quality and quantity. See what it will mean in the coming days when each Son of GOD upon the Earth, with his glorious microcosmic Hierarchical ministries realized, becomes unified with all the Sons of GOD into a cosmic (in so far as it relates to the Christhood that is to be made manifest) revelation of the Divine Mystery, each life a centre of the Divine secret, all held from the seven divine centres by the seven glorious Ones who minister for the FATHER-MOTHER.

See what it will mean when the Messianic Kingdom is realized in the individual, and through the individual, in the communal life! See what it will mean when the whole Christhood in this world realizes that not only individually, but collectively, they are sharing in the glorious Hierarchical ministry represented by HIM Who sits upon the Throne as the Head, and the Four Living Ones who are the Four Eternities, or Elemental Kingdoms of the Divine World in motion containing all the Elements out of which all things have become; and the Elders, or Attributes, ministering and administering unto the communal life, each one being recipient direct from the Inner World, and yet in combination the *whole* one fuller exposition of the sacred Mystery of what goes on in the Divine World of revelation, of manifestation, of interpretation, of realization. Think what it will be for you and all the Sons of GOD who are upon these planes, and who are hastening back to these planes; think what it will mean when the cosmic Christhood is again revealed to the world. No voice will say to the world, even to those spirits or those lives moved by the Zeitgeist or world-spirit—"Look on us! We are holier than thou art;" to men and women in their travail, "Look on us! See how much purer and better we are!" There is never such a thought in the mind of a Son of God. There never is such a feeling in the heart of one who knows the Divine Love and Compassion. Such thoughts are begotten of pride and vanity.

To be like HIM in a Christhood is to represent HIM Who is altogether lovely in HIS Love, unfailing in HIS understanding, and in the outflow of HIS compassion and HIS pity. For such a Christhood will so embody the Hier-archical ministries of the Inner Heavens that the world will feel it and be moved by it, and Jerusalem, the Holy City, or the City that once was holy, shall be restored, and it will have round about, girding it, the sacred Fire. Our GOD is a consuming fire, and with it HE encompasses, HE purifies and illumines and HE exalts.

When the Christhood is making manifest, then shall Ierusalem rejoice and be glad. Then surely shall the children of men, seeking the fulfilment of their life upon the outer plane's experiences of this distraught World, behold and see a radiance streaming from afar, aye, streaming afar from the divine Centre of the Being, and know verily that GOD is in HIS World, not only in its elements, in its breaths, in his kingdoms, in its true life, in its true motion, in all that is exquisitely beautiful in its manifestations, *but He is come.* HE has come to this World and become again in the very flesh, in the substance of the Being, of HIS ancient Children, so that each one is HIS incarnation, that is, the repository of HIS Indwelling, HIS Emmanuel, the realizer of HIS Immanence; HIS Imman-ence filling the whole Being, even to the outer vehicle, making the flesh of the Being HIS own Substance, and the outer body, the vehicle through which the glory of that inward radiance can be revealed.

It is such a day. It is on such a day that the LORD's Feet shall stand again upon Mount Olivet in each one of you. For Mount Olivet is the mountain of recovery, the recovery of all the consciousness of all the past. In that day you will understand the meaning of Zechariah, or the dwelling in the consciousness of YAHWEH, JEHOVAH. For you will understand, as men cannot themselves understand, the Divine Love, and the way of that Love, and the glory of that Love as expressed in the operation of HIS Eternal Law, wherein HIS Wisdom is evermore made manifest. In that day there shall neither be any more day that has a rising and a setting, a setting bringing the darkness, but within the Being the day will be everlasting, the everlasting day. The Light shall not fail, even at eventide, but the radiance in the night watches be even as the splendour of the noonday revelation. And in that day HIS Streams of Living Waters shall flow unto Ierusalem from all HIS children—the living Truth, the truth about yourself, the truth of life, the truth that is the beauty of life, which life is the exposition of the glory of HIS Love, its secret and its law, its operation and its resplendence.

Beloved ones, if these old-world teachings contain so much, they contain them for you. If the meanings were lost, as they were indeed, it was an accentuation for you of the tragedy of your travail; but the day has come when all things shall be made clear.

The LORD HIMSELF doth now stand upon Mount Olivet, and all things shall be made clear.

Ever Blessed be HIS most glorious Name Who is my LORD and your LORD, my FATHER-MOTHER and your FATHER-MOTHER.

I

A MEDITATION UPON THE PROPHET

MALACHI

THE CLEANSING OF THE SOUL

Behold, I will send my Messenger before me that He may make plain the way of the Lord and prepare the hearts and lives of the Children, so that they may know the Lord in His coming when He appeareth within His Holy Temple.

But who shall abide in the day of His coming? and who shall stand upright in the day of His appearing? For like a refiner's oven will He consume away the dross from the Sons of Levi, that the gold which remaineth may be pure and meet for His service; and like fuller's soap which taketh all uncleanness from a garment, shall He wash their robes until the whiteness of them shall reflect His Glory.

I

THE DAY OF HIS APPEARING

The Lord of Hosts hath spoken unto His people Israel; through His Servant whom he did send, hath He declared Himself.

Behold! Behold, ye who are able to see with the Understanding!

The Lord Himself doth come in His Message which he revealeth through His Messenger.

Prepare ye for His coming, all ye who look unto Him; make your ways of life a pathway for the Light of His Revelation.

His appearing shall be within His Temple; and in His coming the Ark of Covenant and Testimony shall be unveiled.

His Shekinah once more will be overshadowing the Oblatory, and the Mercy Seat become the scene of purest sacrifice.

* * * *

Who shall endure in the day of His coming? For His Sacred Fire will burn away all evil, even as the refiner's fire doth purify the gold of its alloy.

As the refiner of all the elements shall He come in His Sacred Fire to make to stand upright as pillars of His righteousness, the Sons of Israel.

MALACHI

The silver and gold of their inheritance shall He again make pure; and they shall possess the power of Mercury to move at His approach in obedience to His Law and fulfil His Commands; and the golden glory of His own resplendence shall crown them, and they shall be the children of His Radiance, and be as Stars in the spacious Firmament that is His Canopy, wherein He holds and embraces all His Sons.

For as jewels shall they reflect His glory in the day when they all become exalted within His Heavens, and the Book of their Remembrance is opened.

I

A MEDITATION UPON
THE PROPHET MALACHI

THE book of Malachi contains the closing cadences
of the Bible as set forth by tradition in the canon of
the Old Testament. It is accounted one of the minor
prophecies, supposed to have been uttered contem-
poraneously with the second visit of Nehemiah to Jerusalem some four hundred years B.C. Like most of the other
minor prophets it opens strangely, and as strangely closes.
It opens with a presentation of the Divine Love and
Wisdom such as is not, could not be, consonant with the
idea we hold of the Divine Love and Wisdom, and it closes
with the threat of a curse, which thing you will understand is utterly at variance with the very nature of Love
itself. However tried in its burden-bearing, however
oppressed in the process of burden-bearing, however
great the Cross of its carrying and its sacrifice, Love could
never do other than bless. It is of its nature to bless. It
would be unlike itself if it did not bless.

But though the opening and the closing cadences of the
Book are not happy in their presentation of the Divine Love
and Wisdom, there are elements in the message it contains of great spiritual value. Yet here, even, as we shall
see, the living message is lost through the national, racial
and local changes, relationships and applications, so that
the book becomes essentially a Jewish story rather than a
transcendent revelation unto Israel of the Divine Love
and Wisdom.

The meaning of the Message of the book is contained
in the name of the Prophet. Even the highest and most
careful scholars consider that the title is not the name of a
man, but has relation to the Message. We will just look
at the name, and then at the four distinguishing features
presented in the book:—

Israel, the Chosen of GOD;

The Temple with its Priestly Service and the Call to the Priests;

The Return of the Presence;

The Recovery by the Soul of the Paraclete.

THE MEANING OF THE NAME

Now, the name Malachi means the Messenger, though there are not lacking amongst the scholars those who believe the name originally was Mala-Chi-Yah, meaning the Servant of the LORD, the Servant of YAHWEH. It is remarkable with this book, as with all the books of the Old Testament, that, after it has passed through the fire of the Higher Criticism as well as the criticism of the more Evangelical Schools, in both the high and the low schools of criticism, the scholars are lost in their scholarship concerning geographical and historical associations, with the result that the Message also is lost in the midst of them. That which the prophet meant is also veiled from them. You cannot discover a Divine Message by intellectual criticism of the book in which it purports to come. That is uttered in no depreciation of a true scholasticism which is humble and ever beautiful in spirit. Nevertheless it is a great truth that Divine Realities can be discovered only through the Soul's approach to the Inner World. No scholarship can bring about an unveiling of the Divine Realities. If it could, verily these books would be unearthed and their glory revealed. But the more you read the Higher Criticism and the evangelical schools of Criticism the more you would become perplexed as to what the Prophet, if there ever was such an one, could have meant.

The glorious Messages of old time, just like the glorious Message of the Manifestation days, fell into the hands of those who could not understand or did not desire to understand; with the result that through the ages there have

been presented views of GOD, of HIS Love, Sacrifice and
Judgement, such as could not be received by one who
knew HIM. These misrepresentations have veiled GOD
from HIS children, and made the day of life which should
have been resplendent with the glory of HIS Love and
Wisdom, as the darkness of a night of travail for all the
children, the youngest Souls and the eldest Souls, in their
search to discover what GOD was like, where HIS vision
could be discovered, how HE might be found and realized.
Divine Revelation appeals to the inner Being; and the
inner Being alone can discover for itself whether it be
Divine Revelation. For the mere announcement that it is
such a Message does not bring to the consciousness the
reality of any revelation. People may recognize and accept
a true Revelation should it come; but many believe other
things which are announced as revelations, which are certainly not revelations in any degree of the Love and
Wisdom of our FATHER-MOTHER. Always try the spirits;
try the beliefs of men and women whether they be of GOD.
If they be of HIM, they will bear the imprint of HIS Love.

The name Malachi is a term signifying The Messenger.
So burdened with secret meaning is the word Mala-Chi-
Yah, that many scholars believe it had relation to the
Presence. And this was even so. It has relation to the
Message of the Angel of the Presence. The Angel of the
Presence gives the Message as high Servant of ADONAI
unto a Servant of the LORD. But you will note that the
Message concerns the LORD of BEING. It is not concerned
with the Servant, nor even with the One who is the
Servant of the LORD in the Innermost. The ADONAI is
always the Regnant ONE, the ALPHA and the OMEGA, the
First and the Last of all Divine Revelation. And this is
always so even to the Human Soul, or to the individual
Planet, or to the Solar Body of the System. If the LORD
be not the ALPHA and the OMEGA of the life, then there
has been something misunderstood. The vision has
become veiled. The heart has not understood its own

motion when it has been moved from HIM. GOD must be the first and last in everything, because HE is the ARCHE— the very Principle of our Being. And the perfect exposition of the motion of that magnetic Principle is surely the fulness of Being. And is not the fulness of Being, even in a Human Soul, an exposition of HIS own Sacred Mystery within it, and a revelation of HIS own likeness, the Mystery of HIS Nature? For when anyone realizes HIM, that one is like HIM; it cannot be otherwise. You understand me? Do not dream you have realized HIM unless you seek to become like HIM. For truly to desire to be like HIM is to realize HIM. To realize HIM is to reflect HIM in every attribute and to be not only the repositories of HIS Love, but the expositions of that Love in everything said and done in the whole deportment of our life.

ISRAEL, THE CHOSEN OF GOD

Now you will observe that the Message of Malachi is unto Israel. How often Israel is addressed by the Minor Prophets as well as by those accounted the greater Prophets! The Message is unto Israel, first; but it is also unto Judah through Israel. Judah is the Planet-Soul, and her children are those of this World. The Message appeals first to Israel because Israel alone can understand those things of which it speaks. Israel had known something of the quality of the Realm whence the Message came, having drunk of the streams of that Realm and basked in the resplendence of the glory shed within it. For the Sons of Israel are those who were the Sons of GOD in their estate long ages ago, before and after they were sent to this World for blessed ministries.

This is the reason for the appeal being made unto Israel. The book almost opens with it. It opens with a chiding, full of rebuke and judgment, and makes the ungodlike and strange pronouncement that GOD loved Jacob and hated Esau, and smote the land of Edom unto utter impoverishment and made of it a place for dragons. Hate is the absolute inversion of the polarity of Love, therefore in perfect Love there could not possibly be present the element of hate. To predicate such a thing of GOD, the FATHER-MOTHER, is to libel HIS Most Sacred Name. Hate is the repellent and hurtful state resulting from loss of the polarity which is the equipoise of Love, and which, in its motion, is the antithesis of the Divine Righteousness because it is the inversion of it. Instead of being the apex, the radiating centre of the glory of the Divine Mystery, the will is turned to the realm of the outer darkness where the glory of the Presence shines not. If men and women could see the images formed by even an approach to hatred and thrown upon the screen of the magnetic plane, they would understand how impossible is the truth of the statement that GOD loved Jacob and hated Esau and wrought the latter dire hurt. For GOD, Who is Love, could not hate any child of HIS. Nor is it possible for any child of GOD who truly loved HIM to have hate towards another child. Every ugly thought and terrible deed is reflected upon the screen of the Planet's magnetic plane, and also upon the screen of the magnetic plane of the individual where hate manifests itself.

You will thus see what a sad perversion of the great truth such a statement is. GOD loves Israel. HE loves those who can dwell in the consciousness of HIM. But HE *loved* such Souls into the consciousness of HIMSELF great ages ago; and HE loves all Souls into such consciousness in due course as they grow in response. The little children grow into the states of the older children, and the older children rise into states of the elder children, and the elder children ascend into further states of consciousness of the Divine Indwelling Presence wherein they become in their degree one with the Presence. For it is thus that the Soul becomes one with its LORD, and enters into the Nirvana.

How greatly the Divine Love has revealed HIMSELF to Israel is manifest in the history of Israel through the ages since the time of the great Descent. The Love manifested itself in making them the people chosen to come here, the children sent on a lovely mission of education unto the children of this World. Is it any wonder that the Prophets continually appeal to Israel to remember the LORD—HIS Love, HIS tenderness, HIS loving-kindness of old time? You find such expressions of tender appeal throughout all the prophetic books, notwithstanding the terrible state of corrupted text in which all of them are to be found to-day. How the Messengers appeal to Israel to remember! For only through remembering the Divine Love, and the gentleness and tenderness of HIS Love unto them, can they come back to that estate of life wherein HE was realized by them and made manifest through them.

So Malachi is the LORD's Messenger unto Israel. HE conveys a Message right from the Presence of the LORD GOD of Sabaoth. It is a Message recalling to Israel their heritage, the glorious Divine nature of the heritage, the wealth associated with that heritage, the Divine Ritual by which they came into the possession of that inheritance, the masonic Mystery of their own inner Being as that Mystery was unveiled within the Heavens to them as they grew up before the LORD. Like all the other prophetic books, it is full of masonic statements. By this latter it is meant that the Truth is revealed in symbols, in signs, and in what might be called "passwords", which signs and symbols and passwords Israel should remember.

The opening is a call to the Ancients. They have grown weary through their travail, but are not to think that the Great Love is weary of them, as they think HE is. For even when the Heavens most sorrow and the Divine Love and Wisdom expressed in the Heavens yearn most for the return of HIS children, the Divine Love never wearies. The burden may be great, the sorrow imposed by means of the burden may be intense, the travail may cover ages, and the servants who are the vehicles of the manifestation of the process of the Passion of the LORD in its ministry may grow weary; but the Divine Love never wearies in the sense of withholding and withdrawing. What a terrible World it would have been if the Divine Love had withdrawn! Notwithstanding the grievous state of the World just now, and all it has been of evil in past ages, the conditions would have been greatly worse but for the sacrificial ministries of the Divine World. Why, we should not have been here but for the Divine Love's Passion! You could not have been here. Judah would have been lost to the Celestial Realms in so far as her planetary exposition as a centre for the generation of Human Souls in ministry for the Divine was concerned.

I would, therefore, bring this home to each one of you that you may understand. O child of Israel! If you be one who longs to be once more in the estate of a Son of GOD, you will not seek for power and dominion, for self-exaltation and glorification, for personal and world ends. If you wanted any state merely for power, then your motive would be wrong. That is often the occult motive, for many occultists love knowledge for power. It is the motive that has led this World to disaster all through the ages. It was the motive behind the cause of the awful cataclysms that rent the Planet's kingdoms. Seek all things that are spiritual and divine for what they are in themselves; then the power which is resident in them will become yours. But if you seek them for power to make yourself great, then in your seeking you will miss them; they will pass you by. You cannot take the Kingdom of Heaven by force, though you may force much out of the kingdom of this world.

O Son of Israel! Seek the power of true Sonship to HIM. Then you will be like HIM. It is the Life that reveals HIS fashion, the Life that is adorable, the Life that is altogether lovely. Why should I want powers and principalities merely to be able to exercise them over other people or over the elements and kingdoms of worlds? But there is a reason why I should wish to be like HIM Who is the

Altogether Lovely ONE, in Whose Love there is Omnipotency and in Whose Wisdom there is Omnisciency. To be like HIM is to share in the Omnipotency of HIS Love and the Omnisciency of HIS Wisdom. Such is the inheritance for the Soul, to realize all things and, wherein necessary, to be able to know all things for service as the Divine Love unveils HIS Mysteries and secrets unto that Soul. Oh, to be like HIM! That is the Secret of a Son of GOD.

Therefore, Child of Israel, hear HIS recall to you. HE loves Ya-Akob-El, the Angel of this most stricken World in the Divine Hierarchy. HE loves the members of the House of Ya-Akob-El, called the children of Jacob in those old Mystery Teachings; these are the members of the Hierarchy. HE loves Israel, for Israel passed through the estate of Ya-Akob-El in a special way. For all Souls, in their journey unto the Hierarchies of Divine Realization wherein, at last, they become one with the Angel of the Presence in relation to this System, must pass along the path set forth as that trod by Jacob.

THE RESTORATION OF THE TEMPLE
AND ITS SERVICES

The call being unto Israel, the next thought is the Temple and the restoration of its service.

The book was supposed to have been written at a period when the Temple had been rebuilt, the law re-instituted by Ezra, and the walls of the city rebuilt by Nehemiah. But these are mystical things. For the Temple of GOD is no earthly house. You may have an earthly house consecrated to the Divine which you may be able to fill with your atmosphere, just as you can your home, through radiating HIS Presence and making the atmosphere sweet and pure, even as a Temple where you come to bow before the High Altar in the worship of HIM.

The Temple referred to by Mala-Chi-Yah is the Temple of the Being. For it has first an individual aspect and then an aspect that is communal. In both it is the Temple of the Christhood. Israel is recalled to the Christhood. That Temple is to be rebuilt. It was the Temple relating to the manifestation of the communal Christhood through the House of Israel. It had long been levelled with the dust. But after the liberation from captivity it was to be rebuilt. But the communal Temple of the Christhood could be rebuilt only in the measure in which that Temple was rebuilt by the Sons of Israel. Therefore, the call is not only unto the communal Israel, but to each member of Israel to rebuild within himself the Temple of the living GOD.

The Temple is the place where HIS Altar is and where HIS Shekinah abides. It is for the exposition of HIM in worship and in service. Worship is a service to oneself, for by means of it the Being expands and ascends. But high worship is the Cherubic service. Thus worship is the Soul's service unto HIM. Service for HIM is Seraphic. The Temple is thus for Cherubic service unto HIM and Seraphic service for HIM. We worship GOD in serving to become like HIM. That is the Cherubic service. We can become like HIM only through the Cherubic motion, which is the inward motion, getting further and further in our state. In the measure in which we are able to realize that motion, so is the strength, the potency, the expansiveness of our true Seraphic service. That which we gain we give. The Temple is for this dual ministry of the Soul, receiving through the giving of itself, and then the giving of that which it has drawn unto and received into itself.

To rebuild such a Temple is no mean piece of work. So many are anxious to accomplish great things in the outer life, and to shine before the world. We have to have an exposition, it is true, in every realm of experience of the active forces of life as well as of the passive forces of life. But if only the Children of the Kingdom could realize that the primary thing in life is to embody HIM again, and to make of Life HIS sacred Temple! Many lustily sing:—

"I worship THEE, O blessed GOD,
And all THY ways adore."
and they would account that worship. But to adore the
ways of GOD is not simply to acclaim HIM, but to walk in
them, acknowledging the beauty, the truth, the glory of
all HIS ways through making them your own. That is how
to worship GOD. It is to love to live for HIM always, to
make all life's action in its inner motion one of worship,
and in its outer motion such as will express that adoring
attitude of HIM in our service, in our speech, in everything
we say and do, in our attitude of mind and heart, in the
gait and the deportment of our life, in every attribute, in
the whole motion of our Being to make of life divine music,
a composition full of the Divine Rhythm as that Rhythm
is expressed through us in every thought, feeling, desire,
purpose, intention, act and attitude to one another. The
deportment of a Soul before the FATHER-MOTHER should
be expressed in its deportment upon these mundane
planes. Therefore, you will understand me, there is no
room for anything that casts a shadow—none! There is
no room whatsoever for that which is unlovely and therefore unlike HIM.

In the book of Malachi the priests are arraigned before
the Divine. They are told that their Temple-service is
wrong; that their oral teaching is a perversion and mis-
interpretation of the Divine Mind, Thought, Purpose, and
contrary to the Divine Love and Wisdom. They are informed that their sacrifices are imperfect. Indeed, stronger
language is used in the book itself, for they are said to be
diseased. But that was not the Message as it was given to
Israel. Yet Israel was reminded of the true nature of the
Divine Sacrifice as offered by a Human Soul: that it must
be perfect in its intention, even though some of its limbs
or attributes had become maimed through the conditions
of this world; for purity is first in the intention, but pure
intention comes to realize itself in purity in the whole
Being. A perfect sacrifice is first in the purpose of the will

begotten of the desire of the heart and the yearning of the whole Being to offer unto HIM a living sacrifice. A living sacrifice is a life vibrant in every attribute, every nerve-centre full of divine magnetic motion, enriched and empowered with the very energy of HIS own glorious Love. Even though the life be maimed and oppressed through the crushing it has received, yet, if the purpose be pure, if the desire be selfless, if the will be truly unto the accomplishment of the purpose of GOD, then the sacrifice is a whole-hearted sacrifice, and will be acceptable unto the FATHER-MOTHER. For the language of the Soul is in the Soul's motion, and the articulation of that motion is in the realm of sacrifice where the Soul finds perfect expression. And though the result in the chronicling of its tones upon the outer attributes may seem to be imperfect, yet the whole sacrifice will make up the Soul's symphony sung before and unto the LORD of BEING.

You see you may have a wrong view of sacrifice, just as the Priests had whom Malachi addressed. You may have misconceptions concerning the Christhood like those which arose and were promulgated in an oral message after the Manifestation, and which led to the disaster or betrayal of the Teachings. It was through the betrayal of the Message held by the Brotherhoods as received from the Master before the Brotherhoods themselves were broken up and an oral message was given which became ultimately the Pauline message and not the Message of the Master, that the false view of sacrifice was perpetuated and the Temple of the Christhood reared by the Master was thrown down. For the whole direction of what has been called historical Christianity was a misdirection and therefore a betrayal of the Master and all He stood for. All that HE gave to HIS intimate ones, and which was once more to become the heritage of Israel unto the finding of whom HE came to seek, in order that they might have the Christhood vision restored again, was betrayed in the oral interpretation more and more as the Pauline and Judaizing teachers gained influence. Nay, as in the faraway days of the Prophet, there were those who divorced GOD from the everyday affairs of life, and said that HE Who is the All-Present ONE, the Omnipresent GOD, knew nothing whatsoever about the mundane affairs of life and took no interest in them. And so Christ became divorced from life, from the real Message of the Master to the individual Soul, and was centred in personality. And of this same betraying spirit we have an active recrudescence to-day, a revival of the effects of the Judaizing and Pauline unseating of the Christ-regnancy as the Master taught it, and in its place the glamour of personality and mental therapeutic panaceas.

It is true that a vast proportion of the mundane affairs are no true reflection of GOD's Purpose; but to those who say that such things are not known to HIM and HIS Divine World we would reply: Then why are ministries sent of a healing and redemptive character to this World? Why are special ministries given to this World, like the Manifestation, if the need be not known? Is it not because the needs are well known that the Messengers are sent and the ministries are rendered? Men and women cannot in reality divorce GOD from the daily round of their life, though they may ignore HIM. Religion is not a set of intellectual concepts, credal beliefs, and ritualistic performances. All these things may be made use of in a beautiful way, and they may be and should be truly contributory to spiritual growth. But religion is the Divine Spirit in us. It is the God-ward motion of that Spirit, and its exposition earthward in life's embodiment. Religion does not build up beliefs. Beliefs are built up around it. Religion in its motion lifts the Being onward and upward into the realms of yet greater realization, until the life knows HIM Who is its Source, and Who ultimately becomes its fulness. Then the Divine Pleroma is its inheritance for evermore.

THE RETURN OF THE PRESENCE

The realization, through the upbuilding of life, of the Temple of the LORD, and the endeavour to give it exposition in the communal life, brings to the individual Israelite and through each ultimately to the communal life, the LORD Presence. The Messenger proclaims that the LORD is coming. HE who is the LORD is the High Priest of the Temple of Christhood. It is said that HE will come suddenly to HIS Temple, and the question is asked, "*Who may abide the day of His coming?*" Though the experience may seem to be sudden at the moment, it must have been prepared for. You can no more climb to the estate wherein the realization of the Divine Presence becomes yours, by a momentary action, than you can climb in a moment on your feet and hands up the great mountains. Indeed it is a far slower process than the earthly experience, but it is a surer one. For if you climb truly, you are sure to get there. There are no obstacles you cannot overcome if you rightly present yourself to them. If you do not present yourselves rightly to them in your willinghood, your desires and actions, then there may be a rebound of their magnetic action unto your hurt. When the LORD comes to HIS Temple HE comes as a refiner's Fire. The refining is at work long before you realize it. The coming of the LORD to HIS Temple as a refiner of silver and gold, is the process of the Regeneration wherein HE is refining the silver of the Being, all the mercurial elements in you, the glorious Divine Elements out of which you are fashioned; and those elements of HIS Mystery which belong to the Innermost Magnetic Centre which are spoken of as gold. When HE comes HE comes as the purifier of all the magnetic states, and all the atmospheres associated with the Divine Mystery, Gold, in your superstructure.

So Malachi, though accounted only a minor prophet, has a great Message. It concerns Mala-Chi-Yah, the Messenger of YAHWEH. It is fragmentary, it is true, like all the messages in the other books. The fragments are scattered here and there. But it is the same Message as is found elsewhere. What a Divine unity runs through those books! It is always the same Message to Israel concerning the LORD of Sabaoth, the worship of HIM in HIS Temple, and the service of HIM as HIS chosen servants unto this World. Unto this end the Message is concerned with the restoration of the Temple in the individual life of Israel and also in the communal life for service. When HE doth come HE is as a refiner to purge the House of Levi, the House of Priests. HE comes in HIS Fire to make pure and beautiful the mediatorial realms of your Being, all your priestly attributes, to make them once more strong and radiant, that you may be able to interpret HIM. For you are to interpret HIM through your priestly attributes, even as it is through your attributes that you embody HIM. Therefore the attributes must be made whole. They must be refined. HE comes to HIS Temple to make the attributes whole and in that sense to salve them, to heal their woundings, to restore them to perfect balance, to give them a perfect equilibrium, to enable them all to come into unified action that you may realize that divine polarity which crowns the Soul who comes into the consciousness of HIS Overshadowing Presence.

Thus you may recognize that Malachi had a wonderful Message for Israel. You may see it grow unto great fulness. For when the LORD comes to HIS Temple, everyone in it is filled with surprise, which means that the whole life is filled with astonishment at the joy of it even amid the travail of life; surprise at the power of it, even whilst there seems to run concurrently with it a refining process and detachment from the earth life. There is the surprise of the coming of a consciousness of the Presence Who Overshadows even whilst it encompasses, and this consciousness intensifies, until the life expands to such a degree that it recovers the past. It remembers. It regains its former estate. It becomes consciously once more a dweller in the very bosom of GOD.

It is recorded in the book as it stands:—

"Then they who feared the Lord spake often one to another; And the Lord hearkened, and heard it, and a book of remembrance was written before Him for them that feared the Lord, and that thought upon His Name."

But the LORD does not require a book of remembrance concerning HIS children. HE knows everything about them. They have a book of remembrance, however. It is in themselves. Everything about themselves concerning their life's history is written in themselves. Your history is written within you. And that is the book that has to be opened. It is sealed upon each plane, and only the Divine Love can break the seals for you. It is not only the book of the Innermost Realm, but the book of your own inner realm. "Then they who loved the LORD spake of HIM one to another." That is the beautiful way. You cannot love someone and know that another loves that one without speaking of that one. Even in earthly relationships is it not a joy to speak of those who have ministered unto your love, and, in a strange way, called forth your love to minister to them? You love to speak of them as well as to them. Then they who loved the LORD spake of HIM one to another. And you see the result? It created an atmosphere. It was the atmosphere of the Presence around the life. And the book of their remembrance was opened.

Then they who loved the Lord spake often one to another of Him, and concerning His Message to them, and the book of their remembrance was opened, and they recalled the days of old, and all that the Lord had wrought out on their behalf. And they remembered that they were accounted as gems in His diadem, those unto whom He had committed His most precious treasures.

THE RECOVERY OF THE PARACLETE

Now it is remarkable that in the closing cadences of the Old Testament Scriptures, the Paraclete should be spoken of as the Remembrancer. For the word means *The*

Remembrancer. You remember in these passages in the New Testament concerning the Holy Paraclete, *"But when He is come, He shall bring all things to your remembrance."* "When the Holy Guest comes to you, you will remember all things which the FATHER-MOTHER hath given unto me to unveil to you." His intimate ones were to remember the past. They were to recover.

So here in the book of Malachi. It was their remembrance that was opened. *"For they are Mine"*, saith the LORD. *"The treasure in them is Mine."* It is the treasure of HIMSELF, the knowledge of HIMSELF, the wealth of HIS own glorious Love and Wisdom built up into the fabric of the Soul. For the wealth of mediatorial potency in the Being is for service in HIS Temple. The wealth of HIS Love and Wisdom is to find expression bye and bye through HIS Israel as venues, interpreters, revealers and manifestors.

O Israel, Israel; Children of the Sacred Flame and the Radiant Presence; Princes of the regnancy of that Presence, awaken ye to the full understanding of that which you would fain believe yourselves to be! Awaken ye to the realization through manifestation of all that which you would fain become! If you be HIS Chosen, it is to make HIM manifest. You are not here simply to enjoy yourselves in any self-regarding way, though it is the most delightful thing in the Universe to live so as to make HIM manifest. Let your Temple be HIS dwelling-place and its sacrifice something living and vibrant and absolute for HIM. Let your priestly motion be a mediatorial ministry wherein there is the exposition of HIS own glorious outflow. Let HIS coming be unto you in such fulness that HE HIMSELF shall be incarnate in you. Let HIM become so immanent that HE shall become manifest through you. In this way you shall radiate HIM and reveal HIM; you will interpret HIM; and you may become a Divine Incarnation. Let HIS Paraclete keep before your vision always HIMSELF in HIS glorious Love, and HIS resplendent Wisdom. Thus you will go out no more from the consciousness of

His Overshadowing and Encompassing, nor from His Inner Court of your Being where His Remembrancer abides.

Lord God of the Heavenly Hosts, even of Sabaoth, Thy Children would adore Thee, even unto the manifestation of Thee.

Thy Children would worship Thee even unto the perfect motion of Being towards Thee, and from Thee in mediatorial service for Thee.

Thus, O Father-Mother, mayest Thou again become the Lord God of Sabaoth in the midst of Thine Israel.

Blessed be Thy Most Glorious Name!

Amen and Amen.

BIBLIOGRAPHY

The prophetic *Logia* and the interpretive addresses by the Rev. J. Todd Ferrier, concerning the Messages of the Minor Prophets, were given at various times and published in several volumes of *The Herald of the Cross* (H), as set out below. Volumes i-vii appeared 1905–11; the new series, from Volume viii onwards, began in 1934.

The Introduction, "The Office of a Prophet", is taken from *The Message of Ezekiel: A Cosmic Drama*, published in 1931.

THE MINOR PROPHETS

Title of Prophecy	When Address was given	When and where Logia were published		When and where Address was published	
BALAAM	1934	1934	H viii	1952	H xxvi
JOEL	1930	1934	H viii	1952	H xxvi
AMOS	—	1908	H iv	—	
OBADIAH	1934	1934	H viii	1934	H viii
JONAH	1935	1935	H ix	1935	H ix
MICAH	1930	1939	H xiii	1951	H xxv
HABAKKUK	1934	1934	H viii	1952	H xxvi
HAGGAI	1934	1934	H viii	1935	H ix
ZECHARIAH	1930	1908	H iv	1952	H xxvi
		1935	H ix	—	
MALACHI *circa*	1930	1908	H iv	1951	H xxv
	—	1934	H viii	—	

INDEX

INDEX

INDEX

Page

232

PITY   COMPASSION   LOVE

The Order of the Cross

SPIRITUAL
AIMS AND IDEALS

THE Order is an informal Brotherhood and Fellowship, having for
its service in life the cultivation of
the Spirit of Love towards all Souls:
Helping the weak and defending the
defenceless and oppressed; Abstaining
from hurting the creatures, eschewing
bloodshed and flesh eating, and living
upon the pure foods so abundantly
provided by nature; Walking in the
Mystic Way of Life, whose Path leads
to the realization of the Christhood;
And sending forth the Mystic Teachings
unto all who may be able to receive
them — those sacred interpretations
of the Soul, the Christhood, and
the Divine Love and Wisdom, for
which the Order of the Cross stands.

SELF-ABANDONMENT

SELF-SACRIFICE

SELF-DENIAL

REDEMPTION

REGENERATION

ILLUMINATION

SERVICE   DEVOTION   PURITY

SYNOPSIS OF MAIN PUBLICATIONS

THE MASTER sets forth the Inner Meanings of the Master's Teachings and gives a true picture of Him as He was in His Life, public and private. The Birth Stories and the Allegories of the Soul are revealed in their true setting; with the Teachings on the profound Mystery of the Sin-offering, and the Allegories of the Soul's Awakening.

THE LOGIA contains the chief utterances of the Master, in the form in which they were spoken by Him. Here they are restored, including the real Mystic Sayings, found in the Synoptic Records, the Gnostic Record, the Pauline Letters, and the Apocalypse, containing remarkable histories of the Soul, the Planet, the Ancient Christhood Order, and the Oblation or Sin-offering.

LIFE'S MYSTERIES UNVEILED gives the Path of Discipleship and Aids to the Path of the Realization. It includes definitions of terms in their relation to these Teachings and many answers to questions asked at Healing and other Meetings. The principal theme of the volume is Initiations of the Soul.

THE DIVINE RENAISSANCE, Vol. I. i. The Message. The Divine Adept. The Superstructure of Man. ii. The Eternal Mystery. A Divine Apologia. The Seat of Authority. iii. The Path of the Recovery. The Redemption. The Divine Purpose of the Oblation. The Mass and the Oblation. Altars and Sacrifices. The Flame before the Altar.

THE DIVINE RENAISSANCE, Vol. II. i. Unto the Great Silence. Science and Religion. The Angelic Realms. Corpus Christi. The Sabbath of the Lord. ii. Beginnings of Historical Christianity. Pentecost. The Advent of Paul. The Stone the Builders Rejected. The Church of the Living Christ. The Seven Sacraments. iii. A Renascent Redemption. The Seven Thunders. The Healer, Manifestor, Redeemer. The Obedience of Christ. Our Lord and Our Lady. The Three Altars. iv. A Divine Oratorio. The Ministry of the Gods. The Divine Government. The Cosmic Consciousness. The Regnancy of Christ.

THE MESSAGE OF EZEKIEL. *A COSMIC DRAMA.* The Office of a Prophet. The Purport of the Book. The Divine World Unveiled. The Distinction given to Israel. The Mystery of Tyre and Zidon. The Pharaoh of Egypt. The Arising of Israel. The *Logia* of the Prophet Ezekiel: with extensive Notes to the *Logia. The Logia of Israel.* Vol. I.

ISAIAH. *A COSMIC AND MESSIANIC DRAMA.* i. The Unity of Divine Revelation. ii. The Prophecy. iii. The Word of the Lord. iv. A Divine Drama. v. The Mystery of the Sin-offering. vi. A Momentous Promise. vii. The Triumph of Adonai. viii. The Drama of Israel. ix. The Sign of the Cross. x. The Daysman of Israel. xi. The Appointed Redeemer. xii. The Five Cities of Egypt. xiii. The City of the Sun. xiv. The *Logia* of the Prophet Isaiah: with extensive Notes. *The Logia of Israel.* Vol. II.

THE MYSTERY OF THE LIGHT WITHIN US. With 17 *coloured plates by Amy Wright Todd Ferrier.* i. The Luminous Cross and the Cross of the Elohim. ii. The Spectra of Souls and Stars. The Solar Fashion. iii. Auric Glimpses of the Master. iv. Celestial and Divine Estates. v. A Holy Convocation. Jacob's Ladder. The Adamic Race. The Secrets of God. The Girdle. The Blessing of Israel. A Divine Rhapsody.

PUBLICATIONS

By the REV. J. TODD FERRIER:

THE MASTER: *His Life and Teachings*	Large Crown 8vo			624 pp.
THE LOGIA: *or Sayings of The Master*	,,	,,	,,	436 pp.
LIFE'S MYSTERIES UNVEILED	,,	,,	,,	480 pp.
THE DIVINE RENAISSANCE, Vol. I	,,	,,	,,	402 pp.
THE DIVINE RENAISSANCE, Vol. II	,,	,,	,,	560 pp.
THE MESSAGE OF EZEKIEL: *A Cosmic Drama*	,,	,,	,,	280 pp.
THE MESSAGE OF ISAIAH: *A Cosmic and Messianic Drama*	,,	,,	,,	436 pp.

THE MYSTERY OF THE LIGHT WITHIN US
With 17 plates. Large Crown 4to 240 pp.
THE HERALD OF THE CROSS (Bound volumes)
Vols. VIII upwards. Large Crown 8vo
HANDBOOK OF EXTRACTS of the Teachings of The Order of
the Cross, from the Writings of the Rev. J. Todd Ferrier.
Vol. I: Extracts A to D; Vol. II: Extracts E to J. Demy 8vo
Further volumes in preparation.

LETTERS TO THE CHILDREN With 5 plates	,,	,,	238 pp.
THE MESSAGE OF SOME OF THE MINOR PROPHETS	,,	,,	240 pp.

SMALLER BOOKS (Paper Bound)

THE MYSTERY OF THE CITY UPON SEVEN HILLS	Demy 8vo		80 pp.
GREAT RECOVERIES	,,	,,	80 pp.
THE FESTIVAL OF THE MASS OF ISRAEL	,,	,,	72 pp.
THE STORY OF THE SHEPHERDS OF BETHLEHEM	,,	,,	72 pp.
SUBLIME AFFIRMATIONS	,,	,,	64 pp.
WHAT IS A CHRISTIAN?	,,	,,	64 pp.
THE SECOND COMING OF CHRIST	,,	,,	48 pp.
THE GREAT TRIBULATION . THE WORK	,,	,,	44 pp.
THE EVANGEL OF ST. JOHN	,,	,,	40 pp.
THE CHRIST FESTIVAL . THE WAYS OF GOD AND THE WAYS OF MEN	,,	,,	36 pp.
THE CROSS OF A CHRIST . THE RESURRECTION LIFE	,,	,,	36 pp.
THE PASSING OF SOULS	,,	,,	32 pp.
THE CONTINUITY OF CONSCIOUSNESS	,,	,,	32 pp.
THE PATH OF DISCIPLESHIP	,,	,,	28 pp.
IF CHRIST CAME BACK?	,,	,,	28 pp.
A MEDITATION ON GOD	,,	,,	24 pp.
THE LIFE IMMORTAL	,,	,,	20 pp.
THE ORDER OF THE CROSS	,,	,,	16 pp.
THE MESSAGE AND THE WORK	,,	,,	16 pp.
THE INNER MEANING OF THE FOOD REFORM MOVEMENT	,,	,,	8 pp.
ON BEHALF OF THE CREATURES	Crown 8vo		128 pp.
THOUGHTS FOR THE DAY	,,	,,	52 pp.
THE ABRAHAMIC STORY	,,	,,	20 pp.

By E. MARY GORDON KEMMIS:

THE "GREATER WORKS" (Cloth bound)	Crown 8vo	64 pp.

FOR USE IN WORSHIP

PSALMS AND CANTICLES FOR WORSHIP	Demy 8vo		96 pp.
HYMNS FOR WORSHIP WITH TUNES	,,	,,	256 pp.

THE HERALD OF THE CROSS

Vols. I to VII (published 1905-11) are now out of print. Vols. VIII (1934) to XXI
(six issues a year) and Vols. XXII upwards (four issues a year) are available
separately, paper bound, in limited quantities. (Vols. VIII to XVII, No. 4, edited
by the Rev. J. Todd Ferrier: subsequent issues edited according to his instructions.)

All prices on Application

Please address all communications regarding Literature, and make remittances payable, to THE LITERATURE SECRETARY, THE ORDER OF THE CROSS,
10 DE VERE GARDENS. LONDON. W8 5AE

Loan copies of any of the publications may be applied for to THE LIBRARIAN

MEETINGS

Regular meetings are held, at which all seekers after the Divine way of life **are** welcome, in the Sanctuary at the Headquarters of the Order of the Cross, as below, every Sunday at 11 a.m. and Wednesday at 7 p.m. throughout the year (except during the Summer Vacation); and there are Groups or Reading Circles for the study of the Teachings in many Centres in the United Kingdom, Australia, France, New Zealand and United States of America. Details will be sent on request, in writing, to the Trustees, at the address given below.

COMMUNICATIONS

Communications regarding the Literature of the Order should be addressed and remittances made payable to, "The Literature Secretary", at the Headquarters.

Further information concerning the Order of the Cross and its activities will be gladly given to any inquirer, on application to:

THE TRUSTEES

THE ORDER OF THE CROSS
10 DE VERE GARDENS, KENSINGTON,
LONDON, W8 5AE

The Order of the Cross

FOUNDED OCTOBER 1904

AIMS AND IDEALS

(FOUNDATION STATEMENT)

TO ATTAIN, by mutual helpfulness, the realization of the Christ-life, by the path of self-denial, self-sacrifice, and absolute self-abandonment to the Divine will and service:

It is of these things that the Cross as a symbol speaks. It stands for the Sign of the Order of the Cross, because its three steps are those which have to be taken in order to arrive at that Estate which it symbolizes. It speaks of the quest after the humble spirit and the pure heart. It speaks also of that further state of realization when the Soul gives itself. in absolute abandonment for the Divine Service. The Three Steps are:

PURITY OF LIVING
PURITY OF THE MIND
PURITY OF THE SOUL

Thus to endeavour by example and teaching to win all men to the love of Truth, Purity and Right-doing.

To proclaim the Brotherhood of Man, the essential one-ness of all religious aspirations, and the unity of all living creatures in the Divine.

To teach the moral necessity for humaneness towards all men and all creatures.

To protest against, and to work for the abolition of, all national and social customs which violate the teachings of the Christ, especially such as involve bloodshed, the oppression of the weak and defenceless, the perpetuation of the brutal mind, and the infliction of cruelty upon animals, *viz.*: war, vivisection, the slaughter of animals for food, fashion and sport, and kindred evils.

To advocate the universal adoption of a bloodless diet, and the return to simple and natural foods.

To proclaim a message of peace and happiness, health and purity, spirituality and Divine Love.

EXECUTIVE COUNCIL (1904)

J. TODD FERRIER, *Founder, Editor,* "The Herald of the Cross."

ROBERT H. PERKS, M.D., F.R.C.S. (Eng.), *Secretary.*

All Offices of the Order are honorary

ACKNOWLEDGEMENT

I would like to thank Maura, my wife for her generous and unwavering support in getting ready this book; she supported and encouraged me along every step of the way; Maura was indeed my voice. I thank my sister Rosemary Kemp, for critically reading the manuscript.

Janet Moody O'Keeffe gave me the benefit of her time and experience at the vital and earlier stages of planning the book- this act of friendship I value. Also I offer my thanks to the makers of Amstrad, PCW 8256 whose technical skills make it possible to compensate for a writing disability which has affected me for the last two years.

Finally, I alone take full responsibility for the truth of all the facts related, all views expressed and all ideas promoted throughout this book.

Denstone Murphy
February 15th 1991

CONTENTS

INTRODUCTION

"Rumour of Hope" is an account of my own life with interspersed theological comment. It is divided into two parts, The Lawn and the High Ground.

Part One is an account of my life from birth until my marriage after leaving the active ministry of the priesthood. At the beginning of Part one is a Prologue: it describes the impressions while attending a Congress of the "International Federation of Married Catholic Priests" held in Holland during August 1990. That sets the scene for a flashback of my own story which is started in the first chapter, "Beginnings" and is continued until Chapter 18 "Decision Time" which deals with my final decision to leave the ministry and get married.

Having studied and taught theology and philosophy from post primary level to seminary level for many years I am anxious to encourage open theological debate and I use various incidents of my own life experience as opportunities to stimulate discussion and perhaps controversy. I have been outspoken in certain places, not primarily to shock, but to cause reaction.

Part Two the "High Ground" deals with a number of experiences which impressed me while living in the country where I spent my childhood between the ages of eight and a half and eighteen. It is an attempt to describe key memories which I cherish. In the hope of striking a chord in readers, the last chapter "The Gathering" draws together into the present some significant people of my country childhood days.

"The Lawn" is a symbol of "white collar" middle-class professional side of my life.

The characters and events described here are all real but in a number of instances I have thought it prudent to change names and circumstances.

Prologue
CONGRESS IN THE NETHERLANDS

Whilst awaiting the minibus to collect us at the station in Amersfoort Maura, my wife, and I spent some time trying to identify possible fellow travellers. We estimated that there were about five other priests and their wives and two of these couples were apparently accompanied by their children. Our estimate was proved correct when those we had earmarked converged together with us on the minibus from Slotemaker de Bruine Instituut when it eventually arrived. While scrambling on board with our luggage, on the invitation of the driver we introduced ourselves. We were all on our way to take part in the Second Congress of the International Federation of Married Catholic Priests to be held in Doorn from August 19th to August 24th 1990.

Maura and I got seats in the front beside the driver, a tall, well dressed genial person who spoke fluent English. After some preliminary small talk I asked,

'Is this your own minibus or do you drive for a firm?'

'Actually', he said, 'this is a rented self-drive which we have for the duration of the congress'.

'What then your day job' I rejoined.

I had slightly overrated his grasp of colloquial English so that the idiom puzzled him slightly at first but when he reflected and got the point he replied,

'O, I am Tony, I am a married priest working as a hospital chaplain in Utrecht'.

Furthermore we discovered that he and I had been in the same year in the University of St. Thomas in Rome.

We expressed some surprise that as a married person he was exercising his priesthood. He assured us that it was quite common to have married Catholic priests acting as hospital chaplains in The Netherlands.

Tony had been a member of the Congregation of the Oblates of Mary Immaculate when he was appointed chaplain. When he left the Oblates to get married he held onto the chaplaincy.

In quite a short time we arrived at the Instituut or conference centre. It consisted basically of a beautiful old building with some tastefully designed extensions, in a woodland setting.

One of the organisers whom we met at the reception desk was Sylvia Dierks a friend and onetime missionary colleague of Maura's. Sylvia had worked as a lay missionary in Nigeria with Maura who had been a Medical Missionary of Mary. Sylvia is now married to Wiess Dierks another one of the key organisers of the congress. Wiess is a priest and as a member of the Society of African Missions had been director of the Pastoral Institute of Ibadan where both Sylvia and Maura worked.

Sylvia showed us to our room which had every modern convenience. Having settled ourselves in we started to make our way back to reception. On our way through the long corridor, a door of one of the other rooms opened and out came a venerable gentleman with aquiline features and episcopal (I speak not in metaphor) in bearing.

'My name is Fernandez', he volunteered.

We identified ourselves in turn.

Maura sensitively enquired,

'Are you by yourself or is your wife with you?'

In a very laboured and heavily accented English he said,

'My wife is resting, she is, how do you say? Poisoned'

'My god', said Maura, seemingly convinced on account of the strong South American accent that something sinister was afoot, 'have you sent for the pol..............the doctor?'

'Not necessary', he replied with reassurance, 'she often feels poisoned after a long flight'.

I explained to the archbishop what the difference was between 'sick' or 'ill' and 'poisoned'. He promised to introduce us to his wife, Carmella, as soon as she was fit and well.

The reception area was brimming over with people, meeting excitedly for the first time or renewing friendships suspended perhaps since the first congress held in Italy three years previously or some other such occasion. English seemed to be the dominant language and amongst the English speakers the prevailing accent was American.

I felt deeply that I was welcomed even by those whom I had not met before. As a group, I had so much in common with them. Somewhat like the way in which women only understand other women due to the sharing of a special emotional and biological background, so priests have a shared and unique background.

The happiness which inspired those women and men present was born of their faith and their shared priesthood yet, ironically, this kind of thing bewilders rather than pleases the official Roman guardian of the rule of faith.

The first community exercise on that first evening was to be dinner. Over two hundred of us, between women, men and children were invited to a spacious dining room in which there was a very large number of round tables.

'I'm Joan Tissant and this is my husband, Pierre. We're from Texas in the United States', announced this attractive woman, who seemed to be in her middle fifties, with whom we shared a table.

After reciprocating with our names and place of origin I asked Pierre, 'Were you attached to a diocese or did you belong to a religious order or congregation?'

Before Pierre had time to answer, Joan had reached into her purse or handbag and produced for us to see, a black and white photographic portrait of a distinguished looking cleric.

'This was taken shortly before Pierre left the diocese, he was a Monsignor. It's now thirty years since he left'.

'How did you do financially, or what did you do for a living after you left?' I asked him.

Joan continued as his spokesperson,

'He wanted to go into Real Estate so he took the necessary training courses. But when he was qualified and set about getting a job, things became difficult. He got plenty of job interviews but in each case when it transpired that he was a priest, resigned from the ministry, he suddenly appears to have become too hot to handle and was promptly given the "don't call us we'll call you" treatment. At least one of those prospective employers had sons priests in the diocese. Almost desperately he applied for a job in a firm of stockbrokers on Wall Street and he was accepted by them. He continued successfully in Wall Street up until his retirement'.

Maura asked Joan to tell us something about herself. Trustingly she shared with us. 'I was born in the United States of immigrant Czechoslovakian parents. In early adult life I entered a convent where I remained for twenty seven years, teaching during most of that time. When I left I continued teaching as a lay person for almost another twenty years and at seventy five years of age I am now retired'.

It seemed incredible that Joan could be that age, she was so young in appearance as well as in spirit.

She continued,

'Both Pierre and I were very involved in ballroom dancing and took part in competitions and through this interest we met and got married, just twenty-five years ago. In fact, coming to this congress is part of our Silver Wedding celebrations.

At this point Joan's hand once again explored in her handbag and she produced a sheaf of photographs of their dancing careers and of their wedding celebrations. What a beautiful couple – the names, Ginger Rogers and Fred Astair easily came to mind.

O, God, I felt, how saintly and sensitive these people are – perhaps they are heralds of divinity, expressions of a spirit refusing to be limited in any scope and influence.

The subsequent four days were demanding, yet refreshing. We had papers by experts, outstanding amongst whom was, I thought, Anthony Padovano from the United States of America. He gave a paper entitled, "The Renewal of the Priestly Ministry", the introduction to which is worth quoting;

> *"It is not healthy to live and work in one world and to believe and pray in another.*
> *The harmony of these two worlds is an issue in the Catholic married priests' movement and in the development of contemporary spirituality.*
> *When our daily lives are at odds with our religious lives, the Church is viewed as extravagance, archaic, quaint and remote.*
> *Those who believe in and pray in this Church become a puzzle or an obstacle to the world at large and to themselves".*

The paper ended with the words;

> *"the Spirit compelled the disciples ever forward, into the whole world, beyond Jerusalem, into a limitless universe. There they found their mission"*

To my mind these words enshrine the essence of the congress.

The only person at the congress, as far as I was aware, who would be construed as belonging to the 'establishment' was the Dutch Dominican Provincial. He came to one of the sessions. As someone who had spent twenty-two years as a Dominican I felt very proud and possessive, like a little boy who wanted to show off his famous father to the rest of his classmates.

A considerable number of bishops and other major clerics had slipped notes of well-wishing and support "under the door" but would not wish to be publicly identified. One particular Catholic religious organization donated over five thousand pounds sterling to help towards defraying the expense of running the congress.

On the night of our arrival, after dinner, we gathered for a short liturgy of readings and prayers.

Since leaving the ministry in 1974 I had been called upon on three occasions to exercise my ministry in celebrating the Sacrament of Forgiveness, twice at the roadside in the case of motor accidents and once in hospital, in the case of a patient in danger of death, when the chaplain was not available. On each of those occasions I felt fulfilled and happy, doing what I am best at doing. Words of Ecclesiastes come to mind when I reflect on those acts of ministry. "There is a reason for everything, a time for every occupation under heaven".

I had, for some reason, at the beginning of the first day of the congress, locked within me, an un-askable question.

'Are we going to have a Eucharistic celebration and if we are who is or who are going to lead the celebration?'

In the course of the day, due to the formal and informal discussions and the sharing of background experiences, the words of Jacob, who had been assured by God in a dream of his constant presence with him, kept coming into my mind. "Truly, Yaweh is in this place and I never knew it!" Then what became quite clear to me was the fittingness of a Eucharist concelebrated by all of us. We were in a holy place. On the following evenings of the congress we concelebrated the Eucharist. Each time it was prepared by a different language group. A memory which remains clearly with me is the wholehearted signing of the Magnificat which was used as a recessional hymn.

Those particular Masses or Eucharists were for me the most wholesome prayer experiences I have ever had. The dichotomy suggested above by Padovano between the world we live and work in and the world we pray in was resolved. The support and strength coming from the earthy realism of having Maura, my wife standing beside me, gave me a fulfillment and courage to exercise my ministerial role with an integrity far removed from the dualism which had been prompted in me by uncertain celibacy. I got the impression that all who attended were completely present in mind as well as in body. The scheduled functions seem to have been, in most cases, fully attended. In this gathering of declericalised priests was a remarkable sense of commitment and responsibility.

To no small degree it seemed obvious to me that the women were the sources of much of the refreshing zeal evident in the priests. The partners enjoyed each other, there was fun between them which they rejoiced to share with those around them. The faithfulness evidenced must surely be the fruit of a striving against the tide to get together and share their lives.

A few of the women were there by themselves. There were at least two widows. Their presence was a touching memorial to their late priest husbands and an eloquent reminder of our ultimate accountability for our discipleship "ever forward, into the world, beyond Jerusalem, into a limitless universe" (Padovano). One was a black South African who had been married to a white English missionary priest. Others who came were married to priests who were unable to come on account of work commitments.

There were a few there whose marriages had failed. They were supported, encouraged and accepted, yet they gave more than they received from the group. Their trust made us focus on the frailty of our own relationships and the need not to take each other for granted but to cherish each other's Real Presence.

Various life stories we heard informally. Many had been treated well by ecclesiastical authorities when they sought dispensation from the ministry, others were victims of disedifying hostility. The decisions of some were accepted or even welcomed by their families, others were disowned and in once case there was physical assault.

Some had been dispensed by the Vatican from the obligations in Canon Law that go with the Priesthood, the principal one being that celibacy, but have nothing to do with the essence of priesthood. Others had applied for dispensations but they were refused. There seems to be a serious inequity on the part of the Vatican in the application of its powers of dispensation. I know one person who applied for a dispensation, refused to give any reason for his request, yet promptly received it. I applied, gave exhaustive reasons for my request and was refused. Apparently, so I have been told, I was too positive. I emphasised the goodness and value of the celibate clerical state for those who positively chose it. Since I became director of a pre-marriage course I had studied in considerable detail the Sacramental Theology of Marriage. I was impressed by St. Paul's teaching in his Letter to the Ephesians that the Christian expectation of married love is that it should symbolise or signify Christ's love for humankind. This I had not appreciated before ordination when all the Moral Theology of marriage had been taught with particular emphasis on the possible ways of sinning in this matter. Accordingly, good though the intentions of my mentors may have been, I have perceived sexuality, women and marriage, largely, as possible sources of moral anger. I saw celibacy as a safe refuge.

In Civil Law and in some other branches of Canon Law, the petitioner is given a hearing but when dispensation from the clerical obligation to celibacy is involved the entire transaction is by proxy. The particular individual as a unique person with special needs is not considered, he is not seen and his voice is not heard. The granting or withholding of these dispensations seems to depend on Papal policy. It is difficult to imagine that civil authorities would get away with such expediency.

In 1974 Maura and I were given to believe that there would be no problems about getting the dispensation as all my colleagues who left at that time had their requests promptly granted. Towards Christmas of 1975 we booked the church and planned a reception, arranged with a priest friend to officiate, but at the eleventh hour got a phone call from Rome to say the dispensation was not granted. We postponed our marriage for six months confident that time would find a solution.

At the end of the six months no further progress has been made. I had resisted some gentle pressure that was put on me to file a request for dispensation supported by negative reasons. The Vatican authorities, it appeared to me, would not acknowledge the fact of seeking dispensation from the obligation to celibacy as a possible growth process for some, just as the taking of a vow of celibacy late in life on the part of a widow or widower would be seen as a movement towards greater perfection.

Because of the apparent lack of interest that the Vatican had in our cause and because "the more travelled road" seemed to have been blocked against us, Maura and I felt justified in going beyond Canonical requirements for a valid and lawful marriage. Having done this we saw clearly that there was not obstacle to our fulfilling the theological requirement, which was, in the spirit of the Letter to the Ephesians, to commit ourselves officially to strive, through the quality of our lives and relationship to show forth or signify the kind of love relationship there is between Christ and humankind.

In the case of the Sacrament of Marriage the couple involved are themselves ministers of the sacrament. The priest who usually "officiates" is only a witness.

We participated in the ordinary daily Mass, which we regarded as our wedding Eucharist, in a local church on the morning of June 19th 1976. Shortly afterwards on that same day we committed ourselves in marriage as we ministered the Sacrament to each other in the Registry Office in Coleraine in the presence of the registrar and four very close friends.

The Congress at Doorn stirred in me an awareness of the need and the freedom to leave nothing underground and gave me a permission that I am now accepting, with Maura's full cooperation and blessing, to celebrate all my experience in the light. In this way I have a wider base on which to build a wholesome future. Doorn focused me on the most deliberate and the most important phase of my life so far, my decision to leave the priest ministry and to get married. But there have been other things which led up to this point and yet other things which resulted from it.

Within the last year, I have had to take disability retirement from teaching on account of Parkinson's disease. This leaves me with the leisure to recall and write about some of the people and events by whom and by which I have been influenced for well over half a century. Every person has his/her own unique experiences. Yet, many lifelines converge for a shorter or a longer time and it is a source of interest and courage for me to run alongside others and see what we share, the sadness, the tragedies, the drolleries and the jokes.

I would also like to add to and in some cases endorse the folklore of places with which I am familiar. For this reason I shall tell the tale of a life started in Kildare, a childhood in Cheshire and Cork and of a career involving farming, medical studies, the priesthood and teaching in secondary school, seminary and university. These things happened over a period of sixty years and on two continents.

***

After seventeen years of waiting, the dispensation from the obligation to celibacy, currently associated with the priesthood, was granted to me by Rome.

Thus one period of my life was closed officially. I see the sequence of all my experience as a process of evolution. The best is yet to come.

RUMOUR OF HOPE

The Challenge of Choosing

Part One

The Lawn

Chapter 1
BEGINNINGS

On February 5th 1931 I was born in Riverstown House, near Kildangan, just outside Monasterevin, County Kildare. Monasterevin is a peaceful and pleasant midlands town of waterways and bridges, once the home of the Irish Tenor, John McCormack and (more recently) associated in world news headlines, with the kidnap of the Dutch industrialist, Dr.Tiede Herema.

My parents' home was in Runcorn, Cheshire, quite near to Liverpool. As was the custom in those days, when she was close to her time for giving birth, my mother went to stay with a married sister Kathleen, called Kit, in order to be looked after and cared for. Kit and her husband, Harry Shorte lived in Riverstown House.

My mother's name was Margaret Mary, called Peggy, daughter of Denis and Maria Callanan of Leap, County Cork. My father's name was Jerome Bernard, son of Dr Jeremiah Edward and Hannah Murphy of Lissarda, County Cork.

My mother's mother died in 1916 leaving my grandfather with a family of ten children, eight girls and two boys. Nellie, the eldest, was twenty one at the time of her mother's death. The younger ones, my mother was seventh in the family, were organised and catered for by Nellie.

Auntie Kit and Uncle Harry during the first few years after they got married and before they acquired the farm in Riverstown, lived in Liverpool. Mother stayed with them there for about two years in order to finish her schooling and take a secretarial course.

Having completed this course she went to work in Imperial Chemicals Industries in Runcorn and there met my father who was one of the doctors in the town. Mother was in digs with a family in the town who owned a newspaper and tobacco shop. Sometimes she helped out in serving the customers, one of whom she discovered was from Lissarda, near Macroom in County Cork no more than 30 miles from her own home place, Leap, near Skibbereen. This was 1927; they were engaged to get married in 1928, and they got married in Leap Parish Church on April 21st 1930.

I was christened Denstone Edward Ainslie in the parish church in Monasterevin within a few days of birth, as was then the custom, prompted by the teaching of Pope John XXll in 1321 to the effect that infants who died without baptism could not go to heaven. Uncle Harry was my godfather and Auntie Bess, my mother's youngest sister, was my godmother. Even though only sixteen years of age, Auntie Bess was on her way from Leap to Liverpool to complete her schooling and eventually seek livelihood. For a few days, she was breaking her journey in Riverstown House.

Edward is easily explained as a family name, Ainslie was thought to be sweet sounding and Denstone was the name of an English public school near Uttoxeter in Staffordshire where my father used to attend as school doctor when he began practicing medicine. My father, born in 1878, was fifty two years of age when I was born. My mother, born in 1908, was twenty two.

**

When I was three months old my father took mother and me to Runcorn where I was to spend the first eight and a half years of my life. As was customary with professional middle class families of the time, in our house in Runcorn, we had a domestic staff which consisted of three young women, a cook, a housemaid and a nursemaid.

My father and his assistant had their surgeries in the house. Usually, the assistant was a young doctor just fresh out of university; in those days there was no post qualification training required in order to register as a General Practitioner. The assistants stayed, on average, about three years before going on to buy or set up practices of their own.

During those years I was brought up mainly by a series of nursemaids. My mother was, it would appear at times, cast in the role of supervisor. My first nursemaid was Eileen Dutton who brought me from weaning to earliest memories. She was so indispensable that she was brought on holidays with us to Ireland in 1933. She had never been in Ireland before and loved the green fields, the trees and the easy pace of life. Apparently, she was enraptured by her association with the men working on the farm attached to Lissarda House, our family home in Ireland. One of them, proposed marriage to her, an offer which she accepted and he presented her with a ring.

Alas, when she returned to industrial Runcorn, she lost her rose tinted spectacles and seeing things again from her restored Runcorn perspective she changed her mind and posted the ring back to Lissarda.

While I have only a vague recollection of Eileen I have a very clear memory of her successor as nursemaid, Betty Harrison, whose home was in Church View. She was an only child and lived there with her parents. She often brought me with her to her home and through those visits, which I remember were frowned upon by my parents, I got a knowledge, which I can clearly recall, of what English working class life and conditions were like at that time. The house she lived in with her parents was well kept but very small. Immediately inside the door was the only room downstairs. There was one bedroom upstairs. Water was piped to the kitchen sink but there was no inside toilet. The toilets for the whole terrace were in a special toilet block about twenty-five yards away.

Betty's father was a First World War veteran and had been wounded in the leg with the result that he walked with a noticeable limp. He worked in the salt works at nearby Weston Point. Since he wore wooden clogs which had steel protectors on the soles and heels, his comings and goings were broadcast, for all on the street to hear, by an identifiable call sign as he laboured by.

Betty had more heart than skill and was considerably overweight. These factors and resultant ungainly deportment would seem to have contributed to her disqualification as nursemaid. Whatever about spiritual qualities, in those days, in that professional middle class there was a preoccupation about the keeping up of appearances and about the transmission of such values to children. After a short time she was moved sideways to the post of housemaid; I can recall being perplexed about this move at the time. Her place as my nursemaid being taken over by Betty Walker who was neat and efficient. One was subsequently referred to as Big Betty and the other as Little Betty.

The third member of the domestic staff, who worked "downstairs", in the basement, but who slept "upstairs", in the attic, was the cook. Her name was Jessie Banbury and she was a stepsister of Betty Walker. Jessie had spent some time as a cook in the officers' mess of the Grenadier Guards somewhere in London and liked to tell me all about them when she sat with me sometimes to relieve Little Betty of, what today we would refer to as, her "baby sitting" duties. Her favourite tune, which she taught me, was their Regimental march,
Some talk of Alexander and some of Hercules,
Of Hector and Isander and such great names as these,
Etc..

Betty Walker left after a relatively short time and was replaced by Lily Lamey who lived just up the street from us.

The River Mersey and the Manchester Ship Canal both passed in front of our house in Runcorn, less than a hundred yards away and in full view. They were separated from each other by a gantry wall. After Lily came to us I became more aware of the canal and the ships that passed up and down to Manchester. Apart from scores of smaller craft several large ocean-going vessels passed each day. Each passing vessel caused excitement to different small groups of people who assembled at the railings just outside the front of our house. These were the families and friends of sailors on board the passing vessels. Lily's father and her brother were seamen so that whenever they passed I was always taken out by Lily to wave at them with her.

Some of the ocean going ships accommodated in the canal were up to forty thousand tons and their passing was always quite a performance. They were skillfully guided by two tugs. The one at the stern was a paddle tug with a large paddle on each side which churned up milky foam as it described an arc, straining industriously, sometimes to port, sometimes to starboard keeping this huge floating mass safely within a relatively narrow channel. The tug at the bow seemed to be towing like a small pony willingly hauling a huge load.

* * *

In 1934 we came on holidays to Lissarda in August as usual. On this particular occasion however, Father went back to Runcorn by himself and left mother and me behind. Then one day he returned again and shortly after his arrival I was banished to the basement kitchen of Lissarda House and kept there very deliberately by Mary O'Brien the cook and housekeeper. Whatever this was all about I didn't know but I felt upset and somehow excluded. I needed to have things explained to me. Eventually, my father did come down and said to me, "The stork has just called and brought a baby sister for you to Mummy". "Is the stork still here?" I asked. "If you go quickly and quietly to the front door you might see him", he answered.

I went as fast as I could and did indeed see the stork clearly, moving away with an empty basket hanging from his beak. That sighting confirmed for me, beyond all doubt, that a new baby had arrived.

I was almost four years of age and I expect I must have been jealous of the spotlighting of the new arrival. I was deprived of the customary attention and behaved badly. Nurse Flynn who was looking after my mother had to speak strongly to me for being a general nuisance. That night I decided to get my revenge on the nurse by bringing all of our thirteen dogs into the house and turning them on her. My father had to intervene to rescue the nurse. He reinforced my banishment and said I would have to stay confined to the kitchen until he gave me permission to leave it.

**

My father had only one sister, Adeline, older than him, born in 1876 and whom we called Auntie Ad. She lived in Lissarda House which my father now owned and looked after it for him. She lived in Lissarda with the housekeeper, Mary O'Brien, who came into the service of the family in 1914. Lissarda house had been the home of the family since my grandfather, on being appointed as the local dispensary doctor in 1873, had come to live there as a tenant. Subsequently my father bought it out.

Our house in Runcorn was by this time, after the arrival of the new baby, considered too small for our family purposes, seeing that much of it was taken up with surgeries, a waiting room, dispensary etc. As a solution my father bought the house next door and by opening several connecting doors and by means of some other alterations he made the two houses seem like one spacious dwelling.

When the builders came in there was dust and noise everywhere. I enjoyed all the fuss and my father bought me a set of carpenter's tools, cut down to size like children's golf clubs, so that I could amuse myself by imitating what the tradesmen were doing. I had a mallet, chisels, planes etc. One of the carpenters in particular had been very kind to me and went to great trouble to show me how to use various tools. One incident, however, in which he involved me when I was little more than four years of age, stands out clearly in my memory.

The original house and the house next door had four stories and just at this time the carpenter in question was in the process of putting down floorboards on the top floor. One day, on coming downstairs to where I happened to be alone, he asked me, "Would you like to come upstairs with me and help me finish nailing down the floor boards?"

Of course I was flattered at getting such recognition for my carpentry skills and went along with him willingly. When we got to the room where he was doing the work he involved me in personal sexual familiarity with him. Then suddenly, he lost all interest in me and moved quickly out of the room. From then on he avoided me. His sudden rejection and change of attitude I couldn't understand. I couldn't figure out why he didn't like me anymore. I wasn't shocked or frightened, I was just confused. There is resilience in innocence, to a large extent, an inbuilt coping mechanism.

I began school in January 1936. In spite of Canon Law and even though there was a Catholic primary school available in the parish, I was sent to a private kindergarten owned and run by two sisters, Misses Gwen and Jessica Nowell. They were Methodists. They were interesting, patient and kind. They had small classes which facilitated them in exercising a degree of dedication which was highlighted for me subsequently by my experience in the next school I went to where one teacher had over fifty pupils in his charge. The local parish priest used to call weekly to our home to instruct me in the catechism and to prepare me for first communion.

The school run by the Misses Nowell was, as well as being small, select and mixed. I started there in the middle of a school year, so that by the time I arrived the others in the class had already got to know each other. My first few days at school were incident free but on my fourth or fifth day there I suffered what I remember as my second rejection in life. During an interval in the course of the morning, the daughter of another doctor in the town produced a bag of sweets and started to go around the class offering them to the other children. When she got as far as me she withdrew the bag just as I was about to take one and then passed on to the next child. This incident worried me for a long time. It would have been, in the general estimation of people, a trivial happening, compared, say, to the child sexual abuse mentioned above, but it hurt me much more at the time and upset me for longer.

My First Holy Communion was a dull occasion. There was no pomp or ceremony at all. I just went to the altar rails and received at the seven o'clock Mass in the local church on an ordinary weekday morning. Apart from one or two regular worshippers and my parents who accompanied me, the dimly lit church was empty. Whether this arrangement was on my father's instructions or whether the austerity of the occasion was a token of disapproval, on the part of the parish priest, of my attending a non-Catholic school, I do not know. Was it analogous to the vestry or sacristy weddings of those of mixed cult or religion?

Bedtime for children under ten in middle class England was very early compared to the bedtime of Irish children generally or of English working class children. I recall that when my sister was small she was expected to go down to sleep after we had been given our baths at about seven o'clock, but I, being three and a half years older, was allowed to read in bed or play with toys up to nine or ten o'clock.

Night surgery began at seven o'clock but my father would call up to see me regularly at least once between the beginning of surgery and nine o'clock. On Thursday nights he used to appear in my room with the comics which had just arrived from the local paper shop and which he had on order for me every week, the Dandy, the Beano, Rainbow, Sunbeam, Playbox, Comic Cuts, and the Knockout. I avidly followed the fortunes of Desperate Dan, Pansy Potter, Lord Marmaduke, Billy Bunter and His Pals etc.

Owing to night surgery our house in Runcorn was alive with comings and goings up to about nine o'clock. I suspect that general practitioners' surgeries were busier then than they are now, due to the fact that in those days people went with minor medical and surgical emergencies to the local doctor rather than to the hospital.

Our house was doubly busy, my father's assistant's surgery also being on the premises. The assistant lived with us as one of the family. The assistants were always unmarried and had a curate/parish priest relationship with my father. Whenever he talked to them or about them he gave them their formal titles.

High tea, called supper, was served formally when surgery was over and guests were often present. Mr.Rutter, my father's bill collector and book keeper came on Thursday nights. His main job was to send bills to and collect fees from the private patients the "on the spot" payment system was not, at that time in vogue. Mr.O'Grady came another night with the money he had collected in rents from my father's tenants; over the years my father had acquired quite a large amount of property. Frequently, there were friends of the family at this meal, local friends or visitors over from Ireland. I was never allowed to attend supper although I did not miss much from a vantage point that I had established at the top of the stairs. Selected visitors were brought up to see me.

***

Auntie Mame, another of my mother's older sisters lived in Liverpool which was twelve miles from Runcorn. Her husband was Uncle Tom O'Callaghan. They had two children, Peggy, just a year younger than me and Denis who was about the same age as my sister Rosemary. Living with them also was Michael, son of Uncle Tom by a previous marriage. Michael and Peggy frequently came to Runcorn to stay with us. These visits I really enjoyed. Michael was about four years older than me and was going to school in St. Francis Xavier's College, run by the Jesuits in Liverpool. He was very clever with Meccano, which was popular then as Lego is today. He engineered the most complex structures. At that stage he was the older brother I never had.

Our house was devoid of any religious emblems or insignia. The ethos might be described as non-religious. On the other hand, Auntie Marne's house in Liverpool, where we used to visit on most Saturdays, used to seem to me so different, with holy pictures on the walls and other pious objects in evidence. Their neighbours had Irish Catholic names and the people in the locality converged regularly at the local Parish Church, St. Hugh's, which was a substantial structure compared to the wooden church in Protestant Runcorn. Michael was an altar boy. I used to enjoy going to Benediction on Saturday evenings to see him perform.

* * *

At the age of six I had my first all-consuming love affair. It was decided that an important resource for a gentleman was to be able to ride well. My mother accompanied me every week to a Riding School in Frodsham run by Miss Gwen Greenway, probably in her late twenties, where we both took lessons. Owing to other pressures and commitments my mother dropped out after a time which meant I had Miss Greenway all to myself for a couple of hours every week. After some schooling in her training paddock she would take me for long hacks along country roads and let me fanaticize and talk and talk. How I loved her.

I believe that these "crushes" have a function. The child is totally open to being influenced by someone of his or her choice, Miss Greenway responded so positively; by her total acceptance of me she gave me the confidence to love. Yet, on one particular occasion I have been devastated by someone who told me it wasn't right that little boys should be loved and hugged like little girls. Alas, little boys, thus disillusioned by having their love overtures unanswered, seek refuge and comfort in aggressiveness.

***

In the nineteen thirties talking films were really coming into their own and they were a coveted pastime for all young people. Even as a very young child I used to hear them being talked about constantly. The great stars like Clarke Gable, Louisa Rainer, Deanna Durban and Spencer Tracey were shining and picture houses were rising up like temples. "Going to the pictures" was becoming synonymous with "going out for the night". Over all available billboards were posters advertising current and coming films. Nearly all the small talk, as I remember hearing it, between young adults, was about films or film stars.

The first film I saw in a cinema was "Who's Afraid Of The Big Bad Wolf" .The Walt Disney cartoon, "Snow White and the Seven Dwarfs" made an impact on the child population in the late 1930's. It led to a plethora of dwarfs fashioned from all kinds of materials going on sale in all kinds of shops. In boys' schools, nicknames such as Happy, Grumpy, Dopey, Doc, Sleepy, Sneezy and Bashful, were likely to be given to boys who demonstrated any of the traits implied by these titles.

On Saturday afternoons I used to go regularly to the matinee performances for children which included a variety of shorter films and at the end a serial, to make sure you returned the following week.

One cigarette company included colour pictures of film stars in the packets it sold. One picture in a packet of ten and two in a packet of twenty.

At that time in the late 1930's the hallmark of healthy desirable adulthood was to smoke cigarettes. "Men" smoked and the assumption was that every boy would smoke when he reached eighteen or thereabouts when he could pay for them himself. He was discouraged from smoking too soon not for any health consideration but because of the cost. It was thought acceptable to dissuade children from smoking by telling them that it would inhibit their growth. My father was a dedicated smoker both of pipe and cigarettes and often gave me a cigarette to smoke while still only a child of no more than 7 or 8. Maybe it was a form of aversion therapy?

**

In a sense we had an ivory tower existence where we lived, in the middle of a working class housing area in Runcorn. I was never allowed out officially to play with the children on the street, whom I could see from my playroom window by day and from my bedroom window by night, enjoying themselves with the various games in due season. There was a time for hop scotch and a time for skipping, a time for whips and tops and a time for roller skating.

Occasionally, I did manage to "scale the wall" and have a really enjoyable break until spotted by "sentries" and hauled back ignominiously to the "tower". On one occasion that I remember clearly I made it to a local chip shop. Hungry after playing on the street, I was tucking into a two penny bag of chips when my nursemaid, assisted by the housemaid in white aproned uniform, literally lifted me from behind the scrubbed top table where I was sitting and dragged me home by the scruff of the neck. I felt so humiliated before my "street" friends.

On May 12th. 1937 the coronation of George VI took place. My "street" friends told me that they were having a party of "pop" (minerals) and cake in the local Church of England Parish School. However, I had been invited to the birthday party of one of my father's colleagues' children, but I never arrived there. After a while the alarm was raised and I was unearthed eventually from a group of "common" children.

Though recaptured I held on to my trophy, a coronation mug which I still have.

Since 1931 my father had decided to record every move of his children as they grew up. He first of all owned a nine point five Pathé movie camera and projector and a little later an eight millimeter Kodak camera and projector. As a result of this interest and industry on my father's part, we now have a comprehensive record of the childhood not only of my sister and myself but also of the childhood of some our cousins and close family friends. This runs to between two and three thousand feet of film.

One of the evils of war is the splitting up of families. This was soon to happen to us. It was 1938 and the storm clouds were gathering.

Chapter 2
SECOND WORLD WAR

At the age of seven while still living in Runcorn I was aware of impending change. The words "Hitler", "Chamberlain", "Munich" seemed to proclaim doom and I suspected that soon there may be war.

My concept of war was real enough. I can recall, amongst my earliest memories, hearing the adults of the household talking about the Spanish Civil War and the Abyssinian War. I can recall photographs of tanks on the front page of the Daily Mail which was brought up to my father's bedroom every morning by the housemaid with his cup of tea and toast. World War 1 or the Great War as it was then called was within living memory of anyone over thirty years of age. As a child I was told many stories of people who were gassed or maimed. Households that I remember visiting as a child had photos of husbands, fathers or sons who never returned. Armistice Day, November 11th. was solemnly enacted by keeping a minutes silence at 11 a.m. in remembrance of those killed in action. The cenotaph in Runcorn became a centre of worship on Poppy Day.

The first song taught to me by Betty Walker, my nursemaid, began:

"Will you come to Abyssinia will you come,
Bring your own ammunition and a gun.
Mussolini will be there shooting peanuts in the air
Will you come to Abyssinia will you come?"

(Sung to the air of "Roll along covered wagon")

The family came on holidays to Ireland in August, 1939 as usual. We were met at the station by Auntie Ad and Mary O'Brien, her ladies' companion, who came for us in the hackney car operated by Tim Walsh of Crookstown. To this day I am hard put to restrain tears of childlike wonder whenever I have the good fortune to witness the train emerging triumphantly from the tunnel on to the expectant platform at Glanmire station in Cork. A sacrament of final arrival home.

For the eighteen mile journey from Cork to Lissarda conversation was not spontaneous. I doubt if Auntie Ad had come to terms with having, in my mother, a sister in law who according to age would more comfortably have been her niece.

Auntie Ad, assuming the role of hostess, wanted to know what it was like over there in England in those days of Munich crisis. "What about Mr.Chamberlain, Jerome?" she said to my father. "Oh! I suppose he's alright, why? "he replied. Thus ended that conversation.

Although my father could cope well with problems he could not discuss them with ease. The abruptness of this reply signified his preoccupation which he showed by being not just silent but taciturn.

Other words added to my vocabulary during that August were "Polish Corridor" and "Danzig".

The cloud burst on Sunday, September 3rd. The family, Auntie Ad and Mary were gathered around the wireless in the breakfast room in Lissarda House on that midday when we heard Mr. Chamberlain's voice announce that England had declared war on Germany.

I was told to go to the village to tell the Warrensgrove people, Uncle Mick and Auntie Nellie, about the war, as they passed in the horse and trap, on their way home from second mass in Killarney.

Auntie Nellie, my mother's eldest sister to whom I have referred already and Uncle Mick, her husband, were employed by my father to caretake a farm he owned called Warrensgrove.

They were not as impressed as I thought they should have been. "When are ye going back to England, a ghile (an Irish word for "beloved" which she liked to use)?" was Auntie Nellie's reaction.

"Daddy has booked us for next Thursday" I said. "Sure they'll stop here altogether now", interrupted Uncle Mick, "What business have they going back to that place?"

Just then the real bonus of the war struck me. Life might now become one prolonged holiday, I thought to myself.

When I got back to the house I could see from my father's demeanour that he was working out a plan of action. Before tea that evening he told us that he was intent on getting back to England as soon as possible; if it could be arranged, even on the very next day. My mother, my sister and I were to stay on in Lissarda for the time being.

The next day, my mother accompanied by Rosemary, my sister, aged four and by me, drove my father to the station to catch the Mail Train to Kingstown, as he called it. In those days one was spared the inconvenience of changing trains and of having to go by bus or taxi from Kingsbridge to Westland Row as this particular train, (called the boat train) made use of the tunnel under Phoenix Park and the Dublin stop was in Westland Row.

My father cried bitterly as he kissed us good bye.

In that year the Warrensgrove threshing of corn took place on September 6th which I would have just missed only for the war.

I had expected that the main topic of conversation amongst the men involved in the threshing would be the war which had just broken out and which was to the forefront of my mind, but I remember distinctly being more and more surprised as the day of the threshing wore on that nobody, at least within my hearing, even mentioned it. Even Sean Arthur O'Leary who was "minding the bags", i.e. bagging the grain as it flowed from the threshing machine, a thoughtful and articulate man in political affairs, chose to say nothing.

Since then I have often tried to figure out a reason for this silence. It has occurred to me that the younger men, may have thought of it as in the distance and therefore irrelevant. Indeed they may not yet, at that stage, have heard about it at all as radios, then called wirelesses, were few and far between. For the older men who knew about it, perhaps it unearthed painful recollections of the First World War, still fresh in the memories even of middle aged men at that time. It may have stirred up memories of the War of Independence or certain misgivings about the tragic Civil War. After all, it was the fourth war within twenty five years that they were to experience and it would take more than the three days from September 3rd to the 6th to come to terms with that. A question for some would have been: "Whose side should I be on?"

From now on as a resident of Ireland the direction of my life was to be considerably changed. I would no longer be the much honoured child. I had been in the role of a very young eldest son of a local doctor who begot me in his early fifty to late fifties and openly treasured me as a child of old age. He showed me off to his patients. To my great embarrassment he often sent a message from the surgery to the house, which was just beside it, to the effect that I was to be brought and exhibited to such and such a patient. Yet this was the genuine external manifestation of a glowing warm love that I felt from him. He spared nothing of himself or his possessions on me or on Rosemary.

Delight in the prospect of staying on in Lissarda indefinitely was considerably diluted by the absence of my father. Mother gave us her all but she would be the first to admit that Rosemary and I were in a sense deprived.

At first my father wrote to mother every single day, not a token letter but a real one and during all the years of separation he never wrote less than twice a week, always signing himself "Daddy Dunkers Jerome". As well as that, so to speak, communal letter to my mother, he also wrote very frequently to Rosemary and me usually enclosing ridiculously large sums of money. He was an over-abundant provider.

My mother, then aged thirty one had to establish herself and her children sharing house with a sister in law over thirty years her senior and who was firmly buttressed by her maid/companion, Mary O'Brien, (who had been with the Murphy family in Lissarda House since before the First War)

Auntie Ad was in the role of retired spinster sister of my father. She had no means of support of her own so my father kept her in return for her caretaking of Lissarda House which in later years was his property. She had considerable experience of certain aspects of life. After some years as a pupil with the Ursuline Sisters in St.Angela's school in Cork she was sent to boarding school in England, to the Ursuline Convent, Upton, Essex.

In 1900, Auntie Ad went to Warsaw, where she stayed for many years as governess to a French family. Hence, she possessed a perfect speaking knowledge of the French language. I never heard her utter a word of Polish though she does seem to have had some Russian. She was quite an accomplished pianist and kept her piano, almost literally in cotton wool, clad with a fitted cloth cover like a loose cover of the kind found covering an armchair or settee. It was like a condition of Victorian propriety.

Mother couldn't have been prepared to cope with these demands made of her as a grass widow, young mother and mistress of Lissarda House under these circumstances. The house she left in Runcorn included the surgery. We lived "over the shop" and a system of housekeeping was well established and working. Supported by my father, her authority was unchallenged.

Mother had the confidence of youth on her side as well as some of its brashness. She had male admirers from whom she protected herself by proclaiming easily what seemed like a filial as much as a spousal regard for my father to whom or about whom she always spoke as "Daddy".

The occasional difference of opinion surfaced between Auntie Ad and mother.I witnessed a few such encounters which upset me, but eventually apologies were exchanged. Looking at things from Auntie Ad's point of view, to have to surrender the role as mistress of the house to a "blow in" sister- in-law young enough to be her daughter was not easy.

Soon after my father returned to England mother set about finding schools for us. It was not that easy as the local primary schools in the parish or in Macroom, the nearest town, taught most of the subjects through the medium of Irish. The nearest suitable school for me, where Irish had only the status of another subject, was Presentation College, Cork. Ideally I would have been sent to Christian College, Cork, where my father went to school, but it was at the other side of the city and would have been awkward for me to get at. Anyway, my father's brother, Edward had been a pupil in Pres, and was remembered by Dr. Connolly, the grand old man of Pres., who interviewed me.

While a great deal of trouble was gone to, to get schools considered adequate for me, Rosemary was quickly catered for in local schools, first of all in Macroom and then in the local National school in Kilmurray.

It was eighteen miles from Lissarda to Cork which meant a journey of thirty six miles for me per day by bus. The cost of a weekly ticket was under seven shillings.

In Pres. I was put into third class under the care of Brother Gregory who taught both second and third class in the same room. Both classes were well taught and his organisation was such that you were never aware that he could only give a class half his time and attention. Still, it fell short of the standards I had been used to in Miss Nowell's.

Mother was totally convinced of the need for a good education and with the help of Mary O'Brien launched me every morning on my quarter to eight bus which arrived at the door of Pres. just under an hour later.

Mother and Mary, without fail, on every school day, together or singly walked the two hundred yards with me to the bus stop. The return bus reached Lissarda every evening at twenty past four.

A short break for play was allowed after dinner and then for as long as necessary I was supervised while I did my homework, both written and oral. There was a break for Lord Haw Haw who was listened to every night he was on. The only wireless programme in our house with a higher popularity rating than Lord Haw Haw was Joe Linnane's Sunday Question Time at twenty past eight.

We didn't listen to Lord Haw Haw out of idle curiosity, but to get some information about the extent and intensity of German air raids in Britain. Merseyside, where Runcorn was situated, took a bad hammering from the air with large numbers of civilian casualties and, at times, when all channels of communication were blocked, we feared the worst about my father.

Coping with a new school in a different culture, travelling a long way every day and worry about my father's wellbeing were factors which seemed to bring about in me a state of moral scrupulosity and anxiety. There was one such dreadful anxiety which I suffered each day I went to school. I feared that on coming home in the evening I would find that mother had died. The first thing I looked for when I came in the gate from school was some sign of the death of my mother, particularly a blind pulled down or curtains drawn. Almost sixty years later my mother is still alive thank God.

On going to Pres. at first, my English accent was an object of amusement and the extraordinary anti British sentiments uttered by some were offensive to my political axioms. Still there were some crypto British fellow travellers who came to me, like Nicodemus who came by night to the Lord, and offered their notional support at least.

To my great joy father came to join us in Ireland for Christmas 1939. He was full of interesting information about the black-out and other matters related to the war. He brought us some gramophone records with war songs such as "We're Going To Hang Out The Washing On The Siegfried Line" and "Run Rabbit Run". He told us that there was no question of the family returning to England until the war was over and won.

When we were promoted to fourth class in school we were taught by Brother Laurence who was a sturdy man with very forthright and definite anti-British views. He taught us "Fontenoy" with great energy. Subsequently, when I met him as a teacher colleague in the West Indies he explained that many years previously he and some others of his young confreres regarded Presentation Brothers College, Cork as a remnant of the British Empire and when he got the opportunity he felt an obligation to expose the pupils there to some wholesome republican values.

After three years of travelling to and from school in Cork every day, which was proving very demanding on my health, my parents decided that I should go to boarding school. Anyway boarding schools were fashionable.

Before we left England my father had considered sending me to Stonyhurst, run by the Jesuits, or Ampleforth run by the Benedictines, but then due to the friendship of a certain Father Haughton he tentatively settled to send me to a boarding school run by the Rosminian Fathers, Radcliffe College near Leicester.

Now in Ireland, my parents gave serious consideration to Mungret College in Limerick run by the Jesuits but since closed down and to Clongowes Wood. However, Auntie Ad had heard a friend of hers, Mrs. Honohan, speak very highly of this new school run by the Benedictines, Glenstal Priory School in Murroe, County Limerick.

Glenstal was reputed to be the wartime compromise for those who otherwise would have gone to Ampleforth or Downside. The fees were high, forty five pounds per term. This factor was bound to make it socially exclusive. The fees of the average diocesan seminary were about the same per annum as Glenstal was per term.

Auntie Ad was delegated to write to Glenstal. Even at the time her letter which was read out to me sounded a bit overplayed in relation to my father and his academic background together with his father's background as a graduate in Medicine from Edinburgh.

A reply came very promptly from Dom Matthew Dillon, the Headmaster since it was by this time mid-August and school was due to start on September 16th. He said it was doubtful if he could accept me for that year. However, he agreed to interview me and my parents in the Windsor Hotel, Cork on an appointed day.

My father was not available so Auntie Ad took his place as chef de mission. We were ushered into a waiting room and very shortly an unusual looking man appeared, dressed in what seemed like second hand clerical attire with trousers too short, of low medium height, with a double upper lip, of ruddy complexion, with very thick spectacles and with hedgehog style grey hair. Smiling, he showered greetings on us, but on first hearing we understood little that he said. By oft repeating himself and with patient and deliberate articulation on his part we eventually got through the agenda.

There was now a very good chance he could fit me in and he promised to communicate the verdict by letter within a few days. The letter of acceptance came from Glenstal. Although the novelty of going away to boarding school appealed to me I was very sorry to leave Pres. where' I had made same great friends after I got over my earlier problems of accent and political allegiance.

By this time I had cultivated a good Cork accent, a nice blend of Montenotte and Macroom. Not without difficulty and hard work had I got rid of the English accent. The real breakthrough came when I managed to say "worrrld" with an Irish "r" sound instead of the English "woeeeld".

I had got to like the Irish language and was quite good at it even though I started it later than usual. For this I owe thanks to the patient tutelage of Brother Nessan who began every day's class in that "remnant of British Imperialism" with half an hour's Irish conversation or "modh direach".

The irony of my conversion to a Cork accent was that the English accent which I felt to be a handicap in Pres. would have been a great asset to have had in Glenstal. In my new school I was to be jeered at for having a Cork accent. I felt annoyed with myself for having been so short-sighted.

With that letter of acceptance from Glenstal came instructions about clothes needed which included a grey suit for Sunday wear. As clothes were rationed at the time my mother could not afford the coupons for another suit for me having got one the previous May for my Confirmation in Pres. One suit would absorb something like forty five coupons which left very few with which to get footwear, shirts, socks etc.. My confirmation suit would have to do for Sunday wear in Glenstal.

Somewhat as in the case of my accent I lost out on the suit. The stipulation in Pres. was that the Confirmation suit should be navy blue serge but my mother had a social block against buying navy blue serge suits. The compromise was to buy me a dark blue flannel suit which was soft in appearance and texture. I was prepared to feel awful about it but on the day I was encouraged when such distinguished class mates as Anthony McHale, James O'Brien and Bernard Buckley turned up in grey.

On my first Sunday in Glenstal I caused a certain wonder when I appeared all alone in this dark blue suit. I felt miserably self-conscious. I was promptly given, the nick name "Policeman Joe". The name partially stuck until I had bestowed on me the nickname "Belly", on account of the fact that I was fat.

Being teased was a constant cross during my earlier time in Glenstal. It was really a form of bullying. On two occasions that I can remember a lay teacher and a monk were involved. The lay teacher called me "Dumbo", a Walt Disney elephant character, on account of my big ears and in somewhat similar vein I was referred to by a monk.

I was almost heartbroken with homesickness during that first term in Glenstal yet I was interested in the studies. Latin was the important new subject and I loved it. Mr.McGraw worked us hard but taught us a lot. There were only four of us in the class. Noel Magner, Oswald Barton, Finbarr Dowdall were my comrades. I have maintained to this day a close friendship with Oswald and Finbarr; I hadn't met Noel for over forty years until the funeral of Father Athanasius in Glenstal, when he greeted me, with disproportionate surprise, as follows: "How on earth are you, Denstone, I heard you were dead?"

Letters from mother and father were injections of joy and consolation, oases in a wilderness. Then came mother's letter saying she was coming to see me at the mid-term break.

Private cars were off the road and taxis were hard to get. The only form of private transport available was by bicycle or by horse drawn vehicle or on horseback.

I was allowed to cycle to Boher station, a distance of about four miles, after lunch on one Friday to meet mother, who brought her bicycle with her, off the early afternoon train from Cork. What a reunion! I do not think that either of us had ever before expressed our feelings for each other so strongly and so openly. We cycled back to Glenstal. She was greeted with great courtesy by Father Matthew.

I showed her around and she took particular interest in where I studied, ate and slept. It was her first visit to Glenstal. The Matron, Nurse Maureen Dwyer, kindly served tea in the College parlour and at about half past five mother and I set out by bicycle on the eleven mile journey to Limerick where we arrived shortly after seven o'clock.

Weekends with parents were permitted at certain times during the year. Mother had already booked into Cruise's Hotel. We were both very hungry and ordered a mixed grill with chips.

When we were finished the waitress chatted with us and when she heard we had just come from Glenstal she said, "And I thought ye were Protestants", "What gave you that idea?" re-joined my mother, slightly flattered. "When ye ordered meat on Friday I said to myself that ye couldn't be Catholics", was the reasoned reply. Mother confusedly began to explain that due to our excitement we had forgotten what day of the week it was; then the waitress was called away and we never found out whether her last statement to us was a covert rebuke or an innocent comment.

Then mother filled me in on all that had happened at home since I left six weeks previously.

Late the next morning we went to the station in Limerick city and caught the train to Limerick Junction. I got off at Boher. A desperately sad separation. I can still recall clearly mother leaning out of the carriage window as she kept waving while the train was fading into the distance. Although I was heartbroken that huge injection of love gave me courage.

Summer 1943 we were given a midterm break at home. Auntie Ad had taken very ill during the previous year, 1942, and died on June 6th.1943, while I was at home. Her body, after being prepared by Mrs. Harrington and some other local women who were skilled in these matters, was laid out in my mother's bedroom since it was the most suitable room for coping with the number who were expected to participate in the wake.

The wake is an impressive and consoling event. It normalises death. It copes with the "sting" referred to by St. Paul. Prayers were said by those present from time to time all through the night. Yarns were told; anecdotes about the deceased were related. The bereaved were supported by the inbuilt therapy coming from the sharing of emotion with the neighbourhood group. A meal was offered to all who came, about twenty in number. Alcoholic drink was freely available yet monitored by Timmy Murphy, our neighbour and consumed by those present in commendable moderation. Although there was a whiskey shortage during the Emergency, May Fitz, our local publican and friend, generously came to the rescue.

The idea of "wake" fits in with the theology of death wherein "life is changed, not taken away". It is an acceptance of the continued presence of the dead person in our midst as a more valued than ever member of the community, in spite of appearances. The common band is that we all await the Resurrection, albeit at different stages.

We phoned my father the morning after her death. He was very shocked, largely because she was his only sister and now he was the only member of his own family still alive. He did not come over to the funeral. That was not his style. Besides, there was in place a travel ban between Ireland and the United Kingdom which would have made even compassionate travel difficult.

Auntie Ad left absolutely no money, whatever money she accumulated from time to time from my father's allowance to her, which was little enough; she spent on her favourite hobby which was backing horses. She was an authority on form, but her luck didn't seem to match her knowledge.

She went to Cork every first Thursday to confession in St.Francis' Church in Broad Lane, now replaced by the Byzantine Basilica, then to Thompson's in Prince's Street for lunch and to the bookmakers. On her way to the Bus Office, then in the Grand Parade which at this stage was cluttered up with air raid shelters, she called to Miss Keohane in Oliver Plunkett Street for a bottle of Jenning's Cream Soda. She found difficulty in not calling Oliver Plunkett Street by its old name, Old George's Street. Likewise she had difficulty in calling King Street by its new name, McCurtain Street.

Before finally boarding the bus for the journey home she sought out Mr. Sweetman, a porter at the bus office, about whose wife and family she always enquired. She was a sincere and consistent Lady Bountiful. She was also on personal terms with Dan Murphy, Con Twomey and Charlie Leonard, three of the conductors on the Cork - Macroom bus route.

On the following day, the first Friday, she came with me on the first bus during the time that I was going to Pres., and went to Mass in Broad Lane followed by breakfast in Thompson's in Prince's Street. For some reason she regarded Thompsons in Patrick Street, their premises are now occupied by Hayes, Conyngham & Robinson Ltd., as inauthentic. After that she visited her carefully chosen shops. For Auntie Ad, shopping was an unchanging ritual. The same goods in the same quantities were always bought in the same shops from the same assistants in those shops. The same words of greeting were announced and answered. Blair's for medicines and toiletries, Russell's for books, Woodford Bourne's for groceries, just to mention the few that come to mind easily. I can remember as a child shopping with her and the reward for her faithfulness to them was the great fuss which was made of her by the various shop owners or assistants.

* * *

In October, 1944 I was taken from Glenstal to St.John's Hospital in Limerick with acute appendicitis. I was put into St.Gerard's ward. In those pre-Pentathol days, getting an anaesthetic was a gruelling and stifling procedure. The rag and bottle method was still in vogue whereby Ether was dripped by any doctor available onto gamagee tissue stretched over a small wire tea strainer-like contraption placed over the nose of the patient. Recovery rooms were not yet common, so that the patient woke up in the presence of his/her fellow patients in the ward, protected from them only by a flimsy screen. It was the common belief that ward mates thereafter knew all the secrets of your life which were said to be revealed in a pre-waking up delirium.

After the operation I discovered that my fellow patients were great company. Just beside me was Pak Sheehan, a butcher from Foynes. He was a man of extraordinary humour. One story or joke of his was better than the next. All this was tantalising for someone with several stitches and clips in place. The laughter hurt even more than coughing would have done.

There was a Mr.Ryan a well-known hotelier from Cashel and a Brother Forde, a Redemptorist student. Brother Forde was full of enthusiasm about "The Robe" which had just been published and which he was reading. There were very few visitors, since private cars were off the road and public transport provided little more than a skeleton service. This had a good side, as we formed our own community with fellow patients as well as with the nursing staff who in those days, as far as I can remember were all religious.

Sugar was very scarce and was not supplied, so to speak, as a condiment. I had brought none in as I came from school in a hurry with an acute condition. Mr. Sheehan offered me a share in his sugar for my porridge but sooner than admit that not having sugar was other than a deliberate decision on my part, I refused.   To this day I have not gone back to taking sugar on my porridge.

About mid-morning every day a young sister came to the ward to say the rosary with the patients. Her name, Sister Domitilla, was so unusual that I could not forget it and, small world that it is, I later married her first cousin.

In early November my mother hired a car from Timmy Kelleher, in Macroom, who did her the honour of driving it himself, and came to collect me from hospital in Limerick and take me home to convalesce. I had been three weeks to the day in St. John's. At the time this was the normal stay for an appendectomy.

In June 1945 the war in Europe ended. My father proposed that the family would go over to spend the summer in Runcorn, My mother and Rosemary went but I preferred to stay with horses, mowing machines and reapers and binders.

The startling event of those holidays was the dropping of the atomic bombs on Hiroshima and Nagasaki. My first reaction on seeing the headline on the Cork Examiner was to say to myself, "How can that be?" Mr. Mulvihill, a teacher whom we regarded as omniscient, had always said it couldn't be done. "The atom is the ultimate and indivisible particle of matter."

***

Mr. Mulvihill was a gifted man who had an immense breadth of knowledge. Quite literally, he could teach Greek or Applied Mathematics at any level, His primary qualification was in Irish. His degree was in Celtic Studies, He gave classes on two afternoons a week in motor mechanics. He covered the theory and then had us all dismantling and re assembling two demonstration cars that he managed to obtain. One of the cars was a Belgian model, a "Metallurgique" donated by Bertie Foy's mother.

He established a Cumann Gaolach in the school, organised debates and Irish musical evenings at which he played the piano accordion. Several years he arranged outings to the Munster Championship hurling games in Thurles. He drove us himself in the school van which ran on a fuel manufactured by two containers, called Gas Producers, attached to the bodywork of the van, wherein gas was "miraculously" extracted from slowly burning solid fuel and then used instead of petrol which was almost unavailable.

Over twenty years after these events, as a Dominican, I used to visit the Morning Star Hostel, a night shelter for men who, as a result of alcohol abuse or for some other unfortunate reason needed to be provided with a minimum of food and shelter. While pouring the tea one evening I was upset and in a sense scandalised to see, of all people, Mr. Mulvihill waiting in line for his supper. Immediately I approached him and he could call me by name. He was down and out and had fallen on very bad times. After the supper we talked about Glenstal and he told me quite openly about how he had come to this. He was suffering a great deal.

I had been asked to chair a discussion group that night which had been organised for the men. It turned largely into a question time about God's existence and the creation and destiny of the world. Mr.Mulvihill was in the group and participated fully. He was solicitous for me and by his interventions made sure that "his boy" acquitted himself well.

I kept up intermittent contact with him after that. Not so many years ago I attended his funeral Mass in St.Peter's Church in Little Bray. Now he rests.

Chapter 3
LATER GLENSTAL

Confidence in my own intellectual ability had been considerably undermined by what I felt was thoughtless treatment in the end of year examinations in 1945. During the last four of my seven years in Glenstal, from 1945 to 1949 there was little motivation for me to study. I was largely distracted by matters of conscience. I could pick up enough in class without really trying. Ultimately it was enough to get through the only public examination I had to do, the Leaving Certificate. The Intermediate Certificate was not done there. It was thought, apparently, that the doing of the Intermediate Certificate course would limit the scope of our education. The ultimate aim of the educators was to produce the Christian gentleman but the proximate objectives towards achieving that end were hardly understood and the teaching was, in great part haphazard.

Thought and talk about sport, rugby and athletics in particular, became the dominating factor in my life at school. I had derived, implicitly, a theology of work whereby I saw prayer as the means to be applied for magically achieving all ends. I had a notion that lengthy and devout prayer was a valid replacement for genuine study effort. The recitation of the Thirty Days' prayer was an integral part of exam preparation and, later, with this was combined a promise to 'do' Lough Derg.

A factor in my unease was the fear that I might have a vocation to the religious and priestly life. Having priests and nuns in the family was a source of satisfaction to most families in those days and to some extent was understood as a sign of predestination to a benign hereafter. I can recall feeling that my family were sadly handicapped and overlooked by God because I had no aunts, uncles or first cousins in religious life. I felt I had the capacity and duty to rectify that state of affairs. Things that were said to me and which I heard were said about me also moved me to want to prove that I was not the pampered poor little rich little boy that some seemed to think I was.

Spiritual directors whom I approached to discuss my 'vocation' problem were so disposed that, without hearing me out, they insisted that beyond all doubt I had a vocation which I should try out. Subsequent frustration at not being taken quite seriously alienated me even more from study and I plunged even more deeply into a preoccupation with sport, prayer, masturbation and subsequent guilt which at times involved daily confession.

***

We had quite good rugby teams in Glenstal in those days in spite of the relatively small number of boys in the school. We won the Limerick under 17 cup in 1947 and that same team went on to defeat Presentation College, Cork, at the time the 'All-Blacks' of Munster Schools rugby, in the Bowen Shield the following year.

I used to play in the front row of the scrum. In a match against St. Munchin's College in 1947 I sustained a Collis' fracture of my left arm when the serum collapsed. I was taken to Barrington's hospital in considerable pain. I was put into bed, still wearing my football jersey. To remove it would have meant cutting off the sleeve and in those days of 'post-emergency' scarcity that was out of the question. I had to wait for many hours in great pain for a surgeon to become available.

In due course I was taken to the operating theatre, garbed as for a rugby game. No doctor was available to administer a general anesthetic so I was given a local which did not seem to be very effective. To reset my broken forearm a tug o' war took place, with the surgeon pulling my fingers and hand against the anchorage provided by the theatre sister who held on firmly to a towel slung around my arm just above the elbow. When the fracture had been reduced and the plaster of Paris sloshed on I was taken back to the ward where I spent a further two days before being discharged, still clad for the playing fields.

In the bed beside me in the ward was a man who was supposed to have the D.T.'s or 'delirium tremens' on account of drinking too much alcohol. He was detained against his will and asked for his clothes in order to escape from what he regarded as unlawful custody. When refused access to his clothes he staged a 'dirty protest' by urinating liberally into a mug and loudly swilling the contents over the floor of the ward. I was discharged before his problems were finally resolved.

***

About six of the senior boys were chosen to act as prefects. These prefects were given considerable power and authority. Their duties involved the supervision of all study in the school and the assisting of the Headmaster in maintaining discipline. In return they were given privileges amongst which were included: a common room of their own, permission to smoke during all free time in specified areas (in those days smoking was a respectable and acceptable social pastime: real men smoked!), free access to the local village of Murroe, freedom to go to Limerick city on free days and half days etc.

Every Saturday night, after lights-out for the rest of the school, there was a prefects' meeting with the Headmaster which normally lasted for about an hour and a half or two hours. It was a relaxed affair, tea and cakes were provided by the Matron. Progress was reported and problems were aired and shared. Father Matthew as Headmaster frequently used the expression,

"Are there any complaints, grievances or suggestions?"

It was assumed by the rest of the school that there was a Cabinet Room secrecy enjoined on the prefects, which assumption the prefects rather liked fostering.

Towards the end of the summer term new prefects were appointed, to form the nucleus of a prefect group for the following year. I had high hopes of being appointed and was very disappointed when passed over, yet I still hoped that I might be appointed in September.

* * *

One of the traditional extras provided in Glenstal in those days was horse riding for boys whose parents requested it for them. If and when you reached a certain standard you were allowed to ride to the hounds. During my last couple of years in the school I was among those who hunted with all the local packs, the Limerick Foxhounds, the Limerick Harriers and the Black and Tans.

During the Summer holidays of 1947, as well as taking part in the routine farm work, I got particularly involved in preparing my grey mare, Lissarda Lass, to compete in a couple of local gymkhanas, at Ballincollig and at Kilmichael. She was unplaced in the Novices' Jumping competition in Ballincollig where she was ridden by Gerry Buckley, the groom employed by our local curate, Father Coakley. With the benefit of that experience Lissarda Lass went on to win the Novice's competition in Kilmichael, on this occasion ridden by my friend and neighbour, Teddy Fitzgerald.

My appetite for gymkhana competition had been whetted during the previous Summer term in Glenstal when a very successful gymkhana was held, graced by the presence of one of the greatest of all Irish National Hunt jockeys, Tim Hyde, who acted as judge.

***

Shortly after the return to Glenstal for the new school year the election of the school captain was scheduled to take place. All the boys, except for the new arrivals, had at least one vote. Those who had just completed their first year in the school had one vote while those about to enter the Leaving class had five votes.

I would love to have been elected captain but had not been appointed prefect and precedent seemed to have it that the captain was drawn from the ranks of the prefects. It was 'not done' to seek election for oneself but friends usually looked after your interests. I was pleasantly surprised to hear my name being promoted and was subsequently thrilled when elected to the captaincy, yet I had the fear that my election might not have been valid since I was not a prefect. However, very shortly after the result of the election was announced Father Matthew sent for me and congratulated me. When I mentioned my difficulty about not being a prefect, he reassured me, saying that I had prefect status ex officio.

Many of my classmates worked very diligently during the year but some of us did very little. The most important requirement to get a place in most university faculties, including medicine, was to have parents who could pay the fees. The average first year fee was then about £30. A pass in the Leaving Certificate in certain prescribed subjects was sufficient for entry into most faculties of any of the constituent colleges of the National University of Ireland. An exception which comes to mind is Engineering, which required a certain mark in the Honours Mathematics paper.

A few pupils did the Trinity Entrance examination, which was regarded as a bit of a disgrace. Those doing it disappeared for a week in early July, as if for a secret confinement. We were not discouraged from believing that Trinity was the earthly habitation of the anti-Christ. Father Matthew is alleged occasionally to have asked the question of some of those leaving, about whose third level intentions he had some misgivings,

"Are you going to 'hell' or to National?"

At the end of that year, in summer 1948 our class sat the Leaving Certificate examination. I felt I hadn't done so well but I was confident enough since I had done a private deal with God. Instead of applying myself to study I had negotiated that I would pass my Leaving Cert. in return for making the pilgrimage to Lough Derg. Everything worked out according to plan.

***

Athletics were at a high point in Glenstal at this time and we were undoubtedly the outstanding school or college in North Munster and one of the leading athletics schools in Ireland. This tradition was initiated by the painstaking coaching and preparation of potential hurdlers by one of our teachers, Mr. O'Riordan, himself an old Cambridge Blue. Amongst many others he trained Douglas Dennehy, the onetime Irish record holder in the 120 yards hurdles. We had sprinters of the highest calibre in William O'Hea Cussen and Eddie Cotter and a middle distance runner, Ian Cotton, whose Munster half mile record lasted until comparatively recent times. If Ian had been given the kind of coaching now available it is pleasant to surmise what might have happened.

I was passionately interested in Athletics but had no talent whatsoever, whereupon Father Peter conferred upon me the honour of non-playing captaincy of the team. This I cherished above knighthood.

The first post war Olympic Games were scheduled to take place in London in August 1948. Eddie Cotter and I discussed the possibility of going over to see them. We both contacted our parents and got the necessary permission. We stayed in London with an uncle of Eddie's who was a parish priest and each day for two weeks we went to Wembley from the Elephant and Castle.

The outstanding athlete of those games was undoubtedly Fanny Blankers Koen of the Netherlands who won all the women's sprint events and the Long Jump. Amongst the men athletes the Jamaican middle distance runners Arthur Wint and Herb McKinley were impressive as well as the Czech long distance runner Emil Zatopec who did even better in the subsequent games in 1952 in Helsinki. Mel Patton, world 100 yards record holder (outside of the Olympic Games the Imperial system was widely preferred to the Metric) lived up to expectations in the men's 200 metres but was beaten into fifth place in the 100 metres after Harrison Dillard, Barney Ewell, his fellow Americans, La Beach of Panama and McCorquadale of Great Britain.

In the evening time on several occasions, Eddie's aunt, Dr. Nora Cotter took us to the great shows which were, in a sense, a celebration of the ending of World War II. These were, 'Annie Get your Gun', 'Oklahoma' and 'Bless the Bride' with stars such as Dolores Gray, Ethyl Merman and Howard Keel, of more recent 'Dallas'' fame.

***

An unchallengeable assumption, as it seemed to me, from as far back as I can remember, was that I would study medicine and follow in the footsteps of my father and of his father before him. I might have gone to University College, Cork in 1948 but for the fact that a regulation had just been introduced, applicable only to the Cork college of the National University, requiring that those entering the Pre-Medical year must have passed at least the combined Physics and Chemistry paper in the Leaving Certificate or its equivalent in the Matriculation examination. On this basis I was ineligible for a place on the Premedical course so I went back to Glenstal for another year to prepare to take those extra subjects in the Leaving in 1949. For a variety of reasons six of our class of sixteen came back to Glenstal to do an extra year.

A particularly notable feature of this year was that we had a new Headmaster, Father Columba. Father Matthew had departed to Dublin to establish a University hostel, Balnagowan.
Father Columba confirmed me in office as captain of the school for another year.

It was customary for the monks of Glenstal to have an extern lecturer in Philosophy or Theology for their clerics. For 1948/49 Father Cahill, a secular priest was appointed. He agreed to give classes also in the school to the Upper Sixth in two subject areas which he called, 'Philosophy of History' and 'English Literature'. He was an inspiring and dedicated teacher, an example to us of dedication to study. His classes/lectures were skillfully delivered to six spellbound pupils. His skill was in his being able to nudge along our interest by sharing with us his own thought processes.

'Hamlet' was on the Leaving Certificate course for that year, so Father Cahill, never a man to do things by halves, decided to produce and direct it himself as a school Christmas drama presentation. Every detail was attended to so far as time and financial constraints would permit.
He arranged for a fencing instructor, a certain Sergeant Brown, to come out from Limerick on a few occasions to prepare Laertes and Hamlet for their confrontation in the last act.

We had a couple of successful performances of Hamlet in Glenstal for the boys, parents and community. Tatler in the 'Irish Independent' gave it an encouraging review. The costuming was executed by the matron, Nurse Dwyer and Nurse Synott and the only flaw was the hose. Tights were hard to come by and would prove too expensive to buy or hire from stage costumiers - those were still the days of stockings and suspenders - so we had to settle for ladies' nylon stockings inefficiently held up by elastic garters. The stage management and electricals were attended to by Rex Murphy under the aegis of Father Malachy.

We were invited to give two 'away' performances, one to the Good Shepherd sisters and the 'penitents' in their care. This was an expression of appreciation to them for attending to our laundry. We were intrigued by all these women ranging from teenage to elderly bedecked in a kind of scullery maids' attire. The 'penitents' sat in tiers behind the nuns and gave us a great reception. They followed the plot with rapt attention and reacted as a model audience.

Our other 'away' performance was in Laurel Hill convent secondary school. We were graciously received by the nuns and 'Hamlet' was well received by the girls. After the show we were whisked away to a generous high tea but to our great disappointment we met none of the girls. They had been ushered away to prayer or study. Nevertheless, years later I married one of those girls, Maura Wall, who still remembers me clearly as the King.

At the end of the year, having gone again to Lough Derg, I passed Leaving Certificate Physics and Chemistry which gave me the necessary qualification to go to University College, Cork in order to study Medicine.

During the school Summer holidays of 1949, Niall Cullen, a school friend, and I set out for France and Belgium with Father John of Glenstal who was a Belgian although he had changed his domicile ('stability' in monastic terms) to Glenstal. We left the quayside in Cobh on the tender 'Killarney' and early in the morning we boarded one of the lesser known of the trans-Atlantic liners the 'Marine Flasher', which was anchored offshore. The few of us who boarded at Cobh were scrutinised, as we stepped from tender to liner, by those already on board who had come from New York and were headed for Southampton or Le Havre. After being shown to our cabin we moved around the ship in an effort to socialise. At first this didn't seem easy, as during the five days that they were already at sea close-knit groups had established themselves. However, one particular large and jovial American group opened up to us before long. They asked us to join them. Less than a week ago they had been strangers to each other but now they acted like friends. Most of them had a particular interest in common; they were ex-servicemen and one ex-servicewoman who had been in the United States Forces in Europe up to and after V.E. day and now four years later were returning for the first time to re-live the battles of long ago.

Over a thirty six hour period Niall and I sampled a group atmosphere different to the kind we had been accustomed to. There wasn't much conversational banter. They sought, as it were, to educate themselves about us as Irish youths who had just embarked at a place they insisted on calling 'Cob H'. They questioned us in detail, yet unobtrusively, about our parents, including our fathers' occupations and incomes, our schooling, our religious beliefs and practice.

They were loath to let us pay for anything, we were their guests. Both Niall and I had adequate French and Belgian money but had been incorrectly advised by our travel agents that sterling and French currency would be accepted on board the liner. As a consequence we had no dollars and they were the only legal tender. I tried to purchase some American currency from one of our new American friends who forthwith presented me with a ten dollar bill but would take nothing in exchange.

I protested that I wanted to do a business deal, whereupon she re-joined that she was not licensed to change money and would not do so in conscience but was free to give money and in this instance was particularly happy to do so. It was a commendable ethic and up to this unfamiliar to both Irish youths.

Father John who was frail and elderly kept to his cabin most of the time going for occasional short walks around the decks. We met him only at meals.

The national stereotype of the French person which somehow had been impressed on me was that of someone who was preoccupied with bodily functions, particularly with matters involving sex and excretion. This prejudice was apparently confirmed when in Le Havre as I stepped on French soil for the first time I saw notices on the walls, 'Defence d'afficher'. This I took to mean, 'not to be urinated against'. 'What a filthy crowd', I said to myself.

On arriving in Paris when I had the opportunity to consult my dictionary I was enlightened, yet perhaps a trifle disappointed as well. I discovered that what the notice in question was really saying was, 'post no bills'.

I was guilty of similar misjudgement when, on seeing the word 'Brasserie' written over many establishments, I took it that therein was practised some form of fetishism. But later my dictionary revealed that the word meant 'drinking-saloon' or 'pub', I was to discover that even the word 'brasserie' for which I had mistaken 'brasserie' did not, as a rule mean 'brassiere' in English but referred to the shoulder straps of a knap-sack or of a child's harness.

Father John left us in Paris and went to Maredsous Abbey in Belgium. Niall and I stayed in a good hotel quite near the Etoile and fulfilled every day a vigorous programme of sightseeing. On most days we attended Mass, either in Notre Dame or in the Madeleine. In fact, we served Mass on a few occasions. After serving Mass one morning in Notre Dame the priest engaged us in conversation and asked if we were clerical students. When we told him that we were about to start studying medicine he seemed quite baffled and said, 'People like you don't serve Mass in Paris'.

Our final sight-seeing sortie during our Paris sojourn was to the Palais de Versailles. What was of particular interest there was the Salle des Glaces where the armistice was signed in 1918. Our interest in that was enlivened by virtue of the fact that it was only four years since the cessation of hostilities of World War Two and scars and signs of war were still evident.

We went by train to Brussels where we had a couple of days of sightseeing before proceeding to the Abbaye de Maredsous which was the monastery from which Glenstal was founded and which was held always in high regard by Glenstal. We benefitted abundantly from the Benedictine tradition of hospitality and every step was taken to ensure that we got the most out of our visit to Belgium. One of the monks arranged for us to spend some time in Ghent as house guests of the family of the Burgemeester or Mayor. In that family there were two boys and a girl in or around our own age. They had the use of one of the family cars, both 1947 Ford V-8's, so we covered quite a lot of ground during a short stay.

The high point of our visit to Ghent was attending a Mystery Play as guests of the Burgemeester. This 'Play of the Mystic Lamb' dealt with a selection of Biblical themes. It was enacted in the square adjacent to the Gothic Cathedral. The beautiful stained glass windows of the Cathedral were illuminated by the lights inside the building and thus formed the backdrop to the stage. There were hundreds of people in the cast and scores of horses. The players mimed to pre-recorded speeches and dialogue which was clearly and easily heard by an attentive audience.

After Ghent we spent sometime in the monasteries of Mont Cezar and Saint Andre. We were impressed by the size and organisation of these Belgian monasteries that we visited. They seemed to have great authority and influence.

Chapter 4

UNIVERSITY YEARS

When I went to register for the Pre-Medical year in 1949 I found myself teaming up again with many of the friends whom I had left in Pres. at the time I went to Glenstal. As well as those of the old friends who were about to start Pre Med. others were doing Science or Arts or Engineering. I was particularly happy to join forces once more with Finbarr Dowdall, who was doing Science and who had been my special friend in Glenstal as well as in Pres.

Although liking the study of Medicine, I was only half committed to it. I was distracted from it on a number of fronts; the most difficult one had to do with my father's spiritual welfare. I had the idea that he was a lapsed Catholic and that I should do something about it. He was now about seventy years of age and I thought that time was running out for him.

From my mid-teens I had felt that God was calling me to the priesthood, even to a strict monastic order like the Cistercians. But then like the rich young man in Mark, chapter 10, who "went away sad, for he was a man of great wealth", I demurred. This was linked to and was reinforced by the imperative to sacrifice myself to try to ensure my father's eternal salvation.

Yet, he never missed Mass on Sunday. He always knelt down and prayed for a long time in the sitting room before going off to bed. As I now understand it, he had a relationship with God and he worshipped God.

Yet, at that time, I was unconvinced, because I never saw him go to confession or communion and in spite of the fact that the household had fish on Friday there was always a special meat dish prepared for him. From the preaching of the day one gleaned that amongst the very signs of predestination were frequent confession, communion and fulfillment of the six precepts of the church of which Friday abstinence from flesh meat was one. This abstinence was regarded so emphatically that a portion of meat even the size of a walnut, taken knowningly and willingly on a day of abstinence constituted a mortal sin, according to the commentary on this law by Bishop Browne of Galway.

This unease about my father began early on while I was still at school and became particularly acute when we went over to England to stay with him on holidays. After the war the decision had been made that the family would stay on in Ireland but visit my father regularly in England.

I confided in my mother about my problem and she thought fit to assure me that actually he did go to communion. He crept out to half past eight Mass on Sunday at which Mass he received Holy Communion, she said, and then he managed to get back to the house, a distance of a mile, and back into bed again beside me before I was awakened to go to the nine o'clock Mass for which he would get up also and come with us. This was an extraordinarily tall story but I tried very hard to believe it. In the end I had to admit to myself that it was a cover up for father and an attempt by mother to appease my conscience.

Furthermore, I had seen him going, in his official capacity as Medical Officer of Health, to Divine Service, organised for the Urban District Council, in the local Anglican Parish Church. In those days the law was that he could not attend such a ceremony but could be represented at it by a non-Catholic.

* * *

When I was about to begin Premed, rather than have me travelling into and out from Cork everyday mother got digs for me with Mrs. O'Regan of Connaught Avenue, just near the University. I got on very well with my fellow students in the digs, some of whom worked well at their studies, while others including myself did not get really involved. There was no counseling service or career guidance person available that I knew of and I and others badly needed some support and direction. The feeling I had about myself was analogous to that feeling a person may have who has a small pebble in his/her shoe. He can walk well enough but is aware of a constant irritant which he cannot get himself around to dealing with.

Getting involved in the rugby club was a partial anodyne. I played for the "Beagles" which was the minor team composed only of students from the Pre medical or Medical faculties. The "Bulldogs" was the minor team to represent other faculties. It was a great interest and socialising opportunity.

Towards the end of the first term I was chosen to play for the University College, Cork Freshmen in a match against our counterparts in University College, Dublin. We had an enjoyable journey by train up to Dublin, feeling self-consciously important as chosen representatives of a well thought of institution. Oh! how an autograph hunter would have substantiated the phantasy!

We were directed to the Caledonian Hotel in South Great George's Street which seemed to specialise in providing for teams. There were two double beds in the room to which I was assigned together with three others. Two brothers shared one bed while I and another member of the team who was Jewish shared the other. The three of us who were serious Catholics did not wish to parade our Christianity before our Jewish friend in an insensitive manner. Out of a badly expressed respect for him we compromised ourselves almost to the point of ridicule. Instead of kneeling down to say our night prayers properly we slunk awkwardly into bed thereby somehow incorporating a kneeling posture for just long enough to rush an Our Father, Hail Mary and Glory be to the Father. The compromise was almost certainly noticed by but lost on Ivor who unwittingly proceeded to teach us a lesson by hoisting his pyjama legs over his head, obviously having forgotten or mislaid the correct headgear, before getting down to reading his psalms.

I cannot recall the result of the match in Belfield but the thing to do afterwards was to go to the "Green Rooster" restaurant in O'Connell Street which indeed many of us did, eating large steaks and chips. The "Green Rooster" was also a popular place for terminating the seventy two hour Lough Derg fast, since at the time it was one of the very few places which served meals after midnight.

When we got back to the hotel we met up with those of our group who had chosen the better part by going to a meeting of the Literary and Historical Society in U.C.D. Some said they were impressed by a student whom they called Ulick O'Connor.

In June 1950 some of us went as usual to Lough Derg in lieu of taking the appropriate means in order to pass our exams. Lough Derg was an impressive place of pilgrimage and prayer, a great leveller and a place of good humour. In the course of nine pilgrimages there I heard only one unpleasant outburst and that was from a man who claimed to have been duped into coming along by friends who thought more of his immortal soul than of himself. Between stations at about three o'clock in the morning he declared loudly for the benefit of those around, in eloquent understatement, "this place has nothing to recommend it".

In those days Lough Derg was a great place to meet the famous. I met Cyril Cusack who was most generous in offering help and encouragement where and when needed by those negotiating the rigours of the penitential "beds". He was in no sense "precious" about his widely acclaimed acting prowess. A question like, "is it difficult to remember the lines for a big part?" he would answer as if he was hearing it for the first time.

***

First Med. the real thing began for us in October, 1950. Professor McConnell assured us that we had status and responsibility as medical students. We were now licensed to dissect the human subject or cadaver. We were assigned in groups of about six to each subject in order to dissect the upper limb, three to each side. A very generous allocation compared to other medical schools. The first incision was awesome but thereafter it soon became quite ordinary. After dealing with the skin and superficial fascia we got to our first muscle, the trapezius. From there on the method of proceeding was that one read out the instructions and descriptions in Walmsley's Practical Anatomy while another dissected, the third person observed and commented.

Professor McConnell went around to each of the groups in turn. He was clad in white laboratory coat with a large bag needle in his top pocket secured to a button hole with twine. This implement he found to be the most useful for helping him to assess the quality of a dissection. He was a man of learning and enjoyed metaphor. For dissecting he approved of the scalpel and forceps but not of the scissors. He referred to using the scissors as "shooting the fox". When he gave a spot test in anatomy, which involved naming the parts of the cadaver indicated by number, he spoke of "doing a round of the anatomical golf course".

Professor McConnell always tried to bring spice and variety into his lecturing. He believed in St. Augustine's directive that if you wish to instruct you must first of all entertain. One day during the time we were dissecting the pelvis he came urgently into a crowded lecture theatre like a ballet dancer making a quick entry from the wings. Bowing slightly forward from the hips he bowed his head, raised his arms cruciform fashion saying, "Gentlemen (ladies were implicitly subsumed into that category), I am the uterus, anteverted and anteflexed. My arms are the fallopian tubes, my fingers are the fimbriae".

How could one ever forget information given with such panache?

Particularly in the light of some stage whispered comments from the auditorium.

***

This was 1950, the Holy Year. My mother agreed that it would be good for me to go to Rome at Christmas for the closing of the Holy Door. My father saw threatening implications arising from such Roman-ising but did not stand in the way.

On the way to Rome my friend and I visited Paris. We felt it would be a good education to visit some night spots so we took a tour of Paris by night. This included a visit to the Bal Tabarin. I was taken aback at the degree of female nudity at this club but tried to assuage my conscience by turning the event into a surface anatomy learning experience.

Immediately we moved to a small night club where there was a hypnotist at work. Champagne was served at this function. I had been a pioneer teetotaller up to that point but I rationalised the breaking of my pledge on the basis that the alcohol might in some way inoculate me against "bad thoughts"!

We arrived in Milan in the snow. While looking at the billboard outside "La Scala" opera house we were spirited away to a nearby park where a couple of confidence tricksters tried to get us involved in their version of the three card trick. They assumed that we were completely naive in these matters and they became rather aggressive when we demonstrated a good deal of common sense developed by observing the goings on at side shows at point to point race meetings in Ireland.

In Rome we stayed in the Hotel Anglo Americana near the Piazza Barbarini. We had good contacts and did a fairly thorough sightseeing of Rome.

We had our Christmas Dinner in the Scoglio di Frisio, beside the Basilica of Santa Maria Maggiore, together with quite a large number of other Irish people. This excellent restaurant was owned by a man, Signor Rossi, who had strong Scottish connections having spent a great deal of his life in Scotland. He had a perfect knowledge of English as well as Italian. Unfortunately, some of the Irish contingent got over lubricated with Italian wine and began to indulge in coarse anti-Italian jokes, mistakenly confident that only those for whom they were meant would understand them. Those of us who knew about Signor Rossi were acutely embarrassed. Signor Rossi, the consummate professional caterer did not turn a hair.

The audience with Pope Pius XII was memorable and touching. Seeing an idea becoming incarnate right in front of me I find tearfully joyful. I had the same experience in 1979, when the Jumbo Jet carrying Pope John Paul ll appeared over Dublin while we were stuck in a train jam somewhere between Westland Row and Amiens Street stations. What struck me particularly about Pius Xll was the gracefulness of his hands as he blessed and touched members of the audience in St.Peter's.

**

Just after Christmas 1952 when I was in my Second Medical year my father got a stroke while at home in Ireland. This was the last straw. I could no longer resist the "hound of heaven". I initiated negotiations about entering some religious order. I began by arranging a meeting with a close friend of mine, Ultan Mc Elligot, in the Imperial Hotel. Ultan was impressed and gave me valuable advice and various contacts. With his help I opted for the Dominicans.

Since by March 1952 I had decided to enter religious life and study for the priesthood I rationalised my way out of studying seriously for my Second Medical examination.

Even though I did not pass the Second Medical exam I was entitled to do the pre-clinical course. It was a great boost to flagging enthusiasm as one would from now on be dealing with real live people instead of with cadavers. It was a medical student's first chance to exercise the skills involved in presenting a good bedside manner. We had lectures in Pathology and Therapeutics in college but our main focus of interest was clinical work in the North Infirmary, South Infirmary and the County Home, now St. Finbarr's.

The first clinic for some of us was under the aegis of a distinguished consultant, complete with morning suit, in the fever section of the County Home. It was on a couple of Diphtheria patients. Diphtheria is seldom heard of now but then it was widely feared as an infectious throat disease. When I was living as a child in England before the war it was rampant, a great deal of a General Practitioner's time in those days was spent in treating such cases. My father was continually negotiating the comings and goings of Diphtheria swabs to and from a pharmaceutical company which had an important base in Runcorn.

Consequently, when this clinic in the County Home was over I rushed home to Lissarda in my mother's car which I had on loan, and secretly burned my underwear but quite illogically did not burn my suit. I took a hot bath lavishly laced with Dettol.

By this stage in Medical school it was professionally and socially permissible to sport a stethoscope casually peeping from a pocket or carefully suspended from the neck with the diaphragm or bell occasionally visible under one's jacket like the pectoral cross of a bishop.

The clinical teachers in general gave us a lot of time and attention and gave good example in their own easy, yet caring relationships with the patients. They were enthusiastic about transmitting their skills and gave plenty of opportunity for us to deal with patients in minor matters, under a watchful eye.

We were shown how to give injections, remove stitches and perform many other important ancillary functions. We learned that generous applications of Glycerine and Belladonna were an effective therapy for minor diagnosable muscle or joint ailments that tended to turn up in the outpatient department.

Being called "doctor" by patients was quite a heady experience. When that same term was used to or of a student by a clinical teacher its significance had to be interpreted.

Our first visit to the operating theatre was to witness a prostatectomy. It was what, euphemistically, was called radical surgery. Many years later that experience was still fresh in my mind when I was faced with the prospect of having my own prostate gland removed. Fortunately, I was able to call on a friend with whom I had shared that first theatre experience, now a distinguished medical practitioner, who assured me that things had changed for the better.

I found it hard to leave all these things behind, now that the pace was "hotting up".

**

In 1951 and '52 I went over to Liverpool to the Grand National. In '51 I travelled with Teddy Fitzgerald of Lissarda, of a family very close to my own for many years. My father had very few whom he would classify as friends, but Dan and Jack Fitzgerald, Teddy's father and grandfather respectively he would have regarded as such. My father met us at Speke Airport in Liverpool.

On the plane over, a Dakota, we had turbulence which was mild but noticeable for most of the flight. There was only one woman passenger who seemed to be unconnected with racing. She was seated just across the aisle from Teddy and me. Many of the other twenty one passengers tended to look at her as if she had surprised them in the shower. After take off the man beside her, as if programmed or as if answering a litany kept repeating at intervals, or whenever there was the suggestion of an air pocket, 'I never felt so bad in all my life, I think I am going to get sick',

After a short while I could recognise his words as coded anti-feminism because he never really looked like getting sick.

In 1952 John Bolzan, an American studying Medicine in Cork, and I went over to the Grand National. By that time my father had become ill and was now being nursed by my mother at home in Lissarda. We stayed for two nights with my father's partners in the practice in Runcorn. We had a very pleasant social weekend of which the Grand National was only like a fringe event. Our friends were most generous to us. On reflection on that weekend I am reminded of a phrase Mervyn Wall used in his "Leaves for the Burning", published shortly before that time, when he described Lahinch as harbouring "priests pretending to be sober and bank clerks pretending to be drunk".

***

Up to that time, I had never seen a condom and was very curious about their mechanical structure. I felt that as a medical student in my third year of study I had a right, nay, an obligation to apprise myself of such details, and anyway, I reasoned, even as a future pastoral priest I would need to know firsthand something of the armory of the evil one.

I knew that the smart thing was to ask for "Durex" in a barber's shop, in a specialist sex shop or in a chemist's shop. I rose early on one of the mornings we were in Liverpool on that Grand National occasion and reached the shops just as they were opening. I looked guardedly into the window of the first sex shop I came to but they had no "Durex" advertised. There was on display an undefined product named "Utex". It was worth a gamble and I had to work fast so I asked the man in the shop for a box of "Utex".

'That will be a gross you want, sir?' he said.

'I just want one', I added quickly.

'One gross then, sir?' he concluded.

I panicked and eventually putting a half-crown on the counter I said,

'I want half a crown's worth'.

'That will be a packet of three sir, without teats,' he asserted with pedantic refinement.

Seizing my guilty purchase I evaporated from the shop. I went with indecent haste to the marbled toilet halls of the Adelphi Hotel where I satisfied my curiosity. Then panic really struck when the toilet, as if briefed not to cooperate, refused to consume them. They defied me with devilish glee as they danced on the waters. I could not just walk away. I might be seen leaving the cubicle or even if I wasn't observed I would be the cause of scandal to the next tenant. Then I reflected that if St. Joseph of Cupertino could get unworthy students through difficult exams he might also help in other areas of embarrassment. Suddenly even before I had requested him formally, the contraband disappeared.

I confessed the escapade on returning back to Cork to a priest who nearly had apoplexy.

Chapter 5

SPACE OF LIFE BETWEEN

After a Sunday morning match played in a sea of mid-season mud, I was picking my way towards the gate when I saw Donal Murphy coming into the grounds. I waved at him but, uncharacteristically, instead of waving back, he just continued to walk purposefully towards me. Before he had come to within twenty yards I read it all in his deportment. Still, I addressed him brashly,

'It's not often we see you around here, Donal?'

He started to reply, 'I called out to Lissarda this morning....'

I interrupted 'My father is sick... how bad is he?'

'He got a stroke early this morning, the doctor was with him, he's paralysed all down one side and his speech is affected. Your mother asked me to go to Cork and tell you.......the other lads in your digs said I'd find you here. I have my Dad's car....I'll drive you out immediately.'

Now, I had to face squarely that which was the pressing preoccupation of my life, the state of my father's soul in the sight of God. Paying minimum attention to Donal's occasional kind words, for most of the time I had my own thoughts for the half hour journey to Lissarda.

'Is my father in the state of grace? How could he be when I am almost certain he never goes to confession or communion and eats meat on Fridays, not to mention his neglect of Easter duties and his occasional attendances at Protestant services....I could do something about it if he were a drunkard or an adulterer or both and kept going to confession and communion, but he is a teetotaller and an agnostic who has great respect for the decencies of life.....I have friends whose fathers fall into one or both of the above mentioned categories of sin and quite rightly they take consolation in the assurance that the just man can fall seventy times seven times......If only my father were a lecherous drunkard who would go to confession and remain submissive, instead of being consumed by that very pride on account of which Lucifer was cast out of heaven...... I am being called to leave all things and enter religious life in order to ensure his salvation.'

We arrived in the coach yard of Lissarda House. Mrs. Bourke, one of the housekeepers, greeted us and said that father was resting and that mother was up with him.

Donal left and I went up to the sick room immediately. I knocked on the door and mother invited me in. I saw father lying there with what looked like a flat hat on his head tilted at a music hall angle. It was an ice bag. It occurred to me that an ice bag might be as useful for the curing of a stroke as a mortar board is for the acquisition of knowledge.

By some slight movement of his head, father was able to signal welcome and by the same gesture convey that he fully understood how foolish he must look. Somehow, he gave me to understand that he saw the stroke he had as a foolish interlude which would be over soon. I kissed him on the forehead and he broke down with all the pathos of the helpless.

My mother was totally committed to him and loving towards him. At only forty four she had all the strength needed to cope. I felt happy for him that he could be afforded every comfort.

I hesitated at first about asking my most important question, but as soon as I got mother out of his hearing range I asked, 'Did the priest come?'
'Daddy's a wonderfully good man, he's a saint', she said, evading my question,
It was quite clear to me that the priest had not been called. We both moved out of the sick room to talk more freely.

'Look mum, can't you understand that he might die very soon, even tonight. You must see that he gets confession and extreme unction as soon as possible. There is no good in saying he is a good man if he doesn't go to the sacraments.'

I replied with passion and continued, 'I'll go to get the priest myself, if necessary. This is too serious.'

'All right so, to please you I'll tell Mrs. Bourke to ask him to call, but your father won't like it',

At that I lost control and said,

'It doesn't matter who likes it or doesn't like it. That's beside the point. What's right is right irrespective of whom it pleases or displeases.'

The priest was sent for that day and did come. I escorted him to my father's room and there my mother took over. She then came downstairs and we waited together in the ball for the priest to come down. He came down after too short a time, I thought, and surmised that all may not be well. The priest said he would come with communion again later in the week.

'That proves nothing', I said to myself, 'he must give my father the benefit of the doubt.'

Then it occurred to me that in my great concern about father's future I had forgotten to express to my mother, a consoling interest in the how, when and where of the stroke.

I spoke to mother and she told me about the circumstances of the stroke. She added seriously that I had no idea of how good he really was. With the best of medical attention and with dedicated nursing, father recovered gradually. He was a good patient. I managed to get home to see him regularly. When he was able to get up and talk more easily I felt that I should look for my opportunity to investigate, first-hand, the state of his soul!.

Recently he had been unable to do the Manchester Guardian crossword but it was a sign of his recovery that he was getting back to doing it again. Sometimes I used to sit with him and marvel at his ability to handle obscure clues.

One day, as if tired of these crossword trivia, he talked with great understanding about John Stuart Mill, the English nineteenth century philosopher and told me how he liked his writings and that he agreed with him on so many points. This dabbling in philosophy continued over a number of our meetings, interspersed with the resolving of crossword clues. One day, in the course of our ongoing discussions the opportunity arose for me to put the question directly,

'Daddy, do you believe in life after death?'

He was silent for what seemed like an age, and then from memory, he quoted, in reply, the following words from Hamlet's "To be, or not to be" soliloquy,

"Who would burdens bear, to grunt and sweat under a weary life,
But that the dread of something after death,
The undiscovered country, from whose borne
No traveller returns, puzzles the will,
And makes us rather bear those ills we have,
Than fly to others that we know not of?"

After a space of many years it makes me happy to reflect on this answer which he gave to my question. It was an answer framed carefully so that I would remember it but which would take years to yield up its meaning to me. He was too serious a thinker to give a simple answer to a question that was burning within him.

In the light of my new discoveries and insights I thought of the play "Hamlet" once more. This time I felt myself in the role of the clergyman, who having rashly judged Ophelia as unworthy of full Christian rites of burial, was addressed by her brother, Laertes,

"I tell thee, churlish priest,
A minist'ring angel shall my sister be,
When thou liest howling".

* * *

My father was able to go into the garden when the summer came and by then could manage visitors. A surprising number of people came over from England to him. One such visit I recall vividly and with good reason. Since father was a nondrinker there was very little alcoholic drink usually available in the house. After a dry forty eight hours one particular visitor was overcome by the thirst. He asked me to go out with him after the evening meal for a few drinks. We drove quite far, to Carrigaline, and the guest, having ascertained that I could and would drive his car home, abandoned himself to Bacchus.

When the time came to leave the public house, I loaded him into the back seat and drove on. The roads in those days were more potholed than now so that the journey was rough. Consequently, he got violently sick all over the jacket of his suit. It was a hired car he had, having travelled over by plane with hand luggage which did not include another suit or jacket. When we arrived home everyone had gone to bed and I got him to his room, he was like a heavy, fat, soft toy.

I went back downstairs to where I had left his jacket and washed out all the stains thoroughly. I put on the two-bar electric fire in the hall and hung the coat in front of it. Alas! While I was not paying attention to it, it went on fire. The entire front left hand side was scorched beyond repair before I got things under control. I was at my wits end. How could I ever tell the man that I had burned his only jacket? How might it upset my father? In fact, I had no difficulty in explaining what had happened to the chastened guest. To cope with the rest of the household he decided to come down to breakfast in his waistcoat and insist that it was his custom always to do this. It was a cold May morning and my mother was worried lest the man in the waistcoat might get cold. She went out into the hall and reappeared with the electric fire which she put down beside him and turned on full blast.

***

In due course, I got peace of mind about my father and could accept his good faith and integrity. During his convalescence the seeds of understanding him were sown in me through our doing of crosswords together and by means of our discussions and conversations, as described above, but these seeds were due to spend many long years gestating.

I had a lot of tensions within me which needed to be released. From talking to confessors and from sermons and retreats I was well aware of certain types of weaknesses within myself but had never been encouraged to get to know my strengths. I used to visit regularly a priest friend of mine who was kind and understanding. He said he admired my courage and unselfishness in being prepared to sacrifice my possessions, family etc. for the eternal salvation of my father.

This priest was an idealist and moved me to come to grips with this demand of conscience. He discussed with me what the fruits of my sacrifice would be and how happy I would be with the peace of mind that would follow.

As I see it now, he measured the value of things against the degree of advancement they brought about in establishing God's kingdom on earth. The problem with this criterion was his interpretation of "God's kingdom on earth". For him this "kingdom" was the official section of the institutional Church as realised in clerical and religious foundations and organisations. The best way, he thought, to promote the common good and the ultimate good of mankind was to have clergy and religious in key positions, even, of secular influence. In this he was reflecting the ethos of the nineteen fifties when the idea of "church" was expressed as an image of the forces of good with divinely enlightened leadership drawn up in battle array against the powers of darkness.

Fortunately, this priest who had an almost fascist zeal for his ideas about things of the spirit, when he was changed to a different part of the country, transferred me into the care of a Dominican.

When I had been put in contact with the Dominican order I became most impressed by the men I met and the ideals they told me about. In the Dominican Order I found a blend of the monastic and choral life, which I was introduced to in Glenstal, with a life of study, counselling, preaching and teaching, a taste for which was developed in me by reading Fulton Sheen's writings and through various personal contacts.

***

Sometime in June 1952, I told my mother that I was thinking seriously of entering a religious order with the intention of studying for the priesthood. At the time she had been totally preoccupied with my father's health and was most understandably terribly upset by my decision. She put up all the arguments against...'it would kill my father....she had looked forward to seeing me married and to seeing my children....I had money and property with which I could do a great deal of good in the world.... I would have a degree in medicine and my father's practice would be kept open for me by his partners until I was qualified and ready..... I would break the family tradition of medicine etc.'

I wasn't to be moved. I was certain that I was following the correct course. Anyway, I felt I could never again be conditioned for the retaking of my Second Medical examination in September.

Early in July 1952, I felt that I would have to face the music and break my news to father. On July 11th I told him that I had made a decision to enter a religious order. He was shaken to the core. It was a pathetic scene. He wanted to know how I could do it to him. He was devastated.

But I was confident that it was for his good and the spiritual advice I had got and which I trusted was that I would have to turn the screw. Any other course, I was advised, would be to turn my back on God. Hard choices had to be made.

My full circumstances were never examined or understood by anyone whom I asked for help or advice. The "call of God" was seen as a signal which could override the natural signs of the same God, almost as if it came from a different source. My father came to me a few days later and said he was going to take his own life unless I changed my mind,

'After all', he said, 'what else have I to live for'.

But I wasn't to be moved by that kind of blackmail!

Very soon after that he lodged some money for me in the bank and provided me with a cheque book. He signed over to me Warrensgrove that large farm of his which I mentioned earlier situated just over two miles from Lissarda and where my Auntie Nellie and Uncle Mick were caretakers. I remember the thought occurred to me that this was just a pathetic bribe!

I applied officially to enter the Dominican Order and after doing an interview was accepted. I was told that the official date for entry was September 4th., Then it was official and I let my decision to change from Medicine to the Dominican Novitiate be known to my relations and friends. I met with a great deal of approval and there was a general consensus that I had made a good decision. Many, ironically, enjoined after an opening congratulatory comment, 'Your mum and dad must be delighted'

My father did not seem to have come to terms at all with my decision in terms of understanding what it was about but he did respect my decision to do what I wanted to do and once I had cast the dye my mother gave me her full support.

A number of friends had farewell parties which I recall with appreciation. I remember particularly a party given for me by my medical student colleagues who expressed approval of what I was doing, although some, I felt were a bit bewildered, in particular my rugby friends who had within the previous few months elected me secretary of University College, Cork rugby club.

I had to explain frequently why I had chosen the Dominicans rather than the Benedictines to whom I went to school in Glenstal. I doubt if I gave the same answer twice to that question.

I got the list of clothes and books to be brought into the novitiate which was at Pope's Quay in Cork. It was a simple trousseau, the black suit and the black tie being the only ominous items. The books to be brought in were a set of breviaries and a couple of dictionaries and a bible.

The fourth of September arrived. My mother came into my bedroom very early and hugged me and said,
'My darling child, your big day has come.'

A priest friend of the family who was at home from the missions in Africa invited me to attend a Mass which he was going to celebrate for me that morning in his mother's home which was about a mile away. On the way back from Mass I came across another neighbour's cattle breaking out onto the public road through a break in the fence. Thereupon, I spent a good hour and a half, between calling to notify the neighbour what had been a providential device to bring me comfortably through what otherwise would have been a long and difficult morning.

It was a difficult morning for the entire household. One of the most touching gestures was a present I got from my sister,

Rosemary, of a New Testament of her own. I went into my father early just for a moment to see how he was and didn't go in again until I was leaving.

Saying good bye to my father and mother was a desolating experience as it was a virtual certainty that I would never again sleep under the same roof as my father. In those times the Dominican students were not, as a rule allowed home, except to attend weddings, ordinations, religious professions or funerals of immediate family members.

Rosemary drove me into the house of my friend Finbarr Dowdall in Blackrock. Finbarr's mother had offered me facilities to change into my black suit and black tie in their house before being driven into the novitiate in Pope's Quay. It was thought that it would be rubbing salt into my father's wounds if I donned clerical garb in Lissarda. Anyway, going via a friend's house provided a comforting stepping stone into a new and quite different life.

I smoked my last few cigarettes, as smoking was not allowed in the Dominican novitiate. At four o'clock we set out from Blackrock and I was delivered, with hair crew cut, black suited and black tied, together with my baggage, onto the threshold of St. Mary's Dominican Priory, Pope's Quay, Cork.

Chapter 6

CLOISTER

The front door of the priory closing behind me cut cleanly and dramatically the umbilical cord. I had made a choice, strictly according to what I understood as the prompting of the Spirit, to leave "father, mother, brothers and sisters" for the sake of the Kingdom. I felt happy at the deepest level although emotionally emptied and raw.

The front hallway was dark tiled, polished but unimaginative with parlours off it for counselling and confessions, particularly priests' confessions. The brother doorkeeper, who greeted me and told me I was expected, squeaked on ahead carrying more than his fair share of my luggage. He pushed open a heavy glass panelled door which had the word CLOISTER on it and beyond which it was forbidden, under penalty of excommunication, to women and girls of whatever age, class or condition to go under any pretext whatsoever.

In response to his beckoning I tiptoed after him onto the holy ground. The Prior, who happened to pass by at that moment, recognised me from the interview and welcomed me by name. After a few words of encouragement he committed me again into the charge of the brother who piloted me to another door marked NOVITIATE.

He rang the bell and we waited a short time during which he told me that even brothers and priests, other than the Master and Submaster of novices were excluded from this part of the priory. As he passed me and my luggage over to the white habited young man who opened the door to us, the brother wished me well.

Brother Ignatius, one of the novices of the previous year and who had opened the Novitiate door then took me over. His opening question to me asked with a kind of nervous compulsion was,

'Did you go to the pictures?'

As if a visit to the cinema might have been his own last request before hanging. Shocked by the worldliness of the question and in my heart hypocritically despising its trivial nature, I condescendingly replied that being local I was able to come more or less directly from home and did not get a chance to go to the pictures, Perhaps it was my subtly superior tone which made his next question like a smash to the backhand,

'You're the guy chucking up medicine?'

We reached the top of the stairs which was immediately inside the Novitiate door. Brother Ignatius flopped to his knees, uttering a prayer in front of a statue of Our Lady. Before I could organize myself to kneel down my guide was up on his feet once more and indicating me through a doorway nearby.

'Wait in there. I'll tell the Master you're after coming in', he mumbled as he disappeared, leaving me alone with my luggage in a vast uncomfortable locker room.

'I've made one awful mistake', I thought.

'I should have listened to my parents'

My desolation was intensified as I looked at my large case and recalled that it had been my mother's very own travelling bag before she gave it to me, in fact only that very morning, although it felt an age away.

The Master came in and quietly shook hands. A man with no small talk, he got down to some organisational details. He said that the Dean, Brother Felix would take over, show me around and introduce me to some other postulants who had arrived earlier.

I felt comfortable with Brother Felix, a late vocation who had spent a number of years in the Civil Service before entering religious life. He brought me to my room immediately, helping me with my bags. Sensitively, he said he would call back in fifteen minutes.

The room which had been assigned to me was better than I had anticipated. The novitiate had been built quite recently, in the mid nineteen thirties, of red brick, symmetrical at all costs and with steel framed windows. The room I was given was bright, south facing with polished wooden floor. The furniture consisted of a steel framed bed, a prie-dieu, desk, wash stand and chair.

Brother Felix came back as arranged and showed me the vestry where our clothes were to be kept. Since he was also vestiarian he could show me the shelves assigned to me for my shirts, underclothes etc. and the place in which to hang my suit. He explained to me that it was in the Dominican Constitutions that clothes should be kept in common. He showed me the small novitiate library which doubled up as a billiard room, the oratory and the chapter room.

Having completed the short tour I was taken to a small garden in front of the novitiate which was pleasant because unexpected but blocked from view in front by the wall of the apse of the public church. There I met some other postulants who were probably as benumbed as I was. Our conversation was trivial and my mind was certainly not with present company. We might have regressed into self-indulgent silence were it not for the remarkable loquacity of Brother Celestine who had been assigned to entertain us and two of whose passions in life were the Irish language and the Gaelic Athletic Association.

I believe that the pain of alienation that afflicted me and probably the other postulants was in some way due to the black garb in which we suddenly found ourselves for the first time on that day. I can recall looking in the mirror and being upset. In the world outside the cloister the black would at least bring with it the bonus of same degree of clerical deference but it just labelled us as "rookies".

We were summoned to tea by the bell and the ten of us were taken to the passageway outside the refectory by Brother Felix. We waited there curiously and heard the community chanting grace before meals,

It seemed like a very long grace, particularly as the 'De Profundis' had been recited just beforehand in the corridor.

When grace was over we were slipped in quietly to places below the novices, yet above the brothers, so, as a clerical postulant I found myself after two and a half hours, senior in rank to the lay brother who had let me in the hall door earlier that afternoon and who was in the order before I was born.

After a good tea followed by chanted grace we were spirited back to the novitiate proper although some did get left behind being welcomed by priests of the community who had known them already.

I met all the novices after tea which had sweetened our dispositions.

After the meal we interrelated more willingly. The few alumni of Newbridge College, run by the Dominican Order, took solace in each other's company. Corkonians always sniff each other out anyway. The Rest was a strong group stretching from Sligo to South Tipperary.

At eight o'clock we were taken to Rosary and Benediction in the public church but tucked away behind the high altar. After five hours of cloistered life, which seemed like deprivation, it was a great feeling to be aware of the presence of "people" again, even if we couldn't see much of them. On returning from

Benediction we had a meeting with the Master who welcomed us officially, spelled out some ground rules and outlined our programme for the next ten days.

On the following night our retreat began. It was laid before us that half measures are not acceptable to God. The dominating and recurring theme from which the preacher didn't spare us during the entire time it lasted was emphasised by his quoting of the message to the church in Laodicea, as found in the Bible in the Book of Revelation, 'I know all about you: how you are neither cold nor hot. I wish you were one or the other, but since you are neither, but only lukewarm, I will spit you out of my mouth'.
Mediocrity was described as the greatest evil.

The exciting interlude in the ten day retreat was getting measured for the habit. It involved leaving the cloister for a few minutes to go to the parlour. The only really important dimension was the length, as we varied between six feet two and five feet six. Since it was a loose fitting garment the other dimensions had vast margins of tolerance. Coming close to the end of the retreat there was an air of expectation and excitement.

At our daily one hour recreation we speculated about religious names that might be given. One of the more gullible was given to believe that Abraham was the name in store for him. Brother Felix, as our Dean and vestiarian prepared us painstakingly for the clothing ceremony or reception which was to be conducted by the Provincial.

In the public church at St. Mary's, Pope's Quay on Sunday, September 14th 1952 after the midday Mass the ceremony took place. The church was full and my medical student ex colleagues had a great representation. I could see a number of them and my mother and sister out of the corner of my eye as we processed out onto the altar.

After going to our appointed places in the choir area in front of the high altar the Provincial formally asked us,

'What do you seek?'

To which we all replied together, 'God's mercy and the mercy of the Order',

The Provincial followed this by a short sermon. The solemnity of the exhortation was relieved for some of us who noted that he was wearing slippers and important points he seemed to stress to himself by moving his big toes. We surrendered our ties and jackets as tokens of our renunciation of involvement in the "world" and we were clothed instead in the Dominican habit by the Provincial, assisted by the Novice Master.

Then came what was, in a way, the most interesting part of the ceremony. We were each brought up to the Provincial once more and given our names in religion,

'In the world you were known as Denstone Murphy in the order you will be called Brother Paul'.

When all were clothed in the habit and named in the order, the inspiring hymn, "Veni Creator Spiritus" was intoned, the hair stood up on the back of my neck and each of us moved clumsily in our unfamiliar attire through the choir stalls, being welcomed and greeted in turn by every member of the community present.

For a short while immediately afterwards I was allowed to meet and greet my ex-medical school classmates and other peers in the sacristy. They were generous in their congratulations, yet somewhat restrained by my "new image".

Then we raced, like children at a party, up to the parlours to meet our families and close friends. The excitement of dressing up and a feeling of importance made me talk more than listen. My father hadn't come along. My mother just said he wasn't able. Conversation all round was bland and strained by the surroundings. One cousin, afraid lest he scandalise me, sought my permission to tell what he quaintly described as a "jocular story". Another uneasy friend, on hearing me describe the novitiate year as a trial year before committing oneself to the Religious life, rather tastelessly quipped in the presence of his wife, that the same kind of arrangement for marriage was long overdue. The design of the habit was scrutinised and the material felt. The new name Brother Paul was a talking point.

Whatever about the theological rationale of such a name change it was for me a great relief to have at last a name I did not have to explain and on occasion apologise for. In England no one ever cross- examined me about the propriety of the name "Denstone", any more than they would question about the names "Sandy" or "Selwyn", but in Ireland about one in three new acquaintances wanted to know if there was a Saint Denstone. Onhearing there wasn't the next comment was in the form of a thinly disguised question,
'How well the priest who baptised you allowed such a name?'

It was and still is a tiresome inquisition. It is irritating rather than upsetting as is the situation of a friend of mine from Mitchelstown who on declaring his town of origin to new acquaintances is greeted with the antiphon "the home of good cheese". Or the Navan person who is likewise reminded continually that s/he lives "abou' an owa from Dublin". Such is the impression of advertising slogans.

Although taking photographs of the new novices was forbidden, there were some clandestine clicks and flashes. My mother innocently asked me to pose but I refused to break the law. The result, as I discovered much later, was that a photo was taken by a camera concealed in a handbag randomly aimed in my general direction.

The time to end the visit came but already some of us were planning the next visit due in a month's time.

On the day after our reception, the novices of the year ahead of us and who acted as our guardian angels and mentors, made their first profession and thus became fully fledged members of the order, albeit at this stage, for only three years.

After the honeymoon was over we got down to a testing monastic life which I got to love, particularly the choral office and the plain chant which I had got a taste for in Glenstal where it was to be found at its best.

We had classes each day, though never more than two. These, strictly speaking were not academic classes but instruction periods in the Rule and Constitutions, the Vows, Plain Chant, the Divine Office, the History of the Order and Clerical Etiquette.

Probably our most interesting class happened on Sunday mornings at about eleven o'clock when James Stack, one of the well-known and distinguished actors and directors of those days, came for elocution class. In his natural flamboyance he looked out of place in the novitiate setting but showed no other signs of discomfiture. For a man who could remember the lines of any Shakespeare character he had great difficulty in remembering our names and in doubt called everybody Brother George. He worked us hard but we appreciated him. Occasionally he could be coaxed to give a one man show which for us was as good as a Royal Command Performance. Sometimes he caused us anxiety about his soul when we were aware of the fact that the twelve o'clock Mass which he attended was about to begin while he was lost in full flight declaiming one or other of Antony's or Brutus' speeches.

The novitiate was a time of probation to allow the novices to better understand their vocations; to let them experience Dominican life and in turn to give the order the opportunity to judge about their suitability. One of those who started the postulancy with us left before Reception. Now he's well known as an entertainer on both radio and television.

The rest of us settled in well as a group and some close friendships were formed and are still in place.

There was great feeling for Brother Luke whose father died in November. The same Luke seldom failed in his ability to give the flavour of an entire situation in a key expression; a master in the art of understatement. When asked once by a simple but harassed fellow novice if a particular prescribed novitiate activity were compulsory or optional, he replied calmly, 'The whole thing is optional'.

My own father died during my novitiate year. He had a few trips to hospital during the year and I was allowed to visit him but I always had to be accompanied to the hospital by a socius or companion. We were allowed out, as a rule only in two's; this proviso was in the constitutions and I have also heard it supported by the maxim of St. Gregory, "inter minus quam duos non potest habere caritatem'. (between less than two there can't be charity). However, the socius always waited for me in the hallway so there was never a question of intrusion.

My father was glad to see me but seemed uneasy about my status so heavily underlined by my black clerical suit. But his uneasiness did not prevent him from one day painstakingly though slurringly telling me that he was sorry for in any way obstructing me in pursuing my chosen vocation. They were the most rewarding sentiments that ever I heard. There was no road to Damascus drama. After saying those words he was his same old Shavian self again and by way of asserting his own individuality, immediately proceeded to ridicule what was certainly a ridiculous picture on the wall of his hospital room depicting the child Jesus pulling St. Joseph's beard.

After Easter of that novitiate year he began to decline fast and I got special permission from the Provincial to go home to Lissarda occasionally to visit him, without socius. He always knew me and owned me. He was a deeply spiritual person, I decided, but one who used a metaphor, since then adopted by many but then unusual enough in Ireland. Perhaps an inscription I saw recently on a poster might be relevant.

"He marched to the beat of a different drum".

Coming near the end, my mother kept me up to date on his condition. He died on June 14th 1953, the feast of St. Basil. I was told of his death in what I am sure was an innocent but remarkably uncaring way. A house boy in St. Mary's who happened to walk across my path in the corridor after completing some work in the refectory, turned to me with the degree of concern and rehearsal of one about to tell me that the metre reader called but missed me, 'By the way, a phone call came a while ago to say your father was dead'.

I'll say no more.................

I was allowed home just after midday and attended the removal of the remains to the church that evening and got special permission to sleep at home on that one night. Friends drove me back to the novitiate after the burial.

* * *

Sometime in June we had an interview and examination based on what we had covered in class during the year. We all passed and were now virtually certain of being accepted for profession in September.

The enormous upsurge in numbers of those entering religious life not only in Ireland but also in the United States and England, amongst other countries, was just about to get under way and was to reach a peak in the early sixties. Practically every order, congregation, every lay and clerical religious institute both male and female and every diocesan ordinary or bishop had a recruiting drive organised. The United States became a mecca for vocations' directors as it to some extent still was, for poets and lecturers of the Dylan Thomas era.

Mastery of selling techniques was pursued at every perceived level from Harvard to Harlem. These were the years following on the book "Elected Silence", by Thomas Merton and following on Father Raymond's "God Goes to Murderer's Row" and "The Man Who Got Even With God".

There was keen competition for candidates. Vocations' salespersons queued up to speak to potential candidates in schools. One vocations' director told the story against himself, that in one "better class" school where he didn't feel very welcome anyway, one of the irreverent pupils asked him if he had any free samples to give away. This competition was not good. The particular and various formal objectives which distinguished the various orders or congregations were too often played down in the interests of the numbers game "numbers are beautiful".

For example, if a young man who quite clearly wished to become a priest doing parish work happened to come first of all to a religious order priest for direction and enlightenment there was a good chance that instead of being recommended to the local diocesan vocations' director he would be encouraged to join that religious priest's own particular order being told that they also did parish work. That a particular religious order did parish work was, more likely than not, only a misleading partial truth. The full truth was that some of the men in that order did parish work for some time and there was no guarantee of ever being assigned to parish work.

In other words, it seems to me that instead of a rational attempt at deployment of the abundant talent on offer, by adequate communication in this matter between the various orders, congregations and other groups, petty loyalties wreaked havoc, particularly in the longer term. Resulting from an unaccountable unwillingness to sort out these matters of definition at the higher levels. For many candidates secular priestly vocations were confused with religious/priestly vocations. This led to a disturbing impatience with religious observances on the part of some, who saw in the religious house of studies and formation, nothing more than an unnecessarily confined and confining seminary. They yearned for the day when they could free themselves from it and get down to "serious" work which would have to be provided for them in a parish somewhere.

The months of July and August were quite free, the students, that is the group just ahead of us had left Cork after their exams and had gone to Newbridge for a month's holiday en route to Tallaght. With the students gone we were looking forward to being the senior citizens when the next group would come in September.

A few candidates or aspirants called to see us during those months apart from those who came on the big day when about fifteen prospective novices were formally interviewed. They spent the night before with us in the novitiate building. Their presence allowed us a welcome variation of company.

Brother Luke and I were asked to refurbish a couple of rooms in preparation for the larger than usual intake of novices due in September. In the course of our work I idly commented that the castors were gone off one of the beds. Brother Luke, a strong and agile countryman, sorely confined by the novitiate, wryly enjoined, 'He won't be going very far'.

Chapter 7

AVOWED

That's all there's left for a fella to enjoy', was Brother Fachtna's unsolicited but reasonable explanation to me as he reached for his fifth slice of bread. He was in great form the day of profession but suddenly now, two days later, he was on a low. He usually ate his way through problems and out of difficulties.

Nine of us had taken a vow of obedience, Dominicans pronounce only one vow but that one implies the other two with exactly the same emphasis as if the three were pronounced explicitly.

Vows as we know them now in religious life are solemn promises made to God. They are also a means of expressing membership of a particular religious grouping. Through declaring such membership you are emphasising publicly a commitment to fulfilling the baptismal promises by exercising the virtues both moral and theological in the spirit of the Sermon on the Mount.

Furthermore, by taking vows according to the rules and constitutions of a particular order or religious congregation you are accepting the norms proposed by them as being a suitable framework within which you can exercise those virtues.

Religious are bound no more nor no less than anybody else to exercise the virtues, but they should be able to depend on the limits defined by the vows as providing the optimal conditions within which they can most effectively exercise the virtues.

Our formal academic studies began consisting of Logic, Philosophical Psychology, Cosmology and Greek. We were a small class and had excellent teachers who inspired us by their dedication. Our lecturer in Logic had just completed his studies in Oxford and was full of the advantages of the tutorial system. On account of this we had an essay every week which had to be read out to him in his room and the contents were discussed.

It was so much better than the remoteness of the process that I experienced in the University.

When we went outside the priory for a walk or when we went to play football or simply had to go into town to get a message we wore the Roman collar. This gave a young student a great sense of importance. There was no way of knowing from the way he was dressed that he wasn't a priest and he was addressed as "Father" by those who did not know who he was. Hats always had to be worn going out and preferably the rim had to be turned up all round. Any trendy shaping of the hat was not acceptable.

We went out to play football twice a week with the novices. We used to borrow a pitch from the army near Collins Barracks. It was a great opportunity to get rid of surplus energy. At that stage of life in the early twenties sexual libido is a very powerful force. Seeing and meeting women caused immense desire which had to be controlled. This was an enormous task and at times seemed almost impossible. Some welcome relief was provided by the regular merciful, abundant nocturnal seminal emissions which seemed to drench the sheets unashamedly and which were sometimes accompanied by those vivid dreams that always finished a bit too early. A considerable part of the motivation not to masturbate was the realisation that you would have to confess it, no longer as just a mortal sin but now as a sacrilegious violation of the vow of celibacy.

Not going to Holy Communion at the community Mass on account of masturbating during the night was equivalent to advertising that you were a sinner. Others would know that you had given in to temptation. Sometimes spiritual directors in speaking to groups, in order to discourage rash judgments, made the disingenuous proposal that even though in the state of grace it was a good thing to abstain from Holy Communion on occasion, "to foster piety". St. Thomas Aquinas was cited as supporting that viewpoint but the reference is as elusive as the reference whereby some would have him favour the legalisation of brothels.

From the sexual point of view these were demanding times, as the negative side of this renunciation was much more obvious than the positive gains. I can't recall emphasis of any kind being put on the positive side of marriage in order to underline the "good" that one was offering up through the dedication of the vow of celibacy. Emphasis on the good of marriage might have been construed as a form of seduction, rather than enlightenment about the good of a Christian sacrament.

If perfect knowledge of what one is doing is a necessary prerequisite for validly taking a vow, perhaps there have been more invalid professions than we dare to imagine.

Poverty in religious life used to be more of a formality than a reality. A quip made on occasion by secular priests, who don't have a vow of poverty, to religious priests was,
'You fellas take the vow of poverty but we keep it'.

In Ireland in the nineteen-fifties there was no evidence of any shortage of food, clothing, shelter or of medical security amongst male religious who even when they did good works operated on a limited company basis so that personal involvement or the putting of one's own life on the line was not a consideration. Many the generous heart, it might be argued, was pressurised into unhappy compromise. At one of our very early retreats we were told that one of the great pressures on clergy was to accept a place in the upper middle class of society.

For the serious religious it was disturbing to hear a materially well provided for colleague protesting that he owned not even the clothes on his back. Such a statement of protest is an unworthy cliché. In many cases a religious in having the exclusive use and control of various things such as typewriters etc. together with a guarantee of maintenance expenses and even of replacement when necessary, is in a position more favourable than ordinary private ownership.

The vow of obedience was meant to serve as a kind of bond or contract for the individual with the government of the religious order or congregation. The leadership of the religious order had to lay out plans and reasonably deploy individuals so that the work of the order could be accomplished. The individual was bound to obey directives given to this end, and s/he then exercised the virtue of obedience by willingly and lovingly corresponding to these directives.

It happened sometimes that there was a despotic leadership which encouraged or even begot a fawning membership; a robot-like response to precepts of superiors was sought and expected and frequently given; in that context the vow came to overshadow the virtue. It might be now taken that the superior took responsibility in very large measure for the propriety of the activities of the community. This state of affairs was harshly driven home to me when a superior refused me permission to shelter a particularly needy person who fitted exactly into the category of the naked and the hungry described in chapter twenty five of Matthew's gospel. To have been virtuous in those circumstances would have cost me more than I had the courage to pay. I succumbed to the luxury of being protected by my vow of obedience - I had done exactly what my superior told me to do.

At the end of the academic year we had exams after which we left St. Mary's in Cork to go to the Dominican House of Studies at St. Mary's, Tallaght eventually, but on the way we were to stay in Newbridge College for holidays during the month of July. We had friends already in Tallaght in those who were just the year ahead of us while we were novices in Cork and with whom we had kept up a correspondence during the year.

The big and sad news which dominated the headlines when we arrived in Newbridge was the death in a motor car accident of the Master General, Father Suarez who had recently been on visitation to Tallaght and who although only a name to us had made a good impression on our fellow students.

It was interesting and exciting to meet over thirty new comrades of whom we stood in certain awe. A couple of them were sub deacons. Like any cross section of society they varied in texture from the sporting types who chose to play and talk only football right across the spectrum to those who rested and read. We had all the recreational facilities of the college at our disposal, swimming in the river, tennis, football etc. and a couple of films in the course of the month. During the afternoons we were allowed to go out cycling in twos at least, and in the course of time got to know well the countryside within about fifteen miles radius of Newbridge. Some got taken up with a Guinness Book of Records type of preoccupation to see who could cycle the greatest distance between lunch and tea. The record established about that time and probably still to the good was attributable to a group who got as far as Roscrea Monastery, greeted the Abbot, and then returned. It is important to bear in mind that they were not on racing bikes, nor clad á la Sean Kelly but wore Roman collars and clerical hats.

**

1954 was the year of myxomatosis, in that sense a year of shame. Grotesquely misshapen and diseased rabbits were to be seen languishing or fighting for life at the roadside, a straightforward parable of more recent human sufferings in the Third World. It was also a year in which hay saving was delayed by the weather and consequently difficult. Five of us with farming experience were asked to stay back in Newbridge for a few weeks of August to help the farm manager, with the saving of the hay.

During those few weeks, we had one night in Tallaght Priory when we went there to celebrate the feast of St.Dominic. It was my very first time in the Dominican Priory in Tallaght but about which I had heard a great deal and of which place I expected a lot. I wasn't disappointed. I loved it at first sight and was to be very happy there.

The five of us on bicycles set out from Newbridge on the eve of St. Dominic's day arriving in Tallaght, then a country village, a bit later than expected. Like Moses seeing the Promised Land from Mount Nebo, I got my first glimpse of St. Mary's Priory from the Belgard road, which was then a relatively quiet road, yet with a small number of factories including Urney's Chocolates, Glenabbey Textiles and Johnson's Baby Powder.

We came into an apparently deserted Priory. The only person we met was the brother "on the door" who greeted Brother Luke and me very warmly after we had been introduced to him by the other three of our group who were already established as senior students. The brother told us that the community were at Matins and Solemn Lauds in the church. As quickly as we could we got into our habits which we had brought with us as hand baggage and went to the church. Since we were late we decided not to go into the choir stalls but to go into the nave of the church. The thrill of coming in on that scene just as Lauds was starting, with full, brightly lit, white robed choir and with the organ providing a gentle background to the Gregorian Chant was an experience I hope I never forget. In my treasury of peak moments it holds a sacred place. For good measure, in the Prelate's stall was Father Michael Browne (later Cardinal), then Master of the Sacred Palace, the Pope's private theological advisor.

***

After the Newbridge hay saving sojourn we got back to another year's work, this time in Tallaght which was quite different to Cork. There was a larger community and the ambience was more obviously monastic and scholastic. The teaching staff was large and the atmosphere was conducive to study with quite good library facilities at our disposal.

What was regarded as an important learning instrument was the weekly scholastic disputation held by each class group every Saturday morning in term time. This, as in the case of many of our lectures was conducted in Latin. A thesis was proposed by one of the students, proved by means of a syllogism and then the basis of each premise was explained in detail. It is the purest and most constructive form of argumentation.

It was an integral part of the teaching method employed by St. Thomas Aquinas and other scholastics in the University of Paris and elsewhere. Points of agreement are first of all sought and laid aside. The real point of contention can then be dealt with without distraction. The more common kind of argumentation is called dialectic. We see dialectic exemplified in parliamentary debates, which so often are confused, marginal to the main issue and belittling of the personalities involved. An important feature of the feast of St. Thomas Aquinas every year was the "Conclusio". This was a major scholastic disputation about some current theological topic conducted by certain selected students in the presence of distinguished guests and all the staff and student body.

During my time in Tallaght I developed a missionary zeal for the Irish language and became organiser, secretary and chairman of the Cumann Aonghusa Naofa in successive years. Through this cumann or society we organised debates, had papers read and got people like Sean Óg Ó Tuama to come and speak to us. We had some moral theology classes in Irish to prepare for hearing confessions in Irish after ordination. There were a few of us who spoke Irish together as often as possible and organised, or rather revitalised an Irish get together once a week after tea. We had the community Rosary in Irish on the feast days of Irish saints. Some non-sympathisers found this irksome so we had to take quite a lot of flak which, even though hurtful, acted as a further stimulus to pursue fruits which obviously demanded sacrifice. Padraig Pearse's conviction and preparedness to sacrifice himself for a Gaelic Ireland was our great inspiration. We organised Irish plays and for a couple of years were able to borrow copies of the Abbey Irish pantomime which we produced ourselves. Even though my background was to some extent West British I became totally involved in Irish republicanism.

I always was convinced and still am that a genuine Irish Republic will grow if we use all the people and resources with respect. Writing people off as terrorists is a sloganistic way of dealing with a matter that needs more than thoughtless retorts which absolve them from accountability. If they were effectively challenged to account for their activity, it is most unlikely that they would reject peaceful means if those means were offered without precondition.

We may have to walk some distance with those who burn with zeal and first learn a lot from them before they can hear us. This strategy has worked before; on the road to Emmaus. Surely anyone who knows what it feels like to be "eaten up with zeal" or "consumed by idealism" must appreciate this.

The student's life was one of basic innocence and good will. People really did make an effort to cope worthily with their commitments. It was a rigorous regime, rising at five forty every morning but it was a wholesome training. On one Thursday each month students were permitted an outing up the Dublin mountains. We usually went in groups of eight, becollared and behatted as always. We travelled by bicycle taking with us food such as sausages and eggs which we would cook in a field or ruined house or even at a deserted roadside. In order to stimulate our camp fire for cooking we always carried a small quantity of coal with us which would give zest to the wood. Topics of interest and value came up for discussion around the camp fire, as well as grudges and gripes which could be eloquently aired and usually defused.

A particularly humorous aspect of these outings was the varyingly startled reaction of the occasional mountain walker who passed by and observed us cooking, enjoying our meal or just sitting around the fire. People generally are quite unaccustomed to seeing a group of "priests" squatting around a roadside fire in a remote mountain setting, like witches on the heath. If thoughts can be conveyed by looks I would hazard a guess that one man who passed by as we were sitting around the fire toasting bread was unsettled by the idea that he may have come upon some expression of devil worship.

At the end of our third year of studies when we had finished our philosophy, came the final commitment or Solemn Vows. By virtue of those vows you were committed to the order and vice versa until death. A significant practical consequence was that you were henceforth obliged under pain of mortal sin to the recitation of the Divine Office every day and if for any reason you could not attend Office in choir you would have to make it up privately. The Divine Office while it would take about an hour and a half to chant in choir would take under an hour to say privately. Canon Law had a number of directives about the recitation of the Office and these had to be studied by us during the summer holidays.

After Solemn Profession came tonsure which was a token cutting of hair by the bishop, by which ceremony you became a cleric. No member of a religious order or congregation is a cleric per se, therefore while they are popularly referred to as clerics no members of teaching or nursing orders of brothers are clerics and are given, only out of courtesy, the titles of Reverend, Very Reverend and Most Reverend.

Tonsure and the subsequent minor orders of Reader, Porter, Acolyte and Exorcist were conferred in Clonliffe College, the

Dublin Archdiocesan Seminary. Very large numbers of students were presented together as the conferring of these orders were usually shared by ordinands of different religious houses of formation.

The usual period spent in the order before priestly ordination was seven years, including novitiate, but mature students, among whom I figured were ordained after six years.

Apart from the normal academic exams in theology conducted by the order there were Vicariate exams run by the Archdiocese of Dublin which every candidate had to sit before every conferring of orders. It was a tedious arrangement and suggested a lack of confidence by the archdiocese either in the standards of religious orders or in their integrity.

In those days the first of the major orders conferred was the sub-diaconate which has since disappeared as its historicity and authenticity were found inadequately established. Being allowed to wear a maniple (since then also obsolete) and a dalmatic for the first time was a great joy and the beginning of a new kind of life experience whereby one was afforded status, however slight. A little recognition goes a long way.

Diaconate came in due course around about Easter 1958. I never for a moment doubted my calling to the priesthood which I received in due course, well supported and encouraged by friends and relations.

Ordination was on July 13th 1958 in Clonliffe. It was a very wet day which weather conditions I remember so clearly because we had to do all our socialising after the ceremony in various corridors and class rooms rather than in the spacious gardens. At a decent interval after the ceremony the Provincial told me my posting for the next two years was to be Rome to study for the Licenciate in Theology.

Although all through the course of studies before priesthood I had been very keen, I had a block against really serious and committed study. I was convinced that I should always work for the remote and greatest good and that it was imperfect to study for the sake of the glory of doing well in examinations etc. Instead of getting down to real study I spent days and weeks fretting about my lack of purity of intention. 'If I really studied', I asked myself, 'wouldn't I be doing it only for vain glory?'

This perfectionism lands you in a "catch 22" situation. You are wasting time by worrying about your impurity of intention, but to ignore that prompting to perfection is also wrong, therefore you can't apparently win. I didn't then, but now I do realise that I needed therapy of some kind but psychotherapy or any form of creative counselling was either not available at all or frowned upon. There seemed to have been the assumption that your confessor could supply any such need.

There was never any direct attempt at personal formation or group dynamics. That kind of personal growth when it happened at all happened by chance. The big thing was to keep hanging on until ordination, if possible.

Ordination was longed for by many, if not all. Many were properly motivated through and through and about them there's no question. But for others it was seen often as a state of redemption from the bondage of student life, a time when one could smoke, go home, visit friends, wear black trousers under your habit instead of the habit pants, have two fried eggs on Saturday night and late sleeps on Sunday mornings on account of being on late Masses. Now, these are all reasonable human values. But I would query the wisdom of allowing their sudden availability to coincide with ordination. I think there can be a harmful confusion of motivation. Sudden release into the land of plenty from the desert of the years of formation distracted one from the desert beyond the post ordination honeymoon. All this may be compared to an over elaborate engagement, marriage ceremony, reception and honeymoon which may shield a couple from facing the realities of living together.

Chapter 8

OVERLAND TO ROME

On that very day of ordination we were allowed home on holidays. For some it was the first time home for seven years. For me it was the first time in six years, apart from a few visits lasting just a few hours, to my father when he was dying and one night at home for his funeral. After those years away it was good to run around freely, go places, meet people and be hailed as if something had been achieved.

In the meantime a great deal had happened. The most obvious event was the death of my father. I still felt his presence around and I found it upsetting, saddening, as I had not before known the house without at least the possibility of his being there. I was glad that my mother was still young, only in her late forties. I encouraged her to start a new life of her own. I discussed with her what she might do. The house and farm at Lissarda which belonged now to my sister, Rosemary, would be a liability for her to look after, so I suggested that she might buy a house for herself in Dublin or Cork.

At the time of my Solemn Profession in 1956 I had signed over to her the farm at Warrensgrove, which my father had given me. Later she sold this farm as it would have been too big a task for her to work it profitably.

During my three weeks of holidays I called on every relation and family friend within a reasonable distance. I was enjoying the role.

Two days after celebrating my First Mass I officiated at the marriage of my sister Rosemary to Philip Kemp at our local parish church in Kilmurry. They had their reception at Lissarda House.

Having enjoyed the warmth, welcome and respect of the people I regard as my own folk, I went back to Tallaght to get ready to go to Rome.

Six of us set out from Holyhead to go overland and by sea which in those days was much cheaper than going by air. Our route was via London, Paris, Lourdes, Nice, Milan and Florence.

As a group, we varied in taste and temperament. We had footballers, artists, republicans and West Brits. The first contretemps was in Victoria Station in London when a porter who saw aggressiveness in what was really a display of good spirits expressed by a heartily shouted greeting, told Brother Celestine that he and his likes were the source of all the misery in the world today. A battle of words was about to get under way in which it seemed likely that religion and nationality were going to get confused. The rest of us moved on Brother Celestine as gently as we could.

After an uneventful journey from Calais to Paris we awkwardly threaded our way by metro to our Paris staging post which was at one of the houses of the French Dominican province. We had been expected and were welcomed, fed and shown to our rooms which were adequate though not luxurious. It was a place of study and work and those I spoke to I liked. I have always been a Francophile and was very envious of some of my fellow students who were sent to do their studies in France.

We arose early the next morning and served each other's' Masses; those were the days before con-celebration was allowed, apart from during the ceremonies of priestly or episcopal ordination. Father Colman paired off with me and opted to celebrate first. He was a strict teetotaller and absolutely inexperienced in wine. The altar wine used in Ireland is usually quite sweet, a lot of it at that time coming from Portugal. The French altar wine looked just like it, but there the similarity ended. Father Colman poured a good half cruet into the chalice at the beginning of Mass. He whispered his way devoutly and decorously until the communion. With the appropriate, angled gestures of piety still novel to him since ordination, he took and consumed the Body of the Lord, made due thanksgiving, took the chalice, raised it to his head and set about consuming the Blood of the Lord when he took a fit of paroxysmal coughing. He went purple in the face and only for the help of one of the French priests who happened to be nearby I think he might have choked on a draught of the driest of dry French white wine.

The coffee and bread for breakfast were delightful. There was a wholesome wholeheartedness about the French Dominicans which I always admired.

They have produced some of the best theologians and biblical scholars of recent years. The École Biblique in Jerusalem, established and run by them is one of the foremost centres of biblical scholarship in the world.

Later in the morning some went on a short sightseeing tour to Notre Dame and the Madeleine. Father David who spoke some French acted as tour leader, confidently, unselfconsciously and easily asking directions and questions of Parisians who are not renowned for suffering smiling stammering tourists gladly. I was waiting uneasily for the snub or rebuff which I felt must explode sooner or later, but it never did. I suppose people only get what they expect.

Father David was hoping to go into religious journalism. He was a good photographer and had a well-informed interest in magazine layout and cover design. In Dublin I had known him as being unable to pass by shops which sold periodicals. His eyesight was not good. He couldn't just glance at his watch to tell the time, he had to scrutinise it. His preoccupation with any object of his attention seemed exaggerated. That afternoon in Paris he was like a child in a sweet shop drawn as if by magnet to every street newsstand, looking at the various cover designs talking to the vendors and flicking through the pages of some of the magazines to see the layout of the contents. We thought that it would have been destructive to discourage such innocent single mindedness but yet on going by newsstands we kept far enough away to seem dissociated from the short sighted cleric peering at the binding of "Paris by Night", nonchalantly unaware that his silhouette was framed very much otherwise than by a display of the "Messenger" or the "Catholic Herald" on a Legion of Mary book barrow.

That night, at the Gare de Lyon, we boarded the overnight train to Lourdes. Judging by attire and deportment it seemed that all the intending passengers were pilgrims; the French typecast themselves, and the Irish and a few English who were on the platform could only have been pilgrims. Those were the days before popular package holidays.

We had couchettes together in the same compartment. We agreed to three quarters of an hour of silence when the train pulled out of the station so that we could all catch up on the recitation of our Divine Office or breviary. That arrangement worked out well and then we felt free to enjoy the journey, looking forward to what was to be only a fleeting visit to Lourdes. After something to eat and drink we settled the sleeping arrangements. There were three bunks on each side. Father Celestine on one of the top bunks soothed himself to sleep with one of his favourite authors, the Gaelic games correspondent of the Irish Press. He felt secure as he dropped off re reading the account of the recent All Ireland Football Final.

I settled for the top bunk on the other side. I was in no hurry to get to sleep as I enjoy train travel. We sped through the French countryside. There was a very short stop at Orleans where a few docile youths accompanied by a traditionally cassocked priest got on board. Owing to excitement and too much French coffee I hardly slept and so I was aware of my surroundings.

Father David had been ferreting around the bottom bunk for ages with the aid of a small pen torch, sometimes wearing his glasses and other times looking for them in order to put documents in order. He would read some more Divine Office then read the latest issue of Informations Catholiques, the Time Magazine of the Church in France. He was out to the corridor a few times and still appeared to be unpacking and packing his cases as day was beginning to dawn when we reached Toulouse.

At this point Father Celestine's travel alarm clock, an ordination present, went off uncontrollably and had to be smothered in the Gaelic sports pages of the Irish Press while the alarm mechanism was being defused.

Father David had only just nodded off to sleep when Father Celestine dropped down from his bunk, fully clad. He was a very correct man and would not venture out unless modestly dressed. About ten minutes after leaving the compartment he returned, shaved, shining, full of bonhomie and set about saying the Small Hours of the Divine Office.

We arrived in Lourdes just as the working day was getting under way. We celebrated Mass in the Basilica, went to the baths and did the Stations of the Cross. We bought souvenirs, sent some postcards home and spent a rewarding time with various groups of invalids. We attended devotions that night and did a short vigil at the grotto.

Two words which come to mind about Lourdes are; courtesy and respect. From me Lourdes demands simplicity and tolerance. There is an immediate presence of God which I find hard to cope with, like Moses, in the Book of Exodus, who covered his face at the burning bush, "afraid to look at God". There is no sophistication in Lourdes, you have to lay pretentiousness aside in order to survive. Being there is to take part in the basic Christian experience which loses in the telling. Any description bears the prejudices of the witness which either irritate or foster our own predispositions. Lourdes, Fatima and Knock are places that in my experience are hallowed. By adapting some of the other words of God to Moses in the same passage of Exodus just quoted, it could be said, that Lourdes, Fatima and Knock are also, in a sense "holy ground".

Some people drink Lourdes water for health of body and soul and others think of such behaviour as superstitious. There is no point in arguing, each of these people is looking ultimately at a different kind of model or metaphor for the expressing of revealed truth; "quidquid recipitur per modum recipientis recipitur" (whatever is heard is heard according to the predisposition of the hearer) are the immortal words of St. Thomas Aquinas. If you really want the truth go and see for yourself.

Indeed, cannot we pray with Mary anywhere, be sponsored by her anywhere? All ground is now holy ground. The Spirit has renewed the face of the earth? Why go to Lourdes? Apart from calling on authority and the "holy ground" tradition of many religions, including Islam, perhaps theology might borrow the licence of literature in this case, by adapting George Orwell's words of "Animal Farm", 'all places are equally holy, but some places are more equally holy than others'?

But again more seriously, the decks are cleared for us in these specially designated holy places. The task is made quite clear and there are minimal distractions.

We said Mass early the next morning and got to the station to catch our train to Nice. This was a very long journey in warm Mediterranean weather, particularly as our clothing was that of inhabitants in a cold north European climate. We read our breviaries, looked at the scenery and speculated about what was before us for the time we were to spend in Rome.

Very late in the afternoon we arrived at the station in Nice. We were met by a kindly priest in a Dominican habit who had rented a minibus to transport us and our luggage to the Dominican Priory. It was very warm by our standards and we were tired. We were a large group of visitors to suddenly descend on any house but for some reason a number of the community were away and we had the use of their rooms.

We had a shower and relaxed for an hour before we were summoned to the evening meal. There was soup first of all which I enjoyed. This was followed by a main course of oysters. I had never taken oysters before. I had always been able to avoid them, but on this occasion as they were the main and substantial part of the meal I felt I should cope with them. The others got them back with obvious satisfaction but I felt all the time that things would not be well with me. Immediately after the meal I felt awful. I had to retire to my room, spent a very bad night and I never again ate oysters.

Although feeling fragile I celebrated Mass the next morning and an Irish Dominican priest who was on loan to that Province to act as chaplain to an American naval installation in Nice took us an a brief sightseeing tour of the town. Although it was very late September there were still a few tourists in evidence. Then before lunch some of us went for a glorious swim in the sea. The humidity was high so the refreshing effect of the sea was particularly enlivening. There were very few on the beach which we were glad about as we felt a bit out of place in our Irish clerical suits and collars.

The following day we went to Antibes by bus to see the Picasso paintings. Before we left the priory to go to the bus terminus our Irish senior colleague insisted that we shed our clerical modesty and go in shirt and trousers to Antibes. We were glad to have got the permission to do this and enjoyed the freedom but collarless granddad shirts and, in at least two instances, braces still did not look quite "comme il faut".

On the way to Milan we passed through Monte Carlo. We had one night in Milan. The following morning we spent doing the appropriate sightseeing of the Duomo and of the Da Vinci Last Supper.

Then it was Florence. But we lost Father David at the station before Florence, called Prato. He had fallen asleep and when the train stopped in Prato the rest of us happened to be out on the corridor. On seeing that we were not in the compartment with him he presumed we had reached our destination so grabbing his baggage he jumped onto the platform and we could see him, unaffected by our calling after him, disappear up along the platform going in the direction of the exit. We had no worries about him. Although absent minded he was highly intelligent, a good communicator and predictable. We confidently waited for the following train which was only forty minutes behind us and as expected, he arrived.

After more sightseeing in Florence on the following day, we eventually got to Rome. So this was it, journey's end and a new beginning.

Chapter 9

STUDIES IN ROME

It was evening time, about six o'clock, when we arrived into the station at Rome. I thought I had some idea about what to expect since I had been in Rome for the closing of the Holy Door at the end of the Holy Year in 1950, but things did appear differently to me on this occasion. Now, I was about to become part of the Roman landscape. Then, I came just to look at it.

We booked a couple of taxis and were driven quickly, though at times frighteningly through the Roman traffic. In those days Roman drivers did not seem to operate according to any objective rules of the road but according to their estimate of what might be going on in the minds of the other road users. They were engaged in a constant competition for space in which to move as quickly as possible. There was no reticence about horn blowing.

We had heard a fair bit about anti-clerical attitudes prevalent amongst the Roman population but our driver showed no signs of that. He was communicative and affable and pointed out things of interest as we sped past them. The number of trams was quite surprising, long single decker snake-like vehicles which had an inbuilt right of way.

Within a quarter of an hour the taxis stopped and our driver pointed to a gateway indicating that someone should go to press the bell in the wall beside it. We were stopped in the very busy Via Labicana just outside the gates leading into the garden and Convent of San Clemente.

In Rome, the term 'convent' is applied to both male and female religious houses. Just down the road we could see the outline of the Colosseum.

We were made to feel welcome by Brother Bernard who came out and acted as our interpreter in settling the accounts with the taxi drivers. Having settled these matters, we shyly followed Brother Bernard into the house, treading carefully on what must have been venerable soil. The Prior was informed of our arrival and came to greet us with a certain raucousness which relaxed the atmosphere. This meeting and greeting took place in a large open area in the centre of the house called the downstairs salone. It had a high ceiling and a tiled floor. It was like an exceptionally large hall and off it there were doorways leading to places such as the library and the refectory. It was insulated from the outside by other rooms around it and the theory was that such insulation would serve to keep the salone area cool in the Summer time. Beside the entrance door to this area was a stairway leading up to the next floor which had a similar salone with priests' rooms off it.

There was another wing at right angles to the main building in which were the rooms of the priests who were students. We had been assigned to particular rooms by the Prior who asked Brother Bernard to show us to them. In this wing there were two floors of study bedrooms, I was to be given a room on the top floor. The floors of the corridors were surfaced with uneven undulating polished red brown tiles. Until you got your "sea legs" the floor undulations tended to make you lurch forward or sideways as you walked along.

About two o'clock one afternoon a phone call came from the British Minister to the Holy See (in those days the British diplomatic representation in the Holy See did not have ambassadorial status). He told the Superior that the Queen Mother who was on holiday in Rome had expressed a desire to see San Clemente and could we accommodate her. He was told she would be most welcome and accordingly it was decided that she would be calling down to us in about an hour's time. Since all churches in Rome close daily between midday and four o'clock there would be no crowd problem and the press had not been informed.

Almost at the stroke of three o'clock the Queen Mother arrived with a small entourage consisting of a lady in waiting, her secretary (a man) and one other man. Besides, there were a few Italian police present. After the Superior met her at the entrance to the cortile in front of the basilica he introduced the community to her individually. I found her very personable and interested in whatever was said to her. She mingled with us and chatted for quite some time and posed with us for photographs. She got her secretary to take a few photos for us so that all could be included in a couple of shots. She told us that her family all found San Clemente of particular interest and liked to call whenever possible. What we didn't tell her was that the room in which her husband's grandfather, Edward Vll, once spent a night and in commemoration of which occasion a plaque had been put over the door, had been transformed into a bathroom by a Prior who was less than enthusiastic about the British Royal Family.

After this socialising the Queen Mother was taken on a guided tour.

The student priests' rooms were quite small, but adequate, with bed, table, washstand, bookcase and bedside locker. The window was small, looking out onto an enclosed back garden. The noise caused by the traffic, including trams passing nearby on three sides was very loud and at first disturbing, but in a very short time you got so used to it that you were distracted when there was a lull, which happened only occasionally.

We got changed into our white habits and met other members of the community before going into supper in the refectory for our first Roman meal, at which wine was served. Four of the new student priests decided to drink wine while two decided to preserve their pioneer teetotal innocence. After the meal we met three members of the lay house staff; Ubaldo, one of the house boys, Umberto the chef and Ernesto who had been in service in San Clemente since 1907 (he died in 1969). The atmosphere was friendly and there was genuine interest in us and concern about our needs. It seemed like a close knit community,

Pope Pius XII had been very ill for some time and within a few days of our arrival in Rome, he died. Due to some distastefully inaccurate journalism his death was reported on the newsstands before it actually took place. The record was set right by a radio announcement and the police were sent around to sequestrate the offending copy from the newsstands. Curio collectors tried to snap up copies before the police got there with the kind of enthusiasm with which stamp collectors pursue overprints.

We went to his lying in state in St. Peter's Basilica and took part in the funeral procession from St. John Lateran's Basilica, the Cathedral church of the Bishop of Rome, to St. Peter's where he was to be buried. The funeral procession was made up of such a large number of clerics because practically all of them had just returned from holidays to start the new academic year. There were columns after columns of us lined up. Franciscans, Augustinians, Dominicans et al. It was all most impressive.

We had a few days of sightseeing in Rome before going to register for the coming academic year in the University of St. Thomas, and then called the Angelicum. Most of us visited the places of more popular interest although there were a couple who had not the slightest interest in the art and culture around them and felt no inclination or obligation to go outside the walls of San Clemente except to go to the university or to the station news stand to get the overseas editions of papers with the English Football results. Arrangements had also been made with Associated Press to get Gaelic Games' results sent out on the wires as they happened.

Registering at the University was quite an experience and what I found an interesting, even if a complicating feature was the number of officials and professors of varying nationalities with whom one had to deal. English was spoken by most of them and, in general, those who did not have it as a first language were anxious to try out what they had on you. The only person with no interest at all in speaking English was the Rector who was French.

There were students from most religious orders or congregations and from dioceses all over the world wandering around; some had everything under control while others were finding it hard even to communicate their difficulties. A detailed report of your academic credentials had to be submitted for scrutiny by the authorities who were concerned to maintain high standards.

In early October lectures began. It was just less than a mile from San Clemente to the University of St. Thomas. We walked the distance in all weathers, clad in our white habits covered with black cappa or cloak and black cappuce or hood as well as a wide brimmed black hat. Taking the bus was of little advantage. The street leading up to the university building was called, imaginatively, Salita del Grillo which means "the ascent of the grasshopper".

The streets of Rome were a colourful sight in the early mornings with students from scores of colleges going to the universities, of which there were four with Pontifical status, besides the University of St. Thomas there were the Gregorian, the Lateran and Propaganda Fidei. Amongst the most colourful of the students were those from the German College who wore a red cassock with a black sash.

After a couple of weeks, when we were acclimatised, the Prior told us that we would have to get tonsured, according to the statutes of the Diocese of Rome. There were different degrees of clerical tonsure. The more usual one was an area about the size of a fifty pence piece shaved on the crown of the head. This was the type made use of by secular clergy and students and modern religious congregations. But the Dominicans as well as some other of the older orders had to undergo quite radical tonsures. For Dominicans the style and dimensions of the tonsure were described in the constitutions; the top of the head had to have the hair cut skin-close to within three fingers' breadth of the ears and a band of hair of that same three fingers' breadth was to be cut less closely around the back of the head from ear to ear, but below that band down towards the neck, the hair was once more to be cut skin tight.

A couple of us who were thought to have hairdressing potential were selected to act as barbers and beyond all doubt we branded our victims as clerics, The mystical purpose of the tonsure, as a sign of vocation, was officially stressed but perhaps the authorities had some practical effects in mind too, akin to the old idea of shaving the heads of convicts. For instance, clerics were not permitted to go to the cinema or to the theatre. This could have been transgressed by some, simply by donning lay clothes, but in the Roman circumstances, such as they were, paramilitary head gear would have been needed.

For a number of weeks after the death of Pope Pius XII the papacy was said to be in a state of "Sede Vacante". Procedures to be followed in the Vatican during this period were laid down carefully in 1945 by Pope Pius XII himself in a special document which seems to emphasise that the Cardinals, during this interregnum, have not got the power of jurisdiction or of making laws, which prerogative has reserved solely to the Pope. They were to be content with maintaining the status quo, Pope Paul VI seems to have gone even further along this line in his document of 1975 whereby all cardinals in charge of departments of the Roman Curia would automatically relinquish their offices on the death of the Pope. One of the few exceptions to this rule was the Papal Chamberlain who took over a kind of chairperson's role as Keeper of the Keys of Peter. Pope Pius XII decreed that the Sacred College of Cardinals was to meet frequently during this time but Paul VI changed that "frequently" to "daily". It would appear that both these Popes wanted to minimise the possibility of any improper ambition on the part of some cardinals if left to their own devices for too long. At any rate, the principal function set out for the cardinals was to arrange for the obsequies of the dead Pope and for the conclave to elect the new Pope.

The Vatican Post Office, with an eye to business, promptly brought out a special "Sede Vacante" commemorative stamp.

**

Although, strictly speaking, he should not have done so, our Prior allowed three of us, who so requested him, to play with C.U.S. Rorna, the rugby club of the secular University of Rome. This involved going for a practice session every Wednesday or Thursday afternoon and a match about every second weekend. Quite a number of clerics played for Roman rugby clubs and were keenly sought after by these clubs. There was some outstanding talent in various colleges, for example the Holy Ghost students had amongst them many who had played on Leinster or Munster Senior Schools' Cup winning teams. There was at least one Irish trialist available and a Junior All Black from New Zealand. The climax of our rugby year was the annual match between the clerical students and one of the Roman clubs. No concessions were made about the wearing of clerical clothes and it was quite a sight to see the clerical team arrive at the grounds complete with cassocks and tonsures, Although the cassocks and collars were stowed in the changing rooms the tonsures made it easier for the referee to know whom or whom not to penalise in a loose maul.

On one particular occasion I was selected to play for C.U.S. Roma against the Sardinian Police in Florence. The Roman clubs were used to seeing fully robed and tonsured clerics arriving into the changing rooms but for the Sardinian Police, my appearance in full clerical dress, defied understanding.

Our lectures in the University were all in Latin which did not cause any difficulty when you got used to it. You had to do essays and papers and ask questions in class in Latin and be able to converse with your professor if necessary. Quite a number of the teaching staff knew some English and were glad to practice it on English speaking students. Father Lumbreras who gave a course in Moral Theology had an endless repertoire of jokes which sounded particularly funny when told in Latin.

One day between lectures I got talking in Latin to a student from the Argentine. He told me he had no English, which surprised me since he had a name which sounded obviously Scottish. He told me that his parents had emigrated to Argentina from the Scottish Hebrides and the language of his home was Gaelic, which he spoke just as fluently as Spanish.

In the course of the year a number of friends and acquaintances came to Rome and I was pleased to be able to show them around. One important reason for liking this task was that it gave me the motivation to read up about the various monuments and places of interest.

***

One of the most interesting monuments in Rome was San Clemente itself, where we lived. It was handed over to the Irish Province of the Dominican Order in 1677 to provide for the formation and education of novices and students at a time when it was not possible at home in Ireland. But it was not until 1857 under the skilled directorship of Father Joseph Mullooly that it began to yield up its hidden archaeological treasures. Between 1857 and the time of his death in 1880 Father Mullooly had excavated under the twelfth century basilica, which was in use then as today as a house of worship, and discovered another fourth century basilica. Under that fourth century basilica he went on to discover a first century Mithraic temple. These three levels are today open to the public.

One afternoon, just after four o'clock I was disturbed from my studies by a call from the house boy, Ubaldo. Ubaldo hadn't a word of English and didn't easily distinguish Irish surnames one from another. Murphy and Mullooly had, for him, enough in common, by both beginning in M and ending in Y, to make them indistinguishable. He told me in Italian that there was someone in the parlour who wanted to see me. I went down drowsy from trying to concentrate on theology on a humid enough kind of afternoon.

I knocked on the door of the parlour. There was a loud reply, 'come in'.

And then, 'Well, well, well, isn't it great to meet you at last, Father Mullooly, I thought it would be nice if my wife and I could call to see you and bring back news about you to your cousin who is a great friend of ours.'

I tried to get control of the conversation to straighten the record but not before he had told me that his name was Farrell, he was a retired bank manager on a coach tour of Europe and that he and his wife broke away from the tour for a couple of hours especially to visit me. Eventually, through the good offices of his wife who insisted that he listen, I got his ear.

'I am sorry, but I am not Father Mullooly', I said.

He began to pour out again, 'I was afraid that he might be out when we called, I was going to ring up but I didn't have your number... and anyway I mightn't be able to manage these Roman phones.....when is he likely to be back?'

Becoming somewhat infected by the craziness of this encounter my next comment, which I must admit, may have been a little impish, only tended to prolong the unreality. I said, 'He won't be back anymore'.

'Why is that?' asked Mr. Farrell.

'He's dead', I said, with as straight a face as I could manage.

'May God rest him, the cousin never told me he was dead, when did it happen?'

Even though I felt certain that it would make him feel ridiculous I had no choice but to give him the whole truth, '1880'.

I perceived in him a momentary irritation but then he burst out in good humoured laughter, obviously deciding not to feel himself as ridiculous or ridiculed but deciding to enjoy a ridiculous situation comedy. Then, as if on cue, Ubaldo arrived in with a tray of tea and biscuits. As Mr.Farrell mused over his tea he turned to his wife and said, 'I'll have at least one funny story to tell them when I get home.'

The conclave to elect the next Pope was called. The conclave was bound by strict regulations. All the cardinals were bound to attend, although later Paul Vl was to exclude cardinals over a certain age. Each cardinal could be accompanied into the conclave by two assistants or servants. Some other named people were also admitted but at an appointed time the conclave doors were locked both on the inside and on the outside. No communication whatsoever was allowed with the outside world until the task of electing a Pope was finished. "Telegraphs, telephone, microphones, radios, cameras, moving picture machines," were all forbidden.

Once the conclave started, smoke was awaited by large crowds thronging in St.Peter's Square. The smoke, when it came was not immediately a clear sign of what had happened because quite a lot of it had to be emitted before you could conclude with any certainty that it was white, signalling, "Habemus Papam", "We have a Pope", or black signalling that there was no result and the voting would have to take place again.

The popular favourite in 1958 was Archbishop Giovanni Montini of Milan but those who were wise in the ways of church politics said that it would be quite unlikely that the College of Cardinals would select someone from outside the conclave.

During the many hours that we waited in St. Peter's Square many names were bandied about in an atmosphere of tangible expectation. Finally, one evening the white smoke did curl up in abundance and everybody, even some of those wary of clichés, echoed,"Habemus Papam". There was to be quite a long wait before the new Pope, whoever he was, would be announced and introduced by Cardinal Tixeront, the Dean of the Sacred College of Cardinals. Whoever was elected would have been asked, by that same Dean, if he would accept the office and as soon as he indicated consent he was Pope with all authority. Sometime would be needed to change into the white cassock as worn by a Pope and in this particular case I suspect that considerable hurried modifications had to be made by the Papal tailors.

While we were waiting for the appearance of the new Pope I noticed people pouring out of the Academy of Santa Caecilia on the Via della Conciliazione which leads into St.Peter's Square. It was the interval during a symphony concert and many of the audience came out for some air and to see if the white smoke had come. I can remember the ushers trying in vain to attract the audience back into the concert hall. I never heard what finally happened to the concert, I presume it had to be abandoned.

'With great joy I announce to you that we have a Pope, Guiseppe Angelo Roncalli who will be called Pope John XXIII'.

There followed the customary cheering, but it was, for the vast majority, a cheer for someone about whom they knew little or nothing. Gradually it got around that he had been Patriarch of Venice up to this and he was a native of Bergamo in the north of Italy. He had been in the army and in the Papal diplomatic service in Bulgaria. He was seventy seven years of age. It was concluded by many there and then that he was just a caretaker Pope, put in by the cardinals until they could really make up their minds.

His choice of name was remarkable because there had been an Antipope, Baldassare Cossa, called by this name, John XXIII, at the time of the Great Schism (1389-1414), who is reputed to have used his skills as a former pirate to trade in indulgences. What makes his choice more interesting is the fact that as an acknowledged church historian Angelo Roncalli must have been fully informed.

The day of the Papal Coronation came and I had a very good place in St. Peter's for the Coronation Mass. I was in the right transept and quite close to the altar. There was one drawback and that was that I and my companion were in the full glare and heat of the lights for the television cameras. One great advantage was that we had a perfect view of the Pope's own family down from Bergamo for what was a big family event. They looked to be of peasant stock and were quite relaxed, unperturbed by the vanities of the occasion.

At the offertory of the Mass I noticed quite an interesting incident at the altar. Whether by prearrangement or by clever improvisation I don't know, the Master of Ceremonies, at a certain moment, so placed the large book from which the Pope was reading the prayers that it acted as a kind of screen, shielding the Pope from the lenses of the cameras and from practically all the congregation. As far as I could see, the Pope hastily consumed a beverage of some description. Suddenly being placed centre stage at seventy seven and expected to spend hours at ceremonies, must have been very difficult, so how wise Pope John was to dispense the fasting law for himself on this occasion. The fasting laws then were quite demanding and dispensations for cases not listed in the law had not normally been granted.

Those long hours of ceremonies in the Vatican can be a source of acute discomfort particularly for older men. A Brother who was well versed in the more prosaic aspects of ceremonial once told me that the flowing robes of the cardinals were designed with a view to camouflaging what he referred to as an "instrumentum" which could be carried for reassurance if not for use.

One of the first functions that a Pope performs after his installation is to visit his cathedral church as Bishop of Rome. This is the church of St. John Lateran which is only up the street from San Clemente. Our Prior thought it would be fitting to ask the Pope to call on us in passing. The invitation was issued accordingly and accepted, so San Clemente became one of the first places to be visited by this new Pope. It was a very short visit and he did not come into the house, although he did sign our visitors' book. The event was, I thought, spoiled by a very obvious, but I presume necessary, police presence. I think the Italian police always feel particularly responsible when a Pope wanders outside the boundaries of the Vatican state.

A Papal audience was arranged for the students and staff of the University of St. Thomas. The audience was arranged for seven o'clock in the Vatican. Those who wished to attend assembled well before time in the appointed audience hall. I suppose we were expecting a dramatic entrance at seven o'clock but it never happened. What did happen was that a small rotund man clad in white, busily stuffing a handkerchief back into his pocket with one hand and adjusting his suchetto or skull cap with the other, shuffled in a few minutes after seven, being pursued it would appear, by two keepers who seemed afraid of losing control.

Pope John XXlll faced the assembled group and smiled a welcome, saying, 'I did not expect so many of you.... if I knew in time I would have gone over to you in the University of St. Thomas'.
He continued on giving a gentle and encouraging talk about our studies.

For someone who had been in the Diplomatic service he showed an extraordinary innocence of protocol or perhaps this was just his way of effecting change?

Chapter 10

SPRINGTIME

Christmas in Rome was a good experience. It was my second Christmas there, my first one having been in 1950 when I was in Rome for the closing of the Holy Door. The Christmas liturgy was well carried out in the basilica of San Clemente and the attendance of the public was impressive. Christmas and Easter are times when Roman people, who are not normally great churchgoers, do make an effort.

The bringing in of the New Year was preceded immediately by the throwing out of rubbish onto the streets on New Year's Eve. It was quite surprising to see windows being opened and refuse being dumped in public - a tradition they could profitably abandon.

The onset of spring was refreshing and you could notice the tourist population growing. Walking in Rome was always interesting but even more so when the tourists were arriving. I was often stopped by lost or particularly enthusiastic tourists looking for enlightenment. Their initial approach was sometimes in their own language. Clerics were presumed to be able to speak more than one language and people took the chance that this particular cleric might know theirs. More often the opening words to you were in Italian which ranged from being quite fluent as in the case of most Germans, Dutch or Scandinavians to being a juxtapositioning of nouns and verb infinitives in the case of so many of the English speaking groups.

On one particular occasion I was addressed by two Americans in very poor Italian. I answered back in English, to their relief. I was able to give them the information they needed but the communication never became personal. In the end, one of them simply congratulated me on my good English and the other said I spoke English better than some Americans he knew! In the case of most Irish tourists or pilgrims it was good fun not to reveal your identity for some time and to draw them out a la "candid camera".

At Easter, Rome reached the peak of its tourism and there was a noticeable influx of German people particularly. At Easter, a number of the student priests took individuals, couples or small groups around on whistle stop tours of Rome. These would more usually be relatives or friends from Ireland or friends of friends. I did quite a lot of guiding through the excavations at San Clemente.

We carried out the ceremonies of Holy Week and Easter with as much care and reverence as possible, but the big event as far as most of the people were concerned was the blessing of the houses on Holy Saturday. There must have been hundreds of families and others living in apartments within less than a half mile around San Clemente. Most of these people, although classified as non-practising Catholics, expected a priest to come and bless their homes. From the point of view of pastoral ministry, this was an important tradition to retain, as it was providing at least a thread of contact with the church.....of which basically, they liked to be considered members.

The Prior called on the student priests to help in this "Operation Blessing". We were each provided with a holy water bucket and sprinkler and introduced to an acolyte or helper who would conduct us around the particular apartment blocks assigned to each one of us. We were advised that the custom was that in return for the blessing the household would make an offering which involved dropping coins into the holy water bucket, which may have to be discreetly emptied several times in the course of the operation. The coins would have to be pocketed or put into a briefcase carried around for that purpose.

The apartments I went into were all very well kept, most of them providing just frugal comfort with a few exceptions. They consisted generally of a fairly large kitchen/living room, two bedrooms and a bathroom. There were one or two youngish children or babies in most apartments. I came across no large families.

***

Seeing these living conditions forced me into reflecting on the church's teaching on birth control, on which I had done a fair amount of work in Moral Theology.

I found myself, as a result of the Holy Saturday "Operation Blessing", looking at several possible sexual arrangements between a couple.

The first is that the married couple plan their family according to secular criteria using whatever contraceptive means are aesthetically acceptable to both of them.

The second is that the couple have intercourse when they both need it and desire it in order to copper fasten or climax expressions and feelings of mutual love at any time during the month and without contraceptive precautions of any kind. They are happy to procreate any number of children.

The third is that the couple use intercourse as a climactic expression of love for each other as in the second situation above described, but responsibly parent only as many children as they can reasonably support. These agree not to have intercourse at all when there is a likelihood of conceiving.

As to the first: pastorally, from the church's point of view, as usually expressed through official channels, this couple are persistent sinners and must in one stroke adopt one of the other two above options if they want to be restored to God's friendship. But more usually they tend to move away outside the reach of pastoral instruction and development. They become alienated from serious thought about human destiny and the purpose of life. They become disheartened and despairing at the well-nigh impossible task imposed on them.

As to the second: it is difficult to credit that a couple with genuine virtue would not provide for the demographic or social situation as well as for the needs of their own loving relationship.

As to the third: a couple in this situation have gone far in the perfection of chastity. They exemplify the ideal as set out by the institutional church.

It appears to me that in effectively not dealing at all with the first group the church has allowed a situation to develop in which the best is the enemy of the good. Surely it is better to encourage what might be considered a less than perfect act of loving with the use of artificial means than to expect people to make a gigantic leap to perfection. The prospect of such a daunting leap is often the source of their spiritual despair and total turning away from the pursuit of final goodness.

Furthermore, what is not getting much publicity in the church is the fact that many Catholics from the middle class, at least in English speaking countries, have taken responsibility for their own decisions with regard to the use of so called artificial means of birth control. The poorer people are not given the help or encouragement to think for themselves.

If the church can get around Pope Innocent the Second's condemnation of usury, which, simply, is the using of money to make money as in banking etc., at the Second Lateran Council of the Church in 1139, "money lenders are to be regarded as absolutely infamous and unless they repent they are to be deprived of Christian burial," then it should be able to show more practical understanding of those who are being ostracized for offending against a theological conclusion.

Others who contravene the explicit biblical teaching of Matthew, chapter twenty five about feeding the hungry and clothing the naked are allowed considerable latitude or leeway.

***

In these tower blocks where we were on Holy Saturday there were usually four apartments to a floor, occupied by four different families. Near the bottom of one of the tower blocks we came across a floor which seemed somehow different. The door was opened so quickly when I knocked that I got the impression that she was afraid that I mightn't call. She was fortyish, well dressed and well groomed. It was coming on towards midday. The first room she led me into was directly inside the front door. It was a nicely furnished and quite expensively decorated room with a number of easy chairs, a large coffee table and a desk in the corner beside which was a drinks cabinet and what looked like a coffee pot on a ring. For a woman who had all the attributes necessary for confidence she seemed nervous. At first it occurred to me as strange to find this kind of person in what was, by and large, a working class area. From the size and shape of her reception room I guessed that she had access to more than the standard two bedrooms. She indicated to me to follow her. When I followed after her I found that we were in a longish room back to back with the front reception room. There were about a half a dozen young women, well dressed and attractive looking, lolling in easy chairs, sipping coffee, smoking, reading etc., I blessed them. It occurred to me that they might be office girls on a coffee break. Then the good woman of the house brought me back into another small corridor, off which there were about six sparsely furnished bedrooms, yet each of these bedrooms contained a "letto matrimoniale" or double bed. At her special request I gave each of the double beds a thorough blessing. By the time I was leaving she was much more confident and gave me a substantial stole fee of two one thousand lire notes.

I had a vague hunch about the nature of the establishment as soon as the woman first opened the door for my acolyte and me, and that was confirmed when I saw the double beds in the bedrooms. I was more shaken than I let on even to myself at the time. This upmarket brothel had about it the antiseptic cleanliness of a nursing home. However, I was glad to have been able to render a service - there was gospel precedent.

***

That year, Easter was very early, March 29th, I was hearing from my mother about the preparations and organisation that were going into preparing our home in Lissarda for putting up for auction. I was really saddened about this but I felt at the time that it had to be done as I thought it was far too lonely for my mother to live there by herself. It was a very large Victorian house built in 1860 and constantly in need of structural attention of some kind. It was really Rosemary's, my sister's inheritance but she had gone to live in England. My mother was young, fifty one and a healthy and active person and would need company and some useful work to do to fulfill her. For this reason it seemed best for her to make a complete break· and go to live in Dublin rather than in Cork city.

Rosemary was very upset by the trauma of selling our home which we loved so much and wrote to me in Rome on April 21st. to say that she went over to Lissarda from Liverpool to collect some things before the auction. She was three months pregnant and very nearly lost her baby. She had to be admitted to the new maternity wing at the Bon Secours hospital in Cork and would have had a miscarriage only for careful nursing and expert medical attention. I was particularly touched by these words of her letter, 'imagine having to empty out every drawer in Lissarda House, it takes a terrible lot of time.........poor old Lissarda is being ransacked ...... the auction at Lissarda is a week next Wednesday and Thursday and mum is moving out that weekend and so ends an era of Lissarda'.

The auction was held on 29th.and 30th.of April. The house, farmyard and ninety acres of land were knocked down for the princely sum of £3,500 and the furniture which mother did not need for the new semi-detached house she had purchased in Sandycove, County Dublin was also auctioned off for what now at least seems like very little. An interesting indication of how badly depressed the property market was at the time is that a few years previously the valuation put on Lissarda House alone, for insurance purposes and quite apart from considerations about the land was £10,000.

On Saturday, May 2nd mother said her final good bye to Lissarda, handed over all tokens of authority and set out to a new life in Dublin in the wake of one of Nat Ross's furniture removal vans.

Chapter 11

ROME CONTINUED

After Easter, the University examinations came very much into prospect and the summer was just about beginning and the walk to and from the University became more burdensome. As a means of keeping the house cool the shutters were kept closed during the day in the convent at San Clemente. As there was little circulation of air in Rome during the hot weather it was considered better, in the interests of keeping cool, to keep out the direct rays of the sun. This blocking out of the rays of the sun served to make the house very dark and, for me, depressing.

My examination for the Bachelor's degree in Divinity was due to begin in early June and was to end on June 25th. Although a Bachelor's degree in name it is essentially post-graduate because you are not admitted to study for it unless you have already qualified by having done a three year course in Philosophy, either in Philosophy alone or else in Philosophy as a major subject with another subsidiary subject or subjects such as, for example, English or History.

The system of examination in Rome was different to the system generally employed in Irish universities. Essentially, in the Irish system the more important element is the written. The oral examination, if there is one, has a relatively minor significance. In Rome it is the other way round. In the minor subjects that for me were; Scriptural Exegesis, the History of Dogma, Church History, Oriental Theology, Mystical Theology and Canon Law, there was a fifteen minute examination/ interview with your professor, in Latin, on which he based your mark. In the major subjects that for me were Dogmatic and Moral Theology there was a forty-five minute examination by three examiners, two of them your own professors and one an extern. At the beginning of the year you were given the titles of twenty-eight propositions taken from the various parts of the three years' work that you would have completed at the time of the examination. These had to be so prepared by you that you could discuss and defend any of them chosen by the board of examiners for the allotted time. The examiners then marked you according to their judgement about your ability and application.

One important advantage of this system, particularly when the student population consisted, for the most part, of overseas students, was that the results were available within days. I got through comfortably, if not brilliantly.

Another advantage of the emphasis on oral examination in the Roman circumstances became clear to me during a few short one-hour papers we were given, as well as an oral, in some minor subjects. The shameless copying that went on was astounding. By some students apparently, it was considered ethical to copy provided you didn't get caught. There were two Italian students near me who were producing hitherto concealed notes like magicians. An American student nearby got tired of this behaviour and strongly indicated his disapproval to the offending examination candidates who angrily replied in a stage whisper,
'Lora fumano' (You crowd smoke)
To which the American replied,
'O.K., you choose your fun, I'll choose mine.'

Of the six of us student priests in San Clemente, four decided to go back to Ireland for the summer holidays. Father David and I decided to stay on and avail of the opportunity to do some sightseeing and touring. As soon as the exams were over we hired a Vespa motor scooter and set out to have a camping holiday in the north of Italy, Austria, Germany and Switzerland. We had about three weeks free in which to do it. The Vespa was heavily laden with two of us, our tent and our clothes for three weeks together with some supplies.

Dr. Jerome B. Murphy with his wife
Margaret (Peggy) Murphy and son Denstone. 1931

The Lawn Lissarda House.
Denstone's ordination reception. 1958

Denstone with his dogs 1943

*UCC Medical Ball 1952
LR Finbarr Dowdall,
Evelyn O' Leary, Avril
Taylor, Denstone Murphy*

*Glenstal Revisited 1986.
Denstone with Dom Athanasius OSB*

The Dominican Community with The Queen Mother, when she visited San Clemente Rome, 1958

Glenstal Rugby Team 1946-7
Denstone centre back row.

Denstone in Garden

Attending Congress of Married Priests and their Wives.
The Netherlands 1990
Denstone and Maura with Colleague from Poland

Denstone taking delivery of his first car! Runcorn 1935

TCD Denstone Kemp's Graduation 1983. L R. Peggy Murphy, Denstone Murphy, Rosemary Kemp, Philip Kemp and Polly Kemp

Medical friends from UCC at Denstone's ordination reception. Lissurda 1958

*Denstone Murphy and
Sean Hurley visiting
the Clarke family at
Warrensgrove 1986*

*Celebrating at "Springfield"
with Ossie Barton*

*Denstone Murphy with friend and
colleague Professor Sean Freyne
outside Commons TCD*

Late on the first night we arrived at a place called Lucca about forty kilometres north of Rome. We sought and got permission from a local farmer to pitch our tent in a field near his house. After we had something to eat we thought it fitting that we should seek out the local parish priest, to whom this farmer was able to direct us, and make arrangements for saying Mass in the morning. The village where he lived was, we discovered, about two kilometres away. We left our tent pitched with our belongings in it and rode up to see the parish priest. He wasn't in the presbytery but an elderly man who answered the door said we would find him in the local village hall where he was attending some function. We went to the hall and saw that there was a bazaar in progress. He received us graciously at first but when we sought permission to say Mass in his church the following morning he became defensive. Perhaps what made the situation a little difficult for him was the fact that we were not wearing clerical garb and, who knows, we might have been English (Anglican) ministers posing as priests. On noticing his discomfort we produced our celebrets, which are identity documents issued to priests who are travelling. These satisfied him but then we almost got disqualified again when he asked us where we were staying. We told him we would be sleeping in a field about two kilometres down the road. His mouth opened in disbelief, so to complete the picture we said we were camping in a field that was owned by and beside the house of so and so, who actually had given us his name. That apparently eased the conscience of the parish priest as, I gathered, this man was one of the stalwarts of the parish whom now the parish priest was treating as our guarantor.

We moved on to Orvieto, Arezzo and Florence where we saw some of the great art treasures. Of particular interest to us were the frescoes of Fra Angelico, the Dominican artist, the most famous of which is his Annunciation, painted about 1440 in the Dominican Convent of St. Mark. As is the case with so many of the historic religious houses in Italy, St. Mark's is now owned by a public state body.

After the identification difficulties we experienced with the parish priest of Lucca on the first night, thereafter we made a point of approaching parish priests wearing our collars and some clerical dress.

We made a great effort to say the Divine Office which it would have been mortally sinful to culpably omit. The night we arrived outside Bologna we pitched camp on a hillside near a plantation of young trees. It was dark and the air was saturated with fireflies. We had not yet said Vespers and Compline so we endeavoured to let the fireflies light the pages of our breviaries for us. In principle the idea worked and one sensed the joy of all creation worshipping the Creator, but in practice is was so slow that, reluctantly, we resorted to our electric torch.

After Bologna we travelled through Modena and Padua to Venice. What one could sense in Venice was a definite change of atmosphere. There was more of the central European there and less of the Mediterranean. There were more of the local people going to Mass in the churches and amongst them almost as many men as women. As you go farther south in Italy the church pews become more and more a female preserve.

When we arrived at Balzano, almost due north of Venice in the Alto-Adige we encountered cultural complications. By the terms of the Treaty of Saint-Germain in 1919, whereby President Wilson of the United States sought to trim down European powers to unthreatening proportions, Austria had to cede a part of her southern territory, now called the Alto-Adige, to Italy. Those who would regard themselves as the indigenous population were Austrian in spirit and refused to speak Italian to us. I expect that the older people just didn't know any Italian. The Austrian and Italian elements in the population seemed to keep quite apart.

We had arranged to stay with the local Dominican community. They had a fine newly built church and convent.

The community, as far as I could judge was made up entirely of Italian priests and brothers. We weren't there over a weekend, therefore we couldn't test our hypothesis that this Dominican church which was also the local parish church, was supported almost entirely by "planted" Italians. Even those thirty seven years ago I had a very strong feeling that the church in Balzano was identifying too uncritically with one national grouping.

From then on we set about exploring the Dolomites, going from hot lowlands to the snow covered heights, covering extraordinary distances on a heavily laden Vespa scooter which was designed basically not for continuous mountain climbing with two persons astride but for getting around one's own locality in comfort and with convenience.

We went eastwards as far as the fashionable Olympic ski resort of Cortina d'Ampezzo where we suffered our only loss, which was a blanket, at the hands of thieves who, I would wager, were fellow tourists in need of a blanket for camping just below the snow line.

We continued our journey by going north to Salzburg in Austria and paid our respects to Mozart, born there in 1756. In the years since the early fifties music was becoming readily available on good quality 33 r.p.m. discs most of which were long playing and stereophonic, in contrast to the old 78's which required high quality expensive gramophones to produce tolerable sound. This breakthrough in recording techniques brought Beethoven and Mozart particularly onto the popular market.

From Salzburg we headed north-east to the city of Linz, where we got our first glimpse of the river Danube. We felt comfortable there. Its Gothic Cathedral attracted us as a symbol of our native northern Europe which we hadn't seen for almost a year. It may have been just the luck of the draw, but the people we happened to meet were outstanding in the attention and time they were prepared to give us and spend talking to us in broken English or in a mixture of English, German, French and Italian.

We plucked up the courage eventually to raise the difficult matter of the Iron Curtain with a man with whom we were sharing a coffee-table in a restaurant. He welcomed our inquiry and gave us full details of how to get there. What is more, he offered to pilot us on his pedal bicycle to the outskirts of the city and set us on the road to Prague which, if we followed for a few miles would bring us to the Iron Curtain. We availed of his offer and reached the Austrian border checkpoint in the heat of the mid-afternoon. The border guard was drowsy with the heat but was able to check our identity. He didn't give us any encouragement at all when we asked him about entering Czechoslovakia. He pointed out to us where Czech territory began. The demarcation was made by a low wooden garden fence, not more than three metres away from his hut, in places broken down and even discontinuous. We established a good relationship with the border guard who showed us his stamp collection that he used to work on during the boring hours of border duty. I didn't feel a bit afraid there but the atmosphere was unreal, sad, strange, eerie, and pathetic.

The Czechoslovakian checkpoint was a few hundred metres further along the Prague road and was clearly visible from where we were standing. Beside it there was a watchtower and running into the distance on both sides, always a few hundred metres back from the actual border, was a double wire fence about nine feet high which was punctuated at kilometre intervals by watchtowers. We could see that broad swathes had been cut through woods so that there would be no cover from which the watchtower guards could be quickly stormed. Apparently once you entered Czech territory at the Austrian checkpoint, or for that matter anywhere along the border, you were under scrutiny, until you reached the Iron Curtain itself, by the Czechoslovakian guard, who decided whether to shoot at you or let you approach.

Just in front of where we were, in a field between the border and the Iron Curtain, a number of men and women were making hay under the supervision of guards armed with rifles. While we were there, within thirty metres of the nearest haymaker, there was a lot of shouting and jibing at the guards who seemed to answer them back by making what seemed like unpleasant and violent gestures. Somewhat foolhardily Father David decided to photograph this scene, but as soon as the Czech guards who were supervising the haymakers saw the camera they lay flat on the ground. Whether or not this was with a view to shooting at David, I don't know. The Austrian guard voiced and gesticulated disapproval, so the camera had to be put away, unwillingly.

What stirred pathos in me was the roadway which had grass pushing its way up through the metalling. How busy a road connecting two important cities like Linz and Prague must have been and now it brought to mind a disused airstrip or a seldom used country laneway. During the time we were there not one vehicle approached.

After camping for the night at what we regarded as a safe distance from the Iron Curtain, on the next morning we went back into Linz and after celebrating Mass in the Gothic Cathedral we set off in the general direction of Munich.

There were some camping sites in those times but they were relatively few in number, used mainly by people with children and people in motor cars. The more usual thing for small groups was to beg a few square feet from a local landowner, which in our experience was never refused. So often the permission to camp was accompanied by an invitation to share an evening meal with the family. I had been of the view that Irish hospitality was unequalled but my camping experiences at this time made me revise this notion.

We crossed into Germany from Austria by crossing the river Inn where it flows between Simbach and Braunau which is Adolf

Hitler's native town. The house in which Hitler was born was at this stage a public library which we were shown. Although there was no public acknowledgement of Hitler's association with the place we did succeed in getting the information we needed. We were in Braunau for the most part of an hour in the vicinity of the house where Hitler was born and during all that time there was a man who looked just like Hitler or perhaps was made up to look like Hitler standing beside the door. Whether he was a family member, an old friend, an old supporter or an eccentric or all those things together we never found out.

Having got to Munich we tried to plan a visit to Dachau, the site of the infamous concentration camp. We made some, what we thought to be, discreet inquiries about how to get there but we met with a mysterious wall of negative reaction on all occasions. It seemed to us that shame had caused a kind of selective amnesia. The most notable example was that of a young man within five kilometres of the place, whom we did establish as being a native, who said he never heard of the place.

Eventually, we got to it by using our map and after some trial and error. Our visit was an experience never to be forgotten. The camp was preserved carefully, in all its horrifying detail, by the Americans and was open to the public. We had as guide a onetime inmate, one of the few who escaped. He spared us no detail in his commentary, yet did it all with the greatest of respect. The physical details were shocking but what was even more traumatic was to reflect on the ingenious efficiency that was cold-bloodedly developed whereby the greatest number of people could be exterminated in the shortest time with the least trouble. As concentration camps go it was small. Three hundred and fifty thousand people had been put to death there.

Chapter 12

A STRANGER IN ZURICH

It is too simple to blame Hitler for what went on in Dachau, The feeling which for me was predominant was one of being in some way co-responsible for this holocaust. Hitler happens to have been the person who acted as agent for the carrying out of the effects of the "sin of the world", that "original sin" which, however it was committed historically, has left us, though essentially good, with a strong inclination to evil. We can be so crafty that we can indulge this inclination vicariously, that is through others. The shock expressed by the willing listener to idle gossip is hypocritical because such "shock" is not revulsion so much as a perverse rejoicing that someone else has said the unkind word for them.

Sobered after being shown through the concentration camp and well-focused on what is really important about life and having celebrated Mass on this first anniversary of our ordination, July 13th. 1959, we set off for Zurich in Switzerland

Our first pause en route was in Friedrichshafen which was en fete with a beer festival which was in sharp contrast to the Dachau scene we had so recently experienced. The footage of sausage being eaten and the volume of beer being drunk was considerable. Fresh as we still were from our tour of Dachau we had no mind for what appeared to us as raucous overindulgence. Since I was a teetotaller I felt as if I were on moral high ground and like the pharisee in Luke's gospel I felt superior.

After a very short time in Friedrichshafen we continued on our way smugly putt-putt-putting along on our hitherto faithful motor scooter, apparently aglow with that pride which precedes a fall.

Father David was driving; I was sitting behind him on the pillion. Coming towards a set of traffic lights on the outskirts of Zurich we were moving at a reasonable pace behind a large furniture removals van. Looking over David's shoulder I could see the warning brake lights of the large van and expected a reaction from him.

'He's daydreaming, he's irresponsible', I thought, but before I could express any impatience David shouted out, 'We've no brakes, my God, we're going to crash'.

When the van in front stopped we thudded sickeningly into the back of it. We both fell to the ground and the laden Vespa pinned us underneath it. My right shoulder and thigh took the impact and I felt a sting just above the ankle bone on my right leg.

'My leg, my leg', cried David. Immediately, bystanders who were only a few feet away on the footpath came to our rescue, as did a policeman, When the scooter had been lifted off us it was revealed that David had a very serious injury to the calf muscles of his right leg. They had been almost torn away completely from their point of origin behind his knee joint and he was in great pain and distress. I was seized with a feeling of aloneness, exile, helplessness, unsmugness. I could identify with the exiles from Zion, in Psalm 137, who sat and wept beside the streams of Babylon. Where could I turn? The pride begotten in Friedrichshafen a couple of hours previously, whereby I despised in my heart simple people innocently enough enjoying themselves, had been shattered here on the roadway.

For whom the bell tolls, or for whom the bells of the ambulance ring, for these were pre-siren days, is usually of little practical interest to us, but now I could hear the warning of the ambulance getting closer and closer. They attended to David as a priority and lost interest in me when they saw I could walk and function effectively. When they had applied first aid to his wound they drove away with him, bells clanging.

'Those confounded bells', I said to myself, 'are telling the whole world that two maverick Irish Dominicans are in a traffic accident in Zurich. I wish they'd stop the bells, we'll be disgraced. What if it gets onto the newspapers and the Provincial reads about it?' These kinds of fears come from an inflated sense of one's importance and significance.

We never seem to understand that the generality of mankind, rightly or wrongly, if I may quote from a perceptive friend - 'Don't give a shit about what we do or do not do provided it doesn't cause them any trouble'.

As I self-pityingly stood alone and tried to imagine what my next move should be, a young man, straight from the pages of Luke's gospel walked over to me and uttered what must be the most loving instruction in the world,
'Come home with me'. It wasn't an offer, it was a command. Then he took charge. Otto Stauffer was his name. He spoke English quite well. He told me that my companion would have gone to the Kantonspittal and he would take me to see him in due course. He then took me to his home by taxi and arranged with a friend to collect the scooter, which was not badly damaged. Apparently, we escaped really serious injury because the removals van, owing to the nature of its function, was very low slung at the back, and it was this structural modification which protected us from going under it.

He told his mother what had happened and introduced me to her. I then told them that both my companion and I were Catholic priests. This fact was of interest to them because, as it transpired, they were Catholics. Whatever might be said about me did not change for them the essential fact that I was "a traveller on his way down from Jerusalem to Jericho". After some coffee and a sandwich Otto accompanied me to the hospital.

The house doctor who had admitted Father David told me that while his injury was serious, the accident surgeon who was working on it was hopeful that she could deal with it successfully. When the house doctor learned that I had also been on the scooter he said he would like to check me over. He discovered that I had quite a deep cut on my right leg and said I would have to go to the theatre to get it stitched.

The theatre had two operating tables and I could see David on one when I entered. I was prepared and put on the other table separated from him by a screen. When the surgeon had finished she came around the screen to where I was prepared for her. I was given a local anaesthetic and she sutured the gash near my ankle.

The hospital authorities could not give us beds that night but recommended a hostel nearby where we got booked in. It was a strange arrangement, considering Father David's serious condition, but we felt confident that they were doing the best they could do for us under the circumstances. It was organised for us by the hospital social worker.

Even though David was in great pain he insisted on getting up with me quite early the next morning and as we were having breakfast Otto arrived with his parish priest, Father Hofliger, who turned out to be quite an extraordinary man. He had been chaplain at an American army base in Germany and spoke English fluently. Apparently, when Otto left me at the Kantonspittal the night before he went to talk to his parish priest to see if anything further could be done to help us and make us comfortable. Immediately, the priest remembered that the Dominican sisters had a very good hospital in Zurich called Sanitas and telephoned them booking us both in there.

As soon as he had been introduced to us and when I had introduced Otto to David, Father Hofliger told us about his provisional arrangements for us, for which we were very grateful. He organised a taxi and brought us to Sanitas. He introduced us to the matron who made us welcome. She got David attended to as quickly as possible and allowed me to share the room with him although I might have been considered as in the category of "walking wounded".

The surgeon was brought immediately and expressed concern about David's condition although he was careful to stress that his colleague in the Kantonspittal had done a perfect job. The trouble was that two large parts of the musculature of the calf of his right leg had been torn very badly and there was considerable shock.

Sanitas was a beautiful hospital obviously very well equipped. One of the most obvious novelties as far as I was concerned was the fact that all glass doors were automatically opened when you approached them. This arrangement is now commonplace but in 1959 it was unusual. The nursing staff were efficient, kind and dedicated.

My leg required minimal attention and I went out quite a lot and often met Otto and Father Hofliger. Otto had taken the scooter to get repaired and also to find out why the brakes had failed. Not a great deal of damage was done, apart from having a badly damaged front wheel which had to be replaced. The mechanic said that the brake cable had snapped due, he thought, to metal fatigue probably brought on by the extraordinary stress put on the braking system while we did almost two thousand kilometres of sometimes very steep mountain work in the Dolomites.

I asked Otto to visit the Kantonspittal with me so that I could get the bill which I assumed would be considerable. The bill which I was given, which covered surgeons' fees, theatre fees, ambulance, injections and dressings for both of us was for twenty four Swiss francs - I kept it for the last thirty- seven years and have it beside me as I write. At the rate of exchange at the time the bill was the equivalent of six pounds sterling.

A source of anxiety to Father David and me was that we were, from the religious point of view, illegal emigrants or travellers, not having applied for or received from our Provincial, the permission necessary to leave the country to which we were assigned, that was Italy. We were anticipating quite a stiff reprimand. We would almost certainly have been granted the permission but we just did not bother to apply. Again our anxiety was probably a function of megalomania, as nothing ever happened to us, the Provincial having much more to occupy his waking hours than the border infringements of student priests.

After ten days when David was up out of bed and able to walk around and after being in contact with our Prior, it was decided that I should go back to Rome, this time by train and bring the scooter as baggage.

With trepidation I approached the hospital administrator to find out what we owed to discover that not only were we attended to by the Good Samaritan on the roadway but the innkeeper waived her/his charge. All that time and attention in Sanitas for both of us was a free gift.

Before leaving, I went with Otto to see Father Hofliger and thank him for all he had done. I told him that we were both deeply touched by his commitment to our wellbeing and particularly grateful to him for fixing us up in Sanitas. His response to this was remarkable, contributing a great deal to one's self-confidence,

'It was your due'.

On leaving his presbytery to go with Otto to the station I said I hoped we would meet again, to which he replied,

'We'll meet at least at last'.

It was a profound sentiment, expressed in a way which I don't think a native speaker of English would risk.

As for Otto and his mother, people like them redeem the human race.

'I was a stranger and you made me welcome',

Chapter 13
ROME AGAIN

When I got back to Rome at the beginning of August the Prior showed great understanding about the accident in Zurich. Choosing the right time he sorted things out for us with the Provincial.

August is a very hot month in Rome, so hot that any Romans who can afford to do so get out of the city for that period. I lent a hand in the running of the public church in San Clemente and tried to improve my Italian.

In spite of the heat there were quite a number of visitors to the excavations at San Clemente and it was always interesting to show groups around. I made friends with many of these people and kept up correspondence with them for years afterwards.

Among the visitors were two Irish public figures who came together. One was John A. Costello, who took over as Taoiseach during the First Inter Party Government from 1948 to 1951 and again during the Second Coalition Government from 1954 to 1957. The other was Sean Mac Eoin, "The Blacksmith of Ballinalee", who had recently been defeated by Eamon de Valera in the Irish Presidential election. After they had been provided with hospitality in San Clemente, Séan O'hEideáin, from the Irish Embassy to the Vatican, took them with me, on an outing to visit some of the castelli or towns around about Rome. John A. Costello spoke but little yet wisely. Sean Mac Eoin spoke at length and in interesting fashion about many things. Our drive through the countryside prompted various topics for conversation. Sean Mac Eoin talked about the shoeing of oxen, something which he said he had done on occasion. With equal facility he gave us a fascinating description of the intricacies involved in the conducting of elections in parts of South America. He also made it quite clear that wherever else we went to that day the one place in the castelli that he wanted to visit was the shrine of Our Lady of Good Counsel in Genazzano.

When we arrived at Genazzano he went into the church, knelt at the shrine and spent quite a long time in prayer. He came away a very happy man and then revealed to us that this visit was for him the fulfillment of a promise he had made to Our Lady of Good Counsel while he was under sentence of death in gaol in 1921 for the killing of District Inspector McGrath of the Royal Irish Constabulary while escaping arrest. He attributed his deliverance to the intercession of Our Lady of Good Counsel. An irony is that the more immediate agent who negotiated his release, was, according to my sources, Eamon De Valera.

I met a large number of Australians. I became friendly with one family in particular, consisting of mother, father and grown up daughter, Mr. and Mrs. Cuthbertson and Jennifer from Melbourne. They had rented an apartment in Rome for two years. They had been in Rome for one year already when I met them in San Clemente. Mr.Cuthbertson had retired from business the year before but always had a great interest in art and had done quite a lot of painting. Likewise Mrs.Cuthbertson and Jenny. A family decision was made to change residence for two years to Rome and take a course which they discovered would help them to perfect their skills.

They had no religious background and although christened in the Anglican Church, neither parents nor daughter had ever been practising Christians in the "formal" sense. I have to put formal in parenthesis because their openness, kindness and respect was quite impressive.

They were fascinated by and curious about the Catholic Church always, they told me, and since they came to Rome that interest was sharpened but somehow they had never been in a situation, up to this, to ask their questions of anybody. I met them about once every fortnight for the next year, either in San

Clemente or in their apartment and discussed with them the church's attitude on everything under the sun.

Those were the days in which considerable numbers of people converted from other faiths or from no faith to the Catholic church, so, as their interest in the faith was increasing so was my secret hope of netting a "good catch" becoming stronger. They got and read regularly the "Tablet", a rather sophisticated English Catholic periodical, and discussed various articles in it with me. Towards the end of the year my exams were looming, I was soon to be leaving Rome and they were soon to be going back to Melbourne yet never had they mentioned anything about becoming Catholics, so one day I decided to ask them directly if they were interested in being received into the Church. Mr Cuthbertson took it on himself to answer for the family, 'No, we are not interested'.

Both the tone and content of the reply quite shattered me, partly because I felt I had made a huge tactical error. In a sense I had cornered them and put them on the spot and the reflex reply, as I now see things was almost bound to be defensive. I had not the experience to interpret properly Saint John's affirmation, 'One sows, another reaps'.

After I left Rome I lost contact with them. But I feel sure that like me they garnered good out of our relationship, even if not the good I had in mind.

Another remarkable person took me aside one day after I had shown a group around. They were a small group of tourists from Canada and she just followed along to get the commentary. She told me she was a nurse and had come to Rome within the last few months. Her name was Gwen Campbell and she was from Yorkshire, recently widowed although only thirty-six years of age. She told me she came to Rome to imbibe the culture and learn the language. She was alright financially but she did take odd jobs, particularly live-in jobs with Roman families, when they were available, in order to gain experience of home life in Rome.

Gwen definitely had made up her mind that she wanted to take instruction and be received into the Catholic Church. I organised a programme of instruction which we followed for about six months. Those sessions were a great education for me too as she would tell me about the attitudes that she observed in Roman families, to the Church, children, marriage, politics etc.. In San Clemente we were quite removed from the mainstream of life.

When the time came to receive her into the Church, I discovered that things were not at all as simple as they would be in Ireland where notifying the Vicar General of the diocese was little more than a formality. At the Vicariate in Rome I had to answer questions about her reasons, as I understood them, for wanting to be received into the Church and questions about many other matters. I had to meet the Archbishop who is Vice Gerent of the Pope; he is the person who attends to the pastoral running of the Pope's own diocese. He was a pleasant man and easy to talk to and said that he himself would come along to San Clemente to administer the sacrament of Confirmation immediately after Baptism. While this is theologically correct it was not normally the practice because in a diocese, say, in the United States or England, where there may have been hundreds of converts received every year it would have been disproportionately demanding on the bishop's time. The morning after her Baptism and Confirmation Gwen was to come to Mass and receive her First Holy Communion.

An evening was arranged and earlier that day I had to collect a document of Profession of Faith and Rejection of Heresy to be used at Gwen's reception and which was to be returned to the Vicariate immediately and I was solemnly forbidden to make a copy of it to keep. It was a desperately harsh document and seemed to assume that the person being received had at some stage actively dissented from Catholic teaching. I hadn't rehearsed this document with Gwen so the tone of it came as a great shock to her as she read it out kneeling in front of the Archbishop. It was a version of the Profession of Faith that had been translated into English. The Archbishop knew no English; therefore the impact of the words on Gwen as she was reading them out was not fully appreciated by him. That is until.....without warning she got violently sick and threw up onto the Archepiscopal lap. The proceedings were interrupted for some time until Gwen regained her composure and until the Archbishop had removed his alb. He wisely dispensed the reading out of the remainder of the offending document and we got through the Baptism without further hitch.

In talking informally with the Archbishop afterwards, quite unwittingly, I diluted the terrible impact of the Profession of Faith document by introducing Gwen to him as "una nutrice inglese" at which he nodded his head as if sympathetically understanding the peculiar demands of that calling. Brother John, whose Italian was near perfect and who was standing nearby within earshot, told me afterwards and not without amusement that I had misled the Archbishop. The word "nutrice" which I used, he told me, meant "wet nurse" when I should have used the word "infermiera", which means hospital nurse!

In learning to speak a foreign language there's a particular phase when your confidence grows and your courage with using the language outstrips your proficiency and you are liable to take risks with words. I had to register a letter from Rome to Ireland and went confidently to the post office where, up until a certain point I transacted my business quite properly. When the post office official had put some stamps and labels onto the envelope he handed it back to me after I paid him. He did not put it directly into the mail as is generally done here in Ireland so I made an attempt to ask him if I should put it into the letter box myself. On the spur of the moment what I uttered in Italian was -

'Should I put the letter into the "bocca del postino"?'

At which the post office clerk looked at me and broke into helpless laughter and said,

'Si, si padre', pointing towards the letter box.

When I got back to San Clemente I asked Brother John what I had said that so amused the post office official. An equally amused Brother John explained to me that the word for post box is "buca delle lettere". "Bocca del postino", he said meant "the postman's orifice".

I had, since coming to Rome, renewed a very old and valued friendship with an Irish poet, Sean O' Criadain, who was at that time working in Rome as the editor of an international literary periodical called "Bottege Oscure". We made a point of meeting regularly and he introduced me to many interesting people on the Roman literary scene.

In due course the opening of the new school year was approaching. I was joined by two more classmates, Father Vincent and Father Nicholas who had been ordained during that summer. I had been ordained a year before them on account of being, technically, a late vocation.

At the beginning of the term I got the great news that my sister Rosemary had given birth to a baby boy. My mother had gone over to Liverpool, where Rosemary lived, for the Christening and while there was prevailed upon to take a trip out to Rome. She travelled by land and sea and Sean Ó Criadáin accompanied me to the station to meet her in late November. We noticed that Cardinal Tixeront, a Frenchman, Dean of the Sacred College of Cardinals had been travelling on the same train. Sean was very generous to my mother all during her stay in Rome.

She was booked in to the Villa Rosa which was a guest house run by the Dominican Sisters. It was a great treat for me to have her and together we went to all the tourist spots. One of her great ambitions in life was to go to the Isle of Capri. This romantic need was created in her to some extent, I suspect, by the words of a song which was very popular in her youth, "'Twas on the Isle of Capri that I met her.... ". Also having just read Axel Munthe's "The Story of San Michele" she wanted to see Anacapri where his house was open for public viewing. The fact that Gracie Fields was then living there was a further incentive. Three Medical Missionaries of Mary sisters were staying in the Villa Rosa at the same time as mother. They had planned to go to Naples to stay in the "Clinica Mediterranea", which was a nursing home staffed and run by their sisters. Mother and I travelled with them. A ride by taxi in Rome can be unnerving but in Naples it was indescribable. Our taxi man drove with extraordinary speed, as if with privileged foreknowledge about the behaviour of every other driver and pedestrian on the route.

We were invited into the Clinica Mediterranea and treated to a generous meal. They couldn't offer us overnight accommodation as they were short of space but they made arrangements for us to stay in a good guest house nearby, the Pensione Ausonia.

The next morning we took the early ferry to Capri which was just over an hour's journey away. After arriving at the quayside we got a funicular railway up to the level of the plateau on which the buildings on the island seemed to stand. Quaint seemed like the most fitting description of what we first saw of the place. We got good accommodation in the Villa Helios, which was run by German Sisters and had been recommended to us. We did a thorough tourist visitation of the island, seeing and doing all that we had planned. Even at the end of November the place was still crowded with tourists.

Instead of returning to Naples we went back to Sorrento on the southern side of the Bay of Naples. And thence to Pompei, the ancient city which together with the city of Herculaneum, was buried four to six metres deep under volcanic ash by the eruption of Mount Vesuvius in 79 A. D. Its rediscovery in 1728 was an important factor in the revival of interest in classical archaeology. Its excavation has provided important evidence of various details of daily life in Roman times. Normally perishable objects such as wooden furniture and paintings were preserved by the ash. Our guide spared us no detail in his interpretation and, I suspect, embellishment of the various structures, graffiti, paintings and other artefacts as we passed through the excavated remains.

After coming back to Rome I arranged a Papal audience for my mother which turned out to be the climax of her visit. With a few days left before she was due to go home she asked to see the catacombs and to visit Tivoli, a town in Lazio just outside Rome. Tivoli was a summer resort in Roman times and to be found there are the remains of Hadrian's villa. Hadrian was Roman emperor from 117 to 138 and be was responsible for many building projects including Hadrian's Wall, which was the northern frontier of Roman Britain, the Pantheon and Castel San Angelo in which he was buried. Later, in Renaissance times, the present Villa d'Este was designed by Cardinal Ippolito d'Este in 1550. The Villa d'Este is known particularly for its water gardens which are so called on account of the elaborate system of water falls and fountains, large and small, which dominate the scene.

When I went to collect mother at the Villa Rosa to take her to Tivoli she introduced me to to another newly arrived guest from England, Mrs. Greenoch. When Mrs. Greenoch showed interest mother said she would ask me if it would be alright for her to come along with us. It was her first time in Rome, There was a certain basic briefing which I tried to give, on the advice of Brother John, to people whom I was showing around and whose first visit it was. I learned the hard way that these instructions were important: carry only as much cash as you thought you would need; carry your passport if you are going out by yourself as a means of identification, not in a handbag, however, but carefully secured on your person; if you are going out with me it is probably better to leave your passport in safe keeping at your hotel or accommodation if they have safe deposit facilities. Then at a more personal level: consume a minimum amount of fluid in the morning if you are going out for the day, particularly if going to a function or a Papal audience in St. Peter's because I am not aware of any toilet facilities in or around St. Peter's and in other places no concessions are made to northern European reticence.

It was not without some misgivings that I welcomed Mrs. Greenoch to come along with us because as I arrived on the scene I noticed that she was finishing off a large glass of orange drink, commenting that it was her second large glass since she rose out of bed at 7.30, it was now 9.30. A briefing at this stage would have been useless, nay, even dangerous as a possible self-fulfilling prophesy, so I opted to say nothing.

We arrived at the Villa d'Este at about 11.00 a.m. and after a fairly short look around the Villa we went to the water gardens. I had been there a couple of times previously so I knew of the hazards that threatened even the forewarned, There was this enormous volume of water being dispensed by hundreds of waterfalls and fountains, stretching as far as the eye could see, making a noise above which it was difficult to make your voice beard. Many is the sphincter muscle that failed under such vivid suggestion. Then I noticed that Mrs. Greenoch was beginning progressively to lose interest in her surroundings. The climax of the sightseeing experience in this water garden is to walk behind a waterfall, that is, there is rock face on one side of the passageway and the other side is a wall of water which is thundering down from quite a height. This apparently was the last straw because Mrs. Greenoch said to my mother, 'I am feeling awful, take me to the ladies'.

My mother turned to me for counsel, possibly not fully grasping the nature or urgency of the malady. But I pointed to the biggest bush at hand, being the nearest thing to a ladies that I could see. Without argument Mrs. Greenoch took cover. I thought of the appositeness of the phrase "any port in a storm".

The following day I took both my mother and Mrs. Greenoch to the catacombs of Saint Callixtus on the Appian Way for Mass, a primitive and memorable experience. In the subterranean passages which contain the remains of early Christians one felt very conscious of being part of a saintly tradition. I have always thought that celebrating or otherwise participating in Mass in the catacombs is the most devotional of all the Roman experiences.

Mother left Rome to go back to Ireland on December 9th. I was really lonely after her. I had enjoyed her company as never before. While with her in Rome I was able to talk to her with a freedom that neither of us would have experienced in home surroundings. I never saw her as happy and relaxed as she apparently was in Capri. In particular, on the first night we were there, after the evening meal she walked out into the garden by herself and to me she seemed transformed as she moved in ballet fashion through the grove of citrus trees. It was one of the few glimpses I ever got of the uninhibited, happy, relaxed side of my mother's character. More usually she felt obliged to adopt a mother role which may in the right circumstances be proper with younger children or adolescents. But as I see it, towards adult children the attitudes of parents need to evolve to a different level.

The most effective service that parents of adult children can contribute to these children is to express themselves as the adults they really are. If role barriers are kept in place there may be some superficial communication over or around these but the formative impact of the essential personality of the one called parent will be lost to the essential personality of the one called child.

In the course of that year we also had an informal visit from President de Valera who was over on a formal visit to the Vatican. He came for afternoon tea with us. He was amused when I reminded him of a time some years previously when I joined Senator Jane Dowdall and Finbarr for lunch as his guests in Leinster House. It was the Saturday of an International Rugby match between Ireland and Scotland in Lansdowne Road in 1950. The lunch went on for a very long time and Finabarr and I were beginning to fear that we may not get to the match at all. Senator Dowdall explained our uneasiness to our host and immediately he understood and solved the problem by sending for his personal driver whom he asked to deliver us to Lansdowne Road as quickly as possible. We caused a slight stir outside the grounds when some people recognised the car and looked forward to getting a close up view of Mr.de Valera as he broke his tradition of abstention from rugby matches. But they were let down. Quite embarrassed, we got ourselves mingled into the crowd as quickly as possible.

Nicholas, Vincent and I did the Licentiate in Theology examination in June 1960. It was difficult. We had to prepare a hundred propositions that had been prescribed for the course and during the examination that would last for an hour in front of four examiners, a few of these propositions would have to be defended by the examination candidate, This was the critical test, but as well we had a written examination in Theology and oral examinations in a number of minor subjects. The results came within a few days and we received our Licences to teach Theology.

At this time, June, 1960, the Olympic Games were about to start in Rome. There would have been no problem about staying on to attend them but even though I would regard myself as a keen sportsperson, my desire to get a break from the ambience of study won out and I took the road home as soon as possible. Yet, I had one very important call to make en route back to Ireland. I really was anxious to visit Zurich again to thank Otto Stauffer, his mother and Father Hofliger, the parish priest for having shown such caring love for Father David and me at the time of our accident the year before. I spent two days in Zurich and saw who I wanted to see and I told them again that they were for us bright lights in a very dark night.

From Zurich I went by train to Mainz and then by boat down the Rhine to Cologne, passing by Koblenz and Bonn. The journey from Mainz to Koblenz was beautiful but from Koblenz on to Cologne it was quite uninspiring. From Cologne to Ostende by train and thence to Dover on the ferry. When I got onshore at Dover and heard all around me a language with which I was connatural. I felt at home and grateful for that. The story of the Tower of Babel sees Yahweh inflicting a multiplicity of languages as a punishment. Speaking the same language as somebody else is a big step towards understanding them and being understood by them. I wonder how many wars have been brought about due to leaders of different states simply misunderstanding each other's language?

I called to Liverpool and saw my first nephew for the first time. Seeing the attention and love that was being demanded and given in that small family made me reflect that celibacy would have to be lived out very lovingly if it were to compare favourably with that kind of dedication. Abstinence of the flesh or deprivation of sexual intercourse is of itself a mere privation. Its value is got from accompanying love.

I flew back to Dublin, I remember that the air fare was £5, I could no longer hold back the tears as I felt the reassuring thump of the wheels on the runway in Dublin Airport and I thought the air hostess was beautiful. I really thought about kissing the ground, long before Pope John Paul II.

Mother was there to meet me and welcome me back home again. Proudly she took me to her new house in Sandycove, County Dublin, where she had gone to live after selling Lissarda House in late spring, 1959.

Chapter 14
HOMETIME

I was welcomed at Sandycove, in my mother's new home, by our housekeeper of Lissarda days, Mary O'Brien who reminded me that she had been with the family for four generations, now that Rosemary my sister, had given birth to a son.

My mother asked Mary to come with her to Dublin. She came, as she said, out of loyalty to the Murphys, but realistically, she had little choice at almost seventy years of age. My mother had promised her security and shelter for the rest of her life.

I have often mused over that fiction called "ownership". In legal justice it confers the right to dispose of property, but not sufficiently emphasised is the corresponding obligation or duty in social justice to exercise that right in harmony with the wellbeing of others. For example, Mary O'Brien had invested the best years of her life in Lissarda House, she had lived there more than twice the length of time that my mother had, her friends were all Lissarda people, it was her home, yet without any reference to her needs, that which she probably valued most was sold from under her without prior consultation. She never said how she felt about all that because she was of that generation of servants who knew their place. My mother had never asked her because she was a faithful conformer to what were regarded as the just practices of a society in which the "good" could be defined as that which was not discouraged in the Tablets handed down to the privileged mentors of Irish society.

Mother was now involved in what she called "social work" with the Legion of Mary. She helped out in the Hostel in Harcourt Street and in the Overseas Club in Harcourt Terrace. She felt free, and liberated from the burden of having to oversee a farm. Mary O'Brien cooked the meals for her and kept the house.

***

I received my assignment for the next year from the Provincial. I was to go to St. Mary's, Cork to do a pastoral course for the year and to act as Sub-master or assistant to the Master of Novices and Students. But before that I was to have some holidays.

***

At the end of July my sister and brother in law and their baby boy called Denstone came over to Sandycove on holiday. I had decided to go to Croagh Patrick to climb the Reek on the traditional weekend at the end of July. Phil, my brother in law was a new keen convert to the Catholic faith and to things Irish so he willingly agreed to accompany me.

We borrowed my mother's car and set off from Sandycove very early on the Saturday morning. We had a leisurely drive across Ireland arriving in Tuam in the early evening. We had a good meal. We finished our meal at about 7.30 p.m. which meant we had some time to fill in since we didn't aim to start climbing the Reek until midnight. I got the bright idea that he would call to see an old friend of mine, Peter, now a veterinary surgeon in one of the neighbouring towns. I knew he had been married within the previous year and a half and recently his wife, Margaret, had given birth to twins.

After making enquiries and following directions, at about nine o'clock we found where he lived. We could see a light on downstairs at the back of the comfortable looking house. It was a dull night, overcast but dry. The doors of an empty garage, which was detached from but just beside the house, were wide open suggesting that both Margaret and Peter or at least one of them was out. The light gave us some hope so we knocked on the front door. It was some time before the light in the hall went on and Margaret who at first did not recognise me in Roman collar and black suit, instead of uttering words of greeting said, 'What's after happening, Father? Is Peter alright?' I quickly cut in and said, 'Margaret, this is Denstone Murphy, Peter's friend and this is my brother in law, Phil, Rosemary's husband. We're on our way to Croagh Patrick and we thought we'd call to pay our respects'.

'Denstone is it? My God, Denstone welcome. Thank God it's you. I'm always scared by Gardaí and priests calling late at night, it usually means something dreadful has happened'.

She then brought us in to a comfortable, Aga-heated kitchen explaining to us that Peter had gone out on business with some English colleagues who were over working on the bovine T.B. eradication scheme. The twins were asleep. If we liked we could wait until Peter came in. It was one of those strange situations in which I felt our welcome was not without some reservation yet, having come, it seemed better to wait on for Peter's return because to go now might be thought of as pique on our part.

Margaret made a cup of tea and the three of us conversed cordially, if superficially, waiting for Peter's return about which Margaret was now becoming more evidently anxious.

At about a quarter to eleven, with that finely tuned perceptiveness of a wife, Margaret heard the noise of a car long before Phil or I did and thereupon moved quickly out through the back door, too deliberately to be welcoming, more likely to intercept or at least forewarn. We heard taps turned on and water being splashed liberally against a background of indistinctly competing voices, In due course, Peter made his entry flanked by two Harvey Smith style characters. He greeted me as "Father", with profound respect. His companions called me "Vicar", at which point Peter told them that he as an Irish Catholic would insist on having me referred to as "Father" in his house and in front of his wife. It was as if they had voiced some obscenity. The subsequent, almost mocking overuse of "Father" went unnoticed. Margaret, with restraint and apparent tolerance suppressing anger with all of us, except perhaps Phil, the innocent outsider, supplied tea and cold meat to the three vets.

Margaret then disappeared in response to the crying of just awakened babies. Peter, as if some routine had been triggered off, strongly and wordily supported the Church's condemnation of artificial means of birth control, affirming, more graphically than he might ordinarily dare, that "rubber goods (a popular euphemism at the time) would never come between him and his wife".

Eventually, Peter came to understand that Phil and I were on our way to the Reek but still could not figure out who we were. Then, as if to copper fasten his professed orthodoxy and his approval of our mission, he said he would accompany us.

As soon as Margaret came down to the kitchen again Phil and I stood up to go, it was now almost quarter to twelve. On going out we noticed that our car was hemmed in by another car in the driveway; it was Peter's, a venerable looking Humber Hawk. He volunteered to move out of our way, using a spanner to engage the reverse gear, the gear lever itself had by some means been eradicated. Having got out of the driveway onto the road we bid a hasty goodbye to Peter and the English bovine T.B. eradicators.

Well over thirty years later as I write down this account, and in spite of the spending of billions of pounds on eradication programmes that same T. B. is still with us.

Margaret very thoughtfully invited us back to early lunch the next day on our way back from our pilgrimage, in the hope of meeting, as she said, "the real Peter". Then we moved away fast, not so much because we were behind schedule but to forestall the unlikely event of Peter's remembering that he said he would come with us.

We arrived at the foot of Croagh Patrick just after half past twelve and parked the car after following signs which conducted us to the lower end of quite a soft, sloping field. At least it was convenient to the starting point of the pilgrimage climb. We got our leaflets with prayers to be said and with instructions. It was a hard climb and a long climb which took us several hours. The physical exertion was brought about largely by the fact that on the shale surface, for every two steps forward you slipped one step back. Many passed us out on the way up, older people who were dedicated and practiced and younger people who were making bargains with God. Some barefooted men and women passed us, as did a few men carrying children on their shoulders.

The summit was a hive of spiritual industry, with various station prayers being said and confessions being heard. There were no confession boxes, nor even places for the priest to sit down or for the penitent to kneel down. Confessions were held standing up and by whispering one's sins into the priest's ear behind a hat held in such a way as to foil lip-readers. Another technique used was to put a coat or rug over the heads of both confessor and penitent, as the old fashioned portrait photographer used to cover himself and his camera. This device safeguarded the seal of confession against listeners and lip readers as well as allowing for dialogue between confessor and penitent.

When we had finished saying our prayers we started the descent. A short way down from the top when we were clear of mist we got a memorable view of Clew Bay and its hundreds of islands. I had been expecting an easy journey back down, but it was not so. Holding oneself back from gathering momentum beyond control was a very strenuous task.

By the time we got back to the car at about ten o'clock we were tired. The problem which might arise when trying to drive a car uphill in a soft field would seem to have been obviated by a tractor which was standing by with a towrope. On enquiry, Phil was told that, if we so wished the tractor would haul us out for a consideration. Since it wasn't in Phil's nature to pay under pressure, he summoned up all his motoring skills and to the surprise of the on-looking tractor driver he just about made it through the gate and onto the road.

We called into a convent, on the way back towards the home of Margaret and Peter, and I celebrated Mass. We were greeted at the door by a radiant and refreshed looking Peter, showing no signs of a hangover. Not a mention was there of the night before. I'd say the night before genuinely never happened for Peter. Margaret communicated a subtle acknowledgement of our sharing in an embarrassing encounter the night before. I fussed over the twins, and Phil, as an experienced father himself, of eight months standing, offered enlightened comment.

We talked through lunch at which Peter poured out wine for Margaret and Phil, I was a teetotaller at the time and he poured none for himself, innocently saying that he wasn't much of a man for the wine at this hour of the day.

We left them in late afternoon to go to Clifden where we intended to spend the night before setting out for Dublin and home on the following day.

**

When the holidays were over I reported for duty in St. Mary's in Cork. I was given two rooms, a study and a separate bedroom, in the Novitiate/Studentate and I was briefed by the Novice/Student Master on my duties as his assistant and deputy if he were not available. A slight complication about St. Mary's was that although the house of formation which was attached to it was primarily a novitiate, that is, a place where aspirants to the Dominican Order spent their first year of probation, it was also a house for the first year students who were studying Philosophy. These two groups, while they chanted the Divine Office together and cooperated in many ways, were not normally supposed to fraternise at recreation.

It was only two years since I had left the studentate in Tallaght to go to Rome and six years since I had left the studentate in Cork but I was aware of a change in attitudes. Novices and students, in particular, were beginning to press for reasons. The more simple docility that I was used to was becoming outmoded even though the Second Vatican Council, announced in January 1959 was not to start for another two years, in October 1962,

I took the novices for class about twice a week but I had no academic function vis a vis the students, I was concerned with their living and understanding of the religious life.

One of the senior priests in St. Mary's with a great deal of pastoral and missionary experience was assigned to take Vincent, Nicholas and me for classes and workshops in Pastoral Theology. We had tutorials with him a few days a week in preaching, counselling and moral theology.

In November we had to go to Tallaght to be examined with a view to being granted faculties, that is being given authority, to hear confessions and to preach. The examination was oral and it lasted for two hours before a board of five examiners and covered the whole range of moral theology and relevant Canon Law. Having passed this examination we were entitled to apply through the Prior for authority from the local bishop to preach and hear confessions in his diocese. However, at that time in the Diocese of Cork there were restrictions on the number of priests in St. Mary's who would be given these faculties. Only eight priests were granted permanent faculties but temporary or limited faculties were granted on occasion and by special request. Those of us doing the pastoral course had temporary faculties for most of our time there and got a great deal of confessional and preaching experience. There were very large crowds going for confession to St. Mary's. On Christmas Eve, of that year I, together with eleven other priests, heard confessions for eight hours.

A short time after Easter of 1961 I got a letter pushed under my door from the Provincial who happened to be on a visit to St. Mary's. In short, it was a letter instructing me that I was to go to Trinidad in September to teach in the new Dominican Secondary School, Holy Cross College, which had recently been established in Arima. I was to teach Biology, as teachers of that subject were then in short supply. I was somewhat shaken by this, firstly, because it was totally unexpected and demanded of me without any " warming up" and secondly, I felt bad that the Provincial who was on the premises did not tell me about it face to face, which he could so easily have done. In his letter he said he was sending me out because someone else whom he had in mind had some problem and couldn't go and I was brought in as a replacement. There was no estimate made of my strengths, weaknesses or capabilities. I had not done Biology for about ten years and during those ten years my training had been in a totally different area. Now suddenly, I was expected to take over all the Biology classes in the school including Cambridge School Certificate classes, with only three months left before the examination. In those days the overseas General Certificate of Education examinations were held in December.

At the time I accepted the assignation without murmur and a few weeks before I was due to fly out and when I had time, I blew the cobwebs off my old Biology books. There was neither time nor opportunity to do any kind of refresher course. Many Provincials and similar Major Superiors in those days seemed to have the idea that the virtue of obedience had magical properties whereby a religious could do anything provided that it was done under obedience. So often the homework needed in getting to

know those committed to their care and charge was not done.
Grace and Virtue perfect nature, they don't change it.

During that year in Cork I instructed six and received five
Christians of other denominations into the Catholic Church.
Why on earth was I not encouraged to develop the strengths I
had?

It was a great privilege to have had that year with the novices
and students with many of whom I made close and enduring
friendships.

Chapter 15
To Trinidad

Four of us young priests were instructed to go to Trinidad in September 1961. Vincent and Nicholas chose to go by boat directly from Liverpool to Port of Spain in Trinidad. Colm and I opted to fly out. We got permission to spend a week in New York en route.

Our respective families and some friends came to see both of us off at Dublin Airport on the day of our departure. Two particularly valued friends of mine turned up, Rosemarie and Billy O'Regan, and presented me with a valuable Ronson cigarette lighter as a going away present. Even though the smoking/lung cancer connection had been well established since 1955, cigarettes, tobacco, pipes and lighters were, still, acceptable and welcome gifts.

Before going on board the Boeing 707 which was to carry us across the Atlantic I drew aside one of my priest colleagues Father Damien Byrne who was a member of the farewell party that came from the Dominican Priory in Tallaght and made a good confession as if it were to have been my last. We walked out across the apron to board and as we passed just under the port wing tip Colm blessed the engines. Even though by this time Jet airliners had been in service for a few years there was still a certain novelty about them as even for Trans-Atlantic passenger haulage not all turbo props had yet been replaced.

Because we were priests, a considerable fuss was made about us, or on account of us, by other passengers sitting nearby. In the tense atmosphere of an aircraft cabin people tend to remind themselves, albeit unwillingly, about their own mortality and are disturbed by it. Some Catholics, in such circumstances, look upon the priest as safe, good and useful company, with power to absolve them from sin, in the unthinkable event of an emergency while in flight.

It was my first trip to the American continent and my flying fears were largely forgotten by my thoughts of anticipation about this "dreamland" we had heard so much about and seen so much of in the cinema. The air temperature that greeted us on landing in Kennedy Airport was much higher and the atmosphere more humid than those conditions which we left in Dublin Airport on that twelfth of September 1961. My cousins, Maureen O'Donovan and Mary and Eileen Calnan, all native of Leap in West Cork, now working as nurses in New York, were there to greet and welcome me. Calm's cousins also came. Calm and I went our own separate ways and planned to meet again in just over a week's time to continue our journey to Trinidad.

We went by cab to Maureen's apartment in Manhattan. I remember being somewhat culture shocked by an unusually explicit cab driver who, unimpressed by my prominently displayed Roman collar, told me how he might organise things for the night if he, like me, found himself in the company of three attractive young women. Of further interest was a large sticker prominently displayed for his passengers to see: "Nasser is a shmuck", Nasser, at the time, being President of Egypt. Even on that journey from the airport I was above all aware of a kind of demonstrative, verbal extraversion shown by so many people. There were middle aged drivers shouting abuse or greetings at teenagers with Bermuda shorts, standing up in convertibles. There were elderly drivers shaking fists at others who were attempting to pass them out. Some carried on a shouted conversation with occupants of another convertible travelling in a parallel traffic lane. All the cars seemed gigantic in size. Those were the days before the oil inflation of the early seventies had happened.

It was just before nine o'clock when we arrived at the apartment. We talked our way through the lovely meal Maureen had prepared and continued talking for long after it. Other relatives and friends, nearly all involved in nursing, called in to offer greetings and welcome. The atmosphere was unreal. Even though it was the early hours of the morning, which time I would associate with sleep, people were coming and going as if it were afternoon or morning. When I enquired how this was it was explained to me that the earlier callers were on their way to take over duty starting at midnight and the later ones were those who were replaced and were on their way home.

By about 3.30 a.m. everybody had gone home and Maureen showed me to my bed. Sleep was out of the question. My mind and imagination were far too active from so much talking to so many people and besides I liked the American coffee so much that I had used it as a thirst quencher, thereby consuming seven cups of it. As well, outside, there was an interminable bin collection going on with machinery which noisily chewed and consumed the trash generated by the hundreds of families stacked ten deep all around where I was spending that night.

Quite early the next morning Maureen took me to meet the pastor of the local Catholic Church where I celebrated Mass. For a weekday morning the church seemed to be quite full. This could be explained, I was later told, by the fact that there was a large Irish population in that part of Manhattan. I celebrated Mass on the high altar and afterwards a few people came to greet me in the sacristy. I was deeply touched by this faithful support, particularly on the part of one woman who said she left Ireland forty years previously and never went back even for a holiday. All her immediate family at home in Mayo had died and she felt now that she never would make the journey back, preferring to leave her Irish memories happy ones, so she said, unspoiled by overgrown graveyards and crumbling farmhouses.

It occurs to me now, thirty seven years afterwards, that the woman from Mayo came to help me with her thoughtful words and not to seek my ministrations. While she would have been too modest to say so, I have a strong feeling that she was one of those many unselfish emigrants who were so generous in sending money home that they never could afford the time or the passage money to travel themselves. Still, there is an outside chance, I like to think, that a woman called Bridget with a mid-European surname was spared, eventually to take the short cut home for even a short visit, through Mayo's own recently established airport at Knock.

As we went back to Maureen's apartment about a quarter of a mile away my eyes were opened to the more ordinary side of New York and American urban life. Men were still rushing to work with what I took to be overalls and lunch bundled under their arms. Women with headscarves evidencing somebody's holiday in Florida or Niagara and some pushing little trolleys for their messages, paced themselves according to successive "Don't Walk" and "Walk" signs, as they used the pedestrian crossings at the various street intersections. How different from the Utopian glitter that I had seen occasionally while viewing American tourists during a refueling stop at Rineanna (now Shannon Airport) in its early days?

I was the beneficiary of generous hospitality particularly from an old friend and room-mate of my days as a medical student in Cork, John Bolzan. He was by this a highly regarded physician in Boston. He was American born of Austrian background and was one of four graduate students who in 1950 came from Fordham University to University College, Cork medical school by some special arrangement.

I wrote to John several weeks beforehand to say I would be passing through the States and that I would like to meet him. In spite of his work load he took time off to drive to New York to collect me and to bring me back with him to Boston. He arrived quite late in the evening. I was ready and waiting for him at Maureen's place, bag packed and formally dressed with Roman collar and black suit.

After preliminary greetings and introductions to Maureen and some other cousins present he turned to me and said:

'I hate to have to say this, Denstone, but you would not be very comfortable where we are going tonight if you are wearing that garb. '

I wasn't prepared for this apparent onslaught on my virtue. I had seldom worn anything less than full clerical attire in public during the nine years that I was in religious life and on those few occasions when I did depart from those standards I was in full control. In these present circumstances I had no idea of what I might be letting myself in for. I gasped some kind of immediate reply while trying to assemble a coherent argument against the idea but before I could do so John spoke again, 'I've got a spare sports shirt and jacket in my car, why don't I go and get them for you?'

By this time my troubled conscience must have been obvious because he jestingly added.

'Sorry to disappoint you, I don't intend to take you to any night clubs or strip joints., ... but I would like to drive you through some of the tougher areas of the city to give you some idea of what happens on the streets at night.....we might see some real "cops and robbers" stuff'.

John got his clothes from the car. To change into the shirt and jacket would be sufficient, my black clerical trousers, he reckoned, would pass as "trendy".

After donning the shirt and jacket I felt like I imagined an Orthodox Jew might feel after eating pork.

I headed out with John into the New York night. As if it had all been pre-arranged, there was some incredible "cops and robbers" activity which we observed from a safe distance.

After that display John drove me on a lightning sightseeing tour around New York in his large and comfortable Chevrolet automobile, which, he assured me, was an inexpensive car, corresponding roughly in status significance to the Ford Prefect in Ireland. He demonstrated an expert knowledge of the place. He took me from Manhattan to Brooklyn to Queens and then over the curiously named Throg's Neck Bridge from Queens to the Bronx. On seeing them for the first time I was intrigued by some of those graphic road signs with which we were not familiar in Ireland, for example, "Squeeze Right", "Soft Shoulder" etc..

I really enjoyed that midnight tour. John Bolzan was one of those people whose company I had always enjoyed. He was a close friend and I was with him now on his own ground. I shared in the pleasure he got in showing me some of the wonders about which he had often told me when we were medical students together in Cork.

It was after 2 a.m. when we set out on the road to Boston. I was surprised by the volume of traffic at that hour, consisting mainly of trucks which were so well and clearly lit. I was sensitive to the matter of truck lighting as there was at that time in Ireland some public concern about accidents which had occurred due to inadequate truck lighting, particularly in the case of trucks parked on busy roads.

Perhaps to educate me, if not to impress me, in those pre-rigid speed limit days John put his boot down on the accelerator and at times reached 100 miles per hour on the Boston turnpike. Suddenly, the anxiety which had gripped me was justified, when the air pressure created by our high speed forced the lock on the hood (bonnet) which jumped up, but only got so far, being restrained by a safety chain which probably saved us from disaster. We stopped to examine the damage, which was very slight. We continued our journey at a more moderate pace.

As we arrived on the outskirts of Boston early morning stirrings were already taking place. Our destination was the St.John of God hospital in Brookline where John was medical director. A generous residence for the medical director was provided in the hospital grounds and since John was still single, living alone with his Airdale dog, the house gave an exaggerated impression of spaciousness. I was to be a guest there for the next couple of days.

During those days in Boston we contacted some other onetime medical student colleagues all of whom were settling down to married life and their careers. Even though I was totally accepted and given a wholehearted welcome by each of them and their spouses I was conscious of a certain estrangement by virtue of my single state. At this stage I was just over 30 years of age and the urge within me to consummate love was very strong. The fact that I had never had sexual intercourse gave me a curiosity which whetted my appetite almost to an intolerable degree, yet this carnal innocence was also a source of strength. I felt I still had the initial bonding, at least with interpersonal celibacy, which gave me a kind of home-ground advantage.

I returned to New York with John and then back to my cousins who showed me some more of the well-known New York sights, Greenwich Village, Times Square, the Empire State Buildings etc. They took me to see 'The Sound of Music' on Broadway, with the original cast including Mary Martin.

Both my cousins and John wined and dined me every day while I was with them. They typified the kind of hospitality that I took for granted. At the time I was not aware of the fact that I was a glorified sponger. I took it that my vow of poverty in some way absolved me from reciprocating such acts of generosity. In religious training and formation at the time there were warnings against the possession of wealth but the subtle hypocrisy involved in putting oneself in the way of enjoying someone else's wealth was not emphasised.

The implications of the practice of the virtue of Justice are too demanding and frightening to be considered seriously by the richer propertied class. This accounts for the fact that Justice has been tailored by the textbooks of Moral Theology to correspond to promptings of an acquisitive social grouping which may include clergy and religious however disguised.

On September 21st 1961 Calm and I flew out from New York to Trinidad via Bermuda, Antigua and Barbados. The three intermediate landings at airports, which might have been more accurately described as airstrips, involving some changes in passenger population lent an informal flavour to the flight.

Chapter 16
WEST INDIES

E ven after a relatively short stay there I had been seduced by the material magnificence of the United States of America. The sensation I was aware of, on coming into Piarco Airport in Trinidad was one of anti- climax. Corrugated iron, which was the near universal roofing material in that part of the world, dominated the foreground scenery while the background was provided by surprisingly lush and green vegetation. It was a shade of green, quite different to emerald green.

It was the wet season and humidity was very high. Walking out of the air-conditioned cabin of the plane down the steps and onto the runway was like walking into a Turkish bath. I began to perspire profusely so that the sweat was flowing off me by the time I had walked the hundred or so metres to the terminal building clad in a black worsted woollen suit and synthetic fibre shirt topped off by Roman collar.

My heart was heavy and I felt emotionally tender, devoid of missionary zeal and exiled. Still, I had to put on a brave face and respond to the welcome extended by the Vicar Provincial, Father Woods and Father Connolly who drove out to meet us. Neither was my morale helped by having to pass by the shanty town district on the outskirts of the capital, Port of Spain.

We were taken to the Cathedral presbytery which, at that time, was the Dominican missionary headquarters. It was a largely wooden building which seemed flimsy by Irish standards but apparently designed thus so as to provide maximum living comfort in tropical conditions.

After having had the evening meal with the priests in the Cathedral presbytery Father Edward Foley, the Principal of Holy Cross College in Arima arrived with some other members of the teaching community to bring me out to the College where I had been assigned to teach. Arima was about seventeen miles from Port of Spain. Nicholas who had arrived out by boat a few weeks before me was already established in the college as Bursar. I felt it hard to understand how all these colleagues of mine could be so settled in this strange environment while I felt so homesick and culture-shocked.

The priests' residence in Arima was a somewhat shanty-like structure in the main square of the town. I was shown to my room at the back of the house. It was very comfortable and more than adequate even though the appropriately descriptive phrase that came to my mind on first being shown into it was "chicken-coop". Partitions between the rooms, as is common in the tropics, were constructed so as to allow for good ventilation rather than with a view to privacy.

The final term of the school year, which in Trinidad and Tobago in those days ran from January to December, had already begun. On the morning after arriving I was taken up the hill to the college and there introduced to the pupils whom I would be teaching. I was to teach Latin, French, English and Religion to First Form in which there were 50 pupils. I had Biology with all the pupils who took that subject and this included the Cambridge School Certificate examination class who were due for examination the following December, in just over two months' time. That latter assignment caused me much more anxiety and trouble than I ever pretended. Being the "perfect" and may I add "proud" religious, instead of asking for open discussion about the matter, I accepted and internalised it all in an unhealthy fashion, not knowing how to do otherwise. In the light of the fact that I had been away from the study of Biology for about ten years I am sure an equitable solution to the problem would have been worked out if I had spoken up.

I did come to enjoy the life and work in Holy Cross College which was efficiently run and our efforts were appreciated by the local community. Living, as we were, in an ordinary modest house in the town gave us acceptability and accessibility to the people. We had about two hundred and fifty boys in the school when I went there first in 1961 and by the time I left there in 1965 we had about four hundred boys and seventeen full time teachers.

In my second year I was made sports master with particular responsibility for cricket, a game for which there is almost a reverential regard in that part of the world. In order to ensure credibility with the boys I became qualified as a first class umpire. This involved doing a two year part time course in cricket practice and theory; certain historic decisions were studied by us as a law student might study decisions of the Supreme Court. There were two written exams and one comprehensive final practical exam before two international umpires.

I found those cricket umpiring classes particularly interesting and inspiring from the social point of view. I was there as a colleague of my classmates rather than as a priest. I felt that I was totally accepted by them and we enjoyed each other's company. For the most part, these were men dedicated to the task of organising and supervising cricket in the community so that others could enjoy themselves. I realised that I had a long way to go.

The scout movement was taken seriously in Trinidad and Tobago and I became patron of the scout troop in the college. Apart from being available to attend the regular meetings this involved having to go on camping holidays with the scouts to various parts of the islands during the holidays. Eating, sleeping, cooking and washing with up to twenty boys for up to a fortnight at a time involved asceticism and a constant willing of oneself to the task.

The most demanding and, in a way, the most fulfilling of such expeditions was the camping holiday for almost three weeks in Grenada with seventeen boys. Grenada is another West Indian island about one hundred kilometres from Trinidad. We left Port of Spain, Trinidad late at night by boat and arrived early the following morning at St .George's, Grenada. Very tired and hungry we eventually reached our camping site which was a school building just outside the town of St. George's. That was to be our home for almost the next three weeks. Various projects and expeditions had been planned, discipline was very good and things went as nearly according to plan as possible.

Camping is a great leveller and as the time passed by I could sense that I was becoming more and more accepted and respected by the boys. I became incredibly tolerant of what sometimes amounted to boisterous behaviour on their part. I could see much more clearly their point of view because I shared, in detail, their living conditions. However, I didn't find it easy as, in a sense, I was on duty all the time, both waking and sleeping. What preserved my sanity was a visit every three or four days to the MacLeish family who lived in St. George's. I had been introduced very early on to this family by Father Adrian Dowling, a Dominican of the English Province which ran most of the parishes on the island. The MacLeish's, an elderly mother and two daughters were the most generous and most undemanding of hosts who provided blessed asylum for the "labourer in the vineyard". Ever since that time I have thought of them when I come across the names of Martha and Mary or Aquila, in whose house, according to St. Paul in 1 Corinthians,c.1, the church used to meet.

At the end of my second year at Holy Cross College I was made Vice Principal and during my third year the Principal went on six months leave, which was then the usual holiday leave after a four and a half year tour of duty. I took over as Acting Principal, a task which I enjoyed and which wasn't too difficult as Father Foley handed over to me a ship in perfect shape.

***

Early in 1964 I got the great news that my mother was going to come out on a cruise to the West Indies and spend about six weeks in Trinidad. The great day came and she arrived on the French liner, the "Antilles". I met her at the landing stage in Port of Spain at 7 o'clock on the morning of March 28th, Holy Saturday. A number of my Dominican confreres showed their typical thoughtfulness in appearing also at the quayside to welcome mother that morning. It was said at the time that she was the first parent of one of the Dominican brethren to have visited Trinidad.

Mother stayed in a house very near us as a guest of the Thomas family who were most attentive to her every need. She developed a close friendship with that family, which still endures. Later, Mrs. Thomas, since deceased, spent a holiday with my mother in Ireland.

Invitations flooded in from virtually all the priests for my mother to visit them in their presbyteries. Likewise a large number of the parents of pupils in the school invited her to their homes. The Holy Faith Sisters and the Sisters of St. Joseph of Cluny were very generous and kind to her. She was also received by the Governor General, Sir Solomon Hochoy and by the Archbishop, Dr. Finbarr Ryan. Indeed, her joy was full!

As Acting Principal I had no secretarial help and my paperwork had fallen alarmingly behind. On hearing of my plight, my mother who was a trained secretary, came up to the college with me every morning and worked hard until the whole backlog was cleared. For me at the time that was the most practical possible expression of maternal solicitude.

On the night before mother was due to leave Trinidad for home the Parents' Committee of the college gave a big dinner in her honour. This was the culmination of a series of parties and receptions which had been held for her under various auspices over the previous few days. There were speeches, tears and presentations.

I sometimes think that, perhaps, some small contribution that mother's visit made was that it might have stated that priests were of flesh and blood and came of human parentage. With so many foreign born priests in Trinidad it was possible that the priest was regarded as the priest Melchizedech in the Book of Genesis who had no stated human roots. Melchizedech appears, performs his priestly duties and then disappears without trace.

During the time that mother was in Trinidad we got word from the Provincial that the tour of duty was being shortened from four and a half to three years. That was great news and it took away most of the pain of my mother's departure for home on Sunday, May 10th, since I would now be due home on leave sometime in June.

In preparation for going home I had to reclaim my black suit from the Carmelite Sisters in Port of Spain, part of whose function seems to have been to take care that the priest's suits were kept free from math and mould. Suits were not worn generally by the priests in Trinidad in those days although a few did have white suits for going to cricket Test Matches and other such functions. A cotton version of the religious habit was worn constantly even when driving and as the standard dress for priests. For going to the beach or for relaxing hot shirts were worn.

Coming back to Ireland again after three years away was a culture shock also. I had flown to New York from Trinidad on Argentinian Airlines and changed to Aer Lingus for the flight to Dublin. My first cultural upset was to hear a record of a group called "The Clancy Brothers and Tommy Maken" "murdering" an Irish song, during my short stopover in New York. I was quite offended by their arrangement. Now I love them ......The next body blow came on the flight to Dublin. I presumed a considerable degree of piety amongst the cabin crew and so proposed that there be an in-flight Rosary recited. The hostess to whom I made the proposal told me that she would see what could be done, but I heard nothing more about it. I had left an unchanging, nay, unchangeable Ireland in 1961 but in 1964 the Second Vatican Council (1963-1965) was in progress and I was upset by what many of my Irish confreres told me about a falling off in religious fervour amongst the faithful. Another novelty which seemed to bode little good was the Irish Television station which was started while I was away.

***

It was so difficult to settle back to work in September after returning from three months at home in Ireland. On going out to Trinidad for the first time there was a certain novelty which distracted from the pain of exile but on this occasion there was no such relief. I can remember that the only balm to salve the raw emotional wound that I felt was in prayer in our oratory before the Blessed Sacrament. I appreciate that I was being offered a share in the true missionary spirit of commitment, "leave all and follow". But I can recall also identifying with the sentiments I heard expressed many years previously by the man on pilgrimage to Lough Derg who declared publicly during the night vigil, 'This place has nothing to recommend it'!

Time is a great healer and it was not too long before life became tolerable once more. I settled down for another three year stint. The first year was almost over when, out of the blue, came a telegram on July 9th. 1965 from the Provincial in Dublin, which read,
'Have appointed you Master of Students Tallaght'.

I was delighted with the appointment, it was just what I wanted and, what in a sense I had angled for. I felt quite capable of doing the job. Also it got me back to Ireland and was an honourable escape from exile and missionary asceticism. The reaction of my confreres was different, probably for a variety of reasons. There may have been jealousy, there may have been sorrow that I was to leave them, and there may have been disappointment that the college would be deprived of an experienced teacher. Most of them, after a preliminary formalised expression of congratulation sympathised with me at length and a few of them even proposed to appeal to the Provincial to change the appointment.

I felt isolated and there was nobody to rejoice with me. I became locked in a vicious circle I felt that if I expressed joy, such would be tantamount to rejecting ungraciously their well-intentioned condolences and this reaction of mine strengthened them in the conviction that I did not want to become Master of Students. It seemed like a custom or at least a fashion in religious or clerical life to suppress healthy ambition for preferment and to protest unworthiness.

I acknowledged the Provincial's telegram immediately, saying, inter alia, that "unworthy though I was, I accepted the appointment under obedience". My prompt reply was to seal things lest, for any reason, the Provincial might change his mind!

I was able to get away from Trinidad at the end of August. I decided to call to Chicago and Dubuque, Iowa, as well as to New York and Boston on the way home. I was anxious to meet some Irish students who were being sent to study in the Dominican house of studies in Dubuque. It was still the era of large numbers of young people entering religious orders and congregations and seminaries. Dubuque was full to overflowing with aspirants to the priesthood and full of enthusiasm about implementing the directives of Vatican ll.

Chapter 17
Return To Tallaght

Ifelt so happy. There was that comforting and awaited thump of the undercarriage on the runway as the plane landed in Shannon. The reassurance of the protective restraint of the safety belt combined with feeling the reverse thrust of the jet engines always affects me emotionally, and evokes within me a feeling of gratitude to some benign power for holding me and restoring me safely to mother earth. The few miles remaining to Dublin seemed like a detail. The cabin crew put on their coats and became less formal. I had no anxiety at all about the next take-off and landing. It was just so great to be home again.

A fellow traveller from Boston was Father Wilfred Harrington from the Dominican house of studies in Tallaght which was my eventual destination. Wilfred was returning home after giving scripture courses at a number of Summer Schools across the United States. He was able to fill me in on matters concerning the Irish Church and the Second Vatican Council which was to end in about three months' time. I was quite out of touch with developments and changes in the Church. The only tangible evidence of change that I had experienced up to this was the gift of several sets of Roman old style Mass vestments which were sent out to Trinidad by the Church in The Netherlands in 1964. In the light of what I got to know later of the updating of liturgical fashion in Europe and at the risk of appearing cynical, I would reckon that these vestments are more accurately characterised by the contributor from the "abundance" of the rich people than by the "everything" of the poor widow. (c. f. Mark c, 12)

On arrival in Dublin Airport I was met, not only by my mother but also by Father Malachy O'Dwyer, then one of the two Sub-Masters of students in Tallaght, and by some members of the student body. I felt flattered by what I like to think was "fuss".

I was impatient to get to Tallaght and get started on the new job. It was a dream fulfilled. I had an ambition to become Master of Students. I felt certain I had something to give. Father Ambrose Duffy handed over to me the reins of office and made himself available for some time to give any help or advice that might be needed. It was an easy transition as I knew Ambrose well. When I was a student he was Master and was held in the highest regard. I knew how hard an act he was to follow.

It was great to be back once more to the monastic life with strict observance, the Divine Office chanted in choir, the Gregorian chant and the special times and places of silence. For me, all this was the breath of life; something I missed acutely in Trinidad, although even there I was able to escape occasionally for a few days at a time to share in the liturgy of the Benedictine monks in Mount St. Benedict. It was a source of pain for me that many Dominicans seemed to be intolerant of this regular monastic side of our life. In spite of the fact that the constitutions of the Order give it high priority, for some it was a tiresome practice, an irrational aberration associated with student life. There were those for whom Tallaght was a necessary evil, an over-repressive version of a seminary for the training of students for the secular priesthood. If I may re-emphasise what I have already said in a previous chapter: a preoccupation with keeping up numbers, particularly in the years of the fifties and early sixties prompted a reluctance on the part of those selecting candidates or directing novices or students, to recommend a person, in particular circumstances, to test his vocation elsewhere.

When I took over as Master in 1965 there were about eighty students and during my two years in office something in the region of twenty decided to leave the religious life. The reasons students may have for leaving, like the reasons they had for entering in the first place, are private and sacred. A Master is bound to respect in absolute confidence any communication the student may have with him. It doesn't help anybody if departures are interpreted as a deficiency in stewardship.

Those were times of rapid and substantial change in the outlook of students in general. Relevance was becoming the "buzz" word. Rules, requests and tasks which a student was asked to fulfil had to be supported by reasons. A lot of new wine was being fermented but the condition of the wineskins was questionable. New attitudes of the world brought into the cloister were often not benignly interpreted. That a new paradigm was necessary wasn't accepted by all the academic and formation staff.

A theoretical and academic foundation in theology is essential for the priest, but there may be more than one way of achieving this. Up until the late fifties there was a simple immutability in methods and systems; you loved, worshipped and thought about God and neighbour, but with the advent of Civil Rights, Joan Baez, Bob Dylan and Martin Luther King et al. the emphasis changed from God and neighbour to God in and through neighbour. The generosity of a large number of those who aspired to the priesthood and religious life in those days was prompted and fostered by these popular movements and singers: but this was a tide which wasn't taken at the flood.

Some students were asking to become involved or were already involved in the organisation of various local youth groups and teams around Tallaght which was starting its growth towards being one of the largest centres of population in the country. Others wished to get involved as spiritual directors of Praesidia of the Legion of Mary or of Conferences of the St. Vincent de Paul Society etc. One student had a study group in one of the local factories.

This outside pastoral activity was barely tolerated and clearly discouraged by an influential few of those involved in the academic side of the students' formation. It was tolerated provided it did not interfere with their studies. What a lost opportunity! This fieldwork could have been used systematically to endorse and consolidate the bond that it is essential to forge between theory and practice. Unless relevance was made evident the need for thought in action subsequently during their priestly pastoral work would not be understood and appreciated.

It is a marvel that so many students rose above the limitations of their formation programme. Others would seem to have become victims of a system which could be construed as dichotomising between study and work, producing, on the one hand the academic, who felt unwanted by the practitioners in the field, or on the other hand the "headless" pastor.

Another of the pastoral involvements of some of the students at this time was to go into the Morning Star Hostel for down and out men to help with the cleaning of the place and the serving of meals as well as to socialise with the men. I went along with the students as often as I could manage. Practically all the men were highly intelligent and many had university degrees. Some of these shelters for the underprivileged in those days tended to be besieged by Social Science students doing theses and conducting surveys. Father Paul O'Leary, then a student, told me that one of the resident men asked him what he was doing his thesis on! As I mentioned already one of the regulars in the Morning Star with whom I renewed a very good friendship had taught me for seven years in school,

***

The students had amongst them some good and enthusiastic footballers; besides being involved in an inter-seminary league they had other occasional fixtures. One of these was against St. Patrick's Prison for young offenders, Mountjoy. Father

Seamus Conway, the chaplain at St. Patrick's, brought out a team and supporters once a year. It was a purifying and loving experience. What was so edifying and moving was the care our students took in bountifully providing for their guests, without in any way patronising them. In return, the appreciative reaction of these young men demonstrated an overflowing goodness. They just happen to be scapegoats for the sins of the rest of us. They are those in whose eyes the "speck"(Luke c.6, v.41) has been seen.

Another annual fixture was a rugby match against the theology students of the Church of Ireland Divinity Hostel, once referred to as the Battle of the Boyne! This match was played on a home and an away basis. On one occasion at least Dr. Simms, then Archbishop of Dublin, joined us for dinner afterwards in the Divinity Hostel. He had the double gift of being able to listen well and speak well. To illustrate some point he was making, I can recall that he quoted from the Book of Ecclesiastics. Never before or since have I heard the dignity and meaning of the text so patently expressed:

Next let us praise illustrious men,
Our ancestors in their successive generations.
The Lord has created an abundance of glory,
And displayed his greatness from earliest times.

Ecclesiastics, c.44, vv.l and 2. The final ingredient of these pleasant evenings was the hospitality provided in the Warden's study for the Master and Sub Master.

***

Father Finian Lynch, the Prior of Tallaght, during my first year as Master, went out of office in October 1966. I, automatically, as Sub-prior (the custom was that the Master on taking up office was also appointed Sub-prior) took over responsibility for the running of the Priory in general. Within a certain designated time arrangements had to be made for the election of another Prior. The political activity was covert but vigorous. To sustain my spirits during those difficult days, Father Luke Dempsey gave me a copy of "The Masters" by C.P. Snow for my bedtime reading. The human vagaries involved in the election of the Master of a Cambridge College, could with little difficulty be identified in the preparations for a prioral election in Tallaght.

Those entitled to vote were, roughly, the priests who were attached to the Priory as members of the academic or formation staff and those assigned to pastoral work in the public church and in the locality. In all there were just aver twenty electors. Those eligible for election were, roughly, all priests of a certain seniority who were not already involved in some other particularly specified offices.

The person elected at the first ballot chose not to accept the post as Prior. We had to go back to the ballot box again, and even for a third and a fourth time. One of the subsequent two was declared ineligible by the Provincial and the third chose not to accept. At the fourth attempt Paul Hynes was elected and took up office at the end of November.

Paul Hynes was only 32 years of age when he became Prior. He was energetic, imaginative, efficient and courageous. He masterminded a number of changes to bring Tallaght up to date, not least of which were the establishment of a Social Services Centre for the people of the fast developing district and the extension of the church to several times its original capacity.

Paul and I had been students together, were ordained together and were in Rome together. We had a very warm relationship and worked happily as a team in trying to provide the best atmosphere possible for the implementation of a good training programme for the students. There was no pretence about him and he was direct almost to a fault; if he was quick to anger he was also quick to apologise.

This was a happy time for me during which I felt fulfilled and happy in the work I was doing. Then I received out of the blue, after a meeting of the Provincial Council, a bombshell of a letter from the Provincial saying that I was being changed from Tallaght and sent to Cork as Novice Master. However, the letter pointed out that since the Novice Master's position in Cork was at that moment filled, I would have to wait for sometime until the present Novice Master left to take up the post of Novice Master in the Irish Dominican mission area in India. In the meantime I was instructed to vacate my post in Tallaght so that someone else could take over. It was traditionally a ten year appointment and I was being moved out of it after two years.

I was very upset, shocked and disillusioned. It seemed like a ham- fisted way of getting rid of me. If I wasn't doing the job satisfactorily I heard nothing about it. I was never hauled over the coals for correction by higher authority and given no warning whatsoever about my impending removal. What made things worse for me personally was that I suppressed all this anger at the time. There are few things more degrading for a person than to be given the run-around by somebody in authority who apparently hasn't the commitment to them or interest in them to confront them respectfully.

To add insult to injury, a few days after getting this notification a member of that Provincial Council who had made the decision about me drew me aside and said, for some reason, possibly to give the impression of letting me in on the rationale of the decision, 'We decided to send Father Anthony to India, because he is the junior of the two of you in the Order and to send you to Cork to replace him as Novice Master'.

That statement I found quite incomprehensible. In fact Anthony was my senior! Which information was clearly printed in the catalogue of membership of the Irish Dominican Province,

I was directed to go to St. Saviour's Priory in Dublin and there wait in the meantime until Anthony got the necessary immigration documents to get into India. The wait was a long one, about two years. Someone else was appointed Novice Master in Cork as if there had never been any arrangement with me. I felt sad and let down.

I was disappointed at the rejection but I could see how others might consider they had reasons for not giving me the appointment that I had been promised. But those reasons were never forthcoming and if I was in error surely I had a right to the correction which was never given.

As Virgil has it, "nothing happens without the connivance of the gods". There must have been better things in store.

DECISION TIME

I was feeling like a castaway but trying to keep the good side out when I was assigned to St. Saviour's in Dominic Street, Dublin. It would have been regarded by many in the Province as a plum assignation. It was where the Provincial resided at that time, which distinction conferred a certain status on the place. Various important provincial meetings were held there. There were the comings and goings of many important persons both clerical and lay. It was within easy walking distance of the city centre. In spite of all that, I had little enthusiasm about going there. Monastic observance was at a formalistic minimum. The choral recitation of the Divine Office which was an integral part of the Dominican vocation was carried out with insufficient evident interest in aesthetics. The legalities were too exclusively attended to; the atmosphere was clerical. To me it seemed little different in practice to a large diocesan presbytery.

When I entered the Dominican Order in Cork and again in Tallaght as also in San Clemente in Rome, I was aware of a poetic beauty in the life, which beauty formed an integral part of my attraction to the order.

There is a romantic dimension and an emotional fulfilment which develops the human as well as the spiritual person in monastic observance. A network of interdependent relationships is established. The transmission of this holiness (wholeness) to others as a "Cistercian in the world" was supposed to be of the essence of Dominican life, "to give to others the fruits of contemplation".

The monastic life in its fuller ritual expression may be possible only in the larger and younger communities but, in essence, a group of two or three can do it equally well, with proper adaptation. The prototype is described simply in The

Acts of the Apostles, c.2, vv. 44-47:"And all who believed were together and had all things in common...... "

In Ireland the model for apostolic work which was adapted variously by male religious was one derived from the work of the secular clergy who up to recent times at least had been successful in keeping up the numbers attending church. The secular clergy themselves had an adequate number of vocations to continue this work. Up to the end of the fifties, indeed, many dioceses in Ireland were having to send their priests overseas just after ordination because no positions were available for them in the dioceses in which they were ordained to serve. They were forced to queue up to get back to work at home. In those days of the fifties and before, if all available secular priests were mobilised, the ordinary pastoral needs of the people could have been fulfilled without the help of religious orders and congregations.

However, there were male religious in practically all dioceses who responded to the needs of the faithful little differently to the way that the secular clergy were doing it. Instead of supplying the particular quality of ministry or service that was intended by their founders, which isn't supplied just by setting up expensive shrines to their own saints and beating the tribal drum, some religious groups seemed to be competing with the secular clergy in exactly the same market. Consequently, to a greater or lesser extent many religious priests correctly perceived themselves not as members of a ministering community but as individual priests who happened to be members of a group whose specific objectives they felt they no longer had the time to take seriously. They based their own living styles on that model which served the secular priests so well.

This movement towards a willing usurpation of the work of diocesan clergy I found disturbing, particularly when it involved the running of parishes by members of religious orders or congregations, at the expense of their own specific contributions to the Church. It would have made more sense to ordain married persons and single women who felt they were called to the diocesan ministry than upset the gifts of the Spirit as found in religious orders and congregations.

* * *

Just after leaving Tallaght and before settling in to St. Saviour's the Provincial sent me for two months to Trinidad. I had been appointed to give a number of retreats in Trinidad and in Grenada. I really appreciated this recognition and this task which involved four six-day retreats to priests and two to sisters. I was given a great welcome back and no hospitality was spared by priests or people.

On the way back from that short visit to Trinidad in 1967, I stopped off in the United States. Before calling on some friends in New York and Boston I went to Kenosha, Wisconsin. I had been asked there to give a retreat lasting eight days, to a small group of Dominican Sisters, many of them from The Netherlands, involved in very intense rehabilitation work with young people in Chicago. Kenosha was for them a kind of sanctuary to which they returned at intervals for rest and recollection. These were still the days of protest and civil rights marches, when an "old fashioned" spirituality was being scrutinised and brought up to date. I'm afraid that lectures which I had not long previously delivered to more traditional groups of sisters in the West Indies were, on some issues, not acceptable in Kenosha. It turned out that I had to listen carefully to their open criticism and redraft a lot of my material. I had to bow to the experience of that right in the front line with some of the underprivileged youth of Chicago.

* * *

Back in St. Saviour's again my work schedule began to fill in. I was assigned to give retreats to different groups in various retreat houses; some were to laypeople and others to religious.

Particularly during holiday periods I went to a number of religious houses both here in Ireland and overseas to give longer six or eight-day retreats. Some weekends I went on camping or hostelling outings with various youth groups to act as their chaplain.

One of these outings made a salutary and lasting impression on me. I was asked to act as chaplain to a girls' group who were going for a few days in summertime to a youth camping site. They went to the camp early on a Saturday morning. I drove to the camp later in a borrowed Austin Mini arriving there about midday. I was greeted anxiously by an ashen faced adult group leader,

'One of the girls has just become very sick. We sent for the doctor. He should be along soon',

This sounded straightforward and reasonable.

'And where is she?' I asked.

'Oh, she was sick in the toilet for a long time but a couple of her friends have taken her to her bunk. I think it's her time of the month'. In spite of this simple and unsuspicious reply alarm bells began to ring in my head and on coming by the toilet building en route to the large tent where her bunk was, I decided to look in there to see if there was any evidence of what I suspected remotely.

I was shaken, frightened and disgusted when I saw a newly born infant in one of the cubicles. He wasn't moving and apparently he wasn't breathing.

'What do I do now?' I said to myself. I was on my own. Bonds of inhibition were tightening on me. Suddenly I became aware of the Roman collar I was wearing,

'What am I, a male celibate, doing in a girl's toilet?' I thought.

I felt a distinct revulsion. Only with great difficulty did I get myself to touch the little body in order to baptise him.

Meanwhile, the doctor had arrived, attended to the "sick" girl and passing back again by the girls' toilet saw me and greeted me heartily but dismissively. A youngish man, he was walking briskly and intently. With difficulty I got his attention and somewhat impatiently he came back. Thinking I was simply curious, he volunteered,

'She'll be fine, she's just at that age, if you follow me, Father', His fragile bonhommie was soon dissipated when the truth of the situation dawned on him. After due examination of the infant he said, 'He's dead, drowned.'

Then he rushed out as I heard him muttering'.......... afterbirth',

On the way back to the girl's bedside he met the group leaders in charge and told them what had occurred in the toilet. They hadn't known that one of the girls was pregnant and knew nothing about the birth.

The senior person in charge contacted the Gardaí. The coroner was contacted. I don't know anything about the contacts, if any, made between the group leaders and the girl's family.

What happened exactly during negotiations between all those legally involved I don't know. However, later that summer's evening I was asked if I could negotiate immediate burial in consecrated ground somewhere and furthermore would I mind acting as undertaker, since apparently there was good reason for not getting the local undertaker involved.

I accepted to do all I could to help. I phoned a particular colleague and friend for advice and practical help. In typical style, when I had finished my explanations to him on the phone, he said,

'Is that all? Now listen to me. Be there (naming the place) at 9 o'clock tonight. I'll get-- to meet you to show you where to bury the corpse and to assist in digging the grave. I myself will arrange with the caretaker that the graveyard is kept open,'

I arrived on time with the tiny coffin made from an orange box stowed in the boot of the Austin Mini. I completed the digging of the grave and after some simple prayers of committal filled in the earth at that small unmarked spot.

Looking back now at a distance in time I see the whole episode as an incredible denial by everybody involved. As it now appears to me the owner of the camp site was a key person in the cover up. Such a "scandal", if broadcast, could be bad for business. Perhaps there was no love lost between the camp site owner and the local undertaker who, at almost any cost, it seems to have been necessary to avoid, lest he spill the beans.

The girl who gave birth under such humiliating circumstances was at the camp disco that same evening while I was burying the remains of her child whom she had never actually seen. She was given no nursing care, nor counselling. Legally, her child never existed. There is no record of his birth nor of his death in either church or state register.

If I may add another detail. When I arrived back at the disco after the burial, I was instructed by 'authority' to burn the afterbirth at a certain specified place some miles away, as early as possible the following morning. To make sure it burned I was supplied with petrol to pour over it. By the way, the afterbirth was to be found wrapped up in newspaper near the girl's bunk. Such was to be the final ritual cleansing of the site and the surrounds.

I am quite certain that all of us involved were acting in perfectly good faith in accordance with the accepted mores of the day. The procedure we adopted went ahead with ne'er a dissenting voice neither of church nor of state. We told ourselves we were acting thus to save the girl and her family from being embarrassed and to preserve her good name.

***

In response to a pressing demand. Father Fergal O'Connor and I established formal pre-marriage courses in St. Saviour's in May, 1968. Fergal had a great deal of experience and expertise in counselling in this area. As well, he had given time and consideration to the positive dogmatic theology of Marriage. I was to be his apprentice and the course organiser. When I was a young student he taught me Philosophy and by proclaiming that he must be one of the best teachers of our time I am only adding my voice to the voices of almost an entire generation of students.

Within a few days of announcing the course it was booked out. We had decided that fifteen couples would be our complement. We did our research and set up a programme which involved two lectures and discussion over a period of two hours per night, once a week for eight weeks. One lecture of each session dealt with some aspect of the theology of marriage, the other lecture dealt with matters to do with physical sexuality, legal and economic implications etc.; these were dealt with by experts whom we brought along specially. When it all started Fergal set the pace in the Theological lectures but by degrees brought me into it so that eventually I was able to take over.

During the four years when I was involved with this course it was made use of by over seven hundred couples. In my last year we ran also a course for our 'graduates' who had been married for some time.

* * *

In September of the year when the pre-marriage courses began I was appointed to teach Theology to the students of the Colleges of Education in Sion Hill. Together with a priest colleague I was involved with the four colleges, St. Catherine's College (Home Economics), The Froebel College, The Montessori College and St. Raphael's College of Physical Education. This was work that I really enjoyed. I got to know the students well as a group and also got to know many individuals. Interest in Theology varied but in general the receptivity was good. Except for just a few who chose Theology as an academic subject it played no part in their assessments. It was important to befriend the students and be accessible to them. It was very clearly a buyers' market. If the students got to dislike you and switched off, there was little you could do about it.

During the years 1968-72, my work in Sion Hill during the day and my pre-marriage course preoccupation with both organisation and lecturing, combined with quite a lot of individual counselling meant that my involvement in community life in St. Saviour's was minimal. During those years also a number of young priests, whom I had previously been in charge of as students in Tallaght, were assigned to the house. Some were teaching Christian Doctrine in Vocational or Secondary Schools. Others were committed to giving retreats to schools, youth groups, to adults at weekends in various retreat houses and to religious sisters.

There was another group of more senior priests involved in publications of various kinds and in University lecturing.

All this meant that there were different interest groups in the house. The basic group consisted of about ten priests with an average age of well over fifty, hardworking conscientious men who attended regularly at Divine Office, celebrated the public Masses, preached, heard confessions in the public church and were constantly available in the parlour for confessions and counselling. These men were faithfully established on safe, conservative ground; as individuals, of great charity, giving the impression of tolerating at least cosmetically, but not embracing the "new" church. Then there were those aged about thirty or under of the post-Tridentine Mass era who individually respected the older men and were respected by them. Yet these two groups were anathema to each other in so many ways. There was a tangible intolerance of one group by the other.

Perhaps even this trivial example will serve to illustrate the last point. One night after having been to the theatre one of the young priests came into the recreation room where a number of the community were watching Television. The young man was wearing a collar and tie in place of his Roman collar. As soon as one of the older men saw him one could see that he was genuinely shocked and fixing his gaze on the younger man, he declared out loud,

'As far as I'm concerned, he's no longer a priest.'

On the other hand there were many cases of insensitivity by the younger group towards the feelings of the older men. Perhaps just as clearly illustrated by the same example above; the younger man should have sensed that his garb would upset others and should have changed before appearing in the recreation room.

These happenings upset and confused me. I was forty years of age in 1971 which, in seniority put me right in the middle, I felt somewhat adrift. There was another matter which at around about that time I found perplexing. I was asked by someone outside the community if I would accept responsibility for a monthly all-night vigil in honour of Our Lady. I agreed willingly to take it on in St. Saviour's and all necessary permissions were granted. It was, in a sense, my olive branch to the 'conservative' church. I found the work fruitful in that there was a very large attendance of people, a great many of whom were looking for confession, counselling or comforting, but with a few notable exceptions there were no takers from any group in my own community who would help or encourage me.

* * *

In 1972 when I had been almost four years in Sion Hill I decided I needed to do some formal study of Education. I got a place on the Master in Education course in Trinity College. I got leave from Sion Hill and just kept on one class of about five students who were studying Theology as an academic subject.

Since well before leaving Secondary School I had been disappointed in my academic record and now I longed to vindicate myself. I felt as if I had come of age in terms of study. From my very first day in Trinity I got down to work seriously. I coped successfully with the disastrous scruple I had which used to inhibit me and prevent me from accepting the motivation to study for any 'unworthy' proximate motive like the achievement of success in examinations. It was such a relief to study in peace. A process of liberation showed signs of stirring within me.

* * *

Sometime before I went to Trinity I was asked by a priest in one of the newer parishes on the outskirts of Dublin if I would give a study evening on marriage to a parents' group. I thought it would be proper to have a woman also addressing the group. I contacted a woman friend of mine who was prominently associated in public life with women's issues.

She was unable to come on the night which had been arranged but she said she could recommend someone else to me who would do the job just as well. I asked her who this person was and she told me,

'This woman was a Medical Missionary of Mary. She left them fairly recently. She is a highly skilled social worker particularly tuned in to marriage and mental health. I think she would be ideal for that study evening....... '

I agreed to contact her. I called her on the phone and she replied,

'Maura speaking'.

'I was in contact with Margaret about helping me to give a study evening on marriage but she can't do it as she already has an engagement so she thought you might be able to do it', I explained. I told her what it was all about. She said she would be pleased to help out.

After putting down the phone I began to reflect that this onetime Medical Missionary sister was so easy for me to talk to. Although comparative strangers there was forged between us an immediate bond of interest. But I thought,
'I must be careful. ... I mustn't let my affections run away with me. There are enough priests running away with women nowadays!'
However, I was adrift and did need a friend.

The study evening took place and seemed to be a great success. At the end of the proceedings a genial priest gave us two envelopes. Mine contained a 'Thank You' card and a generous cheque. Maura got an even more beautiful 'Thank You' card but no cheque! Afterwards when I dropped her back to her flat she invited me in for a cup of coffee. We talked into the small hours. We didn't meet again for quite some time.

***

My overall result for the first year in Trinity was a First Class Honours. I was delighted beyond all measure. It did my self-confidence great good. The post of Assistant Director of the Public Examinations Evaluation Project was being re-advertised. This Project was a research unit established by the Department of Education and was to be operated by Trinity College. A friend who thought well of my capacities suggested that I should apply for this post. I got permission from my religious superiors to send in my application which proved successful.

I began work in this research unit in Trinity towards the end of 1973. The pace was hot, the work was comprehensive and involved a lot of travelling throughout the country. There were four of us employed full time on this Project: John Heywood, Director; Seamus McGuinness, Research Fellow; Nuala Brady,

Secretary and I was Assistant Director. I found community with those colleagues. As a group we were pursuing an identified and clearly defined common objective. We often worked very late into the night or started before cock-crow in the morning. Meeting pupils and teachers all over the country was a great encouragement and spur to success.

***

I was at the stage now when my links with St. Saviour's were becoming very slight. No longer had I a sense of belonging there as part of a team with a common objective to be attained - if ever I had that sense. I was lodging there and getting my laundry done. Most weeks I had a few nights away in Ennis, Cork or Waterford and occasionally in England on business for the research unit in Trinity. I was confident still that I had a vocation to contemplate and communicate but I could no longer express it within the canonical limitations of the order. I was frustrated.

I had done quite a lot of   work in encounter groups and through my work in them I got a clearer idea of the true nature of human and sexual love. The ideas I had from my study of the Dogmatic Theology of marriage were thereby complemented.

I learned quite a lot about my own behaviour and human behaviour in general. I learned about friendship. Friendship for me had been to some extent threatening. Perhaps I had taken too seriously the religious admonition discouraging "particular friendships". I was now feeling a painful need for a human, trusting relationship. It was in one of these groups that I met Maura again.

Finally, I asked for and obtained leave of absence from the Order in March 1974. My mother and sister were totally accepting of my decision and supportive. The Dominican Order was generous in ensuring that, in my new life, I would not want for anything. It augured well for the new beginning.

The actual day of my leaving, March 24th 1974 was in many ways a day of mourning. Yet the pain of that separation was assuaged to some extent by the fact that I got a comfortable flat with an understanding landlord. There was the help and generosity of many faithful friends. What I was going through was analagous to a marital separation or divorce. I knew it was necessary for me to take a decisive step in some direction. I estimated that I had reached a stage when I could best approach the Lord through the sacramentality of human love, through the asceticism of generous sexual encounter. I had followed the celibate way and was happy in it. But as there is time for "everything under the sun" there was a time for me to change and yet throughout, it is always "Time to be Priest".

By this time Maura had left Dublin and was lecturing in the department of Social Administration in The New University of Ulster in Coleraine. I used to drive up to see her, at first occasionally and then more frequently.

After our marriage Maura got a lectureship in Queen's University, Belfast and became a weekly commuter from our home in Dublin. In 1978 she came to work in Dublin. I got the First Class Honours that I yearned for in the Master in Education degree. When my full time contract in Trinity finished I was kept on as a part time lecturer and got a full time post as a teacher in Cabinteely Community School in 1976 where I worked for fourteen happy years until I had to retire in 1990.

"The semester is over. Lecturing is finished;
It was tiresome enough - to me, at any rate.
But the seminar was really good and interesting."

Dietrich Bonhoeffer
(26th February, 1932)
Berlin.

Chapter 18b
HOPES FULFILLED

A number of those who sought dispensation from the obligations in Canon Law that go with the exercise of the priestly ministry had their requests granted with little difficulty. The principal obligation from which dispensation was sought was that of celibacy.

I know one person who applied for a dispensation, refused to give a reason, yet promptly had his request granted.

I applied, gave exhaustive reasons for my seeking of a dispensation and was turned down. Apparently, or so I have been told, I was too positive. I had a strong sexual appetite, deep down I knew it was good but couldn't admit this to myself. All this made me aware of the kind of dedication required of the genuine celibate. However this was not an appetite that I cared to own.

When I became director of a pre-marriage course things began to change. I became aware of marriage as the legitimate and appropriate response to my sexual desires.

During theological studies before ordination it was regarded as important to study, in some detail, negative aspects of the theology of sexuality e.g. a variety of ways of sinning. The declared purpose of this procedure was to prepare us for dealing with matters and problems of this kind that might come up in hearing confessions or in giving spiritual direction. Ironically however, it seemed to me that its main effect was to perpetuate the negative approach by stressing the obstacles that we raised against having a loving and childlike relationship with God. The helping hand of the Father, who would restore us to Himself, if we had grown away, was considered only as pious ornamentation on a psychological/legal process of confession. Father Gerald Vann, O.P. in this respect uses the term 'spiritual valetudinarianism'.

Little had been done to give a positive satisfying slant to sex. The categories used in the standard theology text books bestowed a comforting certainty and stability.

Good though the intentions of my mentors may have been, I had perceived sexuality, women and marriage, largely, as sources of moral danger. The rewards for continence seemed proportionately much greater than an unselfishly managed experience of carnal ecstasy.

How do I make sense of these urges? I was driven to ask. Where is the positive side? I opted out of the argument. I had chosen celibacy as a safe refuge. It should have been a source of courage not a denial of passion.

In Civil Law and in some other branches of Canon Law, the petitioner is given a hearing but when dispensation from the clerical obligation to celibacy is involved the entire transaction is by proxy. The particular individual as a unique person with special needs is hardly considered, he is not seen and his voice is not heard. The granting or withholding of these dispensations seems to depend on Papal political circumstances. It is difficult to believe that civil authorities could get away with such expediency.

In 1974 Maura and I were given to believe that there would be no problem about getting the dispensation as those of my colleagues who left at that time had their requests for dispensation promptly granted. Towards Christmas 1975 we booked the church and planned a wedding reception. We arranged for a priest friend to officiate. At the eleventh hour we got a phone call from Rome to say the dispensation was not granted. We put off our marriage for six months confident that time would find a solution.

At the end of the six months no further progress had been made. I had resisted some gentle pressure that was put on me to file a request for dispensation supported by negative reasons. The Vatican authorities, it appeared to me, would not acknowledge the fact of seeking dispensation from the obligation to celibacy as a possible growth process for some, in the same way that the taking of a vow of celibacy late in life on the part of a widow or widower might be seen as a movement towards greater perfection. Because of the apparent lack of interest that the Vatican had in our case and because 'the more travelled road' seemed to have been blocked against us, Maura and I felt justified in going outside the Canonical requirements for a valid and lawful marriage. Having done this we saw clearly that there was no obstacle to our fulfilling the theological requirement, which was, in the spirit of the Letter to the Ephesians to commit ourselves officially to strive, through the quality of our lives and of our relationship to show forth or signify the kind of love relationship that there is between Christ and humankind.

On June 19th 1976 we partook of our wedding Eucharist which was the ordinary morning parish Mass in a local church. Shortly afterwards on that same day we committed ourselves in marriage as we ministered the Sacrament to each other in the Registry Office in Coleraine in the presence of the registrar and four close friends.

Seventeen years afterwards, to the month, with the formal and official blessing of the Church we had a Nuptial Mass and traditional Catholic marriage ceremony in the living room of our own home.

Chapter 18C
SILENCED BY PARKINSONS

I had the good fortune to have a job already when finally I decided to seek leave of absence from the active priestly ministry and from the Dominican Order. I had been working for more than two years in Trinity College, Dublin as Assistant Director of research on the Public Examinations Evaluation Project (P. E. E. P.) which was based in the School of Education. I did not have any permanency but it was a relatively well paid job and I was in a very good position from which to scout around for other employment in due course.

Many of those who left the active priestly ministry around about that time did have some problems in finding employment. Coming onto the labour market in one's late thirties or early forties is not easy. One friend and ex colleague got a job as a bus conductor. He was very comfortable in the work but ex parishioners of his found it at first a little strange to have their erstwhile curate collecting their fares. In a number of cases he was addressed as 'father' which probably perplexed others of the passengers who were not in on the 'secret'.

The year before my contract in Trinity was up I pursued seriously the task of getting another job. It had become clear to me that the Trinity involvement would not be renewed, I had many interviews and at last in the beautiful long hot summer of 1976 I applied for and was offered a teaching post in Cabinteely Community School in the southern suburbs of Dublin. It had been a girls' private secondary school owned by the Ursuline sisters up to 1975 when the running of it was taken over by the Department of Education and a male lay Principal, Liam Ryder, was appointed. The first intake of boys was in 1977.

I had a fair amount of experience of second level schools - in Trinidad, where I had taught Biology to almost every class in

Holy Cross College, Arima for four years. At the same time I taught Religious Knowledge, Latin, French and English. I had begun to teach Physics and Chemistry shortly before I left the school.

In Ireland, up until my appointment to Cabinteely my experience of second level education was mostly through the giving of schools' retreats.

When I began this work on schools' retreats they were straightforward affairs. Groups tended to be very large, sometimes over a hundred. These pupils would be expected to listen to perhaps ten lectures over a period of three days while they sat upright on hard benches in the convent, college or school chapel. Silence was encouraged and often compulsory. Everyone was expected to go to confession, although not necessarily to the priest preaching· the retreat, another priest or priests were often brought in to assist.

Traffic in ideas tended to be one-way - from preacher to congregation. There was usually a question box into which pupils were told they could, anonymously, place questions concerning matters which they might be ashamed of or shy about asking in person. The answers given were regarded as final definitions of the Truth! The questions in general were trite if not sometimes simply prurient. Religious issues were not thought about sufficiently on a real lie day to day basis to prompt real questions.

A question that turned up in the question box with clockwork regularity was: "What is French kissing'?" followed by: "Is French kissing a sin?"

During the sixties after the Second Vatican Council the schools' retreat scene changed considerably. A number of schools opted for splitting classes up into smaller groups and having residential retreats over a few days, in retreat houses owned by religious communities. Dialogue with the retreat giver, now not always a Priest, was encouraged, Attempts were made to give meaning to the liturgy.

In Cabinteely I taught Religious Knowledge and English at all levels. A teacher has to be at concert pitch facing a critical audience for almost five hours a day, I cannot speak for other teachers but I did find that the teaching of religion was gradually becoming more and more difficult, demanding and frustrating for me as a teacher. English I found demanding of energy but in practically every class there was consolation to be found in a certain number of pupils who manifested a sense of responsibility. There was always the biblical 'remnant'.

No motivation for a pupil to apply her/himself to the acquiring of Religious Knowledge was evident. There was a myth abroad that it was somehow unworthy of Religious Knowledge to have it classified as an academic subject depending on ulterior motivation. However, being in a fallen human condition we cannot spurn intermediate material motivators to achieve ultimate sublime objectives. For example, few if any seminarians would acquire sufficient theological knowledge for ordination were it not for the carrot and stick.

There is a body of truth to be found in the Creeds, in the definitions of accredited councils, in the writings of doctors and saints of the church and above all in the bible. This is the 'deposit of faith'; that which is to be believed; also called objective Christian Faith.

To this objective faith there is the counterpart, subjective Christian Faith. It is the human response to the 'deposit of faith'. This human response is understood as the childlike and trusting acceptance of the Kingdom of God and its demands.

Unless the 'deposit of faith', as laid out generally and as in the catechetical works that are available, is substantially grasped and understood, it is not possible to have a properly formed and informed Christian believer. The besetting dangers of this ignorance are superstition and fundamentalism.

Unless there is grist for the mill there can be no flour.

With such ideas in mind I had the following letter published in the Irish Times of September 19th 1994.

> *"The first public examination in religious education as an optional academic subject was supposed to have taken place in 1985. Such an exam, which given our fallen human condition, would be a powerful motivator for learning, never happened then or since then.*
>
> *The status of religious education in most post-primary schools makes the impression on many pupils that it is irrational, therefore, irrelevant. 'The school leaver is likely.......to consider the entire sphere of religion as insignificant and unworthy of attention by an otherwise sophisticated mind," (Werner Jeanrond: 'Rite and Reason', July 12th.),*
>
> *Religious education classes can become periods during which pupils have to be contained or simply amused due to a total lack of interest by a destructive minority who exert a devastating peer pressure on the well-disposed. Why must those, and there are many of them, who want to learn about their own beliefs and the belief of others be deprived?"*

***

Sometime in 1985 I was becoming aware of difficulty in writing fast, and besides, my writing seemed to be getting smaller and smaller. Before this, for a number of years I had been secretary of one of the local branches of Fine Gael and of the local residents' association, I began to find the speed writing involved in the taking of the minutes at meetings which, up to this I had enjoyed doing, becoming by degrees more and more difficult. Similarly, when called upon hurriedly, say, in a corridor by a pupil whose year head I was, to verify a note from her/his parents by adding my signature, I had difficulty. The ability to exercise fine movement with my fingers and hands was diminishing.

At first I thought that it might have been a blood circulation problem. This, however, was not borne out as the problem persisted even in ideally comfortable and warm conditions. Then it dawned on me that it might be a neurological problem. I discussed it with Maura, my wife, and made an appointment to see the family doctor. After due examination he queried Parkinson's disease and referred me to a specialist whom I had to wait several months to see. Finally, sentence was passed on February 5th 1986, my fifty fifth birthday -- I had Parkinson's.

I felt dejected, rejected and helpless - thrown on the scrap-heap. I remember a similar feeling on getting news of failure in my Second Medical examination many years before. Both days were wet and heavy rain was falling. The world is going ahead and you are being left behind. What the future held I had no idea. The prognosis given was uncertain. Apparently, Parkinson's tends to manifest itself in very different forms. A general description which I have managed to extrapolate from what I hear and read and from my own experience goes as follows:

"It is an incurable disease. There is a progressive degeneration of certain brain cells. This results, in my case at least, in slowness of movement, muscular rigidity, difficulty in initiating movement. Rapid and fine finger movements become impossible, writing becomes small and illegible, and dribbling of saliva is frequent. However, the greatest handicap is a drastic loss of the capacity to speak. It is not congenital or inherited. The cause is unknown. The effectiveness of certain

drugs, now widely used in treatment, varies from patient to patient and from time to time".

Speech began to pose a problem in late 1986. Blocks were tending to occur even in one to one conversation and I became liable to dry up completely while giving a class or lecture. Frequently I became "speechless" - the phenomenon was akin to a sense of dumbfoundedness that can take over when one is "annoyed beyond words". Thereafter I experienced an almost geometric depreciation in speech.

This difficulty with speech can cause someone, who was once communicative, to find her/himself somewhat despondently grunting approval of or disagreement with statements made in her/his presence. The 'bon mot', the apt expression, the key to the problem comes to mind but it is effectively locked in and speechlessness can cause frustration. It is so much more than just a physical deprivation. The French expression 'perdre la parole', to lose the initiative, to lose the limelight, comes near to expressing the heart of the matter - you can no longer chuck your ideas into the melting pot in time. While you are struggling to articulate, someone has got there before you.

The passage from John's gospel which tells of the invalid at the pool of Bethzatha is a source of encouragement for me:

"One man was there who had been ill for thirty-eight years. When Jesus saw him lying there and knew that he had been there a long time, he said to him, "Do you want to be made well?" The sick man answered him, "Sir, I have no one to put me into the pool while the water is stirred up; and while I am making my way, someone else steps down ahead of me". Jesus said to him, "Stand up, take your mat and walk." At once the man was made well and he took up his mat and began to walk. (John c. 5, vv. 2-5).

Being misunderstood or misinterpreted is painful. I am too slow off the mark to adapt or refine views attributed to me. Misunderstanding is more likely to occur when I find myself in the company of strangers. These are people who have not known me in my better days and amongst whom I have never been experienced as a speaking person. They are not in a position to estimate how much I still enjoy involvement in conversation, albeit at the fringes, although I can no longer show it. I can find myself ignored and dismissed as if I were someone churlishly opting to sulk.

The problem with speech made life in the classroom difficult. With such a handicap it was not easy to maintain discipline in some classes who in subtle ways but without any real ill will tended to make one the object of ridicule. Religious knowledge teaching, difficult at the best of times, became almost impossible under these circumstances. I got a great deal of help and encouragement from my colleagues and I appreciated their support and encouragement.

Towards the end of the school year 1988/89 I decided I could carry on teaching no longer. I discussed my situation with Maura and with various friends and colleagues and with Liam Ryder, my Principal, who had great wisdom and experience to apply in these situations. He thought it would be wise of me to resign. First of all I took a year's sick leave and I resigned formally at the end of the school year 1989/90.

Part Two

The High Ground

Chapter 19
LANDMARKS

Rosemary's fifth birthday was approaching. It was early October, 1939. We were just settling down to a new life in new schools and getting used to whatever cultural changes were involved in coming from England to live in Ireland. My mother asked Auntie Ad and Mary O'Brien to draw up a list of neighbours who could be invited to come to a party she was thinking of having for Rosemary.

I had been hearing the name Wall referred to frequently and favourably by Auntie Ad, Mary and by Bridie Harrington who was now helping out in Lissarda House since the two children came to live there. Of course the Walls were to be represented at the party in the persons of the two youngest, Peggy and Billy.

Mary O'Brien brought Rosemary and me with her to visit the Wall family who lived in the next farm to us, in order to invite them along to the birthday party on October 20th. There was a great welcome. We were unexpected, as most country guests are, but that did not matter. Peggy and Billy were doing their homework at the kitchen table in the light of an oil lamp. Mrs. Wall was knitting. Danny Wall, the head of the household, a contemporary and childhood friend of my own father's, was catching up on the news in the Cork Examiner. There was timber burning well in the open fireplace. At the side of the fire was what I now know to have been a bastible or pot oven, covered in red hot ashes or griosach in which a brown wholemeal cake was being baked. The term soda bread was not used and confectionery was referred to as "sweet" cake.

Mrs. Wall began asking us all about ourselves. When she discovered that I liked ponies she went on to tell me about a pony they had in Parkmore when she was a child which used to come into the kitchen like a dog if it got the chance or the encouragement. The possibility of bringing a pony into the house had not occurred to me before. I tried it subsequently with a pony we had, called Molly, but without success. She couldn't climb steps.

At some stage during this conversation, without, I believe, looking at clock or watch and without interrupting her flow of conversation Mrs. Wall moved over to the bastible and with a long fire tongs took the cover off it tipping the burnt out griosach onto the fire. I then saw for the first time one of her brown cakes. Brown cakes are as specific to individuals as finger prints, and probably in some way, reveal character. Using a small jute bag, as oven gloves, first she lifted the edge of the bastible, got a firm hold on one of its three legs and by what amounted to sleight of hand dislodged the cake, which she received from the bastible into her waiting right hand. She listened as she tapped it with the tips of her fingers, the Midas touch; the true expert.

With our eyes we followed her across to the dresser where she put the cake to cool. Even though the dresser was not that clearly visible being in the shadows, well away from the paraffin lamp in the large kitchen, I could still make out an array of basins on its shelves. As I was to discover later, these basins were used as drinking vessels for porter at the annual threshing and as repositories for Rosary beads and pending business documents for the rest of the year.

A sign that the Rosary was about to begin, as it always did in the Wall household immediately after tea, was Mrs. Wall's walk over to the dresser to get the various beads which were then distributed. One touching Rosary trimming which I remember her for particularly, was a special prayer that the whole family would find each other again in heaven.

Billy at some stage of this first visit of mine went out and came back shortly with apples which I remember as being quite tart but this tartness was made up for by the incredible juiciness.

Billy, just a few years my senior became a great friend of mine later.

On other nights we went with Mary to invite other people including Mrs. Tommy Murphy, then probably in her fifties. She had style and was unambiguous in all her statements. She loved a glass or two of whiskey on occasion and as a child I could not understand why she drank it at all because a glass was consumed in one or at most two swigs followed by a painful looking grimace while apparently discarding the glass, placing it as far away from herself as possible. I was later to appreciate that what seemed like a random discarding of the empty glass was really a strategic realignment for a refill. We always loved her visits to our house as she was very generous, always giving each of us at least a half crown, over £5 in today's terms. The money was taken from a purse which was secreted in her stocking and was modestly retrieved while she turned her back on present company. This gift was always bestowed with a warning to tell no one, but on the way out as she was going home she always checked with mother or father to see if we had kept the confidence!

Mrs. Tommy or Big Nell as we affectionately called her was a keen and brilliant card player of 110. As we got a bit older we were allowed to stay up longer when she visited our house, and eventually we were allowed to play 110 with her. She could be unsparing of your feelings if you played a wrong card while partnering her.

On one memorable occasion I fell foul of her. It happened like this: some men around those parts occasionally made use of the expression, "Goan owa dat yu hoar yu", to urge on a stubborn or or sulking horse. "Yu hoar yu" was a colloquial form of "You whore you" and was used sometimes even as a familiar, good humoured, yet distinctly unpleasant form of address or greeting. In my innocence, I genuinely thought that the unfortunate phrase was a shortened or elided version of

"You who are-you", which obviously was quite harmless. It could never have occurred to me that it was derived from "you whore you", since I didn't know the word "whore". So one night at cards in a moment of outlandish and childish triumph, on playing what I knew to be an unbeatable Jack of trumps, I said to Mrs. Tommy in front of my mother and my Uncle Den who had joined in the game,

'Beat that now yu hoar yu'.

There was a shocked and stunned silence, obvious embarrassment all around. After being told that I should never use that kind of language I was asked to leave and go to bed at once.

When Mrs. Tommy had gone, mother came up to me very caringly, probably sorry for overreacting earlier. When I asked her what I had done wrong she conceded that obviously I had no idea of what I had actually said in referring to Mrs. Tommy as a "wicked unmarried lady".

Rosemary's party launched us effectively into the Lissarda social scene. I recall that at the very end a few adults remained back for further chat with my mother. The main topic of conversation was the war, just begun, and what might happen to Ireland. I remember the 64,000 dollar question being asked by Nancy Sweeney,

'Where will we all be this time next year?'

***

As often as possible Billy Wall and I got together at weekends. I used to call to his home and we would go out often kicking a football around or hurling or we would go to a match in Macroom or Coachford on Sunday. A score of bowls, as a road bowling match was called, from the Pillar Box to Carrigadroichead was good entertainment, in those days of the forties attracting relatively large crowds.

Bowling in ways is like cricket. It is unspectacular for those who know nothing about it but is absorbing for those who are initiated. It can be played up to a much later age than football. It is a very inexpensive game to play as there is no upkeep of playing fields nor is there any need for changing rooms, showers etc. A certain amount of physical strength is necessary but a lot of skill is needed. A keen bowler reads the road like a bowler in cricket reads the pitch. Although the method of scoring sounds complicated, the objective of the game is for each bowler to try to get from one place to another, usually a couple of miles away, in as few shots or throws as possible. The difference between the two bawlers, or pairs in a doubles score or match, is measured in terms like" a bowl of odds" or "a shot of odds". The standard iron ball or bowl used weighs 28 ounces and is about the same size as a tennis ball. There is a special way for throwing the bowl which is most effective for covering maximum ground. One of the mast important things in throwing is to land the bowl on the right part of the road in order to get maximum roll subsequently. There was a certain small number of men in every locality who were experts at reading the road and one of the secrets of success was to get one of those men to advise you or to "stand road" for you. They had a particularly important consultative role when a corner had to be negotiated by being "lofted". The distance covered by a loft was measured in units called "spades". A spade was five feet, or two short paces.

There was a rich bawling folklore which was shared in the evenings during the scoruíacht or chat at certain recognised places, outside in fine weather or inside around the fire in a farmhouse or cottage in cold or wet weather.

Be it football outing, score of bawls or any other kind of entertainment on a Sunday or Church Holyday the terminating factor for the farmer or the farm hand was the milking. It was an ever- recurring task but not resented. It was in a strange way a reminder of how enjoyable the break from work on Sunday really was. After milking I often went by bicycle with the Walls, the six miles into Macroom to the pictures.

On hot Midsummer weekday evenings and on Sunday afternoons we frequently went swimming in the River Lee, in a carefully chosen and safe place, somewhere between Holland's Bridge and Coolcower in those pre-hydroelectric days, before so much of the Lee Valley was flooded. Every time I pass by and see Holland's Bridge abandoned and marooned in an artificial lake I wonder what positive net gain there is from such despoliation. It seemed like a very good idea at the time and it's worth little being wise after the event.

Billy used to come regularly to our house to hear the commentaries on All Ireland hurling and football matches broadcast from Croke Park. Wirelesses were quite rare around Lissarda in the early forties. Before rural electrification some had battery wirelesses, but these were quite a liability. The cabinets that the radio receivers proper were housed in were more usually of plywood, bulky and heavy, the pre-transistor valves were fragile and not easily replaceable. The radio receiver was powered by three battery systems; there was a grid dry battery, a high tension dry battery and an accumulator or wet battery which had to be recharged every week, given average use, usually at the creamery. An outside aerial, frequently a cable suspended between two chimneys, and an earthing system were usually required.

We had our own electric generating set, a Lister one and a half horse power petrol engine with an inbuilt 110/120 volt dynamo. The current was stored in ten 12 volt car batteries. At a certain level of discharge the engine was started automatically. It was a satisfactory system until petrol went totally off the market for quite some time in the early forties. Rather guiltily and cruelly we ran it sometimes on paraffin when available, but paraffin seemed to do it a violence.

Then the 11 Shannon Scheme", as mains electricity was still popularly called, came to the creamery in Lissarda. The nearest house to ours was that of the local curate, Father Coakley, who reckoned that for him electricity was essential. Thus, a campaign was pursued as follows: Father Coakley backed our application for electrification very strongly. We proposed that since our house was already wired in accordance with required standards it would be churlish not to give us a line from the creamery which was so close by. But, to reach us, it would have to go through Father Coakley's garden, therefore by a slight variation of our "churlish" argument he got his electricity supply as well.

***

At three o'clock on the morning of January 3rd. 1942 Auntie Ad rushed into our bedrooms shouting, 'the house is on fire'. There was a terrible smell, a sound of wood crackling and smoke was oozing out around the edges of a door which led to the attic area from a wooden casing that gave access to a skylight.

We had no phone and anyway the exchange closed at 10 o'clock every night, so a fire brigade was out of the question. I was dispatched to summon up help where I could. My father was in England and the occupants of the house that night were Auntie Ad, my mother, my sister, Mary O'Brien and I. It was a very cold night but not windy, which was the great blessing, and I ran down to Father Coakley and on through the village clad only in my pyjamas, shouting for help. There was an immediate response and in a matter of ten minutes a bucket chain was organised, there being no adequate hose or indeed adequate water pressure available. That the fire had not got an unquenchable grip on the house before the help arrived was due to the presence of mind of my mother who, with a poor hose and in spite of low water pressure, concentrated on putting out the burning timbers as they fell down onto the floor of the landing.

After about an hour of desperately hard work when some considerable risks were taken the blaze was under control. Such a stench of burning and the noise of water being bucketed in those circumstances never goes away from the imaginations of those who have experienced it.

The cause of the fire was a wooden beam going through the chimney which ignited because the heat of an ordinary chimney fire had caused its plaster covering to come away earlier. We were told that the burning of wooden blocks and turf together brought about the formation of a substance on the walls of the chimney which if it took fire was particularly dangerous.

The heroes who really saved our house from being burned to the ground were Dan Bourke, Tim Harrington, Michael O'Dwyer and Father Coakley.

* * *

Father Coakley was a man from another age of clergy. He kept two thoroughbred hunters and had his own groom. The grooms whom I remember would not have been out of place in any training stables. He rode to the Muskerry Foxhounds, interpreting his way around Canon Law (c.138). He rode to the chapel of ease in Canovee or to the parish church in Kilmurry to hear confessions and did his school visitation on horseback. He kept his German car in mint condition; it was an Adler, front wheel drive, then very unusual, which he kept on blocks, as in a sanctuary, during most of the war because spare parts were not available. He told me that one of its features was a Bosch magneto. He used a borrowed small Austin for his parish duties. He had developed and planted beautifully the garden of the curate's house, for a great part, with his own hands. He read well, setting aside special periods for reading what he referred to as "heavy stuff". His favourite author for light reading was H.V.Morton, the travel writer. He gave Rosemary and me the benefit of his light reading in episodes, during his many visits to our house. He came up to us for a short period every night for a couple of years. He never accepted even a cup of tea except on Sundays when he accepted just a cup and a biscuit. He was a teetotaler and a non-smoker.

Feeding his horses presented no problem; he commandeered fodder from his farmer friends. Diplomacy was not his strong suit but he managed to get away with it

Father Coakley had very strong political views and was openly and avowedly pro-German. At the beginning of the war, particularly in the early part of 1940, when he called to us on his daily visits he used to taunt us effectively by telling us of all the German successes to date and prophesied that it would all be over in June 1940 when Hitler would be victor. Fair dues after all, that might have been an accurate forecast if Hitler had followed on after Dunkirk, but he didn't and Father Coakley dropped the issue. Subsequently he spoke more about Portsmouth where as a young priest he had spent a number of years. I once asked my mother about his attitudes, but she came indirectly to his defence, saying to me that I'd be just as bad at his age if I had no wife.

Father Coakley may not follow comfortably any of the recommended priestly prototypes, but the talents he had, he used.

One of the social irritants of the Emergency and post Emergency years was a certain amount of uncharacteristic behaviour engaged in by some people who got involved in Black Market dealing. Things that were traded on the Black Market included tea, sugar, petrol, bicycle tyres, clothes coupons etc. Many others colluded in buying the stuff. I knew then of people, who although regarded as paragons of virtue in every other way could not resist turning the easy shilling by illegal trading in that most coveted of all scarce resources, tea.

The usual going rate for Black Market tea was a £1 a pound which gave a margin of over 300% profit. Then there was a further important distinction between "honest" Black Marketeers and "dishonest" Black Marketeers. A great confidence trick was the one sometimes tried on people in the bus office in Cork, then on the Grand Parade, about to board a crowded bus back home to the country. For some, being given the option on a pound of tea at a little under the going "legal" Black

Market rate was an offer they could not refuse and uncritically accepted while struggling to get to the nearest available bus seat. Tea wasn't packeted, it came to the retailers loose in tea chests and was usually sold to customers in characteristically slate coloured paper bags, which owing to paper shortage, were reused many times. Therefore, by using such bags the "illegal" Black Marketeer would lull the purchaser into a false confidence. On reaching home she/he was to discover that one inch of tea was topping seven or eight inches of sawdust.

Chapter 20

LISSARDA REVISITED

Lissarda rich with memories from my youth,
Of joys and sorrows, yet inspired by love
Of one I cherished as one does mind the Truth
Which fleshes beauty as does hand a glove,
I sometimes dream of how things might have been
Had guiding spirits otherwise decreed
By casting us into a different scene,
Fulfilling each other's every need.

But as things are is whence we make our start
What seemed as loss can be reclaimed as gain,
If we accept the prompting of the heart,
To change raw hurt into atoning pain.

Atonement which is at the source of love,
Begets the peace betokened by the Dove

Denstone Murphy
(1990)

The turning into the gate at the end of the avenue which led to Lissarda House was considered dangerous. It was quite a blind spot and traffic tended to travel at high speed. There was particular difficulty when turning into it from the eastern side because it involved crossing the line of oncoming traffic. If you were on horseback or in a horse-drawn cart or trap, as we had been so often in the past, the task was even more difficult, because the impact of the horses iron-shod hooves on the hard surfaced road not only made a noise but also created an echo in the roadway cutting, thus obliterating any other warning sounds.

Even after thirty years my reflexes got me safely inside the gate. The avenue first of all ran through a richly wooded hillside before breaking out onto pleasant grassland, which we used to call the lawn, and which swept up towards a large Victorian House with its adequate and well-kept out-offices sitting graciously in a fenced off area, looking south. The view from the house was limited in terms of distance by the fact that it was situated on the side of a valley and looked across at woodland and pasture land on the opposing slope. My Uncle Edward, who had travelled the world as a ship's doctor, said it was the sleepiest place he ever came across and called it "sleepy valley".

My reveries were interrupted as I spotted a notice which asked car drivers to divert into the lawn in order to park their cars. Of course I had to comply, but felt discomfort of the kind that a man might feel if he kept his hat on in church in compliance with a new decree. This pasture surface was only for human or animal feet; a tractor had a special dispensation. Motor cars were intruders.

It was a perfect sunny summer's day, July 15th, the feast of St. Swithin, 1989. Maura and I got out of the car into a warm welcoming atmosphere and walked up the short driveway to the front of the house. The layout of the garden and grounds was substantially the same as I remembered it when I was growing up.

On the gravel and on the grass in front of the hall door happy people were greeting, celebrating and drinking health. Two couples were mixing with becoming diffidence and receiving the blessings of the guests. This was a joint celebratory gathering to honour the occasions of the weddings of Michael and Richard Bourke and their spouses. Transposing the wedding sweetmeats from London to Lissarda was a very kind consideration of the many relatives and friends on both Kay's and Dick's sides of the family.

Thirty-one year's less one day previously, on the feast of Our Lady of Mount Carmel, my sister Rosemary and her husband Philip Kemp had their wedding reception here.

Thirty-one years plus one day previously, on the feast of St. Bonaventure, after celebrating my First Mass my family gave a reception for me in this same place on what was also a very fine day. The predominant sentiment for me on that day in 1958 on which I celebrated Mass for the first time in Kilmurry church was one of joy and happiness. I felt good and totally satisfied that for myself I had "chosen the better part". I did occasionally, in the course of the reception feel pangs of desire for somebody to share it with, particularly when I was greeted with sincere, genuine and physically expressed warmth by some of the women. But this need for a co-operator I felt most keenly at the cutting of the ordination cake.

It was a joyful launching by my relations and friends on a very demanding life. A great pressure to fulfill the expectations of others is put onto those who are ordained. Then just over thirty - one years after rejoicing in the priesthood I was part of this other celebration, not devoid of irony. This was one of the really important moments of my life. It was amongst another group of my own people, my own folk, the people who were the joy of my youth. The party was in the house where my father was born and died, where my grandfather came to live in 1873 and where he was dispensary doctor until 1925, for more than half a century. In Lissarda I learned how to live and above all I learned about love.

"Love does not come to an end", and one special light that was first enkindled in me forty four years ago has never ceased to burn brightly and intensely without ever being the cause of a pang of regret or remorse.

When at home on holidays from Glenstal one of my prayers always was that the beautiful, attractive girl, with golden, waist length hair who used to kneel across the aisle from me would be at first Mass on the following Sunday and might talk to me on the way out. Gradually we got to know each other. Our families became very friendly; particularly one of Kay's older sisters, Mary, and my mother became close. This gave us the opportunity to share a glorious relationship. For a number of years we shared a deep intimacy while maintaining total respect for each other.

During the holidays our days began as often as possible by meeting at daily Mass in the oratory of the curate's house in Lissarda. A couple of evenings in the week we would meet again to go for a walk, perhaps around the lakes at Warrenscourt or else we might go to play hurling with a few more friends. After I got my driving licence, occasionally I got a loan of my mother's car. Then we might travel as far afield as Bantry or Leap. Whatever the exploit was it always ended up with a warm greeting of acceptance from her parents and family in Kay's home in Ballymichael.

During the school term when Kay was in Ferrybank and I was in Glenstal we had regular postal communication. Letters into and out from Glenstal were no problem because there was no censorship of mail but things were different in Ferrybank so I wrote to Kay's home and her mother colluded in forwarding the letters to Kay in a paper or magazine or under cover of another envelope addressed by her own hand.

Ours was an unspectacular relationship, not widely acknowledged, I think, the extent and depth of which was understood by few, yet one of those was Kay's mother who was supportive in trusting us totally. Nobody ever tried to match us or divide us. We were left free to make our own decisions.

In my last year at school I began to get vaguely uneasy and then on leaving school and going to university became very uneasy about our relationship because I felt that I would have to end it in order to correspond to the conviction that had developed in me that I should opt for the celibacy involved in the priesthood.

Two hearts were broken. In time they healed. Now they share a love that is changed but not diminished, in fact increased, because more confidently understood and more clearly defined.

I ungrudgingly enjoyed this celebration, generously hosted by Kay and Dick, yet there was an identifiable pain of the "what might have been" gnawing within me at times. And why not? It wasn't envy. It was a musing on the mystery of life and on the complex draft of a grand design which does require effort to understand and accept.

Sean and Julia O'Mahony, Kay's brother and sister in law, the present owners always afford the most heartfelt welcome, combined with the most keen sensitivity to our special position, to Maura and me whenever we revisit. In a sense, it is as if I never left Lissarda. Maura accompanied me on a tour of what were the land and farm buildings attached to Lissarda House. Most of the land was sold off by owners prior to Séan and Julia and now only fifteen acres go with the house. The farmyard and walled garden now belong to somebody else, as does the site of Lissarda Castle.

We assumed their permission to trespass on the past. Every monument, stick and stone came back to life. We went to the farmyard which has long since fallen into disrepair in response to the different procedures involved in modern farming. How times change and things move on! It was once a little show piece with its well-built and well-appointed cow stalls. For which a lot of the work was done by a tradesman called Billy Harrop brought over from England especially for this purpose by my father.

Before 1930 the farmyard had its own 50 volt direct current electric lighting system with a small Merryweather dynamo turned by a stationary 8 horse-power Bamford single cylinder four-stroke kerosene engine, the main function of which was to turn a mangel/turnip pulper/slicer and a small Bamford grain mill. There was also a pulley available for turning a small threshing drum of the kind used before the advent of the mobile threshing mill with inbuilt winnower and straw shakers. As a boy, I saw that threshing drum in the farm building stored away but it had gone out of use before my time and was well on the way to becoming a curio.

Beside the farmyard was a walled garden facing south which in our time was well kept and fruitful, now it is desolate. My mother had put enormous effort into the developing of that garden. She planted a score of apple trees and laid various paths to make all the fruits easy of access. Just inside the gate on the right she had established a rock garden, thus making good use of a slope falling away from a retaining wall which made possible the laying of a good pathway which could be used by horse or tractor traffic. She grew all kinds of vegetables and fruits. In the middle of the northern wall was a tool house which was a feature of the garden. It was solidly built in stone and mortar, about eight feet square. There was a loft which could be reached by ladder. It had a sturdy wooden floor and a small round window facing south. On it there was a slated roof. On occasion the loft was an ideal refuge from life.

What I can remember the garden for particularly, was the luscious and abundant raspberry harvest. When the raspberries became ripe all hands were called on deck and for a time other duties were postponed while the raspberry picking went ahead. There were bucketfulls upon endless bucketfulls of these slightly furry textured fruits. In a way they were the kindliest of the small soft fruits to pick. They gave themselves up generously and unresistingly. A minimal squeeze and pressure induced them to slip off the central core and you were conscious that no trauma was being caused to the raspberry plant. In this they differed from loganberries which could be quite resistant and coarse by comparison, although superficially similar to the raspberry.

Mother used to give away bucketfulls of these fruits as well as making jam herself. The big pay off, however for Rosemary and I was the plates of raspberries and cream that we were encouraged to consume. Lissarda was the home of a once prosperous creamery and in our day, although no longer producing the cheese for which it was once famous, it was still making butter and separating cream for that purpose. We bought "jugs" of cream rather than pints or half pints. On occasion, I can remember consuming such quantities of raspberries and cream that I began to think of myself as a swollen tick on the soft warm part of a cow's udder or behind a sheepdog's ear or on the tummy of a stumbling still woolly collie puppy bedding and suckling in the hay shed.

The gooseberries were also in abundance but there was never any urgency about picking them. Nor were they of any special interest to children since immediate consumption in the manner of raspberries wasn't involved and gooseberry-fool I always regarded as an adult dish, yet gooseberry or gooseberry and apple jam was a great favourite.

The dreaded garden chore was the picking of the blackcurrants or the red currants. Since these currants were so small it took an age to fill a sweet tin and picking was accompanied by the dilemma about whether to "top and tail" as you picked or to pick less thoughtfully and have a mass "top and tail" session afterwards.

Domestic fruit harvesting (industrial fruit harvesting is a different matter) is a socialising opportunity par excellence like quilting or washing clothes at the communal water hole in other cultures. It is non-competitive, instantly rewarding and involves cooperation; news, views and confidences are exchanged less guardedly.

Beside the orchard and the farmyard is the site of Lissarda Castle of which even in our time the only relic was the castle well. It is thought that the castle was the home of a Baldwin family, one of whom, called James was married to Máire, the sister of Eibhlín Dhubh Ní Chonaill, author of the poem "Caoineadh Airt Uí Laoghaire".

Having viewed all the relics, I was reminded of Anchises and Aeneas viewing Troy in ancient times or of Séan O'Coileáin reflecting on the ruins of the monastery at Tig Malaga (Timoleague) in his poem, "Machnamh an Duine Dhoilíosaigh".

"*Do bhí aimsear ina raibh
an teach so go soilbh subhach.*"

"*Time there was
When this house was happy and replete*".

We got back on to the avenue and were firmly reminded of the present as the strains of a band playing out in the open on the croquet lawn at Lissarda House were wafted down to remind us of the primary purpose of our visit.

Having arrived back we sat around on the lawn in the sun, Maura sang with the band, a song called "The Rose". I talked as much as my Parkinson condition would allow. Everybody was so kind without patronising. In the last couple of years since I was diagnosed I have enjoyed insights into people, based on their reactions to me, which I had missed before. Some great compensations have come my way.

On our way back to our car which we had parked in the lawn I thought of haymaking in that field when all summer days were hot days; how craftily we forget the miserable drizzle that also must have been. At that time there was a clear view of the lawn from the house. My mother could easily see the toil and sweat, and a bonus given by her, in appreciation of such hard work as that involved in making hay in that field on a hot day, was a sweet tin of porter fresh from Fitz's in Lissarda, served with the afternoon tea. It seemed so satisfying to those who partook that my Confirmation pledge was sorely tested.

Another less salubrious memory of that field was the sudden death of a cow which already had been bought and paid for by a butcher. The butcher arrived on the scene very shortly afterwards and at first seemed perturbed but soon appeared consoled as he reflected to himself and to us that nobody would know the difference.

It was also a field once notorious for its buachaláns or ragwort and on occasion mother would enlist all available bodies for weed pulling sessions. This was rather solitary and destructive work without any social advantages. One thing in favour of the buachaláns was that they could be dislodged easily and cleanly from the ground.

We drove down through the field and emerged through a more recently opened gap onto the main road which brought us out by the post office which together with a busy tailor's shop used to form an outer suburb of Lissarda. The tailor's shop which was widely patronised and where I got my first pair of long trousers made has long since gone but the importance of the area is maintained now by the presence of a garage and filling station.

Just west of where we emerged onto the main road or coach road as it was called, is the main village of Lissarda. There used to be a fully self-contained creamery there with accompanying general store and petrol pump. This pump was inside the premises and the door had to be opened in order to get the delivery hose out to customers. I assume the storage tank was directly underneath it so that part of the creamery building was literally sitting on a time bomb. It was a hand petrol pump with two gallon glasses on top. The petrol was pumped up into the glasses, one at a time, by the hand pump and while the second glass was being filled by the pump the first one was being emptied into the car by gravity through the delivery hose.

The only other business in Lissarda proper was Fitzgerald's public house which still flourishes. As a child my favourite drink here was Little Norah lemonade with a flavouring of raspberry cordial soaked up by Marie biscuits which were available in attractively produced small greaseproof paper packets.

About a hundred and fifty yards west of Lissarda village is the bridge which crosses the disused Cork / Macroom railway line on which the last train ran on November 10th 1953, having been opened in 1866. Quite recently driving past I saw a large notice advertising, not a céilí nor a platform dance but Break Dancing in Leacha Riabhach.

Lissarda bridge is on the road which leads to Kilmurry which is about a mile away from Lissarda. The parish church of the parish in which Lissarda is included is in Kilmurry as are the local national schools.

It is a bigger village than Lissarda with several public houses and shops. It is the church in which my father was christened and from which he was buried. It was built in 1860, the same year as Lissarda House.

The parish church was quite large, cruciform, with a high marble altar. It was a cold church in the winter time and there used to be no heating of any kind, which was usual in country churches up to the sixties. It had a timber floor to about a third of the way down the nave and there were stone flags down the rest of the way. The pews which were within the area with the wooden flooring were occupied by families who paid an annual subscription called pew money which gave them a recognised entitlement to the exclusive use of those pews. This arrangement used to be carefully respected and the occasional stray soul who chanced to violate this tradition was sometimes met with considerable disapproval. The warning shot of such disapproval was usually a couple of well-timed coughs. This might be followed by a gentle crowding out.

There were two Masses there on Sunday but as a rule Mass was not celebrated in the church on ordinary week days. The custom was for the local curate to celebrate the weekday Masses in his oratory attached to his house. It was accepted as having the force of custom that priests in the diocese of Cork could celebrate Mass in their own or their parents' home if that home was more than a mile from the church.

One of my most abiding childhood memories of Kilmurry church was the May Mission in 1940. It was given by three Passionists who were eloquent and impressive. Even after fifty years I have a clear recollection of the content and style of Father Austin's passion sermon.

Apart from the obvious spiritual advantages of a mission it can rally a community to get to know each other better. At that time practically everybody in the parish came to the church twice a day by foot, by bicycle, by horse and trap or by car. At that time, even though it was during the Emergency, private cars were still on the road, surviving with a petrol ration of four gallons per month for the average small car. People rose at a very early hour and milked all their cows by hand before setting out for Mass at nine o'clock. Common striving can unite people.

There was a certain flamboyance about the event, the missioners were treated as celebrities. Tents were erected in the church grounds for the sale of pious objects; rosary beads and variations thereof such as seven dolour beads; seven different scapulars or a scapular medal which could replace the seven; crucifixes, statues and prayer books; candles, some with beeswax content up to the standard required for using at Mass, others with the lower beeswax content adequate for Benediction.

After confession and before leaving the box the missioners gave a commemorative leaflet to each penitent which contained Novena prayers to St. Paul of the Cross, founder of the Passionists.

There was a man in the district whom one of the curates suspected of not going to confession as regularly as he should. The priest met him on the road shortly after the missioners had gone and said,

"Did you go to confession during the mission?"

With the confidence of one about to be vindicated he replied,

"Faith an' I did, Father", and taking out of a pocket the leaflet he had received in confession, he added, "And here is the receipt".

The confession boxes in Kilmurry provided little privacy. There was no door to the penitent's section, just a flimsy curtain, which meant that the hard surface of the inside reflected back out without obstruction whatever was said. It would require the gift of deafness not to hear what the penitent in front of you was saying. In those situations it seems that the more you try not to hear the more you do hear. It is thought that some listened quite happily.

The custom in those days was for the women to go to one side of the confession box and for the men to go to the other. On one particular first Saturday there was quite a long queue of women waiting on one side and very few men. Very shortly the only remaining man went into the box and spent what seemed like an extraordinarily long time with the priest. It was noted that he was a married man, highly respected in the parish and people were even a little scandalized at, presumably, his need to sort something out. Eventually he emerged, a little confused, since he was very conscious also of having kept others waiting for so long. He was walking away from the confessional box past a long row of silent, waiting women who may have been tempted to judge him, when quite unexpectedly he stopped in front of one woman, turned to her and said,

'The priest wants you to go in now'
Horror struck, the woman blurted out, as if in self-defense,
'Me?'
As all eyes focused unbelievingly on her and on him the man
hastened to diffuse speculation,
'He's after hearing all the men and he - wants ye to go in on
both sides now',

We had a parish priest who was given, on occasion, to
memorable sayings in his sermons. He was, one Sunday, talking
about the necessity for the congregation to look before being
seated on the pews because some swallows had nested just up
under the roof and their droppings were soiling the church
seating. Hardly had he finished this warning when he suddenly
changed tone, raised his voice and said to those at the very back
of the church and to everybody's surprise,
'Would some of the men down there put the cow out?'

At that we all turned round to look back, and sure enough a
cow had wandered into the church and now was proving quite
obstinate as the men were trying to expel her. When things
settled down once more the priest added in an aside,
'A good job cows don't fly'.

Father Scanlon was a man who did not like fads or the
thoughtless following of whatever seemed fashionable. At the
time the trans-Atlantic air service from Rineanna, now called
Shannon, to Gander in Newfoundland had just begun and a
popular outing , when cars came back on the road again after
the Emergency, was to travel the almost one hundred miles each
way on a Sunday to see the Skymasters and Constellations land
and take off at Rineanna. Since mass air travel was in its infancy
there was a formality attached to arrivals and departures of
aircraft. I can remember that before one of these planes taxied
out to the runway there was a formal farewell from ground staff
who stood to attention on the apron and saluted.

Perhaps one hoped to meet or at least see some film stars or other celebrities in transit to or from Europe or to the United States. In those days, because all trans-Atlantic plans had to take on fuel in Rineanna, the likelihood of getting at least a close up view of someone like Bing Crosby or Betty Grable, in transit, was quite realistic. But Father Scanlon felt it as his function to advice against such trivial pursuits and one Sunday he spoke out about the futility of this exercise, "What an awful waste of time, going to Rineanna just to see people going on a wild goose chase to Gander".

In Kilmurry there were a couple of shops which specialized in Sunday business. After Masses on Sundays and to a lesser extent on Church Holidays the womenfolk frequently had to get details of shopping while the men went to their own groups to fill in on the happenings of the previous seven days. It was the accepted time to make social contacts and arrangements. There was no obvious rationale for the composition of some of the groups of men. Some unlikely people tended to meet in the same group. This was a very good thing which was really far in advance and more real than the token signs of peace now exchanged before communion during the celebration of Mass.

Ponies and traps and cars were always parked in the same places. Cars were left unlocked and keys left in the ignition. To have locked your car and to have removed the keys was regarded as a public discourtesy. It was also a discourtesy for like to pass like on the way to or from the church; a car was not supposed to pass out another car nor a horse and trap another horse and trap.

These customs were a valuable exercise in the acknowledgement of the rights and dignity of others and to my knowledge were well observed.

During the Emergency, yet not for its entire duration, the only Sunday paper available in Lissarda was the Sunday Independent which came out from Cork on the midday bus. When that bus was then taken off we had no Sunday news. Shortly after the bus and Sunday Independent were restored, quite incongruously, the Sunday People became available locally to be combined with or as an alternative to the Sunday Independent.

Chapter 21

HAYTIME

June was, to some extent, a tedious month on the farm. The work to be done consisted of jobs like hoeing and thinning root crops and earthing potatoes. Thinning was a difficult, backbreaking and wrist spraining task. At the time it was considered to be a necessary process which could never be satisfactorily mechanised. A machine sensitive enough to know which small plants to pull out and which ones to leave, it was thought, could not be designed.

Every drill in a field with root crops had to be crawled along on all fours and every tender plant handled. Those which were adjudged the most viable of the young plants were left at eight to ten inch intervals, so that they would have room to swell and grow. The discarded plantlets were left in the furrow, later to be scuffled back into the soil.

In those days labour was plentiful and shamefully cheap. An outdoor labourer up to the early fifties would earn just over two pounds per week. "Outdoor" meant that he did not sleep in the farm where he worked and he looked after his own meals. There were, as a rule, some perquisites such as the use of half an acre of the farmer's land for growing something for himself and his family, usually potatoes. Free milk was, in many cases available for them and their families. The outdoor labourers then were nearly always married men who lived nearby and went home for dinner at midday.

The "indoor" labourer had his meals at the farm where he worked and often slept there as well. His wage was about twenty five shillings a week. There was an officially prescribed wage, called the "Board Wage", which appeared to be recommended rather than mandatory and often was not paid,

There was a subtle class distinction evident in the farming community which is hard to define, yet it was made manifest in certain social customs. The gentleman farmer, besides having a car and probably wearing a soft hat rather than a cloth cap usually took his meals, with his family, in a dining room or breakfast room quite separate from "indoor" men.

The more general practice was for the indoor labourer or labourers to share table with the farmer and his family but even at that there were some examples of apartheid. One heard of families who allowed the labourers to sit at the family table but served them inferior food. One particular family used to put a cloth on the end of the table at which they ate themselves and the men ate off the bare boards at the other end.

***

Even though thinning was strenuous it provided an opportunity for exchange of news and of views with those on either side of you. You could be crawling up and down the field together for up to eight hours in the day. Sometimes extra help was recruited, school children on holidays or else taking time off school frequently helped.

At the end of June the excitement began when Uncle Den went to the machine shed to take out the mowing machine, a Bamford, two horse, four and a half foot cut. It was a simple but solid and efficient machine. It had been laid up since the previous September and now needed oiling and cleaning. The blades, usually referred to as "knives", had to be sharpened, first of all with a file and then with a carborundum stone.

To sharpen, or as they said, to "edge" the "knife" which was constituted by a number of triangular sections, required great skill so as to avoid turning the edge as can happen when trying to sharpen a kitchen carving knife if it is held at the wrong angle to the sharpener.

The first meadows to be cut were those with first crop hay, that is hay from seed that was set the previous year amongst the cereal and this cereal, known as tillage cereal would be that sown where root crops had been grown the year before that.

The hay cutting crew consisted of two men, the machine man who operated the mowing machine and the "edger" who edged the knives. Another task done by the "edger" was to throw out the back sward. This was to allow the mowing machine to cut the hay near the fence which had been trampled by the horses while cutting the first sward. For some reason mowing machines tended to have the finger bar, that is the housing in which the knife operates on the right, and they cut clockwise, while reaper and binders as a rule, tended to cut anti-clockwise.

One of the smells that anyone who has ever experienced it, will claim as her/his favourite, will as often as not be the smell of new mown hay. The mowing machine, when you are beside it, makes a pleasant, yet, machine like noise, but from the far end of the field or further away it seems to sing. I have particularly vivid and happy memories of Tom Twohig's machine as it sang across Lissarda valley. To that smell and sound add the sight of two white faced Irish Draught horses with heads alternately bobbing up and down as they dig their toes into the freshly mown lawn like turf. One of the horses, probably the inside one, nearest the still uncut grass, may have snatched a bite at the last corner and as s/he leans into the collar with arched neck she tries with her tongue to unravel the too- long for grazing grass from around the bit.

Few instructions need be given to such dedicated horses, they seem to be as concerned as the farmer that the job be well done, yet the man on the machine keeps encouraging them through the medium of a kind of Esperanto. I have heard Italian, French and Portuguese farmers utter more or less similar sounds with the same effect.

The draughts or chains by which the machine is drawn go from the hames or curved bars on the horses' collars back to the swingle-tree (called "whittle-tree" in some places) which can swing horizontally in such a way that from it the man on the machine can judge the relative efforts of the animals and can call by name whom he may wish to encourage or restrain.

Con Lynch was the constant team mate of my Uncle Den. He probably knew as much about the practical aspects of farming as anyone. A reliable consultant when judgements had to be made but his great skill was as a ploughman. He "set" a plough as a violinist tunes his instrument. He studiedly angled the colter, the function of which was to cut through the sod for the bar to dislodge and for the board to turn. The setting of the wheels would determine the depth of the ploughing and the depth in turn depended on other factors which were the fruit of the ploughman's experience, contributing to his lore of professional knowledge.

He knew our land, much of which was quite hilly, like an islander knows the seas around him. Guiding machinery in such territory was hazardous but Con's advice about how to cope in various situations was never far wrong.

As soon as it was dry the objective was to put the hay into small cocks as quickly as possible. Sometimes, if the weather had been showery the hay would be turned with a sward turner before being raked into rows. We had a Pierce horse wheel rake which was a demanding machine to operate but a vast improvement on the old drag rake (sometimes called a "skeeter") which often did irreparable damage to horses' hind legs if at a certain stage in the process they stopped going forward at a constant pace.

Making hay was hot work and tiring. One of the great joys of life was to see Auntie Nellie appear on the horizon with the tea and apple cake when the apples became available. She often arrived with an entourage of younger cousins of mine who were also staying in Warrensgrove for their summer holidays. This apple cake was basically a shell of white soda bread filled with baked apple.

After a length of time, depending on the weather, a number of small cocks were put together and made into "strong" cocks from which the hay was eventually drawn in. This was a big operation and involved three of our own horses and carts and about six men. For some unspecified reason we never had a hay float so the hay had to be built into loads on the carts. Around about Lissarda some farmers expressed a distaste for the hay float or bogie, I once heard a farmer say,

'Floats are useless, yerra..........they're only for the shky farmers up the country',

Nowadays there is a shared respect of farmers for each other in all parts of the country but in the forties some southern farmers believed that midland (up the country) farmers made undue profit out of store cattle which were bought too cheaply in the south, and while such cattle were fattening the midland farmers had nothing better to do than look at the sky (shky).

The loading of hay onto carts involved great concentration. Another man piked it up from the ground while the loader gradually and systematically built up to about eight feet off the ground. I loved to travel from the field to the yard on top of the load which was tied firmly with two tightly pulled ropes. Unloading into the hay shed was very hot work yet it was an exciting place for children who loved to romp around, hide and jump in the hay. But jumping in the hay was not encouraged on account of the danger of the presence of lost or abandoned pikes or hay knives.

Searching the hay in the hay shed every day for eggs was akin to a treasure hunt. Some maverick hens stubbornly resisted using the appointed laying boxes and made their nests in the hay. Possibly they were behaving in a very responsible way in relation to the preservation of the species, as it is likely these hens planned to fill a nest with eggs which they would eventually sit on to hatch out by themselves. The only problem was that many if not all of their eggs laid with a view to hatching by themselves turned out to be unfertilised. These eggs were called "gluggers".

Hay was much more important then than it is now as silage was in its infancy and suspect in many quarters since it tended to cause a peculiar taste in the milk of cows fed on it. Besides that, there was a woeful smell from the silage pit.

Balers also were unusual. There was a feeling that the moisture content was generally too high for bales to be used. Not making use of bales made hay saving particularly labour intensive. Anyway tractors necessary to haul and drive a baler were quite uncommon.

However, by the early fifties there were new designs of tractors which had quite high road speeds such as the Czechoslovakian Zetor diesel, the Fordson Major, the David Brown and the Ferguson. These seem to have been used more for road transport than for work on the land. This was largely due to the fact that the cost of implements suited for use with a tractor was very high and the old horse drawn implements in most cases would be inefficient.

They replaced the pony and trap for some of those who did not have motor cars. They were used for going to Mass on Sunday, going to town for shopping and going to the pub at night.

There was one particular man in the locality of mature years who wasn't married but never stopped considering the option.

He was secretive about paying court to an eligible woman some distance away. But in a quiet countryside his Zetor tractor, which was his usual mode of transport, with its characteristic pounding exhaust noise, loudly proclaimed his whereabouts.

Hay was the staple diet of the two most important groups of animals. If the hay was saved in good condition it gave confidence to the farmer for the rest of the year. The ambition of the Tipperary farmer to have "the hay saved and Cork be't" is more than half true. Like bread is a symbol as well as a reality, so is hay. On the other hand, hay heating or rotting in the shed casts a pall of gloom over all. Hay well saved is like scoring an early goal. It gives heart to face even a difficult grain harvest.

***

The onset of the hay season was about the time when visitors began to arrive in Warrensgrove. All during the Summer Auntie Nellie kept an open house for as many of her nieces and nephews as wished to come along. She had an enormous work load yet made work look easy. She delighted in feeding hens, turkeys, geese, ducks, calves and pigs with an audience whom she generously allowed to help within their capacities. She loved livestock particularly ducks with whom she had great patience and believed that duck eggs had particular food value. She engaged the help of her willing nieces and nephews to find duck eggs which were deposited unceremoniously anywhere.

There were, on average, about four of us at a time in Warrensgrove during the summer holiday period although the total annual throughput would average about ten not including occasional visits by parents of these children and indeed their parents' friends.

Auntie Nellie's husband, Uncle Mick, according to the fashion of the day, wore a Hitler moustache. He was a highly intelligent man who read all available material and retained what he read.

He had strong views on everything from farrowing pens to world affairs. He mischievously flew kites which often were not seen as such and was, as a result frequently misunderstood.

Once in Warrensgrove at dinner in a kitchen crowded with harvesters, on spotting a mite box for the foreign missions on a window ledge he said, "Why do the priests waste their time and our money going out to Africa, aren't the black people much better able to look after themselves?"

It was the kind of question that occurred to many but few would have the courage or interest to ask. Some of those present in the kitchen were shocked into dead silence. One of the company thereupon walked out.

Uncle Mick's special interest was the breeding and fattening of pigs. He kept several sows for breeding. He was also a man who liked a drink, a propensity not always approved of by Auntie Nellie, his wife. He didn't feel free to go to the pub per se but had devised ways of getting around the problem. I got on particularly well with him and was witness to a few of his schemes.

One of the local publicans who also owned land, kept a boar. When the boar's services were required the practice for many farmers was that after introducing the visiting sow to her consort they would repair to the pub. The affaire would normally last the drinking time of a couple of pints. After the happening there would be another pint or two when the sow was loaded back into the crib for the journey home.

On one occasion Uncle Mick, after having been to the boar, sang uninterruptedly most of the three mile journey back, "Slievenaman" was his song. He drove the pony and crib home faster than usual and this excessive bumping dislodged the "lynchpin" which keeps the wheel in place on the axle. As soon as we got inside the gate of Warrensgrove avenue the wheel fell off, the pony bolted and Uncle Mick, the sow and I found ourselves wrapped around each other on the floor of the crib.

After quite a short time the pony stopped and we replaced the wheel, using a chip of wood for a lynchpin and continued home in the quietest possible and most sober fashion.

For a man who was so well up in sow management Uncle Mick made some ingeniously inaccurate judgements about the time of heat of his sows, thus ensuring more frequent visits to the boar and consequently the bar. For a short time he had a sow who used to sit down at a critical moment in the procedure. She eventually had to be slaughtered for bacon as she endangered the emotional integrity of at least two boars.

***

The house at Warrensgrove was very large and in very good condition, inside it was basically a new house. There were eight available bedrooms. When, as children, we went there on our holidays we generally chose our own rooms and sleeping arrangements. Whatever we could do ourselves Auntie Nellie allowed us to do. No apology was made for the fact that there was no electricity and no running water in the house. A jug and basin were available for washing, and there was a chamberpot under the bed, the contents of which were collected every morning by Hannah, the servant girl, in a white enamel bucket.

For further purposes, given the run of the farm, one had to make one's own arrangements.

Auntie Nellie was not a "pious" person but she had certain basic standards. We all had to say our prayers. Every night we had to attend the recitation of the family Rosary in the kitchen just before going to bed. She always gave it out while Uncle Mick led the responses. Particularly at the Litany of Loreto which followed and which Auntie Nellie gave out from memory he got progressively more and more out of phase becoming faster and faster so that the number of times he uttered "Pray for us" far exceeded the sum of the invocations.

**

We could hear the men being called in the morning to milk the cows. Auntie Nellie invariably called them by means of the statement:

"The cows are inside".

Likewise she summoned the men to dinner with the statement, "The poppies are strained".

"Potatoes" she regarded as pretentious, and "spuds" as indelicate.

"Poppies" was the compromise.

The "poppies" were boiled in a three legged pot of three gallons capacity capable of holding a bucketful of potatoes. The pot was boiled hanging from a crane over an open fire fuelled by timber. When it was established that they were boiled Uncle Mick or any available man was called upon to strain them. This demanded skill and strength. The technique involved putting a bag over the top of the pot allowing a small aperture through which the water could flow out. The pot was lifted and the water accordingly poured out but was not thrown away as it was used later for "wetting" ration, a balanced prepared diet for pigs bought in the form of a dry flakey meal-like substance.

The potatoes, after being allowed to dry off for a few minutes were spilled out onto a tray, pyramid fashion, and placed in the middle of the table readily accessible to all who sat around to eat. Hence, the old story about the young man freshly immigrated to England who on getting one wet small potato with his dinner longingly recalled the days at home when he couldn't see his brother across the table for spuds.

The potatoes that I remember on those occasions were always of the finest quality, floury and bursting their skins. Kerrs

Pinks, British Queen's, Golden Wonders, Kerry Blues, Epicures, these were the names of some of the varieties whose distinctive flavours and qualities were discernible to the country person as varieties of wine to the connoisseur.

Nowadays, there is a tendency for people to eat the skins of potatoes. Indeed in America, roasted, they are served as a delicacy. Apparently there is a protein layer just inside the skin which is of nutritional significance. But, in my boyhood days in the country potato skins were never eaten by humans. I can remember being warned that eating potato skins would quite likely cause tetanus or lockjaw.

Auntie Nellie began her day by milking more than her share of the close on thirty cows. Hannah usually accompanied her from the start. The men, more often than not, came later, like monks quietly slinking into choir, guiltily late for Morning Prayer. Uncle Mick never milked, claiming he had conveniently convinced himself that since he did not learn as a child it would be well-nigh impossible for one like him ever to master the art.

A favourite beverage was milk frothing fresh from the cow. Some of us drank this for breakfast, dinner and tea. It was unpasteurised and must have been a focus for all kinds of unfriendly bacteria which over fifty years on are still only gestating.

After the morning milking was over Uncle Mick headed off to the creamery in Lissarda, usually with five churns containing between them just under a hundred gallons of milk in high season. At the creamery the cream was separated from the rest of the milk and bought from the farmer. The exact price scale depended on the butter fat content of the cream. The skimmed milk was brought home again to be used for feeding livestock and it was also used when it became sour, for baking brown soda bread. The only constant element in a farmer's income was the monthly creamery cheque. The regularity of that source of income was as important as the amount.

Because farmers had to survive on what they could earn from the breeding and sales of their animals, in some cases they became apparently callous about their treatment of animals. I hated to see chickens being killed for the table. Yet, quite inconsistently, I enjoyed trapping rabbits for fun. The poor little rabbit might have been howling in the trap for hours before someone would come along to finish it off with a rabbit punch. The castration of young bulls and boars I regarded as intolerably cruel.

One of the more spectacular yet revolting moments in the farm calendar was the killing of a pig for curing as bacon. A few days before that event Auntie Nellie, Uncle Mick and Con Lynch would go to the piggery where the fat pigs were kept. Out of about ten pigs one would be selected on the basis of certain criteria. He/she would have to be long in the back, not too fat etc. When the day of execution arrived, usually Ned and Uncle Den went with Con to lead the pig from the condemned cell which was a small cell separate from the other pigs. This was part of a sort of "black" ritual.

The stomach and small intestine were salvaged for the making of puddings, This section of the alimentary tract was kept patent or open by some means and secured just under the surface of a stream for about half a day or until all chyme-like matter was washed away. When this was stuffed with the blood and oatmeal you had a genuine non synthetic pudding all of which could be eaten profitably.

The carcass was cut up into useful portions. These were salted and stored in a barrel for a few weeks before being hung from hooks on the kitchen ceiling.

Just a few cuts were left unsalted including cuts for the local curate, and the local dispensary doctor and certain other special friends.

* * *

Hannah Donovan, the "girl", was from Union Hall, of a family with a sea fishing tradition. Due to the understandable pressure of having to earn a living she came east. Nothing to her, as to most people west of Clonakilty, was left, right, up or down but all things were east, west, north or south. Instead of going to the dining room she spoke of going west to the room. She must have had an inbuilt compass because her cardinal points were never wrong.

Hannah and Auntie Nellie between them spoke an English which deserved to be categorised as a special dialect, Auntie Nellie always referred to those whom she thought to aspire to grandeur as "the quality".

At one stage during the Emergency Uncle Mick through a deal involving the bartering of firewood with a publican, laid hands on two chests of tea. Auntie Nellie, partly out of charity and partly to assuage a troubled conscience began to apportion it to her friends and relations by the pound. When Hannah saw what was happening she said,
"Don't be too flathúil foill u' have the raidhse".
That just about qualifies as an English sentence, yet the key words are Irish. In the Queen's English it would be, "Don't be too generous while you have the abundance".

Hannah had a sense of occasion and was pleased when the "quality" came to visit. She had a special intonation when she spoke about them or addressed them. Her apprenticeship in "service" was done with a Protestant family about whom she liked to reminisce. She had to leave them when they fell on bad times. If she disagreed with any of Auntie Nellie's decisions she was not slow to quote her first mentors. Hannah wasn't a great cook but excelled in preparing food for the cook. I believe that her backroom work set the scene for Auntie Nellie's efficiency. In her own way she was like the good theatre sister who makes it easier for the surgeon.

As Hannah now awaits the Resurrection, while writing these lines I can think only of Luke 1:48 and 52,
"He has looked upon his lowly handmaid...........and exalted the lowly".

* * *

Amongst the men who worked in Warrensgrove outstanding were the Lynch family. Con, the head of the family and Ned the sixth son have gone on ahead of us. Nelius came to Warrensgrove in the late nineteen thirties after considerable experience as a gardener in Jersey and as a farm worker in Peterborough. He had learned the Jersey dialect of French. He read well and conversed wisely. Materially, he had nothing to gain by coming back to Ireland. He obviously opted for other values and from his presence in our midst those of us who frequented Warrensgrove have benefitted. He was a skilled craftsman, knowledgeable about gardening, crops and livestock.

He was a man who gave respect and was respected. My father was very keen on exploring for water and various historical monuments and the man he always wanted to accompany him on these "digs" was Nelius who was an artisan according to the exact meaning of that word.

The phrase "farm labourer" is widely misunderstood. There is in the expression a hint that the work involved is purely physical without need for thought. But of all jobs it is one of those which demands the widest range of decisions, to be made under most difficult circumstances, such as might have to be made in the case of animals having difficult births under adverse weather conditions at a time or place when a veterinary surgeon is not available. They are called on to make decisions about details of crop harvesting or planting which can be made only on the basis of hard-won experience.

**

After the last "sop" or lace of hay has been laid by in the shed as a bulwark against the winter the farmer looks urgently at the fields of corn, then anxiously at the sky. The fields are full of promise but the weather has a veto, we used to blame the atom bomb, now its pollution, the glass house effect or the ozone layer.

Chapter 22

CORNTIME

The hay was in the shed and then there were visits to the corn fields and subsequent discussions about when the first field, usually OATS, would be fit for cutting.

There were differing opinions about when to cut. Some maintained that it was important to wait until the heads were definitely hanging, others maintaining that it was better to cut while the oats still had a green tinge because it would ripen in the stook. If it got too ripe there would be loss of grain in transporting it to the haggard and in handling it prior to threshing. Another problem that could arise was the lodging of the corn or tangling due to stormy weather.

By the late nineteen thirties most of the farmers around the Lissarda area had reapers and binders although a number still depended on the mowing machine and gate. This involved having a gate-like contraption hinged onto the mowing bar which released the cut corn as soon as there was enough gathered to make a sheaf (usually pronounced "shave"). This operation was under the control of a second man sitting on a seat just over the inside of the blade or knife. A dangerous position which has accounted for not a few severed achilles tendons or worse, particularly when the man in that seat has decided, in the interests of having more helpers available to bind, to take upon himself the task not only of making sheaves, but also of driving the horses.

In the case of badly lodged or tangled corn even those with reapers and binders had to resort to the mowing machine.

The "binder" was in a way, a magical machine. It always impressed me more than the later combined- harvester, perhaps, as the steam engine claims more interest than the diesel electric.

There were a few particular focusses of interest. It was the only bit of farm machinery, except for the uncommon two sod horse-chill plough, which needed three horses to haul it. It had a special set of wheels for road travel and had to have working parts dismantled for going from one place of work to the next.

The great mystery was about how it bound the cut corn into a neat sheaf and as far as a young boy was concerned the man who could thread the binder twine was to be highly respected. It was the one thing I felt my Uncle Den kept from me, like a conjurer refuses to reveal the tricks of his trade. The truth is that he did not want me going underneath the machine where there were mechanisms which could cause me injury.

The binder for working purposes went at right angles to the direction in which it was hauled when being moved from place to place. Consequently, the position of the shaft had to be changed through an angle of ninety degrees when the machine was being adapted from road to field. Three sets of moving canvas platforms were used to convey the corn across the width of the binder to the packer where it was packed into sheaves which were then "magically" bound before the "kicker" got rid of them as the name suggests. They were dropped individually at intervals, long or short, depending on the heaviness or lightness of the crop. The function of the reel, a flimsy looking wooden structure, like a paddle mill in the air, was to ensure that the corn on being cut got on to the platform canvass.

Ours was a Hornsby Standard reaper and binder with a left hand five foot cut. Most horse drawn models were five foot cut. Deering, McCormick and Massey Harris were other makes. There was a whole folklore about the driving and management of reapers and binders. Some men, whose names still come to mind, were renowned for the speed and efficiency with which they could cope with this machinery under given circumstances. Some farmers had teams of horses known for their strength and endurance. All kinds of judgments had to be made when setting the height of cut. In this matter factors such as the quality of the straw itself had to be considered. If it were tillage cereal with hayseed sown in it, this was a modifying factor. Decisions were necessary about the size of sheaf, the tightness of the binder, the kind of binder twine, the height and angle of the reel, how to cope with a bad blockage of the blade etc..

At this time of the year in kitchen and at cross-roads, at the creamery and at chapel gates experiences were bartered and views were exchanged. There were schools of thought about whether a sward should be cleared around a field with a scythe for the first round of the binder or was it sufficient to drive right through the corn on the headland and then cut the back sward as in the mowing of hay.

Clearing around the headlands was hard, backbreaking work, above all for the man using the scythe. A person followed close behind him "taking out" or gathering the corn into sheaf size bundles and a few others followed on binding the sheaves. After a period of binding the skin around your nails was inclined to become raw and sore. If helpers were in sufficient supply someone would follow the binders to gather the stray laces or to glean. Since reading the Book of Ruth in the Bible, for me the word "glean" is full of mystery and romance. In chapter two Ruth says to Naomi, 'Let me go into the fields and glean among the ears of corn in the footsteps of some man who will look on me with favour'.

Two men were involved with the reaper and binder; one was on the machine looking after the various controls. The other had as his function to drive the horses, which involved walking beside the machine round and round the field for miles and miles, encouraging the horses and where necessary whipping them on. This man also kept a watchful eye on the delivery of the sheaves in case the twine was breaking or some other hitch was occurring. Just two horses hauled the binder for the first few rounds and when there was sufficient room the third horse was added.

Once we had a black three quarter bred mare whom we used on occasion as the third horse for the binder. She was a graceful creature and, as was, she showed signs of the strength of the quarter Irish Draught that she also was. One day Uncle Den wanted me to ride her out to the field from the stable in the yard but I was too afraid, I never had great physical courage. Thereupon followed an exhilarating experience. I agreed to ride the mare if he sat on her back behind me to hold me so that I couldn't fall off. He did this. I was seated in front of him situated securely between his arms as he was holding the reins. I felt secure and trusting. I agreed to let him urge the mare to go faster and faster until we were galloping. Never once did I panic. I felt, and in a way, can still feel, that thrill of speed and that comfort of being able to trust.

Those not otherwise engaged did the stooking, which was a sociable task as it was helpful to work in twos placing the sheaves standing up leaning against other sheaves. There were eight or ten sheaves in each stook.

We often had a small "meitheal" for cutting the corn, just a couple of the closer neighbours who, in some cases did not have "binders" of their own. They helped us to do our cutting in return for the loan of our machinery. Two neighbours particularly involved in these matters supplied also the third horse for our own work. One was a beautiful white gelding, a big horse, probably sixteen and a half hands high, that is fifty six inches. He was basically Irish Draught with a little bit of Clydesdale. The other third animal was an almost pure bay Irish Draught mare, who was too willing and tended to pull more than her fair share.

***

These neighbours were wise and thoughtful men. The process of making stooks called for gentle cooperation of those involved. That kind of cooperation seemed to encourage serious conversation. For example, during such a cooperative session I discovered that one of them was an authority on the works of early twentieth century Irish dramatists. Another had a comprehensive view of the progress of the Second World War, particularly of the Japanese War. Yet, with an extraordinary fatalism, the latter argued that to be a farmer you had to be a "cábóg" (stupid clown). His argument was that a farmer tended to leave his land to the son in the family who could not achieve in school and university. If the boy was any good (girls did not seem to come into the reckoning) he became a priest or doctor. He entered the Civil Service if he was bright enough and if his parents could not afford to put him through college.

What he said must be taken seriously. It is alarming that leaders in society did so little to stem the development of such an attitude whereby the self-image of the farmer was, in so many cases, as suggested in what Jimmy said.

My own experience is that a large proportion of our real intellectuals, amongst whom I include emphatically Jimmy Herrick, have been amongst the rural and farming population.

An intellectual is someone who searches constantly to reason to an understanding of every detail of his/her experience and endeavours to evaluate its usefulness in assisting them to achieve their ultimate goal in life. This ultimate goal is based on a belief, be it in our Yahweh God or in any god ("god" being the shorthand for "what is good for us").

The enemy of the intellectual is the unquestioning and unquestionable idealist who deals in propaganda which is equivalent to saying, 'I know what is good for you, do what I say and do not ask questions'.

Perhaps at some stage in our more recent history there was collusion between church and state to establish one hedged-in pathway towards an ultimate goal. Divergent thinking which consolidates purchase on the ultimate goal was discouraged. Resulting from this some sensitive souls scrupled about the legitimacy of a pattern of ideas of their own. Some of these made a truce with life. Some became cynical. Some found themselves forced to abandoned reality in mental institutions. Some became alcoholic. One of the most intellectual teachers I had in school I had the pleasure and the pain of meeting up with again after many years, when he was being sheltered as a guest in the Morning Star Hostel in Dublin, trying to come to terms with a bad alcohol problem.

In summary, what Jimmy was crying out for was an enlightened moral leadership to raise him from a kind of depression by reassuring him of the validity and legitimacy of his thoughts, and of his work which he was inclined to decry when compared to the glittering prizes of Medicine, Maynooth or Dublin Castle.

***

One of the less savoury adventures associated with corn reaping was a slaughter of innocents which I actually looked forward to and took part in. Obviously not everything about the "good old days" was commendable.

A ghoulish spirit possessed some of us when only the last few swards of a field of corn remained to be cut. In those pre-myxomatosis days rabbits were pests, doing a great deal of damage to crops both root and cereal and some form of culling was called for. Surely there are ways of attending to this consonant with human dignity.

While the corn was growing the rabbits took up abode in the field, burrowing there, setting up what they thought was permanent domicile. An idyllic life, it appeared, with an abundance of good food at their front door. Many rabbits saw that the writing was on the wall as the binder encroached slowly, sward by sward, on their homelands and could be seen escaping fairly comfortably towards the fences. Others, particularly baby rabbits and does, panicked and retreated into an area of still standing corn that was getting progressively smaller or else made a suicidal effort to reach a now distant field boundary. In making this attempt they were obstructed by sheaves lying on the ground and easily caught by baying humans who put them to death by pulling their necks until the first vertebra, the atlas could be heard disengaging from the second vertebra, the axis, thus crushing the spinal cord as done by the hangman to human beings. Many others had legs amputated or heads severed from their bodies as they tried to jump away as the blade approached, Some jumped onto the platform canvass and were borne up and over to the packers where they were eventually bound up with sheaves and kicked onto the ground. This was all considered great sport by the adults present and the younger folk were encouraged to participate in the "fun".

In those days I remember that callousness towards animals was tolerated and softness and gentleness in this matter had shades of unmanliness about it. Love of animals was regarded, by some, as a slightly Protestant trait, which, in the light of history, is understandable. Many Protestant landlords did treat their human tenants with less compassion than their animals and what I have described above may have been a reaction. Nowadays, I think proper attitudes about animals have been re-established.

As a young medical student I remember putting down a family pet collie dog called "Addie" (after Hitler) because he was getting senile and smelly. I got a portion of Hydrocyanic Acid from a chemist without any difficulty and detachedly administered a drop to Addie.

"O tempora, o mores". (What times, what customs!),

On the other hand, another one of the really nice things about cutting the corn was the arrival of the tea in the afternoon with not only apple cake but also with brown bread and fresh raspberry or loganberry jam.

Pay for overtime for farm workers was then unheard of and the cutting of a field of corn would never be abandoned just because a certain time had been reached. One or two might leave before the end but that would be to turn in the cows and get on with the milking which would take some time. On those days however Auntie Nellie and Hannah would take on even more milking than usual in order that the men might be free to get on with the cutting and the stooking. Any men who may have gone in to help out with the cows would come back to the field again after milking if they were needed. Stopping time was usually governed by the passing of a bus or a train or some other regular happening. I can remember once querying the unpredictability of the local church bell to be told that the bell ringer set his watch by the time of arrival of the bread man in the village on the day before.

The corn was left in the stooks for some time depending on weather conditions. Sometimes it was drawn in directly from the stooks and other times it was put from stooks into field stacks to give every chance to dry out thoroughly while at the same time protecting it against any rain that may fall. The drawing in of the corn was particularly exciting because it was remote preparation for those days of threshing. A meitheal again assembled for this event and there would be about four carts enlisted for the operation. As the corn was transported in from the fields reeks were carefully built in the yard in such a way as to make the piking of the sheaves onto the thresher most economical of labour. Once this work was under way it often continued on after dark. There was a relief shared by all that the fruit of many months' effort and toil was close to being realised. My father at home on holiday from England would, if necessary, floodlight the reek under construction with the lights from his Baby Ford car, all the time keeping the engine running until there were signs of overheating.

My father always took an interest in his farm at Warrensgrove although he delegated entirely the organisation and running of it to Uncle Mick and Auntie Nellie. He had an excellent personal relationship with both of them. In talking about Warrensgrove to me he always referred to it as, "your place", a designation I didn't quite understand at the time. He was quite likely to drive his Baby Ford around the land instead of walking. This looked incongruous in pre-tractor days when the only source of power in evidence on the land was, as a rule, horse power of the flesh and blood variety.

For children, going barefoot was very common. Some walked daily to school, distances of over three miles each way. For some it was out of necessity, to spare shoe leather, for others it was for a complexity of reasons, including the fear of being ridiculed for appearing too affluent. Some went barefoot with ease, others were as tentative as Lough Derg pilgrims. What ultimately tested the mettle was endeavouring to walk on the stubble which consisted of the little cut stalks left after the reaper and binder had done its job. They were called by the Irish word, "coinlíni".

In between days of cutting corn while waiting for some more to ripen or for some corn in stooks to dry out properly, preparation had to be made for the threshing. Coal, when available, was ordered for the steam engine. When coal was off the market, time and energy had to be spent on procuring timber and cutting it up with a crosscut which made a characteristically pleasant musical sound. The resulting shallow cylinders of wood had to be split into firebox-size blocks.

But there was always an underlying problem when it came to getting timber or firewood. My father was "green" long before environmental issues became as widely discussed as they are now. He would never allow a tree of his to be cut down. When I raised the issue with him on two different occasions he rejoined with what might seem an inconsequential quote from Allen's Latin Grammar which he read for pleasure, 'Arbor quae in horto nostro crescebat et quam tantopere diligebam succisa est', (the tree which grew in our garden and which I loved so much has been cut down).

Trees of his were cut down where it was thought he would never miss them and the stumps were carefully camouflaged. Whether or not he ever discovered what had been done we don't know. He tended to keep disappointments to himself.

Lofts had to be brushed and scrubbed to house the wheat, oats and barley after the threshing. Some cosmetic touches were also called for; the day of the threshing was an open day. The fact that the place was going to be on show always generated a pride in the men. I believe they felt that they owed it to themselves to be seen as part of an organisation that worked properly. Work for them was a focus of life they were connatural with, not alienated from.

Chapter 23

Threshing

When the corn was safely drawn in and in ricks in the yard or haggard the next event was to be the threshing. Uncle Mick would go to book the threshing machine or, to use his own idiom, he would "go after steam". At this time Auntie Nellie rummaged through drawers engaging herself in the annual process of unearthing the sheets specially reserved for the engine men in those days before running water and bathing facilities were commonly available in the country.

Within the next few days Warrensgrove would be a source of much of what life could offer to a boy. Depending on the result of Uncle Mick's negotiations, perhaps on that or on the following night the steam engine and thresher would arrive.

On a particular day, after a long time Uncle Mick returned in his pony and cart (the "t" was not pronounced) which he used as a "gad about". He was in particularly good form and his news was good. Bob Slyne had promised to come that night.

After supper, Mary, my cousin and I, listened at the kitchen door for the distant puffing of the steam engine as it hauled the thresher in our direction. The evenings were shortening towards the end of August and it was already dark when we heard the faint but characteristic hard puffing (more like banging) of the Ransome, Simms and Jefferies single cylinder traction engine. As the crow flies it was less than a mile away at his stage but by road that was about two miles. Allowing for one water stop it would be the best part of two hours before it would arrive.

The threshing set was usually accompanied by a small convoy of well-wishers besides its crew of three. Included in the crew were the owner, Bob Slyne who functioned rather as a non-playing captain, his brother Billy, who had almost a love relationship with the engine and helmsman and "feeder" Jer Leary who was the paid professional. Jer's main task was to put or "feed" the sheaves of corn into the drum of the thresher and to steer the engine while in transit from one farm to the next. People like Jer were said to "follow" the engine.

When this "circus" reached the end of the avenue leading up to the yard at Warrensgrove Jer would invite my Uncle Den to take over the steering. Uncle Den was a younger brother of my mother and of Auntie Nellie and was living in Warrensgrove. He was up to date and efficient in matters mechanical. His local knowledge of this half mile long avenue was useful in order to avoid problems that might arise from overhanging branches and culverts unused to supporting the many tons of engine and thresher.

For well over an hour I had been listening to the sheer music of the engine getting louder and louder. Every hair on the back of my neck seemed to stand to attention and I was perfused with delight as this giant black creature puffing out smoke and noisily labouring finally appeared framed in the gateway of the yard. If that moment could be frozen it would do me for eternity.

On arrival, greetings were exchanged between Uncle Mick and Auntie Nellie and Bob on behalf of his crew whilst Hannah, the girl, set about boiling the eggs and wetting the tea. Bob and a few neighbours who were close friends and who came to share in the vigil of the threshing event were summoned down to the "room" where, in spite of the almost midnight hour, anecdotes appropriate to the occasion were traded. Bob's laughter which was an important note of his character and widely imitated by acquaintances and even friends could be heard clearly by those in the kitchen.

While good spirits and fellowship proceeded in the house Billy and Jer got on with the work of lining up the thresher between the ricks of corn. In this lining up exercise Billy and

Jer always gave a virtuoso performance. There was a practiced understanding between them. Billy shunted with fine precision, operating both the steering and the power controls of the engine all by himself, a man totally absorbed and concentrated, in a powerful and romantic setting of noise and steam. In days before walkie talkies, Jer with almost unerring accuracy by nod and gesture transmitted shunting directions to Billy while he dug in one wheel of the thresher and jacked up another, until in the end this large and apparently complex machine, an Allen 42 inch threshing mill, was spirit level, ready for work on the following day.

The unit of movement used in fine shunting was called a "shake". To move the engine forward or backward a "shake" was to move about an inch or two.

When all this lining up was accomplished Billy and Jer would drag themselves, it would seem reluctantly, away from their work which began eighteen hours previously. They had tea in the kitchen. A radiant Uncle Mick came down from the room and after some pleasantries arranged that Auntie Nellie would conduct them to their room with the special sheets on the bed.

Jer rose at 5 o'clock on the following morning to raise steam, which operation involved scraping the ashes out of the fire box and starting off again with paper and sticks. It would take about three hours to bring to the boil the huge amount of water necessary to give the steam pressure required to power this heavy machinery.

At about 8 o'clock the engine began to show signs of life. The large flywheel was set in motion, thereafter continuing to revolve at a leisurely pace. The engine was now said to be "pumping". It was thus being ensured that the boiler was kept topped up with water from the tank. The great catastrophe in steam circles is the "burning of the plug" which happens if the water in the boiler is not kept above a certain level,

At about half past eight the whistle was sounded to notify the surrounding farmers that there was threshing in Warrensgrove on that day. The milking of the twenty eight or so cows had already taken place at a very early hour. This was done by hand by four or five milkers including Auntie Nellie and Hannah, the girl. Milking was a humdrum task easily overlooked by men on such a day when they were disposing themselves for more spectacular happenings. Women controlled such enthusiasms more readily.

The cows and their shared consort, in those times the bull was not penned, had been surprised and bemused as they passed curiously on after carefully smelling and scratching themselves against this unusual equipment.

Uncle Mick went early to the creamery on that morning with instructions to get extra butter for the day's meals as well as other provisions.

The half tierce of porter, as a connoisseur he always ordered Triple X, had to be collected from May Fitz's. He believed it tactical to alternate his custom in this matter between Auntie (Mrs.Murphy) in Crookstown and May Fitz in Lissarda, He would also tell other creamery goers about the threshing so that they could send help along to join the "meitheal" or group of neighbours who would rally around to help or to "cabhair".

At about 9 o'clock the neighbours would start to arrive. As they already knew each other's skills and job preferences there was no need to assign jobs to them specifically. Jackie Wall and Terry Mac would go to the front of the thresher to draw straw, a job only for the tall and the strong. Con Lynch was the undisputed maker of the straw rick, a kind of "king of the castle", Sean Arthur O'Leary was to "mind the bags", that is to look after the grain as it came from the thresher; the abundance of its coming he would sometimes describe graphically.

As soon as sufficient men were in place, like hurlers waiting for the ball to be thrown in, the engine which had been idling, turning the threshing mill slowly was vigorously transformed into life by Billy as he tapped the throttle lever forward with the heel of his hand. A whirring noise from the mill was replaced by a loud droning and then a series of variations in the pitch of that droning indicated that corn was being fed into the drum.

Jer stood thigh deep in the feeding box which was a recess made into the top of the thresher just in front of the opening of the drum, to save the feeder from having to kneel down so as to function. He fed the corn carefully and evenly into the thresher. It was seized greedily from his hands by the bars or beaters of the drum and as the corn was torn past the concave or steel cage within which the drum revolved the grains were beaten out of the ears. The straw was taken away to the front of the thresher to the "shakers" and any grains that had remained in it were shaken free. The grain and chaff went to the winnower, the chaff was blown out to the side of the thresher and the grain was delivered through a number of openings at the back of the mill.

The chaff tended to pile up at the side of the thresher so it had to be cleared away regularly. Clearing the chaff was one of the easier jobs and was usually done by an elder who had given of his best in earlier years. The gentlemanly Dick Cronin frequently did this job which he combined with the raking down and the tidying of the straw rick as it rose with a kind of synthetic grandeur like a castle on a movie set.

The feeder was like a surgeon in the operating theatre or like a high priest involved in some busy liturgy being ministered unto by a team of expert helpers, two opening up the sheaves by cutting the binders. As long as these binders were of twine it was easy enough but hand bound sheaves with binders of straw quickly caused blisters on even the most seasoned of hands. Two more helpers handed the opened sheaves to the feeder who carefully regulated the rate at which the corn was committed to the threshing drum.

A sharp practice known to have been indulged in by the occasional threshing set owner was the loosening of the concave, thus allowing the corn to be threshed very quickly but very inadequately as a lot of grain got left in the ears and instead of being harvested was discarded with the straw. A reputation of integrity in such matters as this made Bob Slyne much sought after.

About half past eleven there was a shrill blast on the engine whistle. This was the signal to stop feeding the thresher. Uncle Mick had appeared carrying two white enamel buckets full of creamy porter. As if in an offertory procession he was followed by a retinue of acolytes bearing basins usually displayed as ornaments on the kitchen dresser.

The thirty or so men who stood around leaning on their pikes, caps off and wiping the sweat from their foreheads and faces, delicately awaited their basins of porter. A sweet tin, originally used as a container for boiled sweets, appeared, full of spring water for the teetotallers or pioneers. There were usually a few secret porter drinkers who were thoughtfully provided for by a special delivery of porter to behind the straw rick, This latter group was often comprised of those who out of deference to a father or other close senior relation present chose to exercise some degree of filial modesty. In some families at that time smoking or drinking in the presence of parents or indeed of a spouse, even though the parents or spouses knew all about these practices of their husbands/wives or children would be thought of as an act of impiety.

There was a large orchard in Warrensgrove and an abundant supply of apples usually available at harvest time. Some of the cousins used to pick buckets of them and give them out to the threshing "meitheal" during the porter break. Throwing apples up to the men on the thresher or on the ricks was a source of good fun at various other times during the day.

During this porter break a preliminary consensus would have been reached about the quality of the yield. Judgements about the quantity would have to wait until later. A good thing to hear said of oaten straw was that it could be fed to livestock, the bad news would be that it was fit only for bedding.

If by this time wheat had been threshed the speculation would be about how it would bushel - in other words how much a bushel measure of the wheat grain would weigh. This determined the scale according to which the millers would pay. The smaller grain gave some advantage.

The oaten grain was usually stored in lofts around the farmyard carried thither half-sack by half-sack. Four or five of the younger men did this job as a great deal of walking and the climbing of rickety stairs was often involved. The oats was spread on the floor of the loft at a depth depending on the estimated moisture content of the grain. On average the depth was about eighteen inches. Its ultimate use, apart from any that may be set aside for seed, would be the feeding of livestock, particularly horses. Crushed or ground oats would be fed also to cattle, sheep and pigs as well as to poultry of all kinds.

Barley was fed like the oats, except to horses, unless it was grown on contract for a malting company. There was a saying current at the time which claimed as a gem of sound agricultural economics that only what could walk off the land should leave the land.

During the Emergency when good flour was difficult to get farmers usually kept some of their own wheat for grinding and using themselves. I can particularly recall the unusual and appetising nutty taste of the wholemeal bread made of flour from milled Diamante spring wheat which was used by our close neighbour, Mrs. Wall of Lissarda.

The bulk of the wheat was put into large two hundred weight jute sacks and collected at the end of the day for delivery to Howard's Mills, Belmont, Crookstown. Although it is nearly forty years since I delivered my last grain to them I can still feel involved as I bake with their "Oneway" flour at least twice a week.

The mill owners are proud of the fact that this "Oneway" wholemeal flour has always been stone- ground. On one occasion I was shown these grinding stones - an awesome experience, somewhat analogous to being shown the Tablets of the Law in the Ark of the Covenant!

Catering for at least thirty extra mouths for dinner and for supper was a big undertaking. Some local friends would kindly offer to help Auntie Nellie and Hannah. In Warrensgrove, a tea dinner as opposed to a potato dinner was the order of the day. Many neighbours opted to serve a potato dinner. Large quantities of Murphy's or Denny's ham bought in Regan's of Crookstown were boiled. For some reason home cured bacon of which there were many cuts hanging from the kitchen ceiling was not used. Someone since suggested it was so salty that it might have been feared lest its saltiness would stimulate an undue thirst for porter.

To help the men relish the ham, bottles of H.P. sauce or thick Yorkshire Relish were on the table. Some of these bottles were already partially used having been purchased originally for the Station back in March.

A pair of boiled eggs was available for those reputed to have bad stomachs. Tasty fresh white bread in "elbow" or "turnover" loaves was available in plenty, lately delivered by Con Duggan of Thompson's. For a period during the Emergency (1939 to 1945) the regulation of the Department of Agriculture was that farmers were obliged to till one third of arable land. This meant that in Warrensgrove there were about fifty acres under crops. Ten acres were planted with Sugar Beet, Turnips, Mangels and Potatoes. The remaining forty acres of tillage were under cereals. It was commonly accepted that twenty acres of average yield would constitute one day's threshing, so in Warrensgrove to my delight we had material for two days' work. This gave the curious amongst us an opportunity to examine, crawl over and investigate the details of the steam engine and the threshing mill. Billy and Jer were more than generous with the time they would spend answering our questions.

The night in between the two days of threshing was an occasion for a threshing dance. Somebody was always found who could play the "gadget", which was a generic term for any kind of accordion-like squeeze box.

Once when an instrumentalist could not be found someone played on a comb with a piece of paper around it. Not a great idea. Tunes like "Galway Bay", "Moonlight in Mayo" and "I've Been a Moonshiner" were the chart toppers.

During the days of the threshing, fuel and water had to be supplied by the farmer. Before and even during the earlier part of the Emergency coal was easily available, easy to use and efficient for the steam engine. The consumption was about one ton per day's threshing, little more than the cost of a ten kilo bag of coal in today's prices.

As the Emergency proceeded and various scarcities became more critical coal was one of those commodities, which, like white flour, was completely unavailable even for the trains. Consequently, only turf and timber blocks were there to provide the heat to keep steam up. Both these fuels proved quite inefficient and even dangerous as sparks from the burning timber were blown into the air, sometimes even in spite of a spark guard. The straw had to be watched very carefully on account of this fire hazard. Also the quantity of ash which accumulated in the fire box inhibited the draught, the fire would go down, and steam pressure would drop. This often meant that all work would have to stop while the fire box was cleaned out, the fire rekindled, and steam was raised once more to the required pressure.

Churns of water were brought by horse and car from a stream nearby. A lot of water was needed and while one man could operate this water drawing system it was distinctly easier work if he had a helper. Not every horse could be used for this job as the noise and unusual appearance of the engine and thresher might quite unexpectedly cause a horse to bolt. One day under such circumstances Uncle Mick's pony did bolt while momentarily unattended. She raced dangerously between the thresher and the reek of straw where there was quite a thick carpet of chaff on the ground. This slowed her down enough for Jackie Wall, then as agile as he was strong, to smother-tackle her.

As the end approached a message was relayed to the kitchen to send out a sweeping brush to the thresher. There must have been some very good reason for not having one of their own. The most disposable of those brushes available was selected and taken out by Hannah herself to the feeder in charge, She warned him, as few others would dare, about what might befall him if it was not safely returned.

While Jer was brushing down the thresher and folding the platform Billy was checking the steam pressure and the water levels in the boiler and tank. On a signal from Jer, Billy shut down the engine and threw off the driving belt.

Thereafter followed another consummate display of engine manipulation, perhaps better described as enginemanship, which the helpers, almost to a man, stayed on to watch as they rested on their pikes, took off or adjusted their caps and as some prepared and lit their pipes.

As if to indicate the beginning of the display and to call those present to attention, through two pipes which opened at the belly of the boiler, Billy blew two deafening jets of steam to clear out the cylinder in preparation for action - rather like a Spanish bull preparing for the fight. The shroud of steam provided a pantomime effect.

Standing on the footplate, left hand on the steering wheel and with right hand available for handling the various levers Billy moved right up to the back of the thresher and Jer promptly attached a short tow bar to the front axle of the engine; he had already hitched it to the thresher.

There were several loud sharp reports as the engine surely dislodged the several tons of threshing mill from where it had become firmly embedded during the previous two days. The engine then went full tilt to the front of thresher trailing clouds of steam, where it was hitched to the drawbar on the fore carriage. Owing to the limitations of the surroundings Billy had to deal with a precarious potential "jack knife" situation which in less skilled hands might have resulted in the capsizing of the thresher. The drama of this "tightrope" act was not wasted on the onlookers who were obviously relieved as the thresher gradually straightened out behind the engine.

The threshing set was parked near the gate of the yard ready for departure and the crew gathered together their various jacks, chucks, sledge hammers etc. which had been left lying around. These were put into a small trailer which was hauled from place to place behind the thresher, thus adding to the circus-like appearance of the outfit.

During the threshing operation Bob's presence wasn't particularly obvious around the yard, but he was far from idle. He was doing a good public relations job in conversing with Uncle Mick, the women in the kitchen and with various other visitors who came along to savour the atmosphere of the occasion,
Bob Slyne was also skilled in tapping half tierces or kegs of porter, not at all as easy a job as one may think. It involved putting a tap in place in such fashion that the contents would not spew all over the place.

He had to meet also a succession of farmers from far and near who had one request in common; that Bob would attend to their threshing requirements at once. In some cases it was claimed that their corn was heating or rotting in the haggard. Bob was a great listener and was concerned. He came as near to pleasing all as anyone could. He had a great way with him.

When the threshing set had been parked facing outwards the "meitheal" and the engine crew came in to share what seemed like a celebratory supper.

When supper seemed almost over and the threshing crew were about to leave Uncle Mick set about paying Bob. Turning his back on the rest of the company, with well-disguised subtlety, he peeled twelve Munster and Leinster Bank pound notes, the ones with the ploughman motif, off a wad he had in a waistcoat pocket since a recent transaction with Murphy the pig buyer. The fee for threshing was six pounds per day during those Emergency years.

The helpers gradually moved out to go home or to go for a "scoruiocht". A "scoruiocht" in our area was a pleasant chat over the fire in a neighbour's house. I am aware that it involves more musical activity etc. in other parts of the country, particularly in Gaelteacht areas. The threshing set had not far to go that night, only as far as Kilcondy House to thresh for Paddy Donoghue.

In Warrensgrove the show was over for another year. Auntie Nellie and Hannah with some other willing helpers quickly got the house back into order.

The sheets reserved for the engine men were put soaking before being washed and laid aside for another year.

* * *

Chapter 24
THE GATHERING

I was disappointed at having missed the funeral. I phoned Maureen that night to sympathise with her and to apologise for not having been able to attend. I had wanted to be in Leap not only to pay my last respects to Uncle Tim, her father, but also to meet the other cousins who had gathered for the occasion from far and near.

The ten children in my mother's family, eight girls and two boys all married and all had children which meant that there was a large number of first cousins. Thirty-three in all.

Auntie Nellie, my mother's eldest sister who took charge when my grandmother died in 1916 extended her interest and solicitude to her nieces and nephews when they arrived.

Auntie Nellie lived in Warrensgrove and loved us all to go and stay with her whenever we wished and for as long as we wished.

In the course of that phone conversation with Maureen who now lives in New York, we decided that as cousins with this strong Warrensgrove bond we needed to meet at times other than those dictated by funerals. We gave ourselves some time to talk it through with as many of the other cousins as possible.

Maureen, who was Auntie Nora's daughter, took it on herself to canvass interest amongst those now living in the United States, Canada, Australia and Cyprus. I consulted as many as possible of those living in Ireland and Britain. We got a positive reaction from everybody with whom we discussed it.

We planned this reunion of all the offspring of our grandparents, Denis and Maria (nee Casey) Callanan for August

1986 in Leap, West Cork, the place in which these grandparents had lived, worked and had their children.

The day came. The celebration was to begin with attendance at Mass in the Parish Church in Leap, the scene of so many Callanan Christenings, Weddings and Funerals. The religious ceremony was followed by a meal in the Leap Inn.

All agreed that their dominant feelings were of thankfulness that they could renew themselves in the presence of those whose influence once impressed them, perhaps half a century previously. In the meantime and in various parts of the world some said they frequently thought about the others. They had known these cousins not well enough, they thought, to feel free to phone or write to them without a fixed agenda, yet too well ever to forget them. The reunion they saw as a chance to get to know them again and probably understand them better. Up to this, these memories had been like sterile daydreams, now they had been transformed into realisable hopes.

That evening of the celebration was wet, so most arrived weatherproofed at the door of Leap Parish Church. This added a touch of drama to the various entries. Each disclosure was a pleasant surprise. Those at home welcomed others from abroad.

Most from abroad were returning emigrants but Auntie Chrissie's children, Peggy (Twomey) Tracey and Anna (Twomey) Turner were born in the United States. I felt that their presence gave particular endorsement to the occasion. While they, like the rest of us were coming back to beginnings they were also venturing out. They had both been in Ireland before but as infants just before World War two.

I can remember that visit very clearly when they accompanied their mother to the wedding of her youngest sister, Bessie, which took place in that same church in 1939. It was a big commitment to bring a three year old child and an eighteen month old on a five day crossing from New York to Cobh. Owing to rumours of war and possible danger from submarines and U-Boats Auntie Chrissie, Peggy and Anna sailed back to the United States earlier than originally planned on the liner George Washington. Auntie Nellie asked my mother, when they returned from Cobh after seeing them on board the liner from the tender, 'Why did Chris cry so much?'

At Cobh (once Queenstown) the liners en route to New York from Liverpool, Southampton or Le Havre remained in the offing and intending passengers, sometimes accompanied by their relatives and friends were brought out the few miles from landing stage to liner by tender.

It was a pleasant journey through a lovely harbour, although lost on many, who having committed themselves with a reasonable but reckless ambition during the sober space of previous months were now consumed by feelings of hopeless regret at having to leave what they knew and loved to face the unknown. They would turn back here it not for the bridges they had burned and, ironically, the encouragement of once reluctant relatives.

Auntie Chris had gone beyond all that.
Just a few years later we got news of her death in New York on Christmas Day.

Three of the participants in that occasion have since died. Séan Coughlan, Auntie Nellie's son, died in Australia in 1988. He left Ireland in 1943 for Kirkintilloch in Scotland at the age of seventeen. Eventually, after many years working in the south of England, Sean went to Australia in the early sixties with his wife Dorothy and four children. Attendance at this function was his first visit to Ireland for over twenty years. He seemed relaxed as he rolled back the years.

He had been gifted with his hands and, as a boy, had shown great promise as a woodworker. He worked as a skilled craftsman all his life. He was interested in argument and serious conversation in spite of the fact that he had been victimised by an education system which in Sean's case, at any rate, confused its proper educative function with totally other instrumental functions. Individual interests and special talents in such a system were hardly relevant.

Sean was just one of many amongst that group of cousins who started off in second-level education but abandoned it when it seemed so totally irrelevant to their needs. In general, while the primary education system was innoculating people against the Irish language the secondary system was providing but few intellectual skills, together with nothing more than a veneer of information requisite to qualify the student for university. The educational organisers seem to have been either unaware of the fact or unconvinced that second level education had a set of objectives of its own.

Mary (Coughlan) Wendsley, Sean's sister, died on Christmas Day, 1988 in Liverpool. Since Sean and Mary were Auntie Nellie's only children Mary's passing completed the passing of a whole family. They were all back in the eternity whence we were allowed the grace of their presence for a moment of time.

Mary travelled over to Liverpool with my father in 1945 to do nursing. She got married to Richard, settled down in Liverpool, and had a family of two boys. She was the older sister whom many of us never had. She was loving and attractive. She lived with us in Lissarda during much of the time while she was at secondary school in Macroom. I know that she continued in the role of older sister to my own sister Rosemary, while the latter was an occupational therapy student in Liverpool. A role which she fulfilled also for the other cousins who did nursing in Liverpool.

Seamus Shorte was our senior cousin, the eldest child of Auntie Kit and husband of Betty. He died in Birmingham early in 1989. He had gone there to live in the nineteen forties, working first of all as a bus driver and later as an inspector. Before leaving Ireland he had trained as a motor mechanic. He was totally committed to the idea of gathering the extended family together. He had an extensive and catalogued range of photographs and colour transparencies of us all which he delighted to show. Sé was a quiet and gentle man, saying little of his own achievements and interests not least of which was his study of modern languages.

We drew up a special Order of Service which contained the hymns, prayers and readings. The readings for the Mass had been carefully selected. The first reading was from the Book of Ecclesiastics to assure ourselves that God approves of and encourages family pride in righteousness. Faintheartedness has no place in His scheme of things,
Next let us praise illustrious men,
our ancestors in their successive generations.
The Lord has created an abundance of glory,
and displayed his greatness from earliest times.
Their bodies have been buried in peace,
and their name lives on for all generations.
The people will proclaim their wisdom,
The assembly will celebrate their praises.

When Mass was over there was an excited mingling in the church. Further introductions were made and old friendships renewed. Joy was expressed about the obvious wellbeing of so many. People talkatively emerged to the outside to be greeted by rain which forced us to go directly to the Leap Inn where we were to have our celebratory dinner.

It was fortunate that there was in Leap a restaurant of the calibre of the Leap Inn because we felt it important that our celebration should be connected intimately to the surroundings. Brian and Anne Sheehan the proprietors were family friends of long standing and understood what we were about.

Denis Calnan (Callanan) the senior cousin present bearing the Callanan name, a native of Leap and a resident of nearby Glandore was asked to take over as Master of Ceremonies, which he did with style. We had engaged a professional musician to play the piano. He mixed Irish and other music with delicate taste.

The meal was excellent and the menu which had been carefully selected was artistically represented by Maura my wife, who fancifully attributed each dish to a place of family significance, for example, "Salmon Leap".

The guests of honour were my mother, Auntie Peg, also affectionately known as "Lady Margaret" and Sadie, the widow of our Uncle Den. They had an important function as representatives of the previous generation.

On the following day, Sunday, we had lunch in Maureen's Leap home, Droum Lodge, a generous and magnificent function at which food, drink and hospitality were abundant. As well as the first cousins and their spouses she also invited along their children, their children's spouses and their children's children, some of the latter category had flown in from the United States. Mercifully, the sun shone on that gathering. It was one of the few fine days in a wet summer.

On the Monday we set out in a convoy of cars to revisit Warrensgrove, almost thirty miles from Leap, where practically all of us had stayed and played as children, as guests of Auntie Nellie.

It was a joyful and sad occasion. I was joyful in the conviction that the happiness I recalled was but a foretaste of an ultimate glory yet to come and sad at being deprived of it for the moment. When I went through those gates I began to relive a whole childhood which continued to unfold as we went up that half mile of avenue. Even thirty years had not diminished my feeling of familiarity with all that passed by. Warrengrove had been my very own for a short time and almost like a prodigal I let it go. I lost it when I loved it. It never got a chance to go sour on me and that is worth everything. I am free to enjoy a past that is not a burden. We arrived into the yard through the arch that framed the steam engine as it was coming in to thresh the corn.

The yard hadn't changed much and memories crowded in. I was completely overcome. Bernie and Inagh Clarke, the present owners, gave us a generous welcome. Even though we arrived unexpectedly they gave us a lovely tea. They showed us over the house, yard and land. Every field, nook and cranny sparked off a story to be told.

After Warrensgrove we drove to Lissarda House, just two miles away, my own old home up to the time it was sold in 1959. Sean and Julia O'Mahony are the present owners and they gave us a great welcome. Very kindly they opened their house and premises for us to go around and reminisce.

Though not as familiar as Warrrensgrove to most of the cousins a number of them had known it and visited there while staying in Warrensgrove. After leaving Lissarda that evening we scattered, starting on the first stages of our respective journeys back to the present.

We did not want to lose each other again so another gathering was arranged for 1989 which had to succeed now that we had established a model that worked so well.

**

Both reunions were recorded on videotape and every family ordered a copy so that the reunions themselves have been relived many times over from Saskatoon to Adelaide.

**

This family event of ours has been described as an intensive extended family experience. One of the fruits of our reunions has been the deepening of the knowledge of our own nuclear families. I feel I understand my own mother better and love her more deeply as a result. I rejoice and feel privileged that I still have her in this my sixtieth year and feel so sad for her when I remember that her own mother died when she was only eight.

I like sharing these reminiscences and reflections. Firstly, because I am encouraged, by happy memories, chastised by awkward ones and purified by sad ones. I find it good mental therapy. Secondly, because by this sharing I might remind or even challenge others to set out their own experiences and discover that there is much to rejoice about in the remembrance of things past.

Epilogue

I left the Dominican order and I abandoned my right to minister ordinarily as a priest. I opted to change course and strive along another pathway with a companion and wife called Maura, who is full of integrity, demanding in her love and rich in her response.

I hope all will be well when it comes to the end. This Hope is the virtue by which we tend with certainty to salvation, anchored to the truths of Faith.

I am full of genuine admiration for all those who have persevered throughout the heat of the day. I hope we shall all be supported by Him 'till the shades lengthen and the evening comes and the busy world is hushed and the fever of life is over and our work is done'. (Newman)